MW00773351

THE FRAGMENTATION
OF A SECT

Schism in the Worldwide Church of God

David V. Barrett

OXFORD
UNIVERSITY PRESS

OXFORD
UNIVERSITY PRESS

Oxford University Press, Inc., publishes works that further
Oxford University's objective of excellence
in research, scholarship, and education.

Oxford   New York
Auckland   Cape Town   Dar es Salaam   Hong Kong   Karachi
Kuala Lumpur   Madrid   Melbourne   Mexico City   Nairobi
New Delhi   Shanghai   Taipei   Toronto

With offices in
Argentina   Austria   Brazil   Chile   Czech Republic   France   Greece
Guatemala   Hungary   Italy   Japan   Poland   Portugal   Singapore
South Korea   Switzerland   Thailand   Turkey   Ukraine   Vietnam

Published by Oxford University Press, Inc.
198 Madison Avenue, New York, New York 10016

www.oup.com

Oxford is a registered trademark of Oxford University Press

Library of Congress Cataloging-in-Publication Data
Barrett, David V.
The fragmentation of a sect : schism in the Worldwide Church of God /
David V. Barrett.
p.   cm.
Includes bibliographical references (p.) and index.
ISBN 978-0-19-986151-4 (hardcover : alk. paper)
1. Worldwide Church of God—History.   2. Church controversies.
3. Conflict management—Religious aspects—Christianity.
4. Church management.   I. Title.
BX6177.B37 2013
289.9—dc23   2012010985

1 3 5 7 9 8 6 4 2

Printed in the United States of America
on acid-free paper

CONTENTS

AUTHOR'S NOTE

Most of my books on aspects of religion over the last decade or so were aimed at the general reader; they have a scholarly underpinning, but they were deliberately written for people who were interested in the subject but did not necessarily have a degree in religious studies, anthropology, or sociology. In a sense they were the religion equivalent of popular science books.

This book is different from my previous work in that it is based on my doctoral thesis. Although it is therefore an academic book which I hope will contribute to social science and religious scholarship, I also hope it will be read by members of the religious groups of which it is a study: the many Churches of God which are offshoots of the Worldwide Church of God. It is, after all, their story. It should also be of interest to anyone who is fascinated by the complexities of contemporary religion, especially in America.

For the sake of readability I have tried to keep jargon to a minimum. In places, however, it is inevitable; sociological phrases like "social construction of reality," "legitimation of authority," and "rational choice theory" are crucial elements in the theoretical discussion of this story; I explain them as they occur, and try not to allow them to dominate the text.

I hope that all readers will find this account of a group of heterodox, millenarian, Sabbatarian, British-Israelite Churches, which splintered in hundreds of directions after their founder died, even a fraction as absorbing as I have for all the years I have been observing them. I don't expect the leaders, ministers, and members of those Churches to agree with or approve of everything I say about them in these pages, but I would like to think that they will feel I have treated them fairly and will find the perceptions of an outside observer of interest.

David V. Barrett
June 2012

ACKNOWLEDGMENTS

This book is based closely on my 2009 PhD thesis in the Department of Sociology at the London School of Economics. I would like to thank:

- my supervisor, Professor Emeritus Eileen V. Barker OBE, one of the foremost specialists in new religious movements in the world, for all that I have learned from her.
- Dr. Don Slater, Doctoral Program Director, Sociology, for his invaluable administrative assistance enabling me to complete and submit my thesis.
- Dr. Amanda van Eck Duymaer van Twist and the staff at Inform (Information Network Focus on Religious Movements), for their encouragement and assistance.
- David L. Biggins, proprietor of User Management Services, for encoding my questionnaire and hosting it online.
- Dr. Dominic Erdozain, for suggesting, during my viva voce (thesis defense), that I use the term "moral capital" for my extension to rational choice theory in chapter 9.

Any social science research benefits immensely from the cooperation of those on the inside who, in a variety of ways, open doors, offer introductions, and provide invaluable sounding boards. I would like to thank particularly Dixon Cartwright, editor of *The Journal: News of the Churches of God*; Alan Ruth of Barnabas Ministries; Gavin Rumney of the *Ambassador Watch* and later *Otagosh* blogs; the late John Trechak, editor of *Ambassador Report*; Craig White, for both scholarly material and some crucial archive material; Barbara Fenney and later Lewis D. McCann for supplying me with the newspapers *In Transition* and *The Journal*; and the many other former Worldwide Church of God members, ministers, and leaders in America, Britain, Australia, and New Zealand who have provided me with huge amounts of information, helped me track down other people, and been willing to answer what must have seemed a constant stream of questions.

Thanks to Dixon Cartwright and Gavin Rumney again, both for reading my questionnaire and making a number of invaluable criticisms and for publicizing it in an article in *The Journal* and online. Because of the delay in copies of *The Journal* reaching subscribers in Britain and Australasia, a copy of my article was printed and inserted in the previous month's issue by the local distributors; thanks to Lewis McCann, Walter Steensby, and Rosemary Morton in Britain, Australia, and New Zealand, respectively, for making this possible. Such practical kindnesses can make a huge difference in the course of research.

Three separate people who must remain anonymous have supplied me with CDs containing massive amounts of original WCG literature. Others have provided me with or pointed me toward both other archive material and more recent studies.

I would also like to thank the dozens of leaders, staff, ministers, members, and former members of Worldwide Church of God and its many offshoots for providing me with their books, booklets, and magazines; for answering questionnaires; and for their help and courtesy in many encounters by email, letter, and telephone, as well as face-to-face. To me it was an academic inquiry; to them I was prying into their lives, their beliefs, their motivations, and their memories. They may not all have approved of my research, and they may disagree with some of what follows, but without them there would have been no thesis and no book.

I must thank my family and friends for their continued support, and their patience when this research took me away from them.

Finally, I would like to thank my examiners, Professor Emeritus James A. Beckford of the University of Warwick and Dr Dominic Erdozain of King's College, London, and the anonymous readers for Oxford University Press, for their perspicacious criticisms and suggestions, which have guided my rewriting of the thesis into this book. My thanks also to the team at Oxford University Press, particularly Cynthia Read for commissioning the book, Lisbeth Redfield, Rick Stinson, Niranjana Harikrishnan, and Natalie Johnson for shepherding it through its many stages and dealing with my many queries, Ben Sadock for his meticulous copy editing, and the marketing staff in both New York and Oxford. Any remaining failings are, of course, my own.

LIST OF PHOTOGRAPHS

1. Betty Bates and Herman Hoeh, the first two students to graduate from Ambassador College, 1951
2. Herbert W. Armstrong radio broadcast, late 1950s/early 1960s
3. Herbert W. Armstrong and Loma Armstrong arriving at Sydney International Airport, 1966
4. Garner Ted Armstrong singing, late 1950s/early 1960s
5. Garner Ted Armstrong, ca. 2001
6. Roderick C. Meredith and Sheryl Meredith, ca. 1992, around the time he left Worldwide Church of God to found Global Church of God
7. Gerald Flurry, founder of Philadelphia Church of God, 1997
8. David C. Pack, founder of The Restored Church of God
9. The former Hall of Administration, Ambassador College
10. The former Ambassador Hall and the Italian Sunken Gardens, Ambassador College

LIST OF TABLES AND FIGURES

LIST OF ABBREVIATIONS

The following abbreviations occur both in quotations and throughout the text of this book. Two sets of father and son, Armstrong and Tkach, are distinguished by using in each case the surname alone only for the father.

HWA or Armstrong	Herbert W. Armstrong (the Founder) (1892–1986)
GTA, Garner Ted, or Ted	Garner Ted Armstrong (his son) (1930–2003)
Tkach	Joseph W. Tkach (Armstrong's successor) (1927–1995)
Joe Jr.	Joseph Tkach Jr. (his son) (1951–)
CGCF	Church of God, a Christian Fellowship (ex-GCG)
CEM	Christian Educational Ministries (ex-CGI)
CGG	Church of the Great God (ex-WCG)
CGI	Church of God, International (ex-WCG)
CGOM	Churches of God Outreach Ministries (ex-CGI)
COGaic	Church of God, *an International Community* (ex-UCG)
COG Eternal	Church of God, the Eternal (ex-WCG)
COGR	Church of God, Restored; formerly WCGR (ex-WCG)
COG (UK)	Churches of God, UK (ex-CGI)
COGWA	Church of God, a Worldwide Association (ex-UCG)
COG7	Church of God (Seventh Day)
COG21	Church of God—21st Century (ex-Living)
GCG or Global	Global Church of God (ex-WCG)
GTAEA	Garner Ted Armstrong Evangelistic Association (ex-CGI)
ICG or Intercontinental	Intercontinental Church of God (ex-CGI)
LCG or Living	Living Church of God (ex-GCG)
PCG or Philadelphia	Philadelphia Church of God (ex-WCG)
RCG or Restored	Restored Church of God (ex-GCG)
SDA	Seventh-day Adventist Church

UCG or United	United Church of God, An International Association (ex-WCG)
WCG or Worldwide	Worldwide Church of God
WCGR	Worldwide Church of God Restored; later COGR (ex-WCG)

Other abbreviations include:

COG	Church of God
FoT	Feast of Tabernacles
MOA	*Mystery of the Ages*
STP	Systematic Theology Project
NRM	new religious movement

The Fragmentation of a Sect

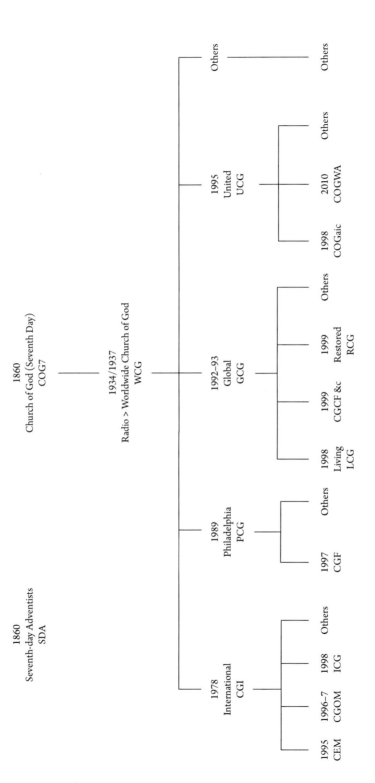

Figure 1.1 A History of Schism: The Main Offshoot Churches

CHAPTER 1

The Fragmentation of a Sect

An Introduction

INTRODUCTION

The September/October 1997 US edition of the *Plain Truth*, for over half a century the flagship magazine of the Worldwide Church of God (WCG), carried a full-page advertisement for a book by Joseph Tkach Jr., pastor general of the church:

> For nearly 70 years the Worldwide Church of God, founded by Herbert W. Armstrong, preached a "different gospel". Then in 1995, only ten years after Armstrong's death, the leadership of the WCG publicly renounced its unorthodox teachings and entered the evangelical mainstream. In this fast-paced and exciting record, Joseph Tkach ... delivers the plain truth. (*Plain Truth* 1997: 31)

That book, *Transformed by Truth*, told a remarkable story; but it only focused on one aspect of it, the changing of the Worldwide Church of God from heterodoxy to orthodoxy; that takes up just one chapter of the present work (chapter 5). Tkach's book glossed over the resultant fissioning of the church as hundreds of its ministers and thousands of its members rejected the new teachings in favor of the old.

This book, *The Fragmentation of a Sect*, tells that story—but it is much more than just a study of one relatively small group of heterodox Christian churches.

The actions of the ministers and members were a consequence of their social construction of reality (see appendix 2) and the legitimation of authority (see chapter 7), both central sociological themes, particularly in the sociology of religion. This book explores these issues through a phenomenological study of the complex process of schism in a new religious movement.

It is in part an examination of problems that ensue when there are conflicting demands of different authority types. Specifically, this intensive case study looks at the issues which precipitated a continuing process of schism in a religious movement following the death of its founder; it proposes an original typological model for the study of what might happen to a religion after its founder dies (see 8.1). It examines issues relevant not only to other religions but also to other social groups; it concludes with a new extension to existing rational choice theory (see 9.8).

1.1 THE STORY

In the mid-1930s an unsuccessful American advertising executive, Herbert W. Armstrong, founded a millennialist, Sabbatarian Christian sect[1] with a heterodox theology, the Radio Church of God. This was renamed the Worldwide Church of God in 1968; although it changed its corporate name to Grace Communion International in 2009 it is referred to by its best known name, or as Worldwide or WCG, throughout this book.

Over the next half century, despite a number of setbacks and scandals, as well as criticisms and attacks from former members and anticultists, amongst others, Armstrong's church grew to around 100,000 baptized members, with a global circulation of between six and eight million for its flagship monthly magazine, *Plain Truth*. In January 1986 Armstrong[2] died in his ninety-fourth year. And then everything changed.

Armstrong's successor, Joseph W. Tkach, gradually withdrew all of Armstrong's books and booklets and started changing the church's doctrines. Shortly before his own death ten years later he announced that the Worldwide Church of God had renounced all of its founder's distinctive teachings and had become a straightforward Evangelical Christian church. Joseph W. Tkach was succeeded as pastor general by his son Joseph Tkach Jr.,[3] who had encouraged his father's changes to the church.

The heterodox sect had, in Bryan R. Wilson's term, been denominationalized (B. Wilson 1990: 109).

The doctrinal revolution in Worldwide which Joseph Tkach Jr. wrote about in *Transformed by Truth* is an interesting story in its own right; the mainstream Christian world has written articles and books about it (Tucker 1996; LeBlanc 1996; Nichols and Mather 1998, etc.), and there have been at least two academic studies on it before this one (see appendix 3.2). But the other side of the story has received far less attention. This is the main subject of this book: the hundreds of

---

1. See "Definitions" (1.6).

2. Throughout this book, except in citations, the use of the surname "Armstrong" on its own always refers to Herbert W. Armstrong and never to his son Garner Ted Armstrong. They are also referred to as HWA and GTA, respectively.

3. Except in citations the surname "Tkach" on its own always refers to the father. With no disrespect intended, the son is sometimes referred to as "Joe Jr." to differentiate him from his father.

ministers and tens of thousands of members of the Worldwide Church of God who refused to "convert" along with their movement.

In a church in which strict top-down authority was a fundamental tenet of belief, Tkach's doctrinal changes set up a conflict in members: How could they continue to accept the authority of the leadership of the one true church which God had caused Armstrong to found and had called them to join, now that it had rejected all the truths which the man they believed was God's apostle, Herbert W. Armstrong, had taught them for half a century?

These conflicting forces—the authority of the leadership and the authority of Armstrong's teachings—are cognitively dissonant elements (Festinger 1957); both are vitally important to the members, but how can the tension between them be resolved? In this study I examine how different members attempted to reduce this tension by resolving the conflict in different ways.

Many senior ministers left the church at various stages during the reform process of 1986–95, encouraging members to repudiate the "apostate" teachings of the Tkach leadership, to leave the Worldwide Church of God and to follow them into new churches which upheld Armstrong's teachings. The three main offshoot churches of this period were:

- Philadelphia Church of God, founded by Gerald Flurry in 1989
- Global Church of God, founded by Roderick C. Meredith in 1992–93
- United Church of God, founded by a group of ministers in 1995

(These and other churches are usually referred to in this book by a one-word name: Philadelphia, Global, United, Living, Restored, etc., or by their initials; see the list of abbreviations on pp. xvii–xviii.)

The three main schismatic churches soon had their own offshoots; by 2009 these were estimated to number over four hundred. I have coined the term "the Worldwide family"[4] to include all those churches and other organizations with their roots in Worldwide. The chart on p. 2 is a partial family tree showing the relationship between the most prominent "offspring" of Worldwide.

Schisms do not tend to be amicable; as James R. Lewis and Sarah M. Lewis point out, because of the negative connotation of the word, "breakaway groups do not typically refer to themselves as schisms" (Lewis and Lewis 2009: 2). Partly for this reason the less loaded term "offshoots" will usually be used for groups which have left a parent church and set up as new churches.

The options available to Worldwide ministers and members can be summarized as:

4. Some detractors, as well as a book title (Hopkins 1974), have referred to this group of related Churches as "the Armstrong Empire" which, while pejorative, emphasizes both the personal focus on Herbert W. Armstrong and the authority he commanded. My term "the Worldwide family" is nonpejorative, emphasizes the "parent" Church, and is also suggestive of both family closeness and the often bitter nature of intrafamily disputes.

1. Accept the new teachings under the Tkach authority (father and then son) and remain in Worldwide (see 5.2 and 5.3)
2. Accept the new teachings, but leave Worldwide and join a mainstream Evangelical Christian church with none of the "baggage" of belonging to a once heterodox sect (see appendix 1)
3. Retain Armstrong's teachings but remain in Worldwide (see 5.3 and 7.2)
4. Retain Armstrong's teachings and join a church led by a charismatic successor with traditional top-down authority: Gerald Flurry, Roderick Meredith, David Pack, etc. (see 6.2.1 and 6.2.2)
5. Retain Armstrong's teachings, but abandon charismatic leadership and traditional authority in favor of rational-legal authority (see 7.1) and join the committee-led United Church of God or similar groups (see 6.2.3)
6. Retain Armstrong's teachings, leave Worldwide but join nothing, worshiping at home (see 6.4.3)
7. Join another (not Evangelical) church—Catholic, Orthodox, etc.
8. Drop out of religion altogether

The ministers and members in groups 4 and 5—those in the various offshoot churches—are the main focus of this study, with some mention of those in groups 3 and 6. The aim of this study is to examine, in a phrase, *who went where and why*. This question is particularly addressed in chapter 9.

1.2 A BRIEF THEORETICAL DISCUSSION OF SCHISM

John Wilson begins his 1971 essay "The Sociology of Schism" with the statement "The history of most of the mainstream Protestant denominations is one of repeated division" (J. Wilson 1971: 1). It is surprising, then, that there has been relatively little sociological work on schism.

This study is not based on any specific theory of schism, nor is it a critique of one, largely because, of the few significant theoretical studies, even fewer have much bearing on the individual case study of the Worldwide Church of God. I shall, however, make some reference to the work of Roy Wallis, John Wilson, Bryan R. Wilson, and Roger Finke and Christopher P. Scheitle where relevant. In a few instances throughout the book, from their work or that of others, I draw comparisons between the Worldwide story and other religions, particularly the Elim Foursquare Gospel Church (a British Pentecostal movement) and the Mormon Church.

Any theoretical conclusions from this inquiry stem from the reality of the case study—theory drawn from evidence—rather than an attempt to fit the facts to a preexisting theory or theories.

In his essay "A Theory of Propensity to Schism" Roy Wallis discusses previous work on schism: Niebuhr on economic factors, Willems on nationalistic feeling, and several writers on social differentiation (Wallis 1979: 174–92; refer to Wallis for specific citations). None of these is particularly pertinent to the present study. He also draws attention to Greenslade on the personal motivations of schismatic leaders, including ambition and personal antipathy—something we shall see mentioned several times during the course of this book.

Other scholars, including Bryan R. Wilson, have focused on the struggle for power; this will be explored in chapter 8 in the context of succession battles after the death of a religion's founder. Wilson's study of three groups—the Elim Pentecostals, Christian Science, and the Christadelphians (B. Wilson 1961)—touches at times on schisms in all three, with sometimes surprising relevance to the present study.[5]

What sort of movements are most prone to schism? Wallis cites Zald and Ash (1966) that "the inclusive organization retains its factions while the exclusive organization spews them forth." An inclusive organization is one which can cope with variations of doctrinal orthodoxy, which, as we shall see (e.g., 4.4), most certainly does not apply to the Worldwide Church of God. He also cites Nyomarkay (1967) making a similar distinction between nontotalitarian and totalitarian movements. In the former "factions can exist without destroying the group" (Wallis 1979: 182); again, that is not the case with either Worldwide or its offshoots.

Wallis refines these two ideas into the concept of uniquely legitimate and pluralistically legitimate groups. The former "will tend to define the boundaries of doctrine rather sharply to distinguish themselves from those beliefs and programs which they reject," while the latter "do not completely reject the validity of alternative paths to truth, salvation or utopia" (Wallis 1979: 183). It is clear which group Worldwide falls into: one of the hallmarks of the historical Worldwide (see 1.6, "Definitions") was its clear differentiation of its teachings from those of the rest of Christendom (see chapters 2 and 3). Wallis concludes that "pluralistically legitimate movements are thus able to tolerate the existence of factional groups more readily than uniquely legitimate movements" (Wallis 1979: 183). Uniquely legitimate movements such as Worldwide, therefore, cannot allow a diversity of beliefs or dissenting voices within them (see chapter 4).

Roger Finke and Christopher P. Scheitle echo Wallis's distinction between uniquely legitimate and pluralistically legitimate groups, but come to the opposite conclusion: "To the extent that a denomination holds claim to an exclusive truth, prophet, historical tradition, or ecclesiastical office, the chance of schism will also be reduced" (Finke and Scheitle 2009: 22–23). It could be argued that it was when Worldwide lost its "inimitability" by replacing its distinctive beliefs with standard Evangelical beliefs that the schisms occurred.

Roy Wallis suggests that schisms occur "more often in decentralized movements" (Wallis 1979: 178), and Bryan Wilson that "schism does appear to be inversely correlated with centralization" (B. Wilson 1961: 341), though Wilson accepts that his

---

5. In an interesting synchronicity, Bryan R. Wilson's book was based on his 1955 doctoral thesis from the London School of Economics.

conclusion is based on a sample of three sects, of which one, Christadelphianism, was the least centralized and the most prone to schism: "Ecclesial independence has undoubtedly been a cause of divisions and schisms: the absence of a central arbitrating authority has enabled schisms to ramify." (B. Wilson 1961: 273). But the opposite is the case with the Worldwide Church of God; it was a highly centralized movement, yet suffered schism both in the 1970s under Herbert W. Armstrong (see chapter 4) and in the years after his death, despite still being centralized under Joseph W. Tkach (see chapter 5).

This study does not set out specifically to test any of these theoretical stances, but the reality of the Worldwide schisms will challenge some of them.

1.3   THE INQUIRY AND OUTLINE OF THE BOOK

In this study I examine, inter alia:

- how the authority conflicts faced by members affected them
- in what ways they resolved these conflicts
- how and why different groups of members prioritized conflicting authority types, choosing one above the others available
- the different forms of legitimation of authority used by different leaders and churches
- why some members choose to remain in a state of cognitive dissonance, where the demands of their beliefs and their organizational affiliation are in a state of conflict
- how various offshoot churches consciously emphasize and maintain the barriers which define and reinforce their separate state, their deviance from orthodoxy (or, within their own social construction of reality—basically, their group worldview—their *adherence* to orthodoxy)
- what can happen to religions after the death of their founder
- what factors affect religious choice, specifically reaffiliation between churches—moving from one church to another.

The differences between the old and the new, the historical and the reformed Worldwide Church of God (see 1.6), are largely doctrinal (see my distinction between orthodox and heterodox sects in appendix 1). In order fully to comprehend the massive disjunction between the old and the new beliefs and the consequent upheaval in the socially constructed reality of ministers and members during the transitional years after Armstrong's death, it is necessary to have a thorough understanding of the beliefs of the historical Worldwide; chapter 2 discusses them, and their origins, in some detail.

Chapter 3 describes the origins and early decades of what would become the Worldwide Church of God, and chapter 4 the decade of the 1970s, the most tumultuous period in the history of the church while Armstrong was still alive, with many of its events foreshadowing the events after his death. In both chapters the figure of Herbert W. Armstrong is center stage, emphasizing both the authority he held within Worldwide and the importance of his memory years after his death: the man and the myth.

Chapter 5 covers the transitional years; it describes the series of seismic doctrinal changes in Worldwide after Armstrong's death in January 1986, through to his successor Joseph W. Tkach's crucial Christmas Eve sermon in 1994 when he announced that Worldwide was now an Evangelical church, and the effect of these changes on ministers and members.

Chapter 6 examines the fallout from those changes: the three main schisms from Worldwide to form Philadelphia, Global, and United Churches of God, and the subsequent splits in these churches to form many more. It describes a wide range of churches and other organizations from large to very small and from hardline to relatively liberal (see 6.1.3), bringing the story up to the present day.

The Worldwide Church of God, as we shall see throughout this study, was a very authoritarian religious sect. The legitimation of authority, not just of the founder, Herbert W. Armstrong, but of his successor, and of the leaders of all the offshoot churches, is examined in chapter 7 largely in the context of Max Weber's ideal typology, specifically tradition, emotional attachment, rational belief, and legality (M. Weber 1993: 81).

The changes to Worldwide occurred in the decade after the death of its founder. Although there have been previous studies of what might happen to new religions when their founders die (e.g., Miller 1991), there has not previously been any attempt to systematize the various possible outcomes. Chapter 8 offers a theoretical model which can be used to do so and applies it not only to the present case study of the Worldwide Church of God but also to a variety of other new religious movements.

Chapter 9 uses the responses to my questionnaire to explore a number of issues, including why people left Worldwide at the point they did and their relationship with church leaders, and considers the question of "who went where and why" within the context of rational choice theory, which holds, basically, that when faced with choices, people select the most rational or reasonable option, bearing in mind the variety of potential costs and rewards associated with any choice and in light of their personal preferences (Stark and Finke 2000: 36–38). It proposes and tests an extension to Stark and Finke's use of two factors, social capital and religious capital, in the religious choices that people make, in particular reaffiliation—joining a new group within their existing religious tradition (Stark and Finke 2000: 114–24)—with the addition of a third factor, moral capital.

Chapter 10 offers a brief summary of the book, including its original contributions to sociological theory.

A number of appendices include additional material which would have slowed down the main text, as well as a short consideration of the future state of schism in the Worldwide family of churches.

1.4 THEORETICAL BASIS AND METHODOLOGY

The theoretical basis and methodology of this study are outlined in appendix 2. Briefly, I have used a phenomenological approach, which I hope will make this work of interest not only to scholars and students of sociology of religion but also to those of religious studies in general, of history of religion, of theology, of anthropology, of psychology of religion, and, as this is very much an American group of religions, of the religious subset of American studies.

Theologically it is essentially a value-free approach. I am not concerned here with the spiritual truth of the beliefs of those I am studying. Because much of the study is based on the literature of the churches, including sometimes conflicting accounts of their recent history, I am also taking the position that all such accounts are of value because they reveal the perceptions of their writers, the leaders and members of different offshoot churches. The personal stories that people tell, even when they are clearly one-sided accounts, are a significant part of the data.

1.5 LITERATURE AND OTHER SOURCES

The literature underlying much of this work is described in some detail in appendix 3. It includes a number of books about the Worldwide Church of God, both external and internal, and large numbers of magazines and newspapers. The factual reliability of the internal source material is discussed in 3.1. I have also made much use of personal communications, including interviews, conversations, letters, and emails with leaders and members.

Leaders, ministers, and members of the Worldwide offshoots are very self-aware about their religion and its fragmentation, which meant that I was able to ask a number of searching questions about their personal history, their decisions, and their motivations, and also a quite complex question about hypothetical choices in my questionnaire. The questionnaire also provided the opportunity for anonymous comments, which were particularly useful for chapter 7, on authority in the churches.

It will usually be clear from the context, and will certainly be clear from the bibliography, whether a citation in the text is to a book or statement from a leader, spokesman, or member of a church, or from a sociologist or other scholar.

1.6 DEFINITIONS

It will be helpful to define certain terms as they are used throughout the book.

First, it is essential to distinguish between the Worldwide Church of God up to 1986 and Worldwide as it is today. In most places it will be clear from the context which I am referring to, but where there could be any ambiguity I shall refer to "the historical WCG/Worldwide" or "the old WCG/Worldwide" to mean up to the death of Herbert W. Armstrong in January 1986, and "the reformed WCG/Worldwide" or "the new WCG/Worldwide" to mean after December 1994, when the church publicly repudiated nearly all of Armstrong's teachings and became Evangelical.[6] The period 1986–94 is referred to as "the transitional years."

To avoid any confusion, the Church of God, a Worldwide Association, the off-shoot church founded in December 2010 when United Church of God split in two, is referred to by its initials COGWA, not as COG Worldwide.

A sociological discussion of how the terms "sect," "cult," and "new religious movement" apply to the churches in this study can be found in appendix 1. This includes a distinction between orthodox and heterodox sects as perceived by mainstream Christianity; with their distinctive teachings (see chapter 2) the historical WCG and today's offshoot churches are defined as theologically heterodox.

In general, theological terms are used in their usually accepted sense throughout this book, with a couple of exceptions noted below. As chapters 2 and 5 include detailed discussion of the original and the changed beliefs of the Worldwide Church of God, most doctrinal terms will be defined as they arise.

Although, as we shall see, Worldwide grew out of common roots with the Seventh-day Adventist Church, I shall be using "Sabbatarian" in preference to "Seventh-day," and "millenarian" or "millennialist" in preference to "Adventist"; these terms will be discussed fully in chapter 2.

Throughout the book I use "British-Israelite" instead of the alternative term "Anglo-Israelite" (see 2.14 and 2.2.3).

Like many Christian movements the Worldwide Church of God had a complex system of ministry ranging from deacons and deaconesses, to local elders and preaching elders, to pastors (including assistant pastors, associate pastors and retired pastors), to evangelists, and, in his lifetime, to the apostle, Herbert W. Armstrong. Variations on this structure have continued in most of the offshoot churches. In most of the larger churches the majority of pastors are normally salaried, but in some, such as the Church of God, International, they are not, and have outside jobs. For the sake of simplicity the word "ministers" is used throughout this book to include all of those who minister to members. Usually I shall distinguish only between founders or leaders of churches, ministers, and members.

The word "charismatic" is used both in its everyday sense of a powerful or winning personality and in the specialized sociological sense of Weber's authority type; context should make the distinction clear. In this book it is *not* used to refer to the Pentecostalist type of church or worship, with its distinctive "sign" of speaking in tongues.

The word "reformed" when describing the Worldwide Church of God refers to Worldwide after its theological changes were substantially completed, i.e., post-1994. In Christian theology the term "reformed" often refers to churches with a

6. See below for clarification of the term "reformed."

Calvinist rather than Arminian theology, particularly with regard to the issue of election or predestination; this is *not* the sense in which the term is used here.

The terms "CE" (Common Era) and "BCE" (Before the Common Era) are used in place of "AD" and "BC," except when the latter are used in quotations.

Bible references are taken from the Authorized (King James) Version unless otherwise stated.

Emphasis in all quotations is as in the original text, unless otherwise noted. Herbert W. Armstrong used and encouraged the use of a variety of typographical emphases such as capitalization, italics, boldface, and underlining in his church's publications; most of today's equivalents have dropped this style, with the exception of some of the leaders of the more hardline churches (see 6.1.3) and some of the more idiosyncratic individual writers (see 6.4.4).

In direct quotations, usage follows the original, such as, for example, "Seventh-Day" instead of the preferred "Seventh-day."

Any square-bracketed interpolations in quotations are mine unless otherwise stated.

1.7 CONCLUSION

In the ten years following the death of Herbert W. Armstrong, his successor as pastor general, Joseph W. Tkach, made major doctrinal changes in the Worldwide Church of God. Eventually all of Worldwide's distinctive heterodox teachings were dropped. Many ministers and members, unwilling to accept the changes in doctrine, left the church and founded new offshoot churches holding, to a greater or lesser extent, to the old doctrines.[7]

Whether later schisms within these offshoots were, in rational choice terms, primarily for doctrinal reasons (religious capital) or family-and-friendship reasons (social capital) (Stark and Finke 2000: 118–24), or whether another determining factor which I have called moral capital might also be involved is a major research question of this book, to be examined in detail in chapter 9.

In the Worldwide Church of God Herbert W. Armstrong taught that there should be a top-down authority: first God, then himself as God's apostle for the End Times, then the evangelists, pastors, and elders whom he appointed. Armstrong, almost from the beginning, constantly emphasized that the Bible did not teach that church government should be democratic (but see 7.3.3). This applied to decisions on doctrine, on members' behavior (including everything from divorce and remarriage to the wearing of makeup), and on the placing of ministers. There are many personal accounts, particularly from the 1970s, of unannounced home visits by

---

7. There had been previous schisms precipitated by changes in doctrine, as well as for other reasons, in the 1970s, when Armstrong was still leader of the Worldwide Church of God (see chapter 4).

senior ministers searching for evidence of noncompliance with church rules (see 8.3.6), and also of ministers from the lowest to the highest level being relocated, demoted, fired, or even disfellowshipped (excommunicated) with no notice and sometimes no stated reason (see 2.2.4). Reports by both ex-members and continuing members speak of an atmosphere of oppression, of mutual suspicion, of backstabbing of those on their way down by those on their way up—whose positions might be reversed six months later.

Memories are long. How much are the choices of today's ministers and members of the Worldwide family affected by their perceived mistreatment thirty years earlier? This is just one of the many questions this book seeks to address.

Such issues arising from authority and its legitimation within a religion with its own very distinctive social construction of reality make this case study of one twentieth-century American religious sect, and its twenty-first-century offshoots, of universal interest within the sociological study of religion.

PART ONE

The Story

CHAPTER 2

Doctrines of the Worldwide
Church of God

INTRODUCTION

In order to understand the shock to ministers and members of Worldwide when their doctrines were changed after Herbert W. Armstrong's death, it is essential to understand the teachings of the church. The beliefs of the historical Worldwide Church included a body of "deviant knowledge" rejected as false by the majority of mainstream Christianity (Bainbridge 1997: 378). The maintenance of this belief system was of major importance to the church.

This chapter and the two following it examine the doctrinal antecedents of Worldwide and many of its own major doctrines, the formulation of Armstrong's distinctive beliefs and the beginnings of his church, and some of the events and controversies of the first half century of the church before Armstrong's death. They thus provide some indication of the significance of the massive shift in value orientation (Glock and Stark 1965: 9) of Worldwide in the ten years after Armstrong's death (see chapter 5), and the consequent determination of the offshoot churches to maintain their existing social construction of reality (Berger and Luckmann 1966) and the conservation of their existing religious capital by rejecting the massive doctrinal remaking of the new Worldwide (Stark and Finke 2000: 121).

Throughout these three chapters it is apparent that observance of God's Law is of paramount importance: obedience to God, and therefore to his appointed representatives, comes before everything else. The Worldwide Church of God under Herbert W. Armstrong, and to a lesser extent the Sabbatarian environment from which it developed, are anything but antinomian. For nonmembers, Worldwide might appear a strictly legalistic church; for members, it is their duty and obligation to obey God's Law, as laid down in the Bible, and as interpreted by the leadership of the church: "But once the *knowledge of the truth* comes, they must OBEY" (H. W. Armstrong 1985a: 55). This is the heart and the framework, the meaningful order, the socially established *nomos* of their lives, and thus the most important function of Worldwide's construction of society is nomization (Berger 1969: 31 and see appendix 2). This is the crucial setting for the issues of authority which lie at the heart of this study.

2.1 HISTORICAL AND DOCTRINAL BACKGROUND OF THE WORLDWIDE CHURCH OF GOD

The historical Worldwide Church of God was a Sabbatarian millenarian sect. The first section of this chapter examines the background of Sabbatarianism and millenarianism from which WCG grew; the coming together of these two distinctive beliefs in the Seventh-day Adventist movement, which shares common beginnings with the precursors of WCG; and finally the history of British Israelism, which formed the fundamental basis for Armstrong's and Worldwide's prophetic ministry.

2.1.1 Sabbatarianism and Observance of the Law

Christianity began as a Jewish sect. Jesus and his disciples were Jews and practiced the Jewish religion. This included the seventh-day Sabbath:

> Six days may work be done; but in the seventh is the Sabbath of rest, holy to the Lord...Wherefore the children of Israel shall keep the Sabbath, to observe the Sabbath throughout their generations, for a perpetual covenant. (Exod. 31:15–16)

Keeping the Sabbath is one of the Ten Commandments. These are still taught within mainstream Christianity, yet in the majority of Christian denominations one of them has been abandoned: the day of rest has been changed from Saturday, the seventh day, to Sunday, the first day of the week.

Christians justify this change by pointing to texts such as "upon the first day of the week, when the disciples came together to break bread, Paul preached unto them" (Acts 20:7), and by saying that honoring Sunday is in remembrance of the day of Jesus's resurrection. The change seems to have begun in Rome in the middle of the second century CE; it may have been a deliberate move, Christians in Rome being predominantly Gentile, to distinguish the fledgling Christian religion from the Jewish religion from which it had developed (Ferguson 1990: 808; GCSDA 1988: 259). According to Eusebius some early Christians observed both the Jewish Sabbath and the first day of the week (Eusebius, *Church History*, 3:27).

Historical evidence suggests that, apart from in Rome and Alexandria, many Christians continued to hold the seventh-day Sabbath as late as the fifth century CE (GCSDA 1988: 259). But with the acceptance of Christianity by the emperor

Constantine in 312 CE, Sunday observance began to be enforced. It has often been suggested that this was an absorption into Christianity of some aspects of the popular cult of Sol Invictus, whose day of worship was Sunday (GCSDA 1988: 259–60). Constantine's edict of 321 CE specifying Sunday as a day for prayer rather than for work (Chadwick 1967: 128; Kee 1982: 57, 96) referred to the day as *Dies Solis*, and he continued issuing coins bearing the symbol of the Sun until at least 323 CE. The church historian Eusebius is clearly presenting a Christian-based apologia for Constantine's edict, which he says is "in memory, I suppose, of what the Savior of mankind is recorded to have achieved on that day"—i.e., the resurrection (Eusebius, *Life of Constantine*, 4:18).[1]

The ex post facto justification of the change to Sunday worship in Christian texts tends to follow Eusebius: "On the first day of the week the Lord rose from the dead, and the Christians began to assemble on that day for worship of the risen Christ. This day is the Lord's Day, and as such is the Sabbath which God had instituted at creation. The commands regarding it have never been abrogated" (Douglas 1962: 1111). Those who maintain the seventh-day Sabbath today would argue that one of the "commands regarding it" is that it must be on the seventh day of the week, not the first.

The Council of Trent (1545–63) openly used the church's change from the (Saturday) Sabbath to the (Sunday) Lord's Day as an example of the authority of the Roman Catholic Church to go beyond scriptural teaching (GCSDA 1988: 261); Worldwide offshoots emphasize this point in order to demonstrate the non-scriptural validity of Sunday worship (Meredith 1997: 34–37).

Sabbath keeping did not entirely die out. There is some evidence that Saints Patrick and Columba observed both Saturday and Sunday, and that this practice might have continued in isolated parts of Britain even after the Synod of Whitby in 664 CE ensured Roman Christianity's supremacy over Celtic Christianity (Leonard 2000: 5).

Sabbatarianism resurfaced in Britain in the seventeenth century with a Puritan minister, John Traske, who was imprisoned for his beliefs in 1617, and a Church of England clergyman, Theophilus Brabourne, who in 1628 published *Discourse upon the Sabbath Day* (Leonard 2000: 5–6). A number of seventh-day congregations developed; the largest group were the Seventh Day Baptists. In 1664 Sabbatarianism was carried to America—specifically Newport, Rhode Island—by Stephen Mumford, a Seventh Day Baptist (Hoeh 1959b: 22–23). It maintained a small but significant presence in America for the next two centuries, until the next major development relevant to the Worldwide Church of God and to this study.

Christian sects are often characterized specifically as being in tension with society (Glock and Stark 1965; B. Wilson 1990: 46–68; Stark and Finke 2000: 144); Sabbatarianism inevitably creates such tension simply because Sabbatarians

---

1. Quotations from this work are from the revised Bagster translation, available online at http://www.fordham.edu/halsall/basis/vita-constantine.asp.

make a point of worshiping and working on different days from other Christians. It should be kept in mind that for its proponents, Sabbatarianism is founded on obedience to the word of God, the authority of the Bible.

For some Sabbatarians this is one aspect of a much more detailed picture, involving the observance of seven Jewish festivals (see 2.2.2).

2.1.2   Millenarianism

Many Christian scholars accept that the earliest Christians, including the New Testament writers, expected the End Times and the Second Coming of the Messiah/Christ to happen in their own lifetimes (Peake 1948: 911; Haggith 1999: 107; see also 1 Peter 4:7, 1 John 2:18, etc.). This needs to be seen in the context of the times, rather than from the perspective of later Christian theology, which had yet to be developed.

Between 200 BCE and 200 CE there was a vast amount of religious writing in the Middle East, in addition to the last books to be added to the Old Testament canon and all the books of the New Testament:[2] the books which were collected in the standard Apocrypha, found in Roman Catholic Bibles but not generally in Protestant Bibles today; the pseudepigraphical writings, which included many gospels and epistles purportedly by disciples or close companions of Jesus; a great number of apocalyptic writings; spiritual poetry and psalms; and rules and regulations of religious communities. There have been numerous collections of these— Cowper 1867, *Lost Books of the Bible* 1963, and Platt 1980, for example—and several more recent translations of what are now often called Gnostic gospels and epistles (Barnstone 1984; Ehrman 2003b; Meyer 2005; Newton 2009).[3] Some of these fit within the broad stream of Judaism of the time; some are clearly Christian; some are Gnostic; some overlap two or all three of these groups. Many display what are now called millenarian expectations.

The purpose of Jewish apocalyptic writing was to answer what would otherwise have to be seen as a broken promise by God. God had promised King David, "Thine house and thy kingdom shall be established for ever before thee; thy throne shall be established forever" (2 Sam. 7:16). Yet four hundred years later Judah was conquered and the Israelites were in captivity, exiles from their own land. So had God lied to them, broken his promise, let them down? Perhaps he was less powerful than the gods of those who had conquered them. Maybe they should turn to those gods instead.

---

2. Although the books of the New Testament had largely been gathered together by the mid-third century CE, there was still dispute about the exact composition of the New Testament canon up to the late fourth century, with some doubts about many of the non-Pauline Epistles, and with the Epistle to the Hebrews and the Book of Revelation in particular often being questioned (*Lost Books of the Bible* 1963: 291–93). See also note 4 to this chapter.

3. Such books are included among the Dead Sea Scrolls and the Nag Hammadi Library, both discovered in the mid-20th century, but some have been known for many centuries.

The prophets, particularly some of the "minor prophets" in the last twelve books of the Old Testament, had an explanation: God was punishing his people for their unfaithfulness to him. If they returned to him, God would deliver his people from their bondage, punish their enemies, and bring the world to a terrible but glorious end. In such prophetic eschatology (apocalyptic writing), "the Jews found a means of accounting for the catastrophic disparity between their votive expectations of national glory and the harsh truth of their miserable history" (Benjamin 1998: 56).

The intertestamental period, after the end of the Babylonian exile around 530 BCE, saw further conquests and foreign rule of the Jews by the Greek Alexander, the Egyptian Ptolemies, the Syrian Seleucids, and finally the Romans. It is unsurprising that apocalyptic writing continued throughout this time, with a fervent Jewish hope for their messianic deliverer from oppression (Manley 1947: 264–97; Cohn 1993: 163–93).

The book of Revelation, crucial to present-day millenarian teachings in many Christian sects including the Worldwide family of churches, was also written in a time of crisis.[4] The Temple in Jerusalem had been destroyed, and both Jews and the fledgling Christian communities faced persecution from their Roman rulers. Had God forsaken them?

The writer of Revelation, one of many apocalyptic books written around that time, used the familiar imagery of Jewish prophets like Ezekiel and Daniel—spectacular visions, complex symbols, esoterically meaningful numbers—to give hope to his readers; whatever troubles they were going through now, they should look to the glorious future when God would step into history and bring them peace and justice, and freedom from their oppressors (Alexander and Alexander 1999, 763, 768). Apocalyptic writing such as Revelation was thus a particular literary genre, with its own rules and conventions, and with a specific purpose—a context which is ignored by most millenarian interpretations of Revelation, Daniel, and other apocalyptic writings in the Bible; for millenarian Christians such prophetic passages in the Bible are speaking to them specifically about their own present day.

Millenarianism is not just the belief in the return of the Messiah or Christ but a specific belief in a one-thousand-year event.[5] Broadly speaking, believers in millenarianism may be divided into two strands: postmillennialists, who believe that Christ will return *after* a thousand years of peace, and premillennialists, who believe that Christ will return first, then establish his kingdom on Earth and reign for a thousand years. Most millenarian Christians today, including the historical Worldwide Church of God and its offshoots, are premillennialists. Some think that

4. Revelation was to become officially accepted in the New Testament canon by Athanasius as late as the mid-4th century CE (*Lost Books of the Bible* 1963: 292), and even then was regarded with suspicion in some areas of Christendom. "Indeed in the Eastern Church in the Middle Ages it was more often omitted from than included in manuscripts of the New Testament" (MacGregor 1959: 41).

5. From Latin *mille*, thousand; the alternative terms "chiliasm" and "chiliastic" are from the Greek for thousand, *chilias*.

true believers will be taken up from Earth in the Rapture to escape the years of suffering that everyone else will experience (pretribulationists), while others believe that Christians too must suffer before Christ returns (posttribulationists), the position held by Worldwide.

Belief in the Second Coming and the millennium is nothing new (Barrett 2001a: 70–81; Benjamin 1998; Bowie 1997; Cohn 1970; Katz and Popkin 1999; E. Weber 1999). No less an authority than Augustine declared in the fifth century that we should treat certain biblical passages such as those about the Second Coming allegorically rather than literally (Thompson 1996: 29–30; this position is known as amillennialism), but his words of caution have frequently been ignored. At many points in the last two thousand years preachers have predicted the imminent return of Christ, many setting dates, some embarrassingly near to their pronouncement, others perhaps more sensibly further in their future.

The teachings of two ministers in the early to mid-nineteenth century would have a marked effect on Protestant Christian beliefs of the next century and a half.

John Nelson Darby (1800–1882), one of the founders of the Exclusive Brethren, or Plymouth Brethren, a Christian sect formed in Britain around 1830, devised the concept of Dispensationalism (Katz and Popkin 1999: 142–44). He taught that there are seven dispensations, or ages, of man: first, the Age of Innocence, before the Fall, followed by the Ages of Conscience, Human Government, Promise, Law, and the current Age of Grace, which was established by Christ. The last dispensation will be the soon-coming millennial reign of Christ; and it was on this that the most attention was focused as "the fulfillment of the theocratic promises to Israel": "The prophecies of the restoration of Israel as a nation to her land with a literal throne, literal Davidic king, literal temple, and literal sacrificial system will be fulfilled *au pied de la lettre*" (Douglas 1962: 390). This literalism is crucial to an understanding of the teachings of Herbert W. Armstrong and the Worldwide Church of God and its offshoots.

Darby's Dispensationalism caught the imagination of many Evangelicals in the nineteenth century, including the famous American preacher Dwight L. Moody, and was taught at the Moody Bible Institute, perhaps the most influential Bible School in America in the late nineteenth and early twentieth centuries. Even more importantly, it was incorporated wholesale into one of the most significant Protestant books of the twentieth century, the *Scofield Reference Bible*, and so became accepted as straightforward biblical fact by millions of Evangelicals, especially in the United States. "For the more naïve reader, there was little to distinguish the word of God from that of Scofield, and his footnotes easily acquired almost canonical status" (Katz and Popkin 1999: 148).

The other significant figure was an American Baptist minister, William Miller (1782–1849). He was influenced by the teachings of a mid-eighteenth-century German Lutheran minister, J. G. Bengel, who had taught that Christ would return in 1836. Miller, basing his calculations on Daniel and Revelation, set the date instead at some time between March 21, 1843, and March 21, 1844, and in his preaching in New England persuaded many Americans of this. Miller himself was reluctant to be more specific than this, but when Christ had not returned by March 1844 one of Miller's followers, Samuel S. Snow, worked out the exact date of October 22, 1844 (J. Greer 2012: 142–50; Thompson 1996: 98–100). Even having been wrong the previous year, Miller and his supporters attracted a lot of followers, in what is known as the Second Advent movement. Some sold their homes and businesses in anticipation of the great event, though stories of them sitting on their rooftops in "ascension robes" are apocryphal. October 1844 became known as the Great Disappointment—but out of it came a church which is still strong today, the Seventh-day Adventists.

2.1.3 Seventh-day Adventism

In his earlier encyclopedias J. Gordon Melton classified the Worldwide Church of God as an Adventist Sabbatarian movement (Melton 1977: 252–53).[6] It grew out of the Church of God (Seventh Day) (COG7), which has common origins with the Seventh-day Adventist Church (SDA).

The name Seventh-day Adventist expresses two of the main distinguishing features of this church: they worship on the seventh day of the week, and they await with expectation the Second Advent, the Second Coming of Christ. Although there is one main denomination with the name, Seventh-day Adventism per se is less a church than a movement; there have been hundreds of offshoots, some no more than a handful of congregations, others considerably larger, like the Worldwide Church of God. William Miller himself, who died five years after the Great Disappointment, never joined or endorsed any of the movements which sprang up in its wake.

The Seventh-day Adventist Church was founded on three main doctrines put forward by different Millerites or Adventists in the 1840s. One was that Christ had not returned to Earth in 1844 but had entered his heavenly sanctuary to cleanse it and sort out the sheep from the goats in preparation for the Judgment. Another was that Christians must obey God's Law, as set out in the Ten Commandments, which include the observance of the Sabbath; this belief was imported from the Seventh Day Baptists. The third was that in these last days the gift of prophecy would come on the church; Seventh-day Adventists believe that the visions and teachings of Ellen G. White are a fulfillment of the Biblical gifts of the Spirit (1 Cor. 12: 1–11).

Ellen G. White (1827–1915), née Ellen Gould Harmon, was brought up a Methodist and joined the Millerites when she was seventeen. She suffered from illness and injury as a child, including fainting and epileptic fits, and some critics believe that her visions were a continuation of these conditions (Sanders 1962: 124).

---

6. In a later encyclopedia Melton classifies Worldwide and its offshoots in a group of their own as "Church of God Adventists" (Melton 1999).

Her first vision, in December 1844, convinced her that belief in the October 1844 date was not an error or delusion, despite the Great Disappointment only two months before.

In her books she taught, among much else, healthy living, instituting several dietary regulations (GCSDA 1988: 280–86) including the Old Testament prohibition on eating "unclean foods" (see 2.2.1). Her writings were regarded as prophetic and inspired, but not as replacing or even adding to the Bible (GCSDA 1988: 227–28). She later married James White (1821–61), a very prominent Adventist minister. After his death she became the acknowledged leader of the movement.

The theology of the Seventh-day Adventist Church mellowed a little over the years as Mrs White grew older, and after her death; her church gradually went through the process of denominationalization (B. Wilson 1990: 109), becoming considerably closer to mainstream Christian doctrine during the twentieth century. For example, many early Seventh-day Adventist leaders were anti-Trinitarian, but today's teaching of the church is conventionally Trinitarian (GCSDA 1988: 22). At one time, the SDA Church taught that Sunday keeping was the Mark of the Beast (Rev. 13:16–17) and that only Sabbath-keepers would be saved; now they say of themselves:

> They do *not* believe that only Seventh-day Adventists will be saved when Jesus returns, or that they are the only Church that teaches Bible truth....
>
> They do *not* believe that humans are saved by Sabbath-keeping. (Stickland, n.d.: 9–10)

Realizing that some of their earlier and more extreme writings were still being quoted against them by Evangelical counter-cultists (Irvine 1917: 154–67; Sanders 1962: 122–35; Davies 1954: 71–82; Sanders and Wright 1956: 18–27), the church produced in 1957 a seven-hundred-page work on doctrine, which clarified many contentious issues. This was followed in 1988 by the more concise 392-page *Seventh-day Adventists Believe...: A Biblical Exposition of 27 Fundamental Doctrines* (GCSDA 1988).

To return to the origins of the movement, the new organization, initially almost a federation of independent congregations, set up its headquarters in Battle Creek, Michigan, in 1855; it took the name Seventh-day Adventist at a conference there in 1860 and was formally organized as a church in 1863.

At the Battle Creek conference in 1860 some people preferred the name Church of God (see 3.2.1), and the matter was put to a vote. Mrs. White made the point that

> the name Seventh-day Adventist carries the true features of our faith in front, and will convict the inquiring mind....
>
> I was shown that almost every fanatic who has arisen, who wishes to hide his sentiments that he may lead away others, claims to belong to the Church of God. Such a name would at once excite suspicion; for it is employed to conceal the most absurd errors. (Hoeh 1959b: 24)

This was quoted with no apparent irony by the Worldwide Church of God's most respected theologian, Herman L. Hoeh.

Those congregations which kept to the name Church of God retained Saturday worship and millenarian beliefs, but rejected some of Ellen G. White's other teachings. They officially took the name Church of God, Seventh Day, in 1884.[7] This small organization was based in Stanberry, Missouri (actually one of the earliest churches in the Seventh-day Adventist movement)—and it had a daughter church in Oregon. It was to this church that Herbert W. Armstrong was to come in 1927 (see 3.2.1).

2.1.4 The Ten Lost Tribes and British Israelism

At the very heart of the millenarian teachings of the historical Worldwide Church of God, and of its offshoots, is the doctrine of British Israelism. Herbert W. Armstrong was to make this doctrine his own, but it was by no means original to his church; indeed, in various forms, it has a long history.

In Old Testament mythology the patriarch Jacob (later called Israel), son of Isaac, son of Abraham, had twelve sons, who fathered the twelve tribes of Israel (Gen. 35:22–26). These eventually formed into two nations, the southern kingdom of Judah, which also contained Benjamin and some of Levi (the priestly tribe), and the northern kingdom of Israel, which contained all the other tribes. These two nations were briefly united under King David.[8]

Both nations—or at least "the cream of the population" (Douglas 1962: 669)— were conquered and taken into captivity in Mesopotamia, first Israel by the Assyrians around 720 BCE, then Judah by the Babylonians around 598–81 BCE.[9]

The general consensus of non-Fundamentalist biblical scholars is that it was during and immediately after the latter captivity that many of the books of the Old Testament were either written or edited into something approximating their present form (G. MacGregor 1959: 17–18; Douglas 1962: 189),[10] and that Judaism absorbed many myths and doctrinal features of earlier Babylonian, Sumerian, and

---

7. There were a number of groups with similar beliefs and similar names. The two largest today are the General Conference of the Church of God (Seventh Day)—the parent group of the church which Armstrong joined—and the Church of God (7th Day), which, with Armstrong, split from it in 1933 (see 3.2.2).

8. Some recent scholarship (Marcus 2000; McKenzie 2000; Cline 2007) has cast doubt on the historicity of the "Golden Age" of David's united monarchy as described in the Bible.

9. Biblical scholarship suggests that, far from being slaves in captivity, as the Bible asserts, the Jews in Babylon were treated as freemen; some rose to high positions; and many stayed there, some of their descendants only returning to Israel 2,600 years later in the 1950s (MacGregor 1959: 15–16; Marcus 2000: 172–75).

10. The psalm beginning "By the rivers of Babylon, there we sat down, yea, we wept, when we remembered Zion" (Psalms 137:1) was clearly written during or after the Babylonian captivity.

Persian religions (Hooke 1963: 103–60), including the Creation story (K. Armstrong 1993: 14, 77), the Flood (George 1999: xiii–xiv), and the Zoroastrian concepts of, among others, one God with an evil opponent, an afterlife in heaven or hell, and, most significant in the present context, a Final Judgment (Crim 1981: 828–29; Hinnells 1984: 362–63; Stoyanov 2000: 54–56).

The books of Ezra and Nehemiah describe how the Jews (i.e., descendants of Judah) were allowed by King Cyrus to return from Babylon to their homeland, by now known as Judaea, in the fifth century BCE—but the other tribes, who had been taken into captivity by the Assyrians, are not mentioned again.

What happened to these "Ten Lost Tribes"? Some may perhaps have returned to Judaea with the Jews and merged with them, the tribal differences of the House of Israel eventually being forgotten. It is also probable that those who were taken to other countries were eventually assimilated into their populations; it was the Assyrian policy to move and merge entire peoples. Indeed, when the Israelites were moved out of Israel, they were "replaced by immigrants from other parts of the Assyrian Empire" (Douglas 1962: 582).

There has been speculation about the fate of the Ten Lost Tribes of Israel for centuries, particularly in an eschatological context. Norman Cohn cites perhaps the earliest reference to their being involved in the End Times, "in the pages of Commodianus, a very inferior Latin poet of (probably) the fifth century":

> For according to Commodianus when Christ returns it will be at the head not of an angelic host but of the descendants of the ten lost tribes of Israel, which have survived in hidden places, unknown to the rest of the world. (Cohn 1970: 28)

So where did the Ten Lost Tribes go? There have been many theories and numerous claimants, some wilder than others, and most with little or no supporting evidence. One theory, dating as far back as Columbus, is that the native peoples of America might be "the barbarized descendants of the Ten Tribes of Israel" (Katz and Popkin 1999: 80).

In a sentence, British Israelism is the belief that the dispersed Ten Lost Tribes of Israel migrated to Europe and settled in Britain. The general theory was first clearly propounded by a Scot, John Wilson, in 1840, but it can be traced back at least two and a half centuries before that.

A French magistrate, Counsellor Le Loyer, wrote *The Ten Lost Tribes Found* in 1590 (Sanders 1962: 136). John Sadler, a town clerk in London, member of parliament for Cambridge, and a favorite of Oliver Cromwell, published the book *Rights of the Kingdom* in 1649, in which he argued that some of the British people were descended from the Israelites (Larsen 1971: 90). A Protestant apologist, Dr. Jakob Abbadie of Amsterdam, wrote in *Le Triomphe de la Providence et de la Religion* (1723), "Unless the ten tribes have flown into the air or have been plunged into the center of the earth, they must be sought for in the north and the west, and in the British Isles" (Sanders 1962: 136; Nettlehorst 1979; Seekins and Seekins 2006).

The Newfoundland-born Richard Brothers (1757–1824), a former Royal Navy officer who described himself as "the nephew of the Almighty," claiming to be descended from James, the brother of Jesus, caused a stir in England in the 1790s with his pronouncements of the imminent end of the world. London was Babylon, and God would destroy it, either by fire or by earthquake, specifically on June 4th, 1795. Believing himself to be the embodiment of the Messiah, he foretold that he would lead the triumphant return of the Jews to Jerusalem—not the "visible Hebrews," readily identifiable in London, but the "invisible Hebrews," who were the descendants of the Ten Lost Tribes. Although Brothers's followers included a member of parliament and a lawyer, among others, this did not stop him being arrested and placed in an asylum until 1806 (Storm 1991: 187; E. Weber 1999: 149–50).

But it is the publication of John Wilson's *Lectures on Our Israelitish Origins* (1840) that really marks the beginning of British Israelism as a recognizable movement (Melton and Baumann 2002: 171). From 1840 to his death in 1871, Wilson taught that the British were the physical descendants of the Ten Lost Tribes:

> The so-called "lost house of Israel", the leading tribe of which was Ephraim…are the modern nations of Europe, and especially those of Saxon race, whose glorious privilege it now is to "preach the gospel for a witness unto all nations ere the end come." (quoted in Katz and Popkin 1999: 172)

These few lines from Wilson include several elements which were to become part of Worldwide's teachings: the mention of all the nations of Europe, the emphasis on the Saxons, the commission to preach the gospel "unto all nations" while there is still time, and, most particularly, the emphasis on the subtribe of Ephraim, the second son of Joseph. In later years Wilson identified America as Joseph's elder son, Manasseh. This identification of Ephraim and Manasseh is central to Herbert W. Armstrong's prophetic ministry, most clearly set out in his book *The United States and Britain in Prophecy*; the dropping of this teaching by Worldwide after Armstrong's death was to be one of the causes of the schisms (see 5.1.2). There were other details in Wilson's teachings which were to turn up again in Armstrong's teachings, such as his derivation of the word "British" and the significance of the name "Dan" in European geography (see 2.2.3).

Wilson himself did not set up any sort of organization, but in the year of his death the first British Israelite organization was founded by others. The next few decades saw a significant growth in the appeal of British Israelism, particularly to the British middle and upper classes. A number of new groups were formed, eventually merging into the British Israel World Federation (BIWF) in 1922. This drew large numbers of members; in 1929 they filled the Royal Albert Hall in London, and in 1931 over 20,000 people attended its week-long annual congress. The BIWF had support from parliamentarians of both Houses (Lords and Commons), some senior members of the armed forces, and a number of clergy; its most senior patron was Princess Alice of Athlone (1883–1981), a granddaughter of Queen Victoria (BIWF website; BIWF Canada website).

The figure of two million claimed adherents in the late nineteenth and early twentieth centuries is often quoted, though without any substantiating evidence (Davies 1954: 121; Kellett 1965: 72; Greer 1997; Pierce 1977). An academic estimate is that "at the peak of its popularity in England in the 1920s, British Israelism may have had as many as 5,000 adherents, in addition to smaller followings in the Commonwealth nations and the United States" (Arthur L. Greil, in Melton and Baumann 2002: 171). But it should be remembered that the Worldwide Church of God, which had British Israelism at the heart of its teachings, had a hundred thousand baptized members at its peak in the 1990s.

British Israelism spread to the United States in the late nineteenth century. The most significant figure so far as this present study is concerned was J. H. Allen (1847–1930), a Methodist minister who promoted the holiness movement in Missouri. Allen moved to Pasadena in California—later, interestingly, to be the home of the Worldwide Church of God—and there he taught British Israelism, specifically that the British are the chosen people, followed by the Americans. In 1902 the first edition of his book *Judah's Sceptre and Joseph's Birthright* was published; this was to be a major, though for many years hidden, influence on the teachings of Herbert W. Armstrong and the Worldwide Church of God, and of most of the offshoots today (see 2.2.3).

Is British Israelism in itself a religion? It is condemned in numerous Christian counter-cult books (Irvine 1917: 34–43; Sanders 1962: 136–44; Davies 1954: 121–35; Kellett 1965: 72–79). Two nineteenth-century comments show how the established church regarded it. The *Church Quarterly Review* wrote of British Israelism in 1880, "Like good Templarism, Plymouth Brethrenism or Freemasonry, it is a quasi-religion, and, once accepted, is looked upon as the most important of all religious truths" (Anglo-Israelism 1880: 319)—which, as we shall see, is certainly the case with the historical Worldwide Church of God and some of its offshoot churches. The newspaper *Church Times* of June 12, 1885, described it as "Chosen Peopleism" and attacked it as a religious equivalent of craving for aristocratic distinction (both cited in Simpson 2002: 8, 9).

A more recent description is "a variety of British nationalism buttressed by biblical references with all the attributes of a religious movement except religion" (Altholz 1989: 130, cited in Simpson 2002: 1). But there is a fine line between nationalism and racism. Because British Israelism effectively claims scriptural support for the supremacy of White Anglo-Saxons, it lies behind the beliefs of some overtly white supremacist groups such as Christian Identity and Aryan Nations today (Storm 1991: 187–88; Katz and Popkin 1999: 187–89; Melton and Baumann 2002: 171). Whether the Worldwide Church of God was openly racist is discussed in 2.2.3.

2.2 DOCTRINES OF THE HISTORICAL WORLDWIDE CHURCH OF GOD

For an appreciation of what made the historical Worldwide Church of God such a distinctive sect, and as a basis for understanding the differences between the many offshoots (see chapter 6), it is essential to look at some of the church's doctrines. First I shall list a number of doctrines in brief and draw some comparisons between Worldwide and its antecedents; then I shall discuss in greater depth Worldwide's own application of the two doctrines discussed above, Sabbatarianism and observance of the Law, and millenarianism, with specific reference to Worldwide's belief in British Israelism. The final subsection, on church governance and authority, is of particular importance to the questions raised in this book (see chapter 7).

2.2.1 A Brief Outline of the Main Heterodox Doctrines

Unlike several other new religious movements (for example, the Unification Church or the Church of Scientology), the historical Worldwide Church of God was always upfront about its beliefs. Every issue of *Plain Truth* magazine contained articles on substantial doctrines and mentioned booklets on a wide variety of doctrinal subjects, which readers could send for and receive free of charge.

The following list includes many of the teachings of the Worldwide Church of God which set it apart from mainstream Christianity, causing it to be regarded by mainstream Christians as a heterodox, deviant, or heretical Christian sect (Campbell 1962; Petersen 1975: 130–43).

- God is a family, currently consisting of the Father and his Son, Jesus (H. W. Armstrong 1985a: 31–57). This is binitarianism rather than trinitarianism.
- Our ultimate destiny is to become part of (the family of) God ourselves (50–51).
- The Holy Spirit is the action of God, not a Person of the Godhead (44–45).[11]
- The Trinity is a false doctrine, devised in the second–fourth centuries, which has been the mark of false Christianity through the ages (51–57).
- The letters to the seven churches in Revelation 1–3 are seen as types of the history of the Christian church through the ages (Hoeh 1959b: 8; H. W. Armstrong 1985a: 282–92). The seven church eras are:
  1. Ephesus (Rev. 2:1–7): first and early second century—beginnings
  2. Smyrna (Rev. 2:8–11): second century to 365—the persecuted church

11. Of all the heterodox doctrines of Worldwide, this is probably the most widespread in other nonmainstream Christian Churches, such as the Jehovah's Witnesses, Christadelphians, etc.

3. Pergamos (Rev. 2:12–17): 365 to the late Middle or Dark Ages—corruption
4. Thyatira (Rev. 2:18–29): 1360 to the early seventeenth century—Reformation, survival
5. Sardis (Rev. 3:1–6): early seventeenth century to 1931—from England to America
6. Philadelphia (Rev. 3:7–13): beginning in 1931—the Armstrong era
7. Laodicea (Rev. 3:14–22): the time of the end—corruption and falling away (Nichols and Mather 1998: 57–58).[12]

- One-third of the Bible is prophecy, relating to the End Times; many current events are specifically foretold in these prophecies, and the return of Jesus is rapidly approaching (Ambassador College 1972a; Ambassador College 1973a; Ambassador College 1973b).
- British Israelism (H. W. Armstrong 1945 etc.): see 2.1.4 and 2.2.3.
- True believers (i.e., WCG members) will be the rulers of the Earth during the millennium, when other people will be given the chance of salvation (H. W. Armstrong 1962).
- After death there is unconsciousness ("soul sleep") until the resurrection at the Second Coming (Hoeh 1956).
- The unsaved will be destroyed, rather than suffering in hell (H. W. Armstrong 1969).
- The Gospel is the Gospel of the forthcoming Kingdom of God, rather than a Gospel of present salvation and being "born again" (H. W. Armstrong 1985a: 224–26, 293ff).
- The Bible is literally true, including the Genesis account of Creation, and evolution is a false doctrine (H. W. Armstrong 1958b; G. T. Armstrong 1967a; G. T. Armstrong 1967b; Armstrong and Kroll 1968; G. T. Armstrong 1969)
- Jesus was crucified on Wednesday and rose exactly three days and three nights later, on Saturday—the Sabbath (H. W. Armstrong 1952c; Hoeh 1959a; H. W. Armstrong 1972a).
- Although salvation is by grace, our reward is according to our works—obedience to God's Law (H. W. Armstrong 1952d; H. W. Armstrong 1969). This is discussed in a little more detail below.
- Observation of not only the seventh-day Sabbath but also the seven annual Jewish festivals is required of all true believers; see 2.2.2 (H. W. Armstrong 1976a; H. W. Armstrong 1985a: 201–2).
- The government of the present Church of God should be hierarchical, not democratic (H. W. Armstrong 1985a: 49, 335); see 2.2.4 and chapter 7.
- Tithing. This was a tenth of gross income to be given to God, i.e., God's church, the WCG. There were also second and third tithes (see 2.2.2) (Hoeh 1959c).

12. See 3.2.2 for the significance of the seven church eras to the founding of Worldwide, and chapter 6 for the present-day significance of the church eras to the offshoots.

- Observation of all Old Testament law is required, including dietary restrictions—e.g., no pork or shellfish (H. W. Armstrong 1958a: 2). Interestingly, this adherence to Jewish law did not apply to circumcision (Hopkins 1974: 136–37), though Armstrong strongly advocated it for health reasons, and to discourage masturbation: "I am sure I have the approval of the Lord in making the most urgent recommendation for circumcision, for sanitary, health and moral protection" (H. W. Armstrong 1981a: 128) (but see 4.3).
- Christmas, Easter, etc. are pagan festivals and must not be celebrated (H. W. Armstrong 1952a; H. W. Armstrong 1952b; H. W. Armstrong 1974a). Birthdays should not be celebrated either.

Several of these doctrines, such as the composition of God, were debated at great length in the first few centuries of Christianity before the generally accepted formulae of orthodox Christianity were devised (Ferguson 1990; Lüdemann 1996; Ehrman 2003a). There are similarities between several of the doctrines and some of those of other unorthodox Christian sects; for example, the Mormons have a version of the "God family" (see 2.3); Seventh-day Adventism (SDA) teaches "soul sleep"; both Jehovah's Witnesses and Christadelphians teach the destruction of the unsaved and emphasize the Second Coming; and the white-supremacist Christian Identity movement is characterized by a version of British Israelism. Many small Christian denominations, both orthodox and heterodox, emphasize tithing, though not usually to the extent that Worldwide did.

Indeed, both the Church of God which Armstrong joined in 1927 and some of the early Seventh-day Adventists held numerous doctrines which he took with him into his own church. One prominent SDA minister, Greenbury G. Rupert (1847–1922), who knew Ellen G. White for forty years,

> observed the Holy Days, eschewed unclean meats, held to the name "Church of God", advocated local autonomy, rejected Christmas, Easter and other pagan holidays, believed in tithing and church eras, emphasized Bible prophecy in his preaching and taught that the United States was part of Israel.[13] (Nickels 1996a)

All of these were to become part of WCG doctrine, though the ideal of "local autonomy" would be dropped as Worldwide grew as a church; this is an area of contention in the offshoots today, and one of the primary differentiations between hardline and liberal offshoots (see chapters 6 and 7, particularly 6.1.3).

As mentioned above (2.1.3), over the years the SDA moved closer to standard Protestant doctrines and practices; for example, many early SDA preachers

---

13. According to one source, boxes found in Armstrong's basement contained old copies of a magazine titled *The Remnant of Israel*, published by G. G. Rupert, containing these teachings and many more which would become Armstrong's "own" teachings ("Herbert Armstrong's Religious Roots," *Ambassador Report* 2).

rejected the Trinity, but by the 1930s it had become accepted doctrine. The Evangelical counter-cult writer Walter R. Martin, in later editions of his influential book *The Kingdom of the Cults*, discusses whether the SDA need still be considered (in his terms) a cult, as its divergences from mainstream Christian belief were now not only few but could largely be found in other churches which were generally accepted within the orthodox Christian fold (see appendix 1 on "orthodox" and "heterodox" Christian sects).[14] One SDA publication carefully distinguishes between the proportion of the church's fundamental beliefs, such as those on God, Jesus, the Scriptures, and salvation, which are also held by all conservative Christians (52%); the proportion which are fairly common "denominational" differences, such as adult versus infant baptism, or free will versus predestination (39%); and the remaining 9% of their beliefs which are quite different from those of other Protestant Christians, such as Christ currently ministering as High Priest, individual judgment before the physical return of Christ, and Ellen G. White being an End Time prophet (Stickland: 8–10). The point of the article is to show that the Seventh-day Adventist Church is broadly mainstream in its beliefs.

In contrast, the Church of God (Seventh Day), the Adventist church which Armstrong joined for a while (see 3.2.2), generally held on to its distinctive beliefs, which included many which were later to be found in the Worldwide Church of God—though Armstrong claimed that these beliefs had been completely lost until he, through his own study, rediscovered them.

2.2.2   Sabbatarianism and Observance of the Law

The historical Worldwide Church of God, like a number of other new religious movements, was often accused of being authoritarian (Hopkins 1974: 192–96, 214); it was also accused of being legalistic (Hopkins 1974: 135–51). While they may not use that precise word, the latter is a charge which they would admit to with pride. Mainstream Christianity does not dispense with the Law—the Ten Commandments are still read in churches—but it emphasizes the point that before Jesus the Jews lived under the Law, while since Jesus Christians live under Grace: the New Covenant of salvation through God's Grace replaces the Old Covenant of obedience to rules and regulations (Richardson 1957: 54–56; Douglas 1962: 264–68).

However, the balance between faith and works is complex. The usual Protestant formulation (Berkhof 1938: 111–38; Hammond and Wright 1968: 136–45)[15] is that we are justified by faith but that our lives should demonstrate the fruits of the

---

14. See (Barrett 2001a: 168–73) for a concise discussion of the theological changes in the SDA.

15. Note that this is Arminian rather than Calvinist soteriology.

Spirit (Gal. 5:22–23); as Jesus said, "By their fruits ye shall know them" (Matt. 7:20). But one verse causes particular difficulty for Evangelical Christians, whose soteriology is centered on justification by faith: "Ye see then how that by works a man is justified, and not by faith only" (James 2:24).

We shall see (3.2.1) how Herbert W. Armstrong came to the belief, which would then underpin the teachings of the Worldwide Church of God, that obedience to the Law is essential, that when God gave a commandment to Israel he meant it for all people, and for all time. This applies perhaps most of all to observance of the Sabbath.

But Worldwide was far more than merely a Seventh-day observance church. Worldwide's use of the term "Sabbatarian" also implies observance of the seven major annual festivals of Judaism: Passover, the Feast of Unleavened Bread, the Feast of Pentecost, the Feast of Trumpets, the Day of Atonement, the Feast of Tabernacles, and the Last Great Day (Hopkins 1974: 139–45). These were of major importance to the historical Worldwide, and still are in the many offshoots. They also necessitate the use of the Jewish calendar to set the date for each festival—like the Christian festival of Easter, they are movable feasts—and this is another of the areas of contention between the Worldwide offshoots (see 6.4.4).

Observance of the Law also applies to the Jewish dietary rules; no member of Worldwide would eat pork, shellfish, or any of the other "unclean foods."[16] And it applies to tithing, which Armstrong applied strictly in his half-century leadership of Worldwide; again, the degree of adherence to this teaching is one of the factors which distinguishes the hardline offshoots from the more liberal offshoots (see 6.1.3). As with some other Christian churches, Armstrong taught that WCG members must give a tenth of their gross earnings to God (that is, to the Worldwide Church of God).

> God's system of collecting from you HIS tithe is just that simple. Since you cannot see God, or go to God's throne in heaven, God instructs you in His revealed Word to pay it to HIS REPRESENTATIVE, who, in receiving it, represents God, just as a collector to whom you pay a debt represents the company to whom you owe it. (H. W. Armstrong 1959)

Unusually, Worldwide also taught that members must set aside a further tenth to pay for their attendance (including travel and accommodation) at the annual Feast of Tabernacles; also, twice every seven years, there was a third tithe for "widows and orphans" (Deut. 14:28–29, 26:12–15; Hoeh 1959c).

16. Like the removal of the need for circumcision, this is an instance where the New Testament specifically negates Old Testament law, by stating that no food is "unclean" (Acts 10:9–16). Armstrong's response to this was to argue: "Not one of our church members—not one of my converts—is eating unclean meats. But I teach it as a physical matter of health, not as a spiritual matter of the true Gospel" (H. W. Armstrong 1986: 560; see also 519). But in reality they were obeying the Law.

This emphasis on obedience to God's Law as laid down in the Old Testament was not just for theological reasons. In a very real sense, Armstrong taught, we (i.e., white Westerners, particularly the British and American peoples) are not just the spiritual but also the physical descendants of Abraham, Isaac, and Jacob; we are the House of Israel; and so what God told Israel over two thousand years ago applies to us today, because of our racial origins. For many, this was an attractive belief.

2.2.3   Millenarianism and British Israelism

The historical Worldwide Church of God had British Israelism (see 2.1.4) at the very center of its teaching, particularly the belief that Biblical prophecies about the subtribes of Joseph's sons Ephraim and Manasseh refer specifically to the modern nations of Britain and the United States respectively.

This first appeared in detail in Armstrong's booklet *The United States in Prophecy* (1942), which was revised as *The United States and Britain in Prophecy* (1945), and then as *The British Commonwealth and the United States in Prophecy* (H. W. Armstrong 1954); it was later greatly expanded in the books *The United States and British Commonwealth in Prophecy* (H. W. Armstrong 1967b) and once again *The United States and Britain in Prophecy* (H. W. Armstrong 1980a). Often referred to as USBP, this booklet and book in its various forms was probably the most heavily advertised and certainly the most requested single piece of WCG literature, according to Aaron Dean, Armstrong's assistant before his death (Dean 2003a). The teaching was also at the heart of many other booklets and magazine articles on prophecy and the End Times from Worldwide; and since the schisms, rewritten versions of essentially the same teaching have appeared from many of the offshoot churches.[17]

In brief, Armstrong taught that the people (Hebrew *ish*) of the covenant (*berith*) became the British (*berith-ish*) people; Isaac's sons became the Saxons; the tribe of Dan (building on the fact that written Hebrew does not use vowels) passed through or settled in, among many other places, Mace*don*ia, the Dar*dan*elles, the rivers *Dan*ube, *Dn*ieper, *Dn*iester and *Don*, and came to the British Isles—in Ireland *Don*egal, Lon*don*derry, and *Din*gle; in Scotland *Dun*dee, *Dun*kirk, and E*din*burgh; and in England, of course, Lon*don*. The famous Tuatha Dé Danaan of Irish legend were simply the tribe of Dan (H. W. Armstrong 1954: 17–20; H. W. Armstrong 1967b: 115–22; H. W. Armstrong 1980a: 93–102). All of this had been taught by John Wilson

---

17. For example, *Europe and America in Prophecy* from the Church of God, International (G. T. Armstrong 1994), *America and Britain in Prophecy* from Global Church of God (R. McNair 1996), *What's Ahead for America and Britain?* from Living Church of God (Ogwyn 1999), *The United States and Britain in Bible Prophecy* from United Church of God (Foster et al. 2001), *America and Britain in Bible Prophecy* from Restored Church of God (Pack 2003), *The Divine Destiny of America* from Church of God Ministries International (Summerville 2004), and *America and Great Britain—Our Identity Revealed!* from Triumph Prophetic Ministries (Dankenbring 2005).

in the middle of the nineteenth century (see 2.1.4) and can also be found spelled out in detail in *Judah's Sceptre and Joseph's Birthright* (Allen 1917; see below).

The subtribes of Ephraim and Manasseh eventually became the peoples of Britain and the United States, respectively—and all the Biblical prophecies about them refer to these countries today.[18] In addition, James VI of Scotland (James I of England) was a direct descendant of the royal line of Israel, and so therefore is the current British monarch—and so, Armstrong claimed, was he himself. The Stone of Scone, Britain's coronation stone, was the stone which Jacob used as a pillow (Gen. 28:18), and was carried to Ireland by Jeremiah in 569 BCE; Jeremiah was accompanied by a daughter of King Zedekiah, Princess Tea-Tephi, whose descendant is Queen Elizabeth II—and so the throne of Britain is a continuation of the throne of David (H. W. Armstrong 1954: 19–22; H. W. Armstrong 1967b: 118–28; H. W. Armstrong 1980a: 99–104).[19]

These ideas had appeared in American books in the last decades of the nineteenth century (Ingersoll 1886; Howlett 1892), the second of these in the year of Armstrong's birth.

This is only the very briefest of summaries. Accepting a few initial premises and making a few conceptual leaps, the whole theory, as carefully presented by Armstrong, seems logical at first glance and has a certain appeal for English-speaking Westerners. Many sects teach that their members are "special"; indeed, this is a common compensator offered by sect membership (Stark and Bainbridge 1987: 36). Members of the Worldwide family of churches (in fact, all British Israelites [Simpson 2002: 9]) are able to view themselves as the chosen people.

The fact that the British Israelite theory is supported by few if any academic historians did not stop Armstrong making it the very heart of his message. It enabled him to apply biblical prophecies to Britain, the then-fledgling European community, and the United States, particularly with regard to the End Times. Any international tension, military buildup, political alliance, or economic development, almost anywhere in the world, was linked to Bible prophecies and presented as evidence that the End must now be very near. Wars, earthquakes, unusual weather patterns, floods, droughts, and famines all appeared regularly in the pages of *Plain Truth* as Signs of the Times.

Armstrong always pointed to the Bible as the source of his teachings, but he gave no credit to anyone but God for his discernment of them. At the May 1974 Ministerial Conference he quoted Paul: "The gospel which was preached of me is not after man. For I neither received it of man, neither was I taught it, but by the revelation of Jesus Christ" (Gal. 1:11–12). To which he added, "I say the same thing, brethren!" He reiterated this in a 1976 sermon: "I came to the truth in a way

18. This is also the belief of most of the offshoots, though at least two believe instead that Manasseh refers to Britain, and Ephraim to the United States (Vincent 1999: 24–25, 202; Dankenbring 2005: 34–54).

19. Note that this ignores the historical fact that the royal families of Europe have intermarried so much over the centuries that genetically *every* European throne must be a continuation of the throne of David, if Britain's is.

I know of no other church leader. I know of no other minister who ever came to it by himself through the leading of God in that way" (Gerringer 1977).

But as we saw above (2.2.1), many teachings Armstrong claimed as unique to himself appeared earlier in SDA minister G. G. Rupert's magazine *The Remnant of Israel* and elsewhere.

Armstrong and Worldwide always gave the strong impression that the church's teachings, including on British Israelism, were a direct result of his personal study (see 3.2.1); it would not be until after his death that the new Worldwide accepted what critics had been saying for decades: that Armstrong's books and booklets on this crucial subject had "borrowed" from (indeed, in places, directly plagiarized) J. H. Allen's *Judah's Sceptre and Joseph's Birthright* (Tkach 1997: 123).

In a letter now in the Armstrong archives, Armstrong wrote to a publisher in 1928:

> What do you regard as the most authoritative and dependable book on the Anglo-Israel theory? I have seen many on this subject which I could not regard as at all reliable. One book which I have read, *Judah's Sceptre and Joseph's Birthright*, by Allen, appears to be more reliable than others I have seen. (Armstrong to A. A. Beauchamp Publishing Co., March 28 1928, quoted in Orr 1999)

In a slightly later letter to the same publisher (who was in fact Allen's publisher), Armstrong says that he is planning his own book on the same subject, and reveals how much this would depend on Allen's book:

> The book I have in mind would follow, in great measure, the line of thought and proof offered by Allen. I would endeavor to keep it as dependable and as sound in its arguments as Allen's. But the ground covered by Allen would be covered in boiled-down form, condensed where possible.... The book would be written, moreover, in an entirely different style....If you believe there is a need and a market for such a book, and you would care to consider the possibility of undertaking to publish it, then I should like to go into the matter further and in more detail with you. (Armstrong to A. A. Beauchamp Publishing Co, May 4, 1928, quoted in Orr 1999)

Armstrong did indeed write his own book, in his own style: *The United States and Britain in Prophecy* in all its versions. But so far as the historical Worldwide was concerned, any connection between Armstrong's "own discoveries" of British Israelism and J. H. Allen's book would be ignored for the next half century or more.

The Worldwide Church of God was not just Adventist—emphasizing the Second Coming (Advent) of Christ—but strongly millenarian. The Gospel is the good news of the coming Kingdom of God here on earth, lasting a full thousand years (H. W. Armstrong 1985a: 294). The true descendants of Israel, the people of God (i.e., members of the Worldwide Church of God), would be rulers on Earth in God's Millennial Kingdom (H. W. Armstrong 1969: 15, 20). Publications included a ninety-six-page booklet by Herbert W. Armstrong and his son Garner Ted Armstrong with the self-explanatory and confident title *The Wonderful World Tomorrow: What It Will Be Like* (Armstrong and Armstrong 1966).

Being so strongly British Israelite, was Worldwide racist (see 2.1.4)? One reason given by the reformed Worldwide for the withdrawal of *Mystery of the Ages*, Armstrong's last book (see 6.2.1), was the implied racism in sections of the book (specifically pp. 147–54);[20] Larry Salyer, appointed director of church administration after Armstrong's death, wrote in a *Pastor General's Report* in January 1989: "Another area of concern is the sensitivity surrounding any discussion of the races" (cited in S. Flurry 2006: 118).

John Halford, UK leader of the reformed Worldwide for many years, told me why, in part, he abandoned British Israelism:

> At worst, what really cemented my withdrawal from it was that we found that so many of the Aryan supremacist groups in the States loved our literature, stockpiled it, and it gave rise to what I consider some of the most foul ideology available....Christian Identity movements, Aryan Leagues, these people. I personally would not want to put my name to anything which would give those people one half of a page of material. The whole redneck, white supremacist, Ku Klux Klan... I think any right-thinking person, whether Christian or not, would want to distance themselves from that. (John Halford, pers. comm.)

The appeal of Worldwide's literature to white supremacists can be judged from the following extracts from an article by Armstrong, "The Real CAUSE of the RACE CRISIS!":

> Christ was WHITE. Adam *"looked like"* Christ. *So Adam was* WHITE!...
>
> The Oriental race is a MUTATION from Adam's stock....The same is true of the Negro....MAN perverts God's Laws by interbreeding and producing a mongrel or hybrid....
>
> *Noah was the ONLY man* on earth who was not guilty of this SIN of intermarriage!... ALL other human beings were *destroyed*—PUNISHED for this sin of interracial marriage....
>
> *GOD is the author of SEGREGATION!* But *man* is the author of INTEGRATION!
> (H. W. Armstrong 1963: 6, 23, 27)

The Aryan Nations and other white supremacists would have little disagreement with this.

---

20. All page references herein are taken from the Philadelphia Church of God C-format paperback edition, which is larger and has different page numbering from the WCG B-format paperback (see 6.2.1).

2.2.4   Church Governance and Authority

One of Armstrong's most prominent teachings in the historical Worldwide, and one of the most prominent teachings in the more hardline offshoots, is on authority and church governance. Six months after Armstrong's death in 1986, his successor as pastor general, Joseph W. Tkach, published a list of "18 Restored Truths,"[21] calling them "Herbert W. Armstrong's legacy." The very first one of these was "The government of God."

> **1. The government of God.** When Christ comes, he will restore God's government to the whole earth. So you can be sure the one to come in the spirit and power of Elijah would restore God's government in His Church. When Mr. and Mrs. Armstrong came among the Oregon Conference era of the Church of God (Seventh Day), the church had the right name, the law, the Sabbath, and the tithing system. But they also had a government of men, with a biannual conference, voting just like they do in the world.
>
> Today, the government of God has been restored to His Church. That's the kind of government you find in Ephesians 4 and 1 Corinthians 12. (Worldwide News 1986)

"God's government" was strictly hierarchical, with Armstrong ("the one to come in the spirit and power of Elijah") at the top, with the absolute power of apostle; below him were the evangelists, and below them the elders and pastors, each with dele-gated power from the level above. Church members had to be obedient to their pastors, who had the power to disfellowship (excommunicate) any member who caused trouble, perhaps by questioning a doctrine or a new directive passed down from headquarters in Pasadena. Pastors could be moved to new congregations, even to new continents, or be bumped down the chain of command at a moment's notice, with no right of appeal; if they complained, they could be disfellowshipped. Even those in the most senior positions found that their jobs were not safe: senior evangelist Roderick C. Meredith found himself "exiled" to Hawaii for six months in late 1979/early 1980, while Armstrong's heir apparent, Garner Ted, was stripped of all his positions for some months in 1972 when his extramarital excursions were revealed (see 7.3.1 and 4.3).

Democracy was an alien concept (see the comments by senior ministers John Halford and John Jewell in 7.2 and 7.3.1); "a government of men...voting just like they do in the world" was not God's way of doing things. Clearly this was a system open to abuse; as will be seen later, there are many reports of such abuse occurring.

The issue of church governance is one of the most crucial differences between hardline and liberal offshoots (see chapters 6 and 7). We shall also see that Armstrong's insistence on "God's government in His Church" was a later development in his teaching, and diametrically opposed to his earlier beliefs on church governance.

---

21. Note: this is not the same as the list of selected doctrines given above (2.2.1).

2.3 A BRIEF COMPARISON BETWEEN WORLDWIDE
AND MORMONISM

The Worldwide Church of God developed ultimately from the febrile atmosphere of early- to mid-nineteenth-century Christian revivalism in America. So did the Church of Jesus Christ of Latter-day Saints, more usually known as the Mormons. Although they are very different religions, there are a number of interesting parallels between the historic Worldwide (and its offshoots) and the Mormon Church.

Both claimed to be restoring the original truth, lost centuries before. Armstrong wrote of "Restoration of God's Truth to Church" (H. W. Armstrong 1985a: 289); Joseph Smith spoke of "the 'restoration of all things' in the last days" (Hansen 1981: 27). Longtime Worldwide watcher Gavin Rumney asks:

> Is it possible that [Armstrong's] borrowings included some from the "Restoration movement" established nearly a century before by Joseph Smith Jr.? And is it possible that there might have been substantial interchange between certain Mormon sects and the Church of God (Seventh Day) prior to Armstrong's separation [from it]? (Rumney 2011)

Rumney cites as an example COG7's adoption of the system of church organization with "Twelve" and "Seventy" (see 3.2.2), which the Mormons had long used (Ludlow 1992: 1300–1305).

Both Worldwide and Mormonism are heterodox Christian sects (see appendix 1) appealing most strongly to Americans. Both have versions of British Israelism (see 2.1.4 and 2.2.3); the *Book of Mormon* contains the story of the Lost Tribes of Israel going to America around 600 BCE (Hansen 1981: 8; Bushman 1984: 115–16; Abanes 2002: 65–67), and many Mormons believe they are descended from Ephraim (Abanes 2002: 108–9). Both churches have faced accusations of racism stemming from their beliefs (see 2.2.3); the main Mormon Church only allowed black priests in 1978 (Abanes 2002: 369–70; Ludlow 1992: 126).

Although the main Mormon Church observes the Sabbath on Sunday (Ludlow 1992: 1241), several small Mormon groups uphold the Seventh-day Sabbath (see 2.1.1), including the Strangite Mormons,[22] a church founded in 1850 which dates back to one of the earliest Mormon leaders, James Strang (Strangite Mormons, n.d.; see 8.2.3).

Both churches stressed obedience to authority (see 2.2.2, 3.2.1 and 7.1), "not just any authority, but an authority derived directly from God" (Hansen 1981: 39).

Both churches have versions of the "God family" (see 2.2.1), though in different ways. Mormons believe that "all resurrected and perfected mortals become gods" (Ludlow 1992: 553); a writer in *The Journal* (see 6.4.5.1) distinguishes between what he called this "totally unbiblical" teaching and "the Church of God teaching

---

22. Church of Jesus Christ of Latter Day Saints—without the usual hyphen.

that man will become a part of the one Eternal Godhead. Men will not become gods but, more properly, God beings" (Boyne 2000: 16).

Armstrong is thought by some to have "borrowed" the seal of the Worldwide Church of God, which shows a child with a lion and a lamb (based on Isaiah 11:6), from the Reorganized Church of Jesus Christ of Latter-day Saints (Rumney 2011; White 2009: 37–38).

Some comparisons between Worldwide and the Mormon Church on the problems of succession and schism will also be drawn in this study (see 8.2.3).

2.4 CONCLUSION

We have seen in this chapter that the beliefs of the historical Worldwide Church of God were by no means new and radical in the present day, or unique to the church, or restored by Herbert W. Armstrong after 1,900 years of being lost, all of which he claimed:

> After many months of virtually night-and-day intensive study, the answers were revealed to me with proof that was positive and absolute....
>
> The revelation of these mysteries was lost, even to the Church of God, although the revelation of them has been preserved in the writings of the Bible. Why, then, has the world not clearly understood? Because the Bible was a coded book, not intended to be understood until our day in this latter half of the twentieth century. I learned, in this night and day study, why it is the most misunderstood book, even though it is the world's best-seller. (H. W. Armstrong 1985a: x–xiii)

Rather, they drew on existing Sabbatarian and millenarian traditions, as might be expected given Armstrong's roots in the Church of God (Seventh Day), as we shall see in the next chapter. Although Armstrong, through his church, focused on certain beliefs which are outside traditional mainstream Christian doctrine, most if not all of them can be found spread amongst a variety of nineteenth-century heterodox sects, including the Church of Jesus Christ of Latter-day Saints.

It was Armstrong's specific combination of beliefs, and especially the way in which he marketed them, that made the Worldwide Church of God stand out from the crowd of heterodox Christian sects in the mid-twentieth century. How he came by his beliefs and how he learned his distinctive style of presentation are addressed in the next chapter.

CHAPTER 3
Origins and History of the Worldwide Church of God

INTRODUCTION

In order to understand the traumatic significance of the doctrinal changes in the Worldwide Church of God to its ministers and members, in chapter 2 we looked at the church's doctrines and its doctrinal antecedents, and saw that it was firmly placed in the already well-established Sabbatarian and millenarian traditions. We also saw how the existing ideas of British Israelism were taken on and made central to the church's prophetic ministry; and we touched briefly on the vital subject of authority, which will be examined a little in this chapter, and in greater depth in chapter 7.

Although this chapter is titled "Origins and History of the Worldwide Church of God," it could as easily be titled "Herbert W. Armstrong: The Man and the Myth." It will show how Armstrong was absolutely central to his church, how a failed advertising copywriter became God's apostle for the twentieth century. This is crucial to understanding why so many left the church when Armstrong's successor began changing and dismissing his teachings; it will also make some sense of the different attitudes of the offshoot churches (see chapters 6 and 7).

First, in this chapter, we shall see how Herbert W. Armstrong, as a young man, began to come to the beliefs which would lead to him founding his church; then we shall look briefly at the early years of what was then the Radio Church of God and its distinctive characteristics and activities, which are still hallmarks of most of the offshoot churches today.

In chapter 4 we shall look at the church's troubled decade of the 1970s, and the schisms during Armstrong's lifetime, which foreshadowed those after his death (see 5.1). We shall see that there were different periods of relative liberalism and authoritarianism in the church in Armstrong's own lifetime, which would later be reflected in the variety of offshoot churches (see chapter 6).

Throughout these two chapters we shall see how Armstrong dealt with challenges, problems, and criticism. We shall look at his own personality, both its strengths and its weaknesses—the root of widely differing reactions to the man and his memory in the offshoots, years after his death. We shall also see how events can be viewed from widely differing perspectives; it is with this issue, and its implications for the historical accuracy of this account, that we begin.

3.1 DIFFERENT PERSPECTIVES

It is a truism that all history is biased. Samuel Butler wrote: "It has been said that although God cannot alter the past, historians can; it is perhaps because they can be useful to Him in this respect that He tolerates their existence" (Butler 1901). Among other sources for this chapter is the two-volume *Autobiography of Herbert W. Armstrong*. In referring to it and quoting from it I am obviously aware both that this was an official internal publication, and so clearly not an objective source, and also that Armstrong's recollections of conversations and detailed events from decades earlier must be, as in any autobiography, imaginative reconstructions. In some cases they might well be relatively accurate in their general sense; in other cases they could be completely fictional; but their importance lies in the fact that this was "the truth" as Herbert W. Armstrong wished to portray it in later years, in the heyday of his church—and not only to members of the church. Considerable portions of the *Autobiography* were serialized in the *Plain Truth* magazine which, at its height, had a circulation of six to eight million,[1] sixty to eighty times the church's baptized membership, at its height, of around a hundred thousand.

John Halford, the British and European leader of the reformed Worldwide through much of my research, in bemoaning the fact that (from his point of view) some of the old Worldwide publications stayed around for far too long, told me, "Herbert Armstrong never went back and rewrote and updated" (John Halford, pers. comm.). This is factually incorrect (see 5.1.2).

So far as the *Autobiography* is concerned, there are differences (in some cases quite significant) between the three editions I have of Volume 1: paperbacks of the 1967 and 1973 editions and a hardback of the 1986 edition.[2] It is not unusual for new

---

1. Both figures were given by WCG and its offshoots, e.g., Taylor 1984: 5; http://www.pcog.org/ourhistory.php. However, as large numbers of copies were put out on free racks at newsstands, stations or in waiting rooms, the actual circulation and readership cannot be ascertained.

2. Each edition of Volume 1 gives a publication history, the latest reading "Copyright © 1957, 1958, 1959, 1960, 1967, 1973, 1974, 1986"; the 1967 edition was the first edition in book form. Volume 2 was published posthumously; the hardback has "Copyright © 1961, 1962, 1963, 1964, 1965, 1967, 1968, 1987"; all but the last date refer to the original serial publication of portions of it in *Plain Truth* magazine, with events from 1959 till Armstrong's death in 1986 being related through excerpts from his co-worker letters (see chapter 4, note 6) and some *Plain Truth* editorials, compiled and edited by the publishers.

religious movements to alter their core texts.[3] In the case of Worldwide, and specifically Armstrong's *Autobiography*, although some of the differences (especially between the 1967 and 1973 editions) are structural, later events sometimes forced a reevaluation of earlier events, a revision of history—and more substantial editing.

One clear example is the treatment of Armstrong's son, Garner Ted. In 1967 Garner Ted was Armstrong's heir apparent, and the main speaker on Worldwide's radio broadcasts. In the 1967 and 1973 editions of Volume 1 of the *Autobiography*, the chapter "Why You Hear Garner Ted Speak Today" includes an event that took place when he was nearly two and a half and had pneumonia. At this age he was unable to talk, and his parents were concerned. Armstrong anointed his son and prayed for God to heal him, and also to restore his power of speech. "His fever left quickly. The very next day he was able to say a number of single words. In about three days he was talking in whole sentences." The point of the story comes a few paragraphs later:

> Words have been pouring like a torrent out of his mouth ever since, as millions of radio listeners on every continent around the world well know! God *gave* him his voice by an unusual divine miracle. And I am *well pleased*, as God was with *His* Son Jesus, that he is now an instrument in God's hands. (H. W. Armstrong 1967a: 450; H. W. Armstrong 1973a: 408)

By the time of the 1986 edition Garner Ted had long been ousted from the church. The description of the miraculous healing is still there, but the chapter itself has been retitled to reflect other parts of its content, and all references to Garner Ted preaching have been removed (H. W. Armstrong 1986: 475).

Some of the most important booklets also went through changes over the years, even before the transitional years following Armstrong's death. In some cases these reflected Armstrong's own doctrinal changes (see 4.2), but at one point in the 1970s Garner Ted Armstrong had sufficient influence in the church to issue edited versions of some of his father's books or booklets on subjects as diverse as British Israelism, sexual morality, and the family (see 4.4). When Garner Ted was ousted in 1978, Armstrong was able to assert, "We are updating, and getting before the world" several booklets which had been downplayed, including "*The United States and Britain in Prophecy*—back to full length!" (Armstrong 1987: 597–98)

The bias in works such as Armstrong's *Autobiography* is countered by the bias both in Joseph Tkach's *Transformed by Truth* and J. Michael Feazell's *The Liberation of the Worldwide Church of God* (two accounts of the process of change in Worldwide

---

3. Critics of, for example, the Church of Jesus Christ of Latter-day Saints of America and of the Church of Christ, Scientist, point out the number of different editions of their respective main texts, *The Book of Mormon* and *Science and Health with Key to the Scriptures*. In these cases the changes were often grammatical corrections, removal of inconsistencies, clarifications, and perhaps minor doctrinal changes (Sanders 1962: 47; Hoekema 1973: 91–92; Abanes 2002: 74, 514n69).

after Armstrong's death, written by the chief architects of that change) and also in articles on the website of the reformed Worldwide. These articles, on the early history of the church; on its doctrines (old and new), especially British Israelism; on why and how doctrines changed; and on the subsequent schisms, are written by the victors from the years of transition. The subtitle of Feazell's book makes its stance very clear: "The Remarkable Story of a Cult's Journey from Deception to Truth" (Feazell 2003).

Herbert W. Armstrong still has an important place in the hearts and minds both of ex-members of Worldwide now in the offshoot churches and also of many long-term members still in Worldwide itself. Perhaps to counter this, some of the articles on the Worldwide Church of God website go to great lengths to show not just that Armstrong was wrong theologically but also that his self-penned personal history was inaccurate and self-serving; this will become apparent in examples quoted below.

The historical account of Armstrong and Worldwide in this and the next chapter draws on (among other sources) both Armstrong's *Autobiography* and the "victors'" history of the current Worldwide. Neither of these sources is impartial, but they are a record of how the history of Worldwide was and is perceived by those involved in it. They present a "before-and-after" picture, from the very different viewpoints of the old Worldwide and the new, each with its own agenda; it is such *perceptions* that form the setting for this study.

There is also a spread of perceptions about the history of Armstrong and Worldwide across the major offshoot churches, as we shall see throughout the book. It is hardly surprising, for example, that the story of Garner Ted Armstrong's "ouster" (see 4.4) is quite different as told by father and son.

This chapter also draws on information from some of the offshoot churches (both from their publications and from interviews and correspondence with senior members; see appendix 3.3), from critical websites run by former members, and from books and other writings both by ex-members and by outside observers, including anticultists and Evangelical counter-cultists.

Historians may indeed, as Samuel Butler wrote, alter the past. Internal church historians—anyone who says anything, or writes anything in any of the many church publications, *about* their churches—create their own pasts for their own purposes.

3.2   ORIGINS AND HISTORY OF THE WORLDWIDE CHURCH OF GOD

3.2.1   1920s: How Herbert W. Armstrong Found the Truth

It is important to look at the very earliest days which led to Armstrong founding what became the Worldwide Church of God, partly to observe the development— and, crucially, the fundamental importance to him—of certain key beliefs; and also for what we can learn from these early years about Armstrong's character, which would have such an influence on his church and on some of the offshoots.

Herbert Armstrong[4] was born in Des Moines, Iowa, on July 31, 1892, "of respected and upright parents who were of solid Quaker stock" (H. W. Armstrong 1986: 11), Horace Elon Armstrong and Eva Wright Armstrong, who were married in 1887. He was their first child; his sister Mabel was two years younger and his brother Russell seven and a half years younger. Probably in the spring of 1900 his family moved to Union, Iowa, where his father went into partnership in a hardware store (15).[5] A younger brother, Dwight L. Armstrong (1904–94) was later to write many of the hymns of the Worldwide Church of God, still used in the offshoots.

Through his childhood Armstrong regularly attended Sunday school and services at First Friends Church in Des Moines. At high school he appears to have been an average student. He left after three years, without graduating; he never gained any formal educational qualifications ("The Insanity Continues," *Ambassador Report* 27).

In his *Autobiography* he recounts "the turning point of [his] life" at the age of sixteen, when the owner of a hotel where he was waiting tables during summer vacation, he writes, "began to tell me that he could see qualities in me that were destined to carry me to large success in life. He constantly expressed great confidence in me, and what I would be able to accomplish, if I were willing to put forth the effort" (20). Until then, Armstrong says, he had never been a leader among boys, but this "created within me the DESIRE to climb the ladder of success—to become an important SOMEBODY." He points out that this was "vanity" which "flowered into grossly overrated SELF-confidence and conceit"; but, he says, "it impelled me to *driving* effort" (21).

All of these qualities, both positive and negative, were to be apparent throughout his life.

At eighteen, on the advice of his uncle Frank, he entered the advertising profession. First he had to decide whether or not to go to college or university to take courses in advertising and journalism, or whether instead to join the want-ads department of a daily newspaper—in his uncle's words, "the freshman class of the

---

4. It seems that Herbert W. Armstrong was plain Herbert Armstrong at birth. According to one source, "Ever wonder what the letter W in Herb's name stood for? Absolutely nothing! Apparently the Apostle thought the extra letter lent him an extra dose of credibility, and he chose W specifically because he felt it sounded distinguished" (Rumney, n.d.; see also "HWA Remembered (Part I)," *Ambassador Report* 36; Thiel 2003: 6–7). In 1970 Armstrong told an Ambassador College student who asked him what the W stood for: "Nothing. It stands for nothing. I added it years ago" (J. Philip Arnold, pers. comm.). He was in good company; President Harry S. Truman (1945–53) also had a middle initial but no middle name. Armstrong could not have been following Truman's example, because he was using his initial as early as 1917, in his signature on his World War I draft card (photograph in *Autobiography*, vol. 1).

5. In this section, page references in the text refer to the 1986 hardback edition of *Autobiography of Herbert W. Armstrong*, vol. 1 (H. W. Armstrong 1986), unless otherwise stated.

advertising school of hard knocks" (25). His uncle's advice to him colored his attitude to formal education from then on:

> "People seem to have the idea that an education is something they have all wrapped up at the university, ready to hand it over to you when you buy it by paying the tuition. But . . . education comes from study—from books—from lectures—from contacts—from travel—from thinking about what you see and hear and read—and from experience. . . .
>
> "Most people are too lazy—most lack the ambition and persistence, the drive—to procure an education outside of schools and colleges. . . .
>
> "Now if you have the initiative . . . you can acquire just as complete an education outside the classrooms as in." (25–26)

Whether his uncle ever said anything approximating to this, or whether these words are the creation of Armstrong, decades later, justifying his lack of a formal education, cannot now be known. But his attitude to higher education, and particularly to academics, was clearly formed early on, and it was an attitude which, as we shall see shortly, has brought criticism from the leaders of the present Worldwide.

Armstrong was successful at selling ads for the Des Moines *Daily Capital*. His approach was to tell prospective clients that the reason they weren't getting the results they wanted was that they weren't professional advertising writers, but that he was. Armstrong himself draws the parallel to years later when Worldwide was to buy expensive advertising space in *Reader's Digest*, *Life* and the London *Sunday Times*—advertisements which brought results: "Two such double pages in English in *Reader's Digest* brought 20,000 new subscribers in India for *The Plain Truth*" (32). The success of the Worldwide Church of God came from its professional marketing, from well-designed and well-written advertisements and magazines.

In January 1912 Armstrong took a short break from advertising to work as timekeeper and paymaster at a major lumber mill in southern Mississippi. It was a job which would involve traveling, and at his first meeting with his new boss, the millionaire W. O. Finkbine, vice president of the Green Bay Lumber Company, he was given advice which again he would follow for the rest of his life.

> "Most people look upon it as an extravagance to ride in the Pullman cars on trains. They are wrong. . . . We humans are influenced by everyone we come in contact with. On the Pullmans you will come in contact with a more successful class of people. This will have more influence than you can realize, now, on your future success in life. . . .
>
> "Whenever you stop at a hotel, the same principle applies. Always stop at the *leading* hotel in any city. . . . You are among more successful people, which will influence your own success." (42–43)

It is perfectly possible that Armstrong was given this advice, typical of success-orientated America (compare such popular books as Dale Carnegie's 1937 *How To Win Friends and Influence People*); but again it could be viewed as a later justification for his extravagant lifestyle, private jets, and determination to be seen and photo-graphed with world leaders (see 3.2.3).

By midsummer that year he was back in Des Moines, taking further advice from his Uncle Frank, and joining the *Merchants Trade Journal*, selling advertising space and writing advertising copy again—and learning how to "grab *attention*" with headlines, subheads, and the creative use of typefaces (57–60 *passim*).

> Use only plain, simple words. Use words that readers of no more than a third or fourth grade education can UNDERSTAND. Try to achieve good literary quality with a *large* vocabulary of common, simple words, and by the *manner* in which you weave those words into the sentence structure. (61)

He would apply these lessons throughout the rest of his life. "And that is one reason why *The Plain Truth* is so avidly read, and its circulation keeps growing so phenom-enally, while other leading mass-circulation magazines are in deep financial diffi-culties" (66).

In all, Armstrong spent twenty years in advertising. Eventually he set up his own business, working for commissions rather than a salary. In 1921, during the Depression, his first business, advertising tractors, collapsed. His next business, advertising laundries, began in 1924; it was grossing $1,000 a month before it, too, collapsed. "It seemed, indeed," he wrote in his *Autobiography* with the benefit of hindsight, "as if some INVISIBLE and MYSTERIOUS HAND were causing the earth to simply swallow up whatever business I started" (287).

In July 1917 Armstrong married his third cousin Loma Dillon. Within a few weeks, Loma had a dream which caused her to write: "It dawned on me that Christ was coming, and I was so happy I was just crying for joy. Then suddenly I thought of Herbert and was rather worried." At this time, Armstrong says, he had "very little religious interest." He writes: "In the morning, she told me of her dream. I was embarrassed" (204).

The Armstrongs had four children: Beverly (1918–92), Dorothy (1920–2010), Richard David (1928–58), and Garner Ted (1930–2003). The sons would become major figures in their father's church but both daughters would leave it. Although she was married to the church's business manager, Vern Mattson, "Dorothy drifted away from her father's church by around 1951" ("HWA Confesses to Incest!" *Ambassador Report* 27), while "Mr. Armstrong had excommunicated his own daughter, Beverly [Armstrong-Gott] because of the make-up issue" (letter in *Ambassador Report* 33).[6] At Armstrong's funeral in January 1986, his three remaining children were all "seated in the front row of the 'unconverted section'" ("Herbert W. Armstrong Goes to His Reward," *Ambassador Report* 35).

---

6. Armstrong taught that the use of makeup was sinful, and a sign of harlots and whores (H. W. Armstrong 1968); female members of the church and students at Ambassador College were forbidden to wear it. See 4.4.

In 1926 Armstrong, through his wife, came to accept the seventh-day Sabbath doctrine; at about the same time he came to the conclusion that the biblical Creation account was true and the theory of evolution false. This was the beginning of his intensive study of the Bible, the beginning of his religious conviction...the beginning of what would become the Worldwide Church of God.

Loma had been an active Methodist all her life, and the Armstrongs had joined a local Methodist church after their marriage, though with little apparent enthusiasm from Herbert. One day Loma was shown some Bible texts by an elderly neighbor, which made her ask, "Do all these Scriptures say that I've been keeping the wrong *day* as the Sabbath all my life?" The reply, once again, is pure Armstrong in both its content and its style:

> "Well, *do they?*" asked Mrs. Runcorn. "Don't ask *me* whether you have been wrong— you shouldn't believe what any *person* tells you, but only what GOD tells you through the Bible. What does He tell you, *there?* What do you see *there* with your own eyes?" (288)

Loma rushed home to tell Herbert of her discovery. "This was the *worst* news I had ever heard! My wife had gone into religious fanaticism!" (289). After arguing for a while, Herbert said:

> "I'll make you this proposition: I don't know much about the Bible—I just never could seem to understand it. But I do have an analytical mind. I've become experienced in research into business problems, getting the facts and analyzing them. Now I'll make a complete and thorough study of this question in the Bible. All these churches can't be wrong. I'll prove to you in the Bible that you are mistaken!" (290–91)

With his business having collapsed, Armstrong wrote, "I had TIME on my hands for this challenge" (291), so "I spent a solid SIX MONTHS of virtual night-and-day, seven-day-a-week, STUDY and research, in a determined effort to find just the opposite" (305). One might wonder why, with a family to support, he was not spending his time searching for new work; but according to his own account, proving Loma wrong was more important.

But the months of study eventually convinced him that Loma was right: there was no biblical justification for the standard Christian practice of worship on a Sunday. During this period of study he also came to believe a number of other things which would be a major part of his teachings for the next half century. One was that Jesus had actually been crucified on a Wednesday, not on "Good Friday," and had risen from the dead, as the Bible says, precisely three days and three nights later, on late afternoon on the Saturday (i.e., still during the Sabbath)—thus removing the one apparently valid argument Christian churches used to support Sunday worship (see 2.1.1), that Jesus had risen on Sunday (339) (H. W. Armstrong 1952c; Hoeh 1959a; H. W. Armstrong 1972a).

Another point which Armstrong realized was the importance of obeying God's Law.

> GOD is the one you OBEY. The word LORD means MASTER—the one you OBEY!
> This [Sabbath keeping] is the one point on which the largest number of people refuse to
> OBEY the true GOD, thus proving they are *not* His people! (303)

Through his studies of the Bible, and endless delving into his local reference library, Armstrong proved to his own satisfaction that evolution was a false doctrine, that Sabbath keeping was enjoined upon man forever, and that whatever the Bible might say about faith and grace, it was incumbent upon man to obey God's Law.

> It was disillusioning to learn, on studying the BIBLE for the first time, that what I had been
> taught in Sunday School was, in so many basic instances, the very opposite of what the Bible
> plainly states. It was shocking to learn that "all these churches *were* wrong" after all! (308–9)

"I began to ask," Armstrong writes, "'WHERE, then, is the real true Church which CHRIST founded?'" (351) It had to be one which kept God's commandments, and one of these was true Sabbath keeping.

> That automatically ruled out all churches observing Sunday. So far as I could learn, it
> reduced the search to three small groups—the Seventh-Day Adventists, the Seventh-
> Day Baptists, and a little, almost unheard-of church called the Church of God, which
> maintained a small publishing-house headquarters at Stanberry, Missouri. (353)

Armstrong examined their teachings. He found that the SDA had "certain points of truth," but the Seventh Day Baptists were indistinguishable from any other Protestant denomination, except for observing a different day of the week. "But of these three churches to which the search had been narrowed, only *one* had the right NAME for the true Church" (354).

Armstrong believed from his study of the Bible that the only name used for God's people in the New Testament—in twelve places[7]—was "the Church of God," and hence this was the only acceptable name for a church. When looking for a church to join, this restriction narrowed down his choice—hence his choosing the Oregon church of the Stanberry-based Church of God. "These verses prove the NAME of the true Church. Denominations *not* bearing this name could *not* be God's true church," writes WCG theologian and historian Herman L. Hoeh (Hoeh 1959b).[8]

---

7. Acts 20:28; 1 Corinthians 1:2, 10:32, 11:16, 11:22, 15:9; 2 Corinthians 1:1; Galatians 1:13, 1 Thessalonians 2:14; 2 Thessalonians 1:4; 1 Timothy 3:5, 3:15.

8. This is an example—by no means restricted to Armstrong—of building a doctrine on "proof texts," then ignoring any texts which might be seen to run counter to that doctrine. In this particular case, believers are referred to in several different ways throughout the New Testament: churches of Christ, the body of Christ, and so on. Of 109 New Testament references to "church," only twelve refer to "church(es) of God" (Hopkins 1974: 55).

According to Armstrong the Christian church had lost its way in 69 or 70 CE. The mainstream of Christianity had been wrong ever since—but there had always been a few, somewhere in the world, who had followed the true way. Among these were Constantine of Mananali around 650 CE and Sergius a hundred years later. Around 1000 CE there were the Paulicians and Bogomils of Bulgaria, and a century later a preacher called Peter de Bruys in the south of France. Even the Cathars, almost wiped out in the Albigensian Crusade of the early thirteenth century, are claimed as forerunners of the Worldwide Church of God, albeit with no doctrinal justification. The Waldensians had the truth, said Armstrong, and so did the Lollards. There were Sabbatarians in the seventeenth century; one of these, Stephen Mumford, took the true gospel from London to America in 1664, setting up in Newport, Rhode Island (Hoeh 1959b: 18–22).

Armstrong's picking out of these particular religious movements and leaders appears to rest on any one or more of four points: their keeping of the Saturday Sabbath, the name "Church of God," their rejection of the standard idea of the Trinity, or their persecution by the established church. In reality, few if any of them could be seen in any way as antecedents of the Worldwide Church of God, in doctrines, practices, or organization.

With each of these movements, Armstrong said, either mainstream Christianity had destroyed the small group of true believers, or the Devil, seeing God's Truth preached, had encouraged the beliefs to be watered down or distorted. This was the case, Armstrong taught, with the Seventh-day Adventist Church, which under Mrs. White's influence had abandoned the only scriptural name for God's church (see 2.1.3).

And so, in 1926–27, Herbert W. Armstrong and his wife, Loma, joined the Church of God headquartered at Stanberry, Missouri, having fellowship with members between Salem, West Virginia, and Eugene, Oregon. The church was small, with fewer than two thousand members in all, scattered in rural areas; none of its individual church congregations had as many as a hundred members; there were fewer than fifty altogether in the state of Oregon. According to one source, "Its pastors, even its leaders, were men of little education" (Hopkins 1974: 32). Even before formally joining the church, Armstrong found himself challenging them, as we shall see shortly.

He also "continued the first three and a half years," he wrote, "of my ceaseless night-and-day STUDY of the Bible—of history, especially as connected with Biblical history and prophecy—and of pertinent allied subjects" (358). The reformed Worldwide today is heavily (though politely) critical of the sort of study practiced by Armstrong:

> Biblical understanding is corrupted further when its interpreters do not consider the multifaceted nature of biblical literature. While it is not difficult to grasp the moral messages of the biblical prophets, understanding many other facets of their messages requires a better-than-casual approach to each text. Exegesis benefits from an appreciation

of the intricacies of the biblical languages and modes of expression. It requires consideration of the prophets' literary genres, and it demands an awareness of a text's original circumstances. Wise interpreters pay close attention to linguistic, literary, historical, cultural and canonical contexts. Unfortunately, too many Christians have read the Bible according to the literary and cultural standards of their own day, without considering that the Bible at its core is a collection of ancient Semitic and Greco-Roman texts. In some circles, people have a quickness to reject and ridicule informed scholarship that should have otherwise tempered their opinions. (Orr 1999)

This is a clear, albeit veiled, put-down of the quality of Armstrong's study and scholarship.

Armstrong wrote up his studies as articles. His wife began to show these articles to other church members, and "soon they began to urge [him] to preach before them" (359). The articles also began to be published in the church magazine, *The Bible Advocate*, published in Stanberry, Missouri.

Before that, though, Armstrong had challenged the Church of God twice. He believed that Christians and churches must grow in the Truth, and thus acknowledge any error in their beliefs. Ironically, in view of what would happen to his own church after his death, he says in his *Autobiography*, "I knew of no church or sect or denomination that had ever publicly confessed error or embraced new truth" (360).

The first challenge was a sixteen-page refutation of an unnamed "certain minor point of doctrine" (360). According to Armstrong, the church leader acknowledged that he was right, but declined to change the doctrine on the grounds that some members, "especially those of older standing and heavy tithe payers" (361), might lose confidence in the church if it started admitting error. "He said he feared many would withdraw their financial support, and it might divide the Church" (361).

This is exactly what was to happen sixty or seventy years later, when Joseph W. Tkach publicly admitted doctrinal errors of the Worldwide Church of God, including its teaching on tithing. As we shall see in chapter 5, thousands of members withdrew their financial support for the church, which became divided. The hypothesis that the continued process of schism today is primarily the result of doctrinal differences rather than stemming from other causes will be tested in chapter 9.

Armstrong's second challenge to the church he was joining was to send to the church leader, who was also editor of the church magazine, a nearly three-hundred-page typed manuscript in which he laid out in detail his discoveries on British Israelism (see 2.1.4 and 2.2.3):

After exhaustive study and research, I had found it PROVED that the so-called "Lost Ten Tribes" of Israel had migrated to Western Europe, the British Isles, and later the United States—that the British were the descendants of Ephraim, younger son of Joseph, and the United States modern-day Manasseh, elder son of Joseph—and that we possessed the national wealth and resources of the Birthright which God had promised to Abraham through Isaac, Jacob and Joseph. (361)

Thus, Armstrong was already setting out the prophetic basis of his own future church. Note that he makes no reference in this account to J. H. Allen's *Judah's Sceptre and Joseph's Birthright*, which was the basis of his own "discoveries"; yet we have seen (2.2.3) that he wrote to the publisher of Allen's book twice in 1928, suggesting that he write his own book, which "would follow, in great measure, the line of thought and proof offered by Allen" (Armstrong to Beauchamp, May 4, 1928, quoted in Orr 1999).

The leader of the Church of God, Andrew N. Dugger (1886–1975), wrote back to him on July 28, 1929 (H. W. Armstrong 1945: 1), saying, "*I was most certainly right*—that this was a wonderful new truth revealed by God, and that God surely had a special reason for revealing this new truth to me" (362). This "new truth" would be revealed in Armstrong's most requested book in all its editions beginning with *The United States in Prophecy* (1942), and still forms the center of the prophetic teaching of the offshoot churches in their own books and booklets (see chapter 2, note 17).

Only *one* of those, United Church of God's forty-eight-page A4 booklet (Foster et al. 2001: 38), mentions J. H. Allen's book, alongside John Wilson and others, as "Advocates of British-Israelism," in a historical sidebar. All the others either cite Herbert W. Armstrong as the source of the teaching (Ogwyn 1999; Pack 2003) or simply present it as their own.

3.2.2 1930s–1960s: Birth and Growth of a New Church

By 1928 Armstrong was preaching, and in 1931 he was ordained a minister by the Oregon Conference of the Church of God (Seventh Day), a state-focused offshoot of the main church headquartered in Stanberry. In the early 1930s, at the time of Armstrong's involvement in it, COG7 was going through a series of internal crises over doctrine and leadership clashes which led to schism between the Stanberry and Salem groups in 1933 (Nickels 1996b). Armstrong was a member of the breakaway Salem group under A. N. Dugger, which held a stricter adherence to doctrines on unclean meats (i.e., not eating pork, etc.), the use of tobacco, church governance, and the date of Passover (Nickels 1999: 213).

In 1933 Armstrong gave a series of lectures around Eugene, Oregon, and in 1934 he began two of the three activities which characterized his church for the next half century: in January the *Radio Church of God* program (renamed *The World Tomorrow* in 1942) on a small, 100-watt local radio station, and in February the *Plain Truth* magazine—around 250 copies of eight mimeographed sheets.[9] According to

9. This is Armstrong's own estimated figure; other sources give the figure as "a circulation of 106 readers" (Nichols and Mather 1998: 28).

Armstrong, writing in the 1970s, "The Work from this point grew in power and scope at the rate of 30% per year over the next 35 years" (Ambassador College 1972b: 15)[10]—though the *Plain Truth* actually ceased publication after the July 1935 issue, not returning to print until January 1938 (623). The combined May/ June 1938 issue was the first to be printed, albeit on newsprint paper, rather than mimeographed. It was only eight pages long, but it was the first issue to carry the words "a magazine of understanding" under the title, which continued until well into the Tkach era after Armstrong's death. Around April 1942 the radio broadcast became daily (H. W. Armstrong 1987: 50), and in August it went nationwide for the first time (H. W. Armstrong 1987: 66).

During the 1930s, according to one internal church historian, "Mr. Armstrong came into increasing conflict with the Church headquarters in Salem because of his teachings" (Ogwyn 1995: 64). Armstrong puts the blame on his opponents, saying the conflict began almost from the very beginning in 1928:

> It is simply the fact that from this point on—from the very second "sermon"—if those early talks could be called that—opposition from other ministers, both within this church and without, was met at every turn continually. (365)

In his *Autobiography* (e.g., 409) and elsewhere Armstrong distances himself from any formal connection with the Church of God (Seventh Day). For example, in 1974 he wrote:

> For some years I worked in cooperation with the [Seventh Day] Church of God.... I never joined them—never became one of their members....
>
> I received no salary or remuneration of any kind from either the Salem or Stanberry organization....
>
> The story that I went out from them is 100% false! I was never even a member of them. (Armstrong 1974c; brackets in source)

This is challenged by former Worldwide member Richard C. Nickels, who did intensive research into the history of COG7. Nickels interviewed many people who were involved in COG7 in the early days of Armstrong's ministry (Nickels 1996d: 222–29). Elder John Kiesz (1903–96), who edited the COG7 magazine *The Bible Advocate* in the early 1930s, and thus published some of Armstrong's earliest religious writings, states unequivocally:

---

10. Armstrong is not speaking of church membership or *Plain Truth* circulation but of Church expenditure. According to one former senior member, instead of Armstrong budgeting within the church's income, "For many, many years he purposely over-extended the budget for broadcast, publishing and general expenditures by 30 per cent. He would then plead, beg, cajole and occasionally threaten his adherents with the *lake of fire* if they didn't come to his aid and 'SAVE THE WORK!' " (M. McNair 1977: 37). But for nonmembers, the way Armstrong phrased his claim made it appear that the church was blessed with this remarkable increase.

In his autobiography he [HWA] maintained that he never was a member of the Church of God (7th Day), which is incorrect for we did not grant [ministerial] credentials without one being a member. (Nickels 1996d: 226)

On November 4, 1933, Church of God ministers from all over the world met at Salem, West Virginia, for a major reorganization of the nearly half of the church that split from Stanberry, choosing "the twelve spiritual leaders" and "the seventy to go forth two by two, *all Church of God elders.*" The list of the Seventy (see 2.3), from all over the United States, Central and South America, England, India, and Palestine, includes "Herbert Armstrong, Oregon" (Nickels 1999: 210; my emphasis).

Armstrong's assertion that he never took any payment as a minister is refuted by copies of correspondence between Armstrong and COG7 from the 1930s. In fact, in contradiction to his own statement quoted above, he states in his *Autobiography* that he received a salary of $3 a week until 1933 when after a major disagreement he "refused further salary" (524). "But from that 'all-day wrangle' I was independent of them and their ministers, financially. From that time I was dependent, solely, on God" (526). According to Nickels, however, "A ledger book from the Church of God Publishing House in Salem, West Virginia, in 1937, also shows that Armstrong received pay at that time" (Nickels 1996d: 228).

But rather than simply accepting that his ministry developed out of COG7, Armstrong drew a determined line between them. With reference to the seven church eras of Revelation 2–3 (see 2.2.1) he wrote:

From the year 1931, exactly 1,900 years (a century of time cycles) from the foundation of the Church, this small remnant of the original true Church of God began to take on new life as the Philadelphia era. It had come to "the time of the end." ...

The Sardis era (Rev. 3:1–6) was by this time spiritually dying and had become impotent in spreading the true gospel of Christ. Indeed they had by this time lost knowledge of the true meaning of that gospel. (289)

As with many new religions (Barker 1992: 75–76), the Worldwide Church of God developed its own terminology as its doctrine developed. Armstrong believed that God worked in nineteen-year time cycles (Hopkins 1974: 56), a concept which will be referred to again shortly. Of the seven church eras (see 2.2.1), the Sardis era ("I know thy works, that thou hast a name that thou livest, and art dead"—Rev. 3:1) was identified by Armstrong as the Church of God (Seventh Day); the Philadelphia era ("thou hast a little strength, and hast kept my word, and hast not denied my name"—Rev. 3:8) began with his founding of the Worldwide Church of God.

The question of the accuracy of the "official" history of the Worldwide Church of God is well illustrated by this apparently straightforward quotation from Herman L. Hoeh, Worldwide's senior theologian and historian for many years:

Not long after his ordination in 1931...a momentous juncture occurred. A movement was under foot to organize the local congregations of the Church of God under human government—a financial board of seven men. By 1933 certain leading ministers demanded that no more *new* truth be preached to the brethren. They were refusing to repent and allow the Holy Spirit to work through them to establish the truth that was ready to perish!

Most of the congregations succumbed to spiritual DEATH. The age of the Church of Sardis was over. *The Church period of Philadelphia was to begin!* (Hoeh 1959b: 26)

Here we see three explicit or implicit statements about Armstrong's break with the Church of God (Seventh Day) to begin his own church—all of which are later revisions of history.

First, there is the clear implication that it was Armstrong who left COG7 because it was deviating from the truth. In fact, COG7 revoked Armstrong's ministerial license at the end of 1937, effective beginning in 1938;[11] "he was asked to turn in his credentials for continuing to preach contrary to Church doctrine" (Ogwyn 1995), particularly on keeping the seven Holy Days and on British Israelism. There may also have been another, more human reason; Elder John Kiesz, editor of *The Bible Advocate*, later said, "The real reason seems to have been because of his uncooperative attitude.... Nobody can work with him" (Nickels 1996d: 228).

Second, Hoeh, writing in 1959, emphasizes COG7's deviation from God's prescribed hierarchical form of church governance (see 2.2.4) as the reason for Armstrong leaving in 1931–33. In fact, as late as 1939 Armstrong wrote an article making the biblical case for collegial government rather than hierarchical government (Nickels 1996c: 32–41; see also 205–9). The crucial issues of authority and church governance, which still divide the offshoots, are discussed in chapter 7; see 7.3.3 for further mention of Armstrong's 1939 article.

Third, the strong implication is that at this point, around 1933, Armstrong led the Philadelphia-era church out of the Sardis-era church—that he began his own true ministry, leaving behind the corrupt COG7. In fact, he continued as a COG7 minister until the end of 1937, and the June 1938 *Bulletin of the Churches of God in Oregon*, which he edited, gives commendatory news of work by other Church of God ministers and members. As late as September 1945, in the *Good News Letter*, Armstrong says he is expecting two COG7 elders, including Elder John Kiesz, to be present at his Feast of Tabernacles site at the end of that month; the October issue that same year confirms that he paid Elder Kiesz's expenses at the festival (Edwards 1999).

In other words, although he might by the late 1930s have been operating independently rather than as a minister within a denomination, *at the time* he clearly saw himself as a part of the wider Sabbatarian Church of God movement, rather than the founder of a new church.

11. COG7 ministerial licenses were renewed annually.

Looking back from thirty years later, however, Armstrong commented on the beginnings of his ministry:

Coincidence?—or DESIGN!

This brings us to a series of almost incredible facts....

First, Jesus Christ began His earthly ministry at about age 30. God took away my business, moved me from Chicago, started bringing me to repentance and conversion preparatory to inducting me into His ministry, *when I was 30!*

Second, Jesus began the actual *teaching and training* of His original disciples for carrying His Gospel to the world in the year 27 A.D. *Precisely 100 time-cycles later,* in 1927 A.D., He began my intensive study and training for carrying His same Gospel to all nations of today's world....

But *that is not all!* Consider further!

More Amazing Parallels!

Christ started out His original apostles preaching the *very* Gospel of the Kingdom which God had *sent by Him,* and *which He had taught the apostles,* in the year A.D. 31. For exactly one 19-year time-cycle this preaching was confined to the continent where it started— Asia. After *precisely one 19-year time-cycle,* A.D. 50, Christ *opened a door* for the apostle Paul to carry the same Gospel to EUROPE!...

Now consider *this* amazing parallel!

God first *opened a door*—that of radio and the printing press—for the mass proclaiming of HIS ORIGINAL TRUE GOSPEL *the first week in 1934!* The exact date was January 7, 1934. *Exactly one time-cycle later,* January 7, 1953, God opened wide the massive door of the most powerful commercial radio station on earth, and RADIO LUXEMBOURG began broadcasting Christ's Gospel to EUROPE and Britain!

What startling coincidences!—or *are* they mere coincidences? (H. W. Armstrong 1986: 427–30)

Besides what this passage says about Armstrong's self-image, the point here is that official Worldwide history had the Gospel of the Kingdom lost until the advent of Herbert W. Armstrong as today's apostle. This is part of the foundation myth of the Worldwide Church of God (Barrett 2000; Barrett 2001a: 17). His origins in the Church of God (Seventh Day) and his borrowing of already-existing doctrines (see chapter 2) are completely ignored.

Armstrong "borrowed" more than doctrines. In 1965 an attorney representing Ambassador College wrote to COG7 asking them to stop publishing the booklet *Has Time Been Lost?,* since Ambassador College had a copyrighted booklet of the same name and subject written by Armstrong in 1952. COG7 "dug into their files and found that they had a copy of the booklet dating back into the early 1930s," and the title was included in their 1925 literature list. "It was clearly written before Herbert Armstrong ever began his ministry," writes Worldwide family historian Norman S. Edwards. Not only that, but in about half of their content "the two booklets are word-for-word identical" (Edwards 1999: 9).

As we shall see (7.3.3), in stark contrast to the hierarchical church that Worldwide was to become, as late as 1939, when his own ministry was well established, Armstrong was strongly opposed to centralized church governance (H. W. Armstrong 1939, quoted in Nickels 1996c: 32–41).

In addition to the magazine and the radio broadcast, a third institution was to be of both vital importance to the church and great pride to Armstrong: Ambassador College (much later briefly to become Ambassador University). This was originally intended to be a liberal arts college founded on biblical principles (H. W. Armstrong 1987: 212); effectively it became the training college for Worldwide's ministers and their wives (Ambassador College 1974). (Most if not all the leaders of offshoots mentioned and quoted in this book, all those I interviewed, and a quarter of my questionnaire respondents are Ambassador College alumni.)

Ambassador College began with eight faculty members and four students in October 1947; the students were Herman L. Hoeh ("pronounced 'hay,' not 'hooee'" [Trechak 1985]), who was quoted above; Raymond C. Cole, who was to be one of the first senior ministers to leave Worldwide to found a significant offshoot, the Church of God, the Eternal, in 1975; Armstrong's elder son Richard;[12] and a Miss Betty Bates (H. W. Armstrong 1987: 229). The following year brought three more, including brothers Marion and Raymond McNair (H. W. Armstrong 244). Marion was later to leave and write a critical book about Worldwide (M. McNair 1977); Raymond will be mentioned again in chapter 6. The third year brought five more new students, including Roderick C. Meredith (H. W. Armstrong 1987: 255), who was to become one of the most significant figures both in Worldwide and as the founder first of Global, then Living Church of God (see 6.2.2).

By December 1952 the Radio Church of God had grown sufficiently for Armstrong to ordain five evangelists under himself; these were Herman L. Hoeh, Raymond C. Cole, and Richard Armstrong from the first year's intake of students; Roderick C. Meredith from the third year; and his uncle C. Paul Meredith (died 1968); in January 1953 he ordained Marion and Raymond McNair from the second year's intake.

Not only are many of these very earliest students at Ambassador College of vital importance to the development and history of Worldwide, some are also important players in the story of schism.

The tiny college established in 1947 at Pasadena, California, the headquarters of Worldwide, was the first of three campuses for Ambassador College; the other two were at Bricket Wood, near St. Albans, Hertfordshire, UK (established in 1960, closed in 1974) and at Big Sandy, Texas (established in 1964, closed in 1977, reopened in 1981, and closed again in 1997). The original Pasadena campus closed in 1990. At its peak in 1974, Ambassador College had a total of 1,400 students.

---

12. Richard David Armstrong was to run the church in Britain in the early 1950s, and was clearly HWA's chief lieutenant. He died in a car crash in July 1958, aged twenty-nine.

From the start the college was coeducational; although women never had any positions of authority in any of Armstrong's organizations, "in the early years [the college campuses] were particularly viewed as sources of wives for those who would be going into the ministry" (Dewey 2001: 5).

Armstrong originally aimed "to insure full accreditation before the graduation of the first senior class" (Ambassador College Catalog, 1947–48, quoted in Zola 1977b). There was talk of accreditation in the 1960s and the 1970s; it came to naught largely because of the closeness of the college to the Worldwide Church of God, and because "several persons [held] major roles in both the church and college" (Zola 1977b).

The lack of accreditation means that Ambassador College degrees, including the master's degrees and doctorates held by some of the offshoot leaders (such as Dr Roderick C. Meredith, head of Living Church of God), are not recognized outside the Worldwide family of churches.

Accreditation finally came in June 1994, from the Southern Association of Colleges and Schools; nearly fifty years after its founding, Ambassador College became Ambassador University. For alumni from before 1994, the new university made this somewhat deceptive recommendation:

> As Ambassador University gains a reputation as an accredited institution, the date of accreditation and the name will cease to be issues. (When graduates apply to graduate schools or for jobs, they should use the name Ambassador University. Accreditation should not be raised unless others raise it. Then merely state that Ambassador University is accredited, not when it was accredited.) ("Ambassador Finally Accredited," *Ambassador Report* 56)

The change was, so to speak, academic. In December 1996 it was announced that the last remaining campus of Ambassador University, at Big Sandy, Texas, would close at the end of that semester.

Although the date of the founding of the Worldwide Church of God is usually given as 1937, that is really just the year when Armstrong began preaching independently; the *Plain Truth* magazine and the *Radio Church of God* (later *The World Tomorrow*) broadcast, hallmarks of Armstrong's ministry, had begun in 1934. The Radio Church of God was not incorporated as a church in the state of Oregon until 1946, a year before it moved to Pasadena, California; it changed its name to the Worldwide Church of God in 1968. The post-Armstrong church cut one more tie with the past when it changed its name to Grace Communion International in April 2009.

3.3   DIFFERENT PERCEPTIONS OF WORLDWIDE: A BRIEF SUMMARY

As with many new religious movements, there are several quite different versions of what life within Worldwide was actually like in its heyday, with huge differences between public image and insiders' perceptions.

For the outside world the Worldwide Church of God was a glossy magazine, *Plain Truth*, and a professional radio and television broadcast, *The World Tomorrow*. (In the United Kingdom, only the radio broadcast was available, on Radio Luxembourg and pirate stations.) Magazines, many booklets, and a few full-length books were offered free to anyone who requested them. They contained, among much else, photographs of beautiful college buildings, smart young students, and Herbert W. Armstrong meeting many world leaders. The main emphases were analysis of troubling world news, prophecy of the End Times, Creationism, and very conservative teaching on morality. The End Time teaching was very prominent. "Signs of the Times" were listed—earthquakes, famines, wars, diseases, assassinations, plummeting morality—to show that Christ's return must be very near.

For those who received the more doctrinal magazine, variously titled *The Good News of Tomorrow's World*, *The Good News*, *GN*, and *Tomorrow's World*, there were more detailed teachings on these doctrines, and on the wrong days (Sunday, Christmas, Easter, etc.) versus the right days (the Sabbath, the seven Old Testament festivals), and on the importance of tithing.

Unsurprisingly, the strict requirement for multiple tithing (see 2.2.2) caused some resentment within the church, as poor members saw HWA flying around the world in his personal plane (a Grumman Gulfstream II jet), wearing expensive clothes and watches, and living in some luxury,[13] while they scrimped and saved to pay their tithes. Armstrong's philosophy (in common with some other American churches) was that only the best is good enough for God (see 3.2.1).[14] Photographs in *Plain Truth* and elsewhere frequently showed Armstrong with great world leaders—kings, princes, presidents, prime ministers—which gave him kudos and credibility. According to some former senior members, these photographs were intended to show Armstrong's importance by the circles in which he regularly moved and the caliber of people who consulted him; but very often, the critics say, the great world leaders had little idea who this short, elderly man was who asked to be photographed shaking hands. Garner Ted Armstrong disapproved of his father's many foreign trips, calling them "the world's most expensive autograph hunt" (G. A. Armstrong 1992: 40).

According to Herbert W. Armstrong, writing in the *Plain Truth*, "The remarkable thing is that I did not seek or initiate these meetings—not once! I was invited." He put the meetings down to a series of "miraculous occurrences" (Bowden 1973: 3). But his son later wrote:

13. Cf. the criticism of Elizabeth Clare Prophet, leader of Church Universal and Triumphant, for her clothes and jewelry (Barrett 2001a: 379).
14. Although Armstrong did not specifically teach the "seed-faith giving" of American televangelist Oral Roberts and others (Roberts 1970), he did teach that the more you give to God, the more he will bless you. Another indication of what might be called "the ethos of 20th century American religion" was his booklet *The Seven Laws of Success*.

While I knew his advance man, a Japanese immigrant, was giving away golf clubs, gold pen sets, free trips to the United States, and many other gifts to various of his contacts through Japanese embassies, in order to buy my father's way into these various meetings, my father was kept in the dark. Over $900,000 was spent in only one year by my father's advance man, arranging for him to meet various dictators, premiers and presidents, like Jomo Kenyatta, Haile Selassie, and President Marcos.... I could not help feeling this was a terrible waste of tithe-payers' money. (G. A. Armstrong 1992: 40)

On many occasions Armstrong, as chancellor of the Ambassador Colleges and head of the Ambassador International Cultural Foundation, is alleged to have effectively "bought" meetings and photographs by making donations to charitable causes supported by a world leader. (Similar criticisms have been made of the leaders of other new religions, including Rev. Moon of the Unification Church and Daisaku Ikeda of Soka Gakkai International [Barrett 2001a: 206, 306].)

A different view comes from Armstrong's personal assistant for the last five years of his life, Aaron Dean (later on the council of United Church of God). In a long email to me he accepts that money was spent on Armstrong's world-leader visits, but disputes the "autograph-hunting" scenario.

One thing I would like to clarify is the notion that HWA went "autograph hunting". Those who make these statements (whether in the church or out) never travelled with HWA nor really understood what he did or said to world leaders. They were jealous and did not like the money spent on this function, and as is the human tendency, ridiculed what they didn't understand or want. I will grant that some of this was because of a hatred for Stan Rader [Armstrong's attorney, a powerful person in the church] and events of the 1970s, but each of those making accusations had their own agendas....

"Buying" meetings and his being "unknown" with just short few minute visits is also inaccurate. Yes, there were some meetings "bought" prior to my being his aide, and a lot of money was spent. HWA never knew this and was upset when I told him. Others around him did a lot of things he didn't know.

The last 5 years, when I set up all the trips, never was a meeting bought. I also cut the travel budget 75% and we saw more leaders in any given year than he did in the whole decade of the 70s. Meetings that were scheduled for 5 minutes often lasted 1 or 2 hours. King Hussein of Jordan kept the Egyptian ambassador outside waiting for an hour while he talked to HWA. (Aaron Dean, pers. comm)

But Dean's statement accepts that the criticisms were valid before he became Armstrong's aide.

For years Worldwide was attacked as a cult by both anticultists and Evangelicals, the former in part because of the strict tithing policy and the perceived authoritarianism of the church, the latter because of its "heretical" beliefs. It featured as a matter of course in books about cults (William Martin 1967; Petersen 1975; Harrison 1990). There were full-length books against it from an Evangelical viewpoint

(Hopkins 1974; Benware 1977) and from the viewpoint of former members (M. McNair 1977; D. Robinson 1980; Tuit 1981). There were booklets against it by Christians (*Herbert W. Armstrong: Mr. Confusion*, published by the Back to the Bible Broadcast [Campbell 1962]) and non-Christians (*Herbert W. Armstrong and His Worldwide Church of God: An Exposure and An Indictment*, published by the Rationalist Association of New South Wales, Australia [Bowden 1973]).

Some of the opposition was trenchant:

> In the past year or two a religious body calling itself the Scientologists have been banned [in Australia]. But the operations of this sect were minor compared with those [of] the Armstrong Church, which is a highly-organized racket with world-wide ramifications. It is a huge vested interest, a financial colossus. We can look upon it as a bloated octopus with hundreds of tentacles reaching to every corner of the inhabited world.
>
> What is perhaps most contemptible in regard to the Church and its activities is its professed concern for the "spiritual well-being" of the victims of their depredations. Nothing could be more hypocritical than this pretence; it makes Mr Pecksmith stand out as a model of rectitude and propriety. (Bowden 1973: 34–35)

But the church continued to prosper, both in membership and financially. The 1960s in particular saw a period of rapid growth (D. Robinson 1980: 27).

And then came the 1970s, a turbulent decade for the Worldwide Church of God, and in many respects a foreshadowing of what was to occur after Armstrong's death, as doctrinal disputes and personality clashes disrupted the church and precipitated a number of schisms.

3.4   CONCLUSION

In outlining the origins and history of the Worldwide Church of God this chapter has also presented in some detail a portrait of a complex man: he was dedicated, hard-working, and ambitious, and yet, from the testimony of some who worked closely with him, he could be arrogant, difficult, and perhaps even deliberately deceitful; even his supporters admit that he "had a temper" (Thiel 2003: 6).

We have seen in particular how his own account of his "discovery" of the truths taught in Worldwide, truths revealed to him directly by Christ, truths laboriously worked out through his own in-depth studies, were in fact a rehash of doctrines (outlined in chapter 2) already taught in several nineteenth-century sects, in the Seventh-day Adventist Church, and most of all in the Church of God (Seventh Day). In particular his "discovery" of the modern-day identity of Ephraim and Manasseh as Britain and the United States, the very heart of Worldwide's prophetic teaching, was taken directly from an earlier book and never credited, while another of his booklets was largely a copy of a COG7 booklet. How much all of this was deception, and how much self-deception, is probably impossible to ascertain.

We have also examined the beginnings of "the Work" (see 6.1.2) in the launch of the *Plain Truth* magazine and the radio ministry, the Radio (later Worldwide) Church of God itself, and Ambassador College; and we have looked briefly at different perceptions of both the church and Armstrong himself.

The complex nature of Armstrong's personality, and the way that it molded the Worldwide Church of God and the various offshoots, will be explored further in chapters 4 and 7.

CHAPTER 4

Schism and Scandals in the Seventies

INTRODUCTION

Until the 1990s the most traumatic and controversial period in the history of the Worldwide Church of God was the 1970s, though most readers of the *Plain Truth*, nonmembers, would not have known it. The decade began badly when the church went through "a very serious financial storm" (H. W. Armstrong 1987: 496),[1] but much worse was to come.

This book mainly studies the schisms after the death of Herbert W. Armstrong, but there were also several while he was still alive and running the church. According to the current pastor general, Joseph Tkach Jr., "We started making doctrinal changes in 1987, but a number of splits occurred before that—thirty-four, actually. Fourteen of those thirty-four are splits of splits" (Tkach 1997: 104). This suggests twenty "primary" schisms from Worldwide. A chart of "Worldwide Church of God Organizational Splits" at the end of his book, however, lists a total of fifty-six Worldwide offshoots up to and including 1987, thirty-nine of them primary schisms (Tkach 1997: 209–10).[2]

Of these thirty-nine, twenty-nine primary schisms from Worldwide, i.e., three-quarters of them, occurred in the 1970s. Most of them were very small—just one or two ministers leaving to form their own independent church—but a few were more significant, either because their founders were quite senior in Worldwide (several of

1. This may or may not have been the case; according to one former senior minister, Armstrong habitually used "financial crisis" and similar terms whenever planned expenditure exceeded anticipated income, to persuade members to make greater contributions to the church (see chapter 3 of M. McNair 1977: "Armstrong's Second Secret: How to Get Money").

2. Joseph Tkach's book contains a number of inconsistencies and inaccuracies; he gives the size of United Church of God as both "about seventeen thousand members" (71) and "about eighteen thousand members" (105), for example, and says that Philadelphia Church of God (which he misnames as "The Church of God, Philadelphia era") has "about three thousand members" (105) instead of the five to six thousand members it has had for much of its existence.

them at evangelist level and/or vice presidents of the church), or because more than a handful of members left Worldwide to join them, or because they are still functioning—and vocal—years later.

There were three main causes of schism in the 1970s. First, some conservative ministers left when Armstrong made two doctrinal changes, on the date of Pentecost (see 4.2.1) and on divorce and remarriage (see 4.2.2). Second, around the same time, a number of more liberal ministers left in protest over Armstrong's hardline policies (see 4.2.3). Third, Armstrong's own son and heir apparent was ejected from his father's church for both his repeated sexual misconduct and his attempts at liberalizing his father's church (see 4.4).

But the decade began with a very different problem.

4.1 WHEN PROPHECY FAILS

Many in the church believed that 1972 would be the beginning of the End Times. In a booklet titled *1975 in Prophecy*, first published in 1956, Armstrong quotes a weather authority who fears the *"big drought of 1975,"* then says, "But the indications of prophecy are that this drought will be even *more* devastating than he foresees, and that it will strike *sooner* than 1975—probably between 1965 and 1972!" (H. W. Armstrong 1956: 10). A little later he says:

> But again, I repeat—IT'S LATER THAN YOU THINK!
>
> Yes, time is running out on us, *fast*, and we're too sound asleep in deception to realize it! . . .
>
> Then, suddenly, before we realize it, we'll find ourselves in the throes of FAMINE, and uncontrollable epidemics of DISEASE. Already we're in the beginning of a terrible famine and we don't know it . . .
>
> All this is now only a few years off . . .
>
> Yes, millions of lukewarm inactive professing Christians will suffer MARTYRDOM— and that *before* the anticipated push-button leisure-year of 1975 dawns upon us! (H. W. Armstrong 1956: 18, 19, 20)

The booklet, like many others, was illustrated with photographs of floods, starved cattle, and marching troops, and with graphic drawings by Worldwide's resident artist, Basil Wolverton,[3] displaying scenes of "utter destruction," with captions such as:

> Unrepentant human beings will be stricken with excruciatingly painful boils—no position of the body may give relief from their agonies—as God destroys the evil works of sinning mankind to bring the nations to repentance and peace. (H. W. Armstrong 1956: 26)

---

3. Better known to the general public as a cartoonist for *Mad* magazine.

In the introduction to his 1967 book *The United States and British Commonwealth in Prophecy*, Armstrong wrote:

> Events of the next five years may prove this to be the most significant book of this century.
>
> People of the Western World would be STUNNED!—DUMBFOUNDED!—if they knew!…
>
> The events prophesied to strike the American and British peoples in the next four to seven years are SURE! (H. W. Armstrong 1967b: vii, xii)

The 1980 edition of the book, retitled *The United States and Britain in Prophecy*, leaves out the first sentence of these quotations and changes the last sentence to read "in the next few years." (H. W. Armstrong 1980b: xii).

The repercussions of "when prophecy fails" (Festinger, Riecken, and Schachter 1956) are not the subject of this study, but because prophecy was so central to the teachings of Worldwide, the problem must be mentioned.

Movements deal with the failure of prophecies in different ways (Barrett 2001a: 79; Barrett 2011: 115–16). Sometimes, as with the Seventh-day Adventists' rationalization of the Great Disappointment of 1844, they say that the event *did* occur, but on the spiritual plane; sometimes they say that God, in his mercy, stayed his hand; occasionally, as with the Jehovah's Witnesses in recent years, they admit that they made a mistake through their overenthusiasm.[4]

Armstrong had made specific prophecies previously, during World War II.[5] When they did not come to pass, they were either quietly forgotten or rephrased in rather less specific language in later articles or later editions of booklets. In any case,

> during those years the church was small, and the members were, for the most part, simple rural people who, considering the difficult times Europe and the world had been through, did not generally take as very serious the fact that Armstrong's predictions of the end-time were not on schedule. (O'Connor 1997: 177)

One source, however, suggests that Armstrong's move from Oregon to California in 1947 was to distance himself from those who had seen his prophecies fail and were losing trust in him (M. McNair 1977: 174).

4. "The wrong conclusions were due, not to malice or to unfaithfulness to Christ, but to a fervent desire to realize the fulfillment of God's promises in their own time. Consequently, A. H. Macmillan explained later, 'I learned that we should admit our mistakes and continue searching God's word for more enlightenment'" (Watch Tower Society 1995: 9).
5. E.g., "Hitler MUST BE THE VICTOR in his present Russian invasion! A settlement will be reached, giving Hitler the supplies and resources he must have and undoubtedly part of Western Siberia. The terms will give Hitler assurance that the Red army is unable to attack him, as Hitler turns his wrecking machine to the British Isles, the United States, and Palestine. Hitler will emerge from this Russian campaign stronger than ever, free to turn the entire might of his forces against Britain—and AMERICA!" (Armstrong 1941: 7)

But in the early 1970s there was such a strong expectation in the church that Christ would return that the matter could not be brushed under the carpet when the event failed to occur.

> These people had been taught authoritatively from the pulpit that 1972 was going to wind up everything in this country [the United States] and the faithful would be taken to a place of safety in Jordan, there to await the return of Christ to rule the world. By the summer of 1972 it was obvious to all that Herbert Armstrong had failed in his prophecies, and had failed miserably. (D. Robinson 1980: 29)

When 1972, and then 1975, passed with no great increase in famines, floods, or plagues of boils, and without Christ's return, a significant number of members—"It was a lot more than 2,000 from memory" (Gavin Rumney, pers. comm.)—left in disillusionment.

Armstrong never really dealt with the issue of his failed prophecies. In February 1972 he was backing away from his earlier certainty: "As of the present I, and a majority of our historians in Ambassador College, and researchers in the School of Theology, feel that it is utterly unsafe to try to set dates in regard to prophesied events" (H. W. Armstrong 1972b: 1). By 1977, five years after the Tribulation should have begun and two years after Christ should have returned, he was showing still more caution: "During this generation—within 60 to 90 years or less—from 1927—Christ will come again" (H. W. Armstrong 1977). The early limit of sixty years after 1927 was 1987, ten years after Armstrong was writing, and ninety-five years after his birth; although he very nearly reached that age, by the later limit he would be long dead and safe from further embarrassment.

The offshoots deal with the problem of Armstrong's failed prophecies in different ways. Richard C. Nickels, of Giving and Sharing Ministry (see 6.4.5), quotes Armstrong himself from an early *World Tomorrow* radio broadcast:

> A terrible famine is coming on the United States, that is going to ruin us as a nation inside of less than twenty more years. Alright, I stuck my neck out right there. You just wait twenty years and see whether I told you the truth. God says, if a man tells you what's going to happen, wait and see. If it doesn't happen, he was not speaking the word of God, he's speaking out of his own mind. If it happens, you'll know God sent him. (Nickels 1996d: 215)

Nickels comments, "The twenty years is long past! Herbert Armstrong labeled himself a false prophet."

But Richard T. Ritenbaugh, of Church of the Great God, comes to a different conclusion. Although he accepts that Armstrong "made many predictions during his ministry, and many of them have not come to pass. Some were plain wrong. Some were vague. Some were specific," he then argues:

So what are all those predictions Herbert Armstrong made? Rather than call them prophecies (which they were not) and him a false prophet (which he was not), his predictions were more correctly speculations, theories based on true but insufficient and unclear evidence. Speculation is not sin. (Ritenbaugh 2000)

Such prophecies, predictions, or speculations included among many others these front page headlines in *Plain Truth*: "The POPE Plans to Move Vatican!" (October 1951), "HITLER *May Be Alive!*" (June 1952) and "HITLER *Did Not Die*" (August 1952).

4.2   CHANGES IN DOCTRINE

A few conservative ministers left Worldwide in 1974 when there were disputes over changes to two doctrines: the correct date of Pentecost and remarriage after divorce. Both doctrinal topics need to be examined briefly, partly for what they show about Armstrong himself, both his personality and his attitude to authority (see chapter 7); partly for what they show about how Armstrong was regarded by some within his church; partly because they illustrate the huge importance of doctrinal correctness to Worldwide Church of God ministers; and hence, as the result of all these, because of their continuing importance to the offshoots today.

By looking at the schisms of the mid-1970s, we can gain some insights into the later schisms following Armstrong's death (see chapter 6).

During the 1970s there were also more liberal ministers, some of them at the highest levels, who had doubts about some of Armstrong's doctrines, or about the perceived authoritarianism in the church. They had no wish to leave the church they believed in and loved, but felt the need for debate on certain issues. Armstrong's characteristically over-the-top reaction, turning honest questioners into opponents into enemies is a classic case of demonization and deviance amplification (L. Dawson 2002: 98):

> ...ministers turning false, and leaving God's Church, trying to draw away members after them, and trying to destroy the Work of God...
>
> Yes, there was a conspiracy....
>
> Co-Workers, Satan exists! And Satan hates this work of the living God, and seeks by every subtile [*sic*] deception and maneuver to destroy this Work!... The handful of dissident and disloyal ministers took a certain number of deceived brethren with them.... They were deceived. They may not have realized Satan was using them....
>
> Yes, Satan did strike a blow at this new dimension in God's Work. (co-worker letters, March 28 and May 21 1974, in H. W. Armstrong 1987: 548, 550)[6]

6. "Co-workers" included people who might not be baptized or attending members of the Church, but who gave it financial support. They received regular letters from Armstrong in addition to *Plain Truth* and other literature.

Some of the offshoot churches founded then by "dissident and disloyal ministers" are still in existence today. The way that Armstrong dealt with challenges to his own authority will be examined in more depth in chapter 7.

4.2.1   Pentecost

For Worldwide throughout its half century under Armstrong, and for many of the offshoots today, holding the Old Testament festivals has meant holding them at precisely the right times, and this has necessitated a concentration on the calendar which, to outsiders, might seem obsessive.[7]

Some of the offshoots follow the same calendar as today's Jews follow, which was standardized by Hillel II in 359 CE; others follow the calendar they believe was followed in the Old Testament or by Jesus. This can mean that different churches which otherwise are almost identical in their beliefs celebrate the festivals, including the all-important Feast of Tabernacles, on different dates, sometimes a few days apart, but sometimes a full month.

The proponents of each position marshal complex arguments from the Bible and from history to prove their points. This is a hugely complicated issue, and not one to be examined here. A much simpler question, one might think, is whether the Feast of Pentecost should be held on Sunday or Monday. This was linked to the issue of whether Passover should be celebrated on Abib 14 or Abib 15 (all the Worldwide family use the Jewish months).

For many years Armstrong taught that Pentecost should be held on Monday. The dispute went right back to the earliest days of his ministry.

> Emil Heibel was trained as a minister and ordained by HWA to assist him in the Eugene Church. Heibel took charge of the Eugene Church when HWA moved to Pasadena [1946–47]. Along with Oscar Spires, Heibel espoused a Sunday Pentecost and led a number of the original Church to form a group separate from Armstrong. (Nickels 1996d: 224)

That must have been one of the earliest schisms from the church. If this was a big enough issue for someone to form a separate group, it was big enough to disfellowship people.

---

7. In addition to articles in the magazines, booklets include *The Original Calendar for Our Day* and *God's High Days* from the Church of God Talents Ministries, *Postponements* from the Church of God in Truth, *The Passover Controversy: 14th or 15th?* from the Philadelphia Church of God, *Holidays and Holy Days: Does It Matter Which Days We Keep?* and *God's Holy Day Plan: The Promise of Hope for All Mankind* from the United Church of God, and many others. Fred R. Coulter, leader of the Christian Biblical Church of God, wrote the 574-page *God's Plan for Mankind Revealed by His Sabbath and Holy Days* and the 482-page *The Christian Passover: What Does it Mean? When Should It Be Observed—the 14th or the 15th?*

A shocking fact is that in the late 1940s and early 1950s Armstrong put members out of the Church for keeping a Sunday Pentecost when he kept a Monday Pentecost. In the mid-1970s Armstrong abruptly changed to a Sunday Pentecost and put members out for keeping a Monday Pentecost! The important thing seemed to be obedience to him as "God's Apostle" no matter what. Those who refused to toe the line on any issue, no matter how small, were summarily removed. (Nickels 1996d: 215)

The date of Pentecost had been one of several subjects which kept cropping up over the years, quietly being discussed and debated behind the scenes in Worldwide. According to Raymond C. Cole, founder of Church of God, the Eternal, from 1972 there were different factions of ministers and some lay members, leading to "two different, and for the most part opposing, sources of authority." From his conservative viewpoint, "The result was fear, distrust, resentment and acts of rebellion." There was a strong feeling amongst the "liberals" that doctrinal questions should be discussed openly. "The result was the creation of a new doctrinal committee—made up of evangelists, college instructors, and other better-known headquarters personnel" (Cole 1999b). Because Pentecost was a perennial topic, this is what they started with—and they decided it should be Sunday, not Monday as Armstrong had always taught.

Why was this so important to Raymond Cole? In 1948–49, Herbert W. Armstrong had discussed the dates of Pentecost and Passover with his early students, many of whom, as we have seen, later became evangelists in the church. Raymond Cole and Herman Hoeh believed from their study that Passover is on Abib 15 rather than Abib 14 (Nickels 1996d: 217), disagreeing with Armstrong. Cole had "wanted to see tangible and technical proof" of Armstrong's position, but Armstrong "continually insisted God had revealed to him that which he was preaching." Cole then came to the realization that despite the lack of evidence "Mr. Armstrong was right—God reveals His Truth to a chosen servant." From that moment on, Cole writes, "I lived with the absolute conviction that the Truth had been given to him and that it could not, nor ever would, be changed" (Cole 1999b).

This, then, was a matter of faith, of belief that Herbert W. Armstrong had been chosen and appointed by God, and that God revealed the Truth to him. Trust in Armstrong's divinely appointed position came before technical proof.

Now, in 1973–74, a committee was discussing Pentecost, on purely technical bases: "In the length and breadth of the meetings little, if any, emphasis was given to divine revelation. But, plenty of scorn was heaped on Mr. Armstrong. He was not a student, they said. They felt his grasp of history and languages was at best, very limited" (Cole 1999b).[8] This was bad enough to Cole. When the committee recommended changing Pentecost from Monday to Sunday, Cole was certain that Armstrong would reject this. But he sent word that he would accept the change.

8. Compare the criticism of Armstrong by today's Worldwide; see 3.2.1.

"I was shocked beyond belief. What happened to divine revelation?" (Cole 1999b) But there was worse to come for Cole.

4.2.2   Divorce and Remarriage

The church's policy on divorce and remarriage (known as D&R) caused schisms by both liberals and conservatives.

For years Armstrong held a very strict position. Members who had remarried after divorce, or who had married a divorced person, even before they joined the church, were required to end their marriages. This caused a tremendous amount of pain and unhappiness, as couples who might have been together for many years and raised families were forced to separate. They were taught that if they had sex, they were adulterers.

This was still the case in 1973, when Armstrong released a new edition of the booklet *Marriage and Divorce* (the previous 1953 edition had been entitled *Divorce and Remarriage*, hence D&R). He quotes Romans 7:3, "So then if, while her husband liveth, she be married to another man, she shall be called an adulteress; but if her husband be dead, she is free from that law," then states firmly, "Anyone who thinks he has found a loophole to allow divorce and remarriage does violence to this clear, plain statement of GOD'S LAW! Any scripture that would allow divorce and remarriage would contradict the above-quoted scripture" (H. W. Armstrong 1973b: 7).

Later in the booklet he says unequivocally, "In the Bible, what GOD has joined together, man is FORBIDDEN to separate or UNbind—man is UNABLE to UNbind what God has bound for LIFE. Only God could—and God WON'T!" (46). And he makes it clear that this applies to all marriages: "God is witness to all marriage covenants. He, and He alone, joins the marriage bond. It is He who 'glues' the marriage, not the minister, rabbi, priest, judge, Justice of the Peace or other human" (51).

At the end of the booklet he describes "tragic cases" where a "hasty and ill-considered" early marriage ends, and someone remarries and has children—and then, "perhaps one—either a husband or wife—has become a begotten child of God—knows he or she cannot continue living as an adulterer or adulteress. What TRAGEDY!" Tragedy, because under his church's teaching, the couple must now separate.

> There are children. There are now property rights and considerations. There are family and relatives. If one now dares obey God, the persecution will be heavy and full of self-righteous indignation. The Church will be persecuted, accused of "breaking up families." (53)

But obeying God is more important than what the world thinks.

For many ministers, the pain that the church's policy on D&R caused was not acceptable. They had studied Armstrong's teaching, and found it to be at fault. Armstrong's son Garner Ted agreed with them. Matters came to a head in 1974 when at least thirty-six ministers, some of them senior, challenged the implementation of the doctrine. One minister, Gary Arvidson, wrote to me about this crisis:

Ken Westby, Regional Director for the Washington Region, had over 50 D&R cases on his desk. He knew about the serious problems with the current teaching. He knew that Ted knew this as well—and confronted Ted about it. Ken knew that it was not right to break up all those homes—over something that Ted himself knew was doctrinally contrary to what he himself believed. But Ted would not go to his father as Ken asked—because of his own problem (i.e. HWA would not look into D&R because of Ted...). So the hapless members were made to suffer under the then-current D&R doctrine.

So, on that score, Ken told Ted that he couldn't in good conscience process all those D&Rs. Ted told Ken to process them—or that **Ted would fire Ken**. Ted fired Ken. Then all of Ken's men (who were willing to stand for the truth) were ambushed individually and collectively.

I was on the HQ side of things working in Church Administration as David Antion's assistant, while Ken was in the field. Ken & I were close as college buddies. Ken wanted me to keep Al & Dave focused on the need to be strong—and continue their stand—so that the ministers would have a chance to present their case about the doctrinal problems. They folded. Al accepted a settlement. David received an expense-paid trip to Hawaii. We were eaten by the sharks.[9] (Gary Arvidson, pers. comm.)

Despite this "divide-and-conquer" stratagem, thirty-six ministers left Worldwide because of the church's hardline attitude, founding Associated Churches, Inc. (later Association for Christian Development) under Ken Westby's leadership. They took around two thousand members with them. In some ways this 1974 offshoot was a precursor of the more liberal offshoots such as United following the death of Armstrong (see chapter 6).

Early in 1974, Armstrong reiterated the church's teaching on D&R in a policy statement. Then suddenly, in a letter to co-workers dated May 14, 1974, everything changed.

> Dear Brethren in God's Church:
> New light on marriage and divorce has been announced!
> The CHURCH OF GOD GROWS in grace and the KNOWLEDGE of our Lord and Savior Jesus Christ! (Armstrong 1974d)

In the letter Armstrong now shows great compassion for the "spiritual widows" in the Worldwide Church of God:

> Of prospective Church members—those applying for baptism—somewhere near one in five, or one in four, have been divorced, and most of these remarried. In order to qualify to be baptized and accepted into God's Church MANY have been required by the Church, knowing this teaching, to separate from a second marriage—in many cases a happy marriage with children.

9. Gary Arvidson, Ken Westby, David Antion, and Al Portune were senior-level ministers in Worldwide.

> This brought on a growing class of what came to be called "spiritual widows"—women separated from such a second marriage, unable to support themselves (and often children) and therefore living on third tithe. Also many divorced from a former marriage were plagued with the desire to remarry—forbidden by the Church. (Armstrong 1974d)

The "new light" was that marriages of unbelievers, though legal by the law of the land, are not specifically sanctioned by God. Therefore if the marriage breaks up, and one partner becomes converted, there is no barrier to remarriage to another converted person, because God had not blessed the previous marriage; effectively, in God's eyes, they had not been married.

By 1976, the new policy was stated even more clearly: "The church accepts new converts in whatever marital state they enter the church....A previously divorced person who has entered fellowship is free to remarry within the church" (Chandler 1982: 12).

This was explosive stuff. For some couples, it was the best of all possible news; they would not have to separate after all. But for others, who had broken up their marriages on Armstrong's orders, it was devastating; there was now no reason for all the years of pain and heartache they had been forced to go through. And for others, it was unacceptable for another reason: Armstrong had "found a loophole to allow divorce and remarriage" and so was breaking the "clear, plain statement of God's Law."

For Raymond C. Cole, already seriously troubled by the change of the day of Pentecost, such further liberalizing of long-held church doctrines was unacceptable. "The concept of the 'faith once delivered' became foundational to me," he wrote. In a realization prophetic of events ten to twenty years later:

> "The thought flashed through my mind, 'Now nothing will be restrained from them.' The way was paved. Doctrine after doctrine will fall at the hands of those who had no love for the truth. I knew my days within Worldwide Church of God were limited" (Cole 1999b).

Believing that "there was not one other person who stood for the truth which had been taught for forty years," he reluctantly left the Worldwide Church of God and founded the Church of God, the Eternal.

Other ministers left to join Cole, taking their members with them. Cole died in 2001, but his church, although small, continues. The front page of its website shows that his founding principle still holds:

> Church of God, The Eternal is a remnant of the Worldwide Church of God still teaching the original doctrines first proclaimed by Mr. Herbert W. Armstrong.

> We accept these doctrines as the divine revelation of Jesus Christ to His Church of the last days, given through the inspiration of a chosen servant; teachings that were blessed by God, producing an annual growth of 30% over four decades, with incredible blessings in the lives of those who practiced the same in faith.

What makes this remnant group truly different from the 300+ splinter groups of our parent organization? No one else believes what Mr. Armstrong *originally* taught about Truth—that it comes only by revelation to a chosen servant, and even that servant has *no authority* to change what Christ gave! Read it for yourself:

From *The Plain Truth*, July 1965. [http://www.cogeternal.org/theplaintruth1965.html]

In April 1973 Mr. Armstrong prophesied what would happen if the church's doctrine on Divorce and Remarriage were ever changed! Again, read it for yourself:

From a Bible Study on Divorce and Remarriage; Pasadena, April 1973. [http://www.cogeternal.org/text/hwa1973d&rquote.htm] (Cole 1999a; URLs are hyperlinks in website)

Ironically, this church, which upholds Armstrong's original teachings, is headquartered in Eugene, Oregon—where Herbert W. Armstrong began his ministry.

In some ways this 1975 offshoot was a precursor of the doctrinally more hardline offshoots after Armstrong's death, such as Philadelphia Church of God and Restored Church of God (see chapter 6).

The D&R doctrinal change may have been explosive, but the real dynamite was to come a year later, when Armstrong announced, precisely ten years after the death of his wife Loma, that he was about to remarry. He was eighty-five; his bride-to-be, Ramona Martin, was thirty-nine—and a divorcée. We shall return to Ramona shortly; suffice to say for now that "Armstrong had been dating Ramona previous to the time of the new ruling by the WCG, actually several years before the ruling" (Nichols and Mather 1998: 37). The word "dating" here means a sexual relationship ("The Insanity Continues," *Ambassador Report* 27) (see 4.3).

4.2.3   The Liberal Dilemma

Part of the problem faced by the more liberal ministers in the 1970s was that they knew that Garner Ted Armstrong (GTA) agreed with them on doctrinal changes. Indeed, he initiated much of the debate within the church on doctrinal change. But when it came to the crunch—when his father would not back down—he supported his father. The following extract from a letter by two senior ministers, David Antion and Al Carrozzo, to Herbert W. and Garner Ted Armstrong, clearly illustrates the dilemma for dissenting ministers at the time.

As both of us have stated to you verbally and in written reports, these men are reacting genuinely to issues and circumstances that have been developing for a long period of time. Certainly these men are disturbed, distraught, and emotionally beset. But it is over bonefide issues that you yourself, Ted, have agonized over to both of us and before dozens of other of the Headquarters and Field Ministers for a long time.

You, Ted, yourself, have decried the dictatorial and unbearable rule and labeled it as being out of the dark ages. You, personally, have agonized and been one of the primary ones to repudiate your own father's methods and conclusions in the Divorce and Remarriage booklet. You, Ted, yourself, have been one of the most outspoken of us all about the opulence, ornate buildings and hundreds of thousands of dollars—even millions—spent on paintings, punch bowls, gold fixtures, vases, sculpture, jewelry, bric'-a-brac' and the like.

You, Ted, yourself, have spoken out before forums, assemblies, and in the pulpit about the dominance over the personal lives of students, ministers, and laymembers alike concerning hair styles, clothing, marriage and many other issues.

You, Ted, yourself, have agonized over the "inviolable" doctrinal issues that just could not be brought to your father because he would "just not go into them."

And we could go on and on.

Yet, because finally under the weight and pressures of these same issues (which you yourself have helped to create) many of the ministers have been pressed beyond measure in their lives and ministerial responsibilities. Now they are suddenly "demon-influenced, collusionists, detractors and defectors." This is simply not the justice of God!…

We are not making impossible demands. Is it unreasonable to ask for an official open forum to discuss these things? Is it unreasonable to ask you to openly restore the confidence of these men by showing true willingness to deal with these issues?…

Even if both of us did turn our backs on these men and the issues the problems wouldn't go away. But you can stop it by simply showing by fruits and acts that these problems will be solved openly and in brotherly love—not by bringing the full weight and strength of this organization to bear to stamp out this rebellion. (Antion and Carrozzo 1974)

Later in the decade Garner Ted Armstrong was to seize the opportunity to push through some reforms, though it would eventually cost him his position, and even his membership, in the church (see 4.4).

4.3   SEX SCANDALS

The Worldwide Church of God was also hit by sexual scandals in the 1970s; some of these leaked out to the wider world in newspaper reports.

In 1971–72, some senior ministers went to Armstrong with their concerns about Garner Ted's moral fitness to be senior evangelist in the church because of his extramarital relationships, including with Ambassador College female students. Armstrong suspended his son for two brief periods, in autumn 1971 and spring 1972 (the second time disfellowshipping him), but then reinstated him with increased power—enabling him to reassign other evangelists in the church to less powerful positions. At one point in the mid-1970s he demoted Roderick C. Meredith

to pastor over a small church of around 100 in the ghetto area of Los Angeles with no active work in any of the literature. The same happened to Mr Raymond McNair who was demoted to a similar small church in the Ozarks of Missouri. (Waite 2000: 229)

It appears that one reason Armstrong brought his son back so quickly is that he was such a gifted preacher on *The World Tomorrow* radio and TV broadcasts, and the show was nowhere near as successful without him—success being measured not just in requests for literature but in how much revenue was brought in.

> For six long months Ted's golden voice was not heard on the church's radio broadcast, and no new television programs were filmed. Although old broadcasts of HWA were aired across the country the church's income plummeted. The old legend did not have the drawing power of his son. Shortly thereafter, a fully "repentant" GTA was reinstated into his father's church with all of his former rights and privileges. (Zola 1977a)

> Most of those present were convinced that Garner Ted had to return. Too much time had already elapsed, causing the organization's income to plummet by the millions. (Carrozzo 1977)

It should also be noted that although Armstrong had removed his son because of his sexual behavior, "members of the church, however, were led to believe that Ted had been removed for health reasons" (Carrozzo 1977).

Ministers in Worldwide had complex feelings about Garner Ted Armstrong. Al Carrozzo wrote:

> One Worldwide Church evangelist summed it up succinctly: "Ted can charm the rattle off a snake." Unfortunately, he charms people too. Glib as an orator and possessing awesome mental dexterity, Ted can change black into white, turn silk into wool, and refine sin into baseless allegations and rumor. (Carrozzo 1977)

Another minister, later to be a senior leader in one of the offshoots, told me off the record, "Ted is a great man, and great men tend to have great sins."

There have been other allegations of sexual impropriety by senior evangelists in WCG. Such accusations about leaders of new religious movements are not uncommon; sometimes they might be blatant slanders, but sometimes there is a basis of truth to them. Garner Ted Armstrong said on tape at a ministerial meeting in March 1974 at which he was challenged over his own sexual behavior:

> I know of about five or six or eight or ten [Worldwide Church of God ministers] who have committed adultery and who upon repentance have been allowed back. You want some leveling done here today? I am not the FIRST CASE! (Zola 1977a; brackets in original)

Herbert W. Armstrong, author or coauthor of the very morally conservative book *The Missing Dimension in Sex*,[10] scarcely led a blameless life, either, if the reports of those close to him are to be believed.

10. HWA is credited as the author of the third edition (1981), but the nearly identical second edition (1971) and the first edition (1964, under the title *God Speaks Out on "The New*

Longtime readers of *Ambassador Report* know how Herbert's intimate relationship with Ramona predated their marriage by a number of years. In recent months Ramona has admitted to friends that she and Herbert maintained a sexual relationship for three full years prior to their marriage. At some point along the way Ramona had some misgivings and so asked Herbert what he would do if he discovered some man in the church was involved in a nonmarital sexual relationship with one of the church women. He answered that he would immediately disfellowship them both. "But," questioned Ramona, "isn't what we are doing also wrong?" To her surprise Herbert said, "No." When she asked why, Herbert explained, "Because I am an Apostle!" ("How Not to Have a Happy Marriage," *Ambassador Report* 27)

This from the man who had written, "Sexual intercourse prior to the actual marriage vow is FORNICATION, and the Law of God is inexorable—it will exact the penalty—CAPITAL PUNISHMENT! It is, in the sight of God, as great a crime as MURDER!" (H. W. Armstrong 1981b: 192)

There were further sexual scandals, revealed in 1980 by a former senior minister, David Robinson. In his book *Herbert Armstrong's Tangled Web*, written six years before Armstrong's death, Robinson made two sexual allegations about Armstrong. The first was that the man who taught that "masturbation is a form of PERVERSION. It is a SIN!" (Armstrong 1981b: 173) himself masturbated regularly. "He extracted a small black book and showed me the last entry, in his own hand. HE HAD KEPT BOOKS ON HIS OWN MASTURBATION! He said, when checking over the record, it occurred about every two weeks" (D. Robinson 1980: 80).

Immeasurably more serious than this, Robinson alleged that Herbert W. Armstrong had an incestuous relationship with his younger daughter, Dorothy, for ten years in the 1930s and 1940s, starting when she was thirteen, with full intercourse starting when she was sixteen. "I learned of this in the summer of 1979 from members of his own family," wrote Robinson (D. Robinson 1980: 266). Garner Ted Armstrong learned the story directly from Dorothy in 1971; she also told David Antion, Garner Ted's brother-in-law, and Lois Chapman, widow of Ted's late elder brother, Richard ("HWA Confesses to Incest!" *Ambassador Report* 27).

WCG lawyers managed to block distribution of Robinson's book for a short time after publication, but the incest allegations were never publicly denied by either Armstrong or his daughter. The matter was also discussed in several issues of the critical news magazine *Ambassador Report* (see appendix 3.4); according to this, Armstrong confessed to the incest to at least two named people, including his second wife, Ramona. The story was also confirmed by Dorothy's husband, Vern Mattson, later the business manager of Radio Church of God, and by attorney and former member Jack Kessler in an open letter to the board of Worldwide (Kessler 1981). (Some ministers, though, dismiss the story altogether; John Jewell, who

---

Morality") are credited to "Faculty Members of the Graduate School of Theology, Ambassador College with HWA, Chancellor." The authorship of booklets is discussed further at 6.1.4.

knew HWA for many years, told me in a telephone conversation that it was "absolute nonsense." It should be noted that although neither Armstrong nor his daughter ever denied the story, neither did they ever confirm it publicly.)

Garner Ted confronted his father over the incest in 1978, in response to Armstrong's accusations of GTA's sexual improprieties, in what was the last face-to-face meeting between the two. Armstrong threatened to destroy his son by making public information about his personal life. Garner Ted responded that he could destroy his father with the information he had:

> Ted charged his father in no uncertain terms, yelling: "You fucked my sister!" Herbert, shocked at Ted's knowledge of the incestuous relationship, could only reply, "Well there have been times in my life when I have gotten far away from God." ("HWA Confesses to Incest!" *Ambassador Report* 27; D. Robinson 1980: 265–68; Nichols and Mather 1998: 37–38)

They never spoke again.

4.4   THE OUSTING OF THE HEIR

This was the end of what had been for some years an increasingly difficult relation-ship between father and son. From the accounts on both sides, it would appear that Armstrong ousted his son and heir for a number of reasons. As Armstrong had grown older, Garner Ted had increasingly taken the helm, doing most of the radio and TV broadcasts and much of the writing, and practically running the church. Herbert W. Armstrong, however, found it difficult to relinquish the reins, and GTA frequently found his decisions overturned.

There were also doctrinal differences between them; Armstrong later claimed that GTA had begun "to water down, liberalize and secularize Christ's true doc-trines!" On a more personal level, he wrote, "I learned that Ted had a somewhat normal attitude of resentment against his father," and, "He has accused his father of senility." Worst of all, "His sole effort has been to destroy his father and God's Church, and draw tithe payers after him!" (H. W. Armstrong 1979: 25) In his letter to co-workers telling them he had disfellowshipped his son, Armstrong said he began "to sense there was a CONSPIRACY to 'retire' me as being now too old, and for Garner Ted to 'TAKE OVER' as the supreme HEAD of the Work" (H. W. Armstrong 1978: 8).

Unsurprisingly, Garner Ted's version of the dispute is considerably different. He had effectively been running the entire organization for several years, while his father spent up to three hundred days a year on his foreign trips. He consulted his father on major decisions; but often, after they had agreed a policy and Garner Ted had implemented it, Armstrong would suddenly change his mind and countermand his son's actions.

> No, I did not "try to take over", but you gave the reins to me, and then continually snatched them back out of my hands until I was once more in a complete power vacuum—every decision second-guessed and suspect

Garner Ted wrote in a long and very emotional letter to his father (April 25, 1979, in G. T. Armstrong 1992: 72).

As Armstrong became older his eyesight and hearing deteriorated badly, and he became more and more forgetful, and also more prone to falling out with his son. According to Garner Ted, among Armstrong's closest aides were several people who deliberately fed his confused father lies about him, which his father believed. "To most, I am viewed as being very conservative, far-to-the-right. But to some who had my father's ear unbeknownst to me, I was being subtly painted as a 'liberal'" (G. T. Armstrong 1992: 52).

Matters were made worse by Armstrong's marriage in 1977 to Ramona, a divorcée eight years younger than his son; GTA disapproved strongly of the marriage, though he eventually conducted the wedding himself. The confrontation over sexual misconduct in 1978 was the last straw.

Armstrong expelled his son and heir apparent from the church. Armstrong's legal adviser Stanley Rader offered GTA a large retirement payoff to go away and keep quiet. GTA wrote a letter to all Worldwide ministers, beginning:

> I have recently received a letter from Mr. Rader, offering me a $50,000 (before taxes) salary per year, for retirement.... In the letter, he goes into great, legal detail about my remaining silent about certain confidential information I have concerning the work. Further, he offers me the free-rent use of the Tahoe Cabin. However, it is stated that this "retirement" salary and the access to the cabin may be terminated at any time "with or without cause."...I utterly reject all such offers, and all such strings attached.... Such offer is tantamount to taking God's tithes...and paying me not to preach the gospel with those tithes! (July 25, 1978, quoted in "Garner Ted Strikes Back," *Ambassador Report* 5; ellipses in the article)

Turning down the payoff, Garner Ted Armstrong went off to found the Church of God, International, based in Tyler, Texas (see 6.3). Some other ministers and members left with him. "Some 'liberals' who wanted to water down God's truth are being sifted out," said his father (co-worker letter, January 18, 1979, in H. W. Armstrong 1987: 602).

Some months after expelling his son Armstrong wrote a short and very personal piece in *Good News* magazine: "Why My Son No Longer Stands 'Back to Back' with Me." It began: "Six years ago my son, Garner Ted, and I often said, 'As long as we two stand *back to back* TOGETHER, no one can overthrow God's Church!' How many times we said that! And as for me, *I meant it!*" (H. W. Armstrong 1979: 25). This is an uncanny echo of the rift between the president and the secretary-general of the Elim Pentecostal Church in the 1930s; Bryan R. Wilson quotes the church president: "It seemed that *as long as we two were united in purpose* nothing could stand against us" (B. Wilson 1961: 48). In the Elim case "the struggle was between the two dominant figures of the movements, the titular leader and the expert administrator"; in Worldwide's case it was between two very powerfully charismatic men, father and son. There was another similarity. "The laity were left utterly uninformed of the differences between the men at the top" (B. Wilson 1961: 49) for a long time.

After he had been ousted Garner Ted became, for his father and for the Worldwide Church of God, a nonperson. In Volume 2 of Armstrong's *Autobiography*, compiled in 1987 after Armstrong's death and long after Ted's ouster, the 143 pages covering the 1970s contain almost no references to any of the troubles the church went though in that decade; as noted in 3.1, official histories can be very selective. In the whole of that decade there is just one mention of GTA, who was the church's chief evangelist for most of the decade, and who ran the church in his father's absence. This was when Armstrong suffered a near-fatal heart attack in August 1977, and reads in total: "I think Ted anointed me" (H. W. Armstrong 1987: 591).

At about the same time as GTA was expelled there was another doctrinal shake-up, with Armstrong reversing certain recent liberal moves. The background to this was the Systematic Theology Project (STP), a doctrinal review led by Garner Ted Armstrong in 1972–74 "to sift our accumulated teachings." It was later adopted as the doctrinal statement of GTA's own churches, prefaced on their website for some years by this account:

As the Church developed into a substantial institution, Mr. Garner Ted Armstrong, Executive Vice-President of the Church, recognized the need for a more organized, thorough systematic presentation of the Church's doctrines and beliefs, and thus commissioned the present Project.

During the final months of preparation, Mr. Garner Ted Armstrong presented the STP to his father, Mr. Herbert W. Armstrong, in its rough draft form. On several visits to the elder Armstrong's home in Tucson, Garner Ted Armstrong and other ministers read through various segments of the STP which they knew might be of special interest to the elder Armstrong, particularly the sections on Healing and Tithing. Some minor edits were made, and Mr. Herbert Armstrong approved the project.

He was fully aware of the development of the STP through all its phases. Repeated mention of the project was made in the "Pastor's Report" to all the field ministry, and repeated solicitations for input from the entire ministry of the Church were made through that medium.

Later, after the rough draft was typewritten, printed, and placed in a loose-leaf binder with spacers and vinyl cover, Mr. Herbert Armstrong told the ministry he had "never seen" the document; said he had not authorized it, and repudiated the entire project.... Others influenced Mr. Armstrong to come to such an outrageous conclusion— they shall bear their own responsibility....

Since the leadership of the Worldwide Church of God repudiated the entire STP, required that all ministers turn in their copies, and presumably destroyed them, taking the document out of circulation, it was understood the Worldwide Church of God had relinquished all claims to the material. (ICG Doctrines, n.d.)

Nevertheless, during the 1970s there had been certain doctrinal changes, as we have seen (4.2), and some shifts in emphasis within the Worldwide Church of God.

Once Garner Ted had been ejected, his father put the church "back on track." In 1981 Armstrong wrote about the STP in an article titled "How Subtly Satan Used MAKE-UP to Start the Church off the Track: How Satan Began Injecting Liberalism into God's Church."

In early fall of 1974...it was a time when certain "scholars" among our leaders were engaged in "doctrinal research." I had not realized until later that most of them were actually researching to try to prove Church teachings were in error, rather than to discover truth. I admit now and repent of the fact that, not realizing the real motive, I approved this doctrinal research team. (H. W. Armstrong 1981a)

But in 1985, in a special edition of the internal church magazine *Worldwide News*, Armstrong denied all knowledge of the STP.

I had not gotten very far out over the Pacific Ocean that afternoon, until in the afternoon session of the conference a voluminous printed work called "Systematic Theology Project," or "STP" for short, was distributed to the ministry with specific instructions that this was a definite outline of basic Church doctrines, and no minister was to preach anything contrary to this treatise.

I knew absolutely nothing of this STP, or that it had been in preparation. It had been carefully concealed from me. It was a flagrant violation of the promise made to induce me to leave so this doctrinal change in Church teaching could be given to all ministers without my knowledge. I knew nothing of this STP, in spite of claims made by others, until a copy was brought to me by some loyal ministers in late April or early May of 1978 when I then notified every minister in the world to return his copy immediately and ignore all its liberal doctrines and teachings.

It has come to my attention that some of the liberals, no longer members of God's Church, have claimed that I did know of this infamous STP project. That is positively NOT TRUE. A few papers on one or two subjects, which were not liberal, had been brought to me in Tucson, Ariz., but no clear mention was made of the preparations under way for producing this STP project. None of the liberalized teachings in the STP were shown to me or approved by me at any time.

Some of these liberal ministers who worked on and produced the STP and the one who was in charge of executive administration in my absence were disfellowshipped and others left the Church. (H. W. Armstrong 1985b)

One of the "liberalized teachings" had been on the wearing of makeup by female members. Garner Ted allowed it; Armstrong had always been against it—in fact, according to one source he "personally disfellowshipped both of his daughters for its use" (Nugent 1976).[11] Now that GTA was gone Armstrong claimed that the "watering down" of the policy against makeup had been the first step toward liberalism.

> My mother and grandmothers did not wear make-up—nor did your great-grandmothers of the same era. How did it get into our mid-and-latter-20th century society? FROM PROSTITUTES!...
>
> Women do not use make-up to PLEASE GOD today—for I can tell you ON HIS AUTHORITY it is NOT pleasing to HIM!
>
> Satan used human reason and make-up and WOMEN to START the ball of LIBERALISM AWAY FROM GOD and TOWARD SIN to rolling in the Church beginning October, 1974....
>
> Christ is GETTING US BACK ON THE TRACK! (H. W. Armstrong 1981a)

Classic "Armstrongite" booklets which had been downplayed or rewritten while Garner Ted was in charge were brought back into print, including *The United States and Britain in Prophecy*—"back to full length!" (co-worker letter, July 25, 1978, quoted in H. W. Armstrong 1987: 598)

In a further cementing of his authority, in 1979 Armstrong purged the editorial staff of *Plain Truth*—for the third time that decade (previous purges were in 1974 and 1976). The critical news source *Ambassador Report* commented acerbically:

> Interestingly enough, almost 85% of those who ever worked for the editorial department have become "dissidents." The reason is obvious: if you are truly qualified to analyze, edit, and write—and if you have a conscience—you will also be sensitive to the gaping holes in Armstrong theology and the gross hypocrisy that permeates the church hierarchy. ("Plain Truth Staff Purged," *Ambassador Report* 11)

Armstrong's son and heir was ejected from his father's church, and this time there was no reversal. There were moves from GTA in the spring of 1981 for a rapprochement, and Armstrong apparently considered it, but Stanley Rader and Armstrong's Advisory Council of Elders—who included Armstrong's eventual successor, Joseph Tkach—all opposed GTA's return and advised Armstrong against it.

> He took the matter to the WCG's council of elders to test the waters. It was there that Herbert discovered that anti-GTA feelings now run very deep in the WCG and that bringing Ted back at this juncture could again not only divide the WCG, but cause a widespread revolt by the church's ministry....

---

[11] Both daughters left the church in the 1950s.

But the council of elders knows that if Ted does return, it could well mean curtains for them. Some of those almost sure to be demoted, if not let go altogether, include Roderick Meredith, Raymond McNair, Bob Fahey, Dibar Apartian, and Herman Hoeh. Virtually every area of the church and college would see a major shakeup. Naturally, those in charge have a lot to lose and little to gain if Ted returns. ("GTA Rebuffed," *Ambassador Report* 16; see also "GTA Strikes Out," *Ambassador Report* 17)

The first two of these names were to be significant in the schisms after Armstrong's death.

4.5   FURTHER PROBLEMS

The ejection of Garner Ted was not the end of the church's problems that decade. In 1979 the state of California put the church into receivership after allegations of financial impropriety based, according to Armstrong, on "false charges...by malcontent former members." With characteristic overstatement Armstrong referred to this in his co-worker letter of January 18, 1979, as "this most monstrous and outrageous travesty of justice ever heard of by any state government!" (quoted in H. W. Armstrong 1987: 601, 603).

The allegations came from members who, in their lights, were loyal to the church and trying to protect Armstrong from some of his chief advisers, especially his attorney, Stanley Rader, who (although at least initially a nonbeliever) had huge influence in the church, and was eventually ordained a minister, and even an evangelist—this last being the final trigger for the resignation of senior minister Fred Coulter, founder of what became the Christian Biblical Church of God (Coulter 1979; Coulter 2003). In a decade full of bitterness and backstabbing, Rader was probably the man most hated by others in the church organization: "He was spoken against everywhere. Smoke had boiled around Stan for years, great billowing clouds of it. I didn't know a single minister who spoke well of him in private" (D. Robinson 1980: 146–47). He and Garner Ted were open opponents; at the time of GTA's "ouster," Rader was HWA's closest adviser. Two years later Rader too was gone, resigning from his position as general counsel and treasurer in 1981 with a $250,000 net bonus (H. W. Armstrong 1981c). He died in 2002, aged seventy-one.

Despite their rivalry for top positions, Roderick Meredith, later to be the founder of Global and then of Living Church of God, agrees with GTA that Armstrong was often badly advised during this period (see 4.4).

He did not know fully what was going on.... He had been misguided and misinformed. When Mrs. Armstrong was alive, she would spot the phonies around him and the bad guys. Once he lost Mrs. Armstrong [in April 1967, a few months before their Golden Wedding Anniversary], he tended to have people, and I won't name their names, take advantage of him. As he got older, he couldn't see well or hear well, and those things happened and men took advantage of the situation. (Barnett and Pomicter 1995)

John Jewell, in an interview when he was the CEO of United Church of God in the United Kingdom (see 6.2.3), provides another perspective on this. If HWA had a weakness, Jewell says, particularly in a church where there was a lot of politicking by strong personalities, it was in "his evaluation and selection of people. He always thought the best of people, and gave them the benefit of the doubt" (John Jewell, pers. comm.).

Meanwhile, Armstrong's marriage to Ramona had fallen apart. One source cites "Ramona's unbelief and unwillingness to submit to her husband's leadership" (Nichols and Mather 1998: 37), something of a contrast with how Armstrong had initially described her to the church, "a woman truly led by God's Holy Spirit," and had described their relationship, which had "grown into true love and like-minded rapport" (co-worker letter, April 18, 1977, quoted in H. W. Armstrong 1987: 585). One report, however, says that when Armstrong was confronted with the allegations of his incest by senior members, he had pleaded that Ramona not be told—but she had already seen a copy of Robinson's book, and was in the next room, listening to the whole thing ("HWA Confesses to Incest!" *Ambassador Report* 27).

Armstrong filed for divorce in 1982. He was finally granted it in 1984, after a long and acrimonious court battle, which allegedly cost the church somewhere between $1 and $5 million, and included (among much else) discussion of Armstrong's senility ("Court Documents Reveal: Herbert Armstrong Decrepit!" *Ambassador Report* 23).

The Worldwide Church of God recovered from its rough times in the 1970s, and Armstrong continued to lead it and to preach his uncompromising message of God's impending judgment of the corrupt world, and his gospel of the forthcoming Kingdom of God, until his death in January 1986.

4.6 CONCLUSION

In this chapter we have seen some of the tensions and problems of the Worldwide Church of God during the 1970s, particularly on doctrinal issues. We have seen how Herbert W. Armstrong dealt with liberals in the church, including his own son; debate and dissent, even in a constructive spirit of love, were not allowed. Ministers, including some at a senior level, were disfellowshipped; they left to found a number of offshoots, some of which are still in existence today.

We have seen too how the doctrinal changes which Armstrong did allow also caused friction, in this case because God's revelation to Armstrong was overturned by a human committee. In the founding of Raymond C. Cole's Church of God, the Eternal, we see a clear example of belief in Armstrong as God's chosen apostle for the End Times.

In the offshoots today, many love and revere Armstrong's memory, still referring to him as the apostle, and some as the Elijah; others, while to a greater or lesser extent still following his teachings, accuse him of arrogance, an overbearing nature, manipulation, deception, and authoritarianism. These different attitudes will become apparent in the next two chapters, which examine what happened after Armstrong's death, when his successor changed many of the core doctrines of the church and many ministers followed the example of their 1970s predecessors and left the church, taking their members with them, and in chapter 7, which examines Armstrong's authority. We shall see how Armstrong is perceived within the different offshoots which sprang up in response to the changes in Worldwide after his death.

CHAPTER 5
Revolution and Schism

INTRODUCTION

The Worldwide Church of God today has abandoned all of Herbert W. Armstrong's distinctive teachings, those doctrines which were the mainstay and hallmark of his Church and which, by his own account, he had begun to discover, through his own intensive study, back in 1926 (see 3.2.1). These teachings were set out in the dozens of free books and booklets which readers of *Plain Truth* were encouraged to request.

This chapter describes briefly how under Armstrong's successor these fundamental books and booklets were withdrawn as the new leaders of the church began to examine their beliefs. New booklets were written setting out doctrines very different from those Armstrong had taught for decades. As the process of doctrinal change continued, ministers had to struggle with their understanding of new beliefs which overturned those they had previously taught their congregations. Ministers who questioned the new doctrines were disciplined.

Faced with the conflicting demands of two sources of authority, the leadership of God's church and the teachings God had revealed to Herbert W. Armstrong, ministers had to choose. In less than ten years after Armstrong's death hundreds of ministers left Worldwide to found new churches holding to the old teachings, leaving behind them a shell of their former religion.

5.1   A DOCTRINAL REVOLUTION

5.1.1   Joseph W. Tkach, Armstrong's Successor

Herbert W. Armstrong died on January 16th, 1986, aged ninety-three and a half. When a prophet, founder, or leader of a movement dies, there are frequently problems and complications; some of these are examined in the context of a typological model in chapter 8, while the authority issues of succession are explored in chapter 7. But first we shall look at the story, the events of the succession in Worldwide.

In 1981 Armstrong had set up a committee of nine senior ministers, the Advisory Council of Elders (ACE), to choose his successor after his death. According to Stephen Flurry of Philadelphia, this was largely to ensure that his son Garner Ted could not gain control of the church (S. Flurry 2006: 34), but according to Aaron Dean, HWA's assistant in his final years, it was to keep out Stanley R. Rader, his hugely powerful attorney,

> so if he died those around him on his death bed couldn't say his last wish was for SRR [Stanley R. Rader] to be in charge. He was afraid of this. He actually let SRR think he was winning the battle while he had set up ACE in motel rooms away from his home when Mel Olinger would take him for his "afternoon drive." In printing this [information] it totally closed the door on SRR who never returned. (Dean 2009)

In the months before he died Armstrong changed his mind. Flurry and Dean agree on the reason: "Later he felt that certain men on ACE would try to take over, and might succeed by lobbying others on ACE, so he felt he had to name a successor" (Dean 2009). Flurry names the person Armstrong did *not* want to succeed him: Roderick Meredith. "'He just might succeed in getting control,' Mr. Armstrong told [Dean], 'and he should never, ever be over the church'" (S. Flurry 2006: 35; see 7.3.1).

According to Dean, Armstrong considered a number of people:

> So, he'd pick someone. For about a month. And then they'd give a sermon or do something, and he'd look at them and say, Naw, he can't be it! And, he'd pick somebody else. Then he'd look at them and they'd give a sermon or something, and he'd sit there and...(Dean 1996)

On January 7, 1986, just nine days before his death, he named his successor as pastor general: Joseph W. Tkach ("pronounced Ti kotch" [Trechak 1989: 1]). Aaron Dean comments:

> Most of you don't know that Mr. Armstrong had a stroke about two months before he actually died. Almost died that week. Thought he was going to. Had he died that week, someone else would be in charge! Not Mr. Tkach! But he got well. Well in the sense of getting better, not "well." And so, another couple of months went by, and Mr. Tkach happened to be the one that was appointed at that time, when he did die. (Dean 1996)

In the Worldwide Church of God it had always been assumed that as God's End Time apostle Armstrong would be here to see Christ's return, and to receive his reward for his work, though Armstrong never explicitly taught this. Indeed, in a co-worker letter dated March 19, 1981, he wrote, "I have NEVER SAID I expect to live until Christ comes" (Pack 1999: 75). But the general perception was that he would. His appointed successor Joseph W. Tkach's letter to co-workers (January 16, 1986) announcing Armstrong's death dealt with this first problem:

> Perhaps God saw fit, as He describes in Isaiah 57:1, to spare Mr Armstrong, at his advanced age, from the persecutions and trials prophesied to come as we finish the work of God for this age. (H. W. Armstrong 1987: 647–48)

At this stage Tkach was still expecting the imminent return of Christ following the turmoil of the Last Days, as Armstrong had taught for half a century.

Six months after Armstrong's death the church's internal magazine, *Worldwide News*, published a list of "18 Restored Truths" under the title "God Restored These 18 Truths: How Thankful Are You for Them?" The introduction read:

> The Editorial Services staff has compiled here, for the first time in any of the Church's publications, 18 essential, basic truths that God restored to His Church through our late Pastor General Herbert W. Armstrong.
>
> As you prepare spiritually for the coming Feast of Tabernacles, please spend time with this important article, reviewing each of the 18 truths and thanking God for restoring them to His Church.
> —*Pastor General*
> *Joseph W. Tkach* (Worldwide News 1986)

The "18 Restored Truths" were effectively a summary of the distinctive teachings of the Worldwide Church of God under Armstrong. At the end of the article was the comment: "Where would we be without these truths? Without them—without Herbert W. Armstrong's legacy of these 18 restored truths—there isn't much left." There is the most remarkable irony in this statement, as the church was about to start dropping these truths one by one.

5.1.2 Literature Withdrawal and Reassessment

A new leader brings the opportunity for change (see chapter 8). There was no doubt that many in the Worldwide Church of God had seen things over the years which they felt needed attention (see chapter 4). Some of the doctrines were perhaps a little askew,[1] some of the literature was perhaps a little overwritten,[2] and some of the members were unhappy about the authoritarianism (see 7.3.2). Within a year of Armstrong's death a full literature review and a top-level doctrinal review had been initiated by Tkach, though these were not announced to the members; books and

---

1. Garner Ted Armstrong's Systematic Theology Project of 1972–74 (see 4.4) had been a conscious attempt to revise the church's doctrines.
2. Again, GTA's influence on Church literature in the 1970s had meant fewer stylistic excesses.

booklets simply became unavailable. When asked, the leadership said that they were being checked or revised, so that "minor errors" could be corrected.

Joseph Tkach Jr., J. Michael Feazell, and Greg Albrecht, the three most senior members of the reformed Worldwide below the new pastor general, explain this process:

> Even before HWA's death, his books and articles were edited before they were reprinted. In some cases he made the edits himself, and in other cases he approved edits made by others. Often the edits were stylistic. Sometimes they were doctrinal. When articles and books were reprinted, HWA did not knowingly perpetuate errors. When he believed his previous understanding to be in error, he edited the text, just as any author would when it came time to reprint.
>
> After HWA died, this process continued at a faster pace. Since HWA was a full-time employee of the church and writing was part of his job, and since the church paid for all of his publication costs, his writings fall into the legal category of "work done for hire." The copyright was held by the church, not by HWA, and therefore the church could continue to edit his works as we saw the need.
>
> After Herbert W. Armstrong died and his booklets came up for reprinting, they were reviewed to see if edits were necessary. If we saw statements that were erroneous or unlikely, we would delete them. This was the only sensible course of action. There is no point in publishing things we know to be in error. But we would edit only according to what we understood, and we did not understand at first the magnitude of HWA's errors. Initially we saw a great deal of truth in HWA's booklets and felt that they *should* be reprinted as a service to our readers, if we just took out the errors. We certainly had no thought of giving the misimpression that Herbert Armstrong's teachings were all without error.
>
> As time went on and we learned more, and as our inventory of booklets was depleted and we needed to reprint, we realized that it was better to simply cancel the reprinting of his booklets. (Nichols and Mather 1998: 123–24)

As with all accounts quoted in this study, this needs to be taken with some caution; in this case it is the version of history as written by the victors (see 3.1 and appendix 3.3). The reclassifying of "God's Apostle" as "a full-time employee of the church" whose teachings were "work done for hire" displays a monumental shift in attitude, if not a certain triumphalism, putting Herbert W. Armstrong firmly in his place. Note also that this account contradicts the assertion of the then British and European head of Worldwide, John Halford, that Armstrong never rewrote anything (see 3.1). (The copyright issue mentioned in paragraph 2 of this quotation was to have major repercussions, as will be seen in 6.2.1.)

The background to the words "As time went on and we learned more" is a contentious matter. In spring 1990 Joseph W. Tkach's son, then known familiarly as Joe Jr., had attended graduate school at a nondenominational Christian university, Azusa Pacific University, along with a WCG friend, Michael Feazell, and Feazell's assistant, C. W. Davis (Tkach 1997: 56–58; Feazell 2003: 28). With one or two others they started to question the teachings of their own church—initially, it seems, in response to a Roman Catholic priest challenging an anti-Trinitarian letter in *Plain Truth*. Joseph W. Tkach encouraged a few very senior leaders in Worldwide to discuss the church's core doctrines, though for some considerable time this was not known outside the church's headquarters in Pasadena, even by other senior ministers.

At what point were the Tkachs converted to Evangelical Christianity? When did they accept the concept of being "born again," as Evangelicals understand it? When did they become full-blown Trinitarians? Opinions differ on the exact sequence of events, and of cause and effect, over the next few years. Some ex-members have suggested to me off the record that Joe Jr. and Michael Feazell were converted, then set to work to convince Tkach Sr., and then launched their transformation of the church, quite deliberately in small steps that they could slide through without too many people noticing. Indeed, some former members believe that Joe Jr. had planned the whole thing from the start: the conversion (or, as they see it, subversion) of Worldwide (S. Flurry 2006: 57–65; Edwards 1997: 5).

Joe Jr. denies this in his own account of the transitional years, arguing that they were led, step by step, to the truth; after they had made one change—doubting the truth of British Israelism—all the others inevitably followed. The title of one of his chapters sums this up: "The Central Plank Cracks." This is why British Israelism was covered in such depth in 2.1.4 and 2.2.3.

> Our acceptance of Anglo-Israelism affected practically everything we did. It helped shape what we preached, to whom we preached, how we spent our money, where we spent our time, how we related to various ethnic groups....
>
> In June 1988 my father withdrew *The United States and Britain in Prophecy* from circulation. Soon thereafter all mention of Anglo-Israelism disappeared from the church's publications. We stopped sending out *The Book of Revelation Unveiled at Last*. We stopped sending out *Who Is the Beast*, which essentially identifies Sunday-keeping (as opposed to Sabbath-keeping) as the mark of the beast. (Tkach 1997: 130, 131)

And so, in this account, End Time prophecy and Sabbatarianism—two other central planks of Worldwide—also cracked.

Other accounts put the issue of the Trinity (as mentioned above) as the first domino to start to wobble, while others make the first actual change in doctrine Tkach's reversal of Armstrong's teaching on healing, which forbade medical treatment. According to one internal source this was "in the Spring of 1987" (G. Flurry 1994: 19); according to an external one it was "in the Spring of 1988" (Rube 1999).

One by one over the next few years, Joseph Tkach, with the support of his son and a small handful of other people at the center of things in Pasadena, gradually introduced doctrinal changes to the church. Initially these were accepted by most members, because of the authority of the leadership (see 7.2). There had been some changes in past years under Armstrong (see 4.2); his authority had guaranteed their acceptance by most, though in the late 1970s the church had lost some members over his reversal of the former strict policy on divorce and remarriage. But now the changes kept coming, until eventually the church was taking a diametrically opposed stance on many of its former core beliefs.

> Seemingly, Mr. Tkach enjoyed a four- or five-year honeymoon period with most ministers and other members. But, by the early 1990s, there were increasing hints of change, and many ministers and a small percentage of other WCG members began asking: "I wonder if there is a doctrinal agenda?"
>
> As time passed, the question became: *"I wonder what the agenda is?"*
>
> Then the question was refined to: *"I wonder **whose** agenda it is?"*
>
> Growing numbers of ministers and lay members began to conclude that there was indeed a clear agenda to reform the WCG into a mainstream Protestant organization or to "lead a cult to Christ," as some have characterized the goal of top WCG leaders. (Overton, Robinson, and Smith 1995)

Very slowly and tentatively, the church was beginning the process of "denominationalization": "the loosening rigor; the loss of the sense of dissent and protest; the reduction of distance from other Christians; and the muting of claims that the sect's distinctive teachings are necessary for salvation" (B. Wilson 1990: 109). For example, on British Israelism, the core of Armstrong's entire prophetic teaching, the church eventually announced:

> After having carefully researched the tenets and history of its belief that the United States and Britain are the descendants of the ancient Israelite tribes of Manasseh and Ephraim, the Worldwide Church of God no longer teaches this doctrine. While it may be an interesting theory, there is simply a lack of credible evidence, either in the biblical account or the historical record, to support a conclusion regarding the modern identity of the lost 10 tribes of Israel. We recognize that there were hermeneutical and historical inaccuracies in the Church's past understanding of this issue. (WCG: Israel, n.d.)

Thus "Ephraim = Britain, Manasseh = USA," the central tenet of Armstrong's prophetic teaching for several decades, was discarded completely by the church he had founded.

WCG leaders now also admitted what critics of the old WCG had been pointing out for decades: that Armstrong's *The United States and Britain in Prophecy* (in all its versions) was at least in part a plagiarization of the 1917 A. A. Beauchamp edition of *Judah's Sceptre and Joseph's Birthright* by J. H. Allen, first written in 1902 (Hopkins 1974: 67 and see 2.2.3).

For decades Armstrong had preached that Christ would return very soon. Like the Jehovah's Witnesses and other millenarian movements, he pointed to the "signs of the times": drastic changes in the weather, drought, wars, famines, pestilences.

His booklet *1975 in Prophecy* did not say definitively that Christ would return by that year, but it strongly implied that he would—with consequences for the church when he did not (see 4.1).

Looking back through its own history, the new WCG later said:

> In the 1970s, growth continued, but at a slower pace, as the Church learned important lessons about avoiding predictive prophecies. Christ did not return as expected, but he did lead the Church to a deeper understanding of the Bible. (WCG 1995b: 16–18)

On Armstrong's "startling coincidences" between the beginnings of the early church's ministry and his own (see 3.2.2), a WCG spokesman told me in 1995, "Regarding 19-year time cycles, we no longer have any formal statements or beliefs on this particular topic."[3]

Another great passion of both Armstrongs, father and son, had been attacking the theory of evolution. They and their associates wrote dozens of highly illustrated articles, some of them reprinted as full-color A4 booklets, claiming to prove conclusively that evolution was a false doctrine. Titles included *Some FISHY STORIES About an Unproved Theory*, *The Amazing Archer Fish Disproves Evolution!*, *A Theory for the Birds*, and *A WHALE of a TALE, or The Dilemma of Dolphins and Duckbills!* But in 1994 a church booklet said:

> We have firm confidence in the inspired declaration of Genesis 1:1, "In the beginning God created the heavens and the earth." We do not deny, however, evidence from science that indicates a long history of life on this planet. We do know that only God can create life, and that the Creator has not revealed exactly how he has done this. Therefore we do not presume to speak for him on this subject. (WCG 1994: 6)

One of the main doctrinal differences separating the Worldwide Church of God from conventional Christianity was its rejection of the Trinity, which it taught (quite correctly) was a doctrine developed in the first few centuries of Christianity, and unknown to the apostles. The Trinity limited God to three persons instead of the "God family" which Armstrong taught (see 2.2.1). In his last book Armstrong said of the Trinity, "By that doctrine, along with others, Satan has DECEIVED all traditional Christianity" (H. W. Armstrong 1985a: 42). The WCG had always taught that Jesus is God, but the Holy Spirit is simply the power of God, an It rather than a He.

But by 1994 the church taught, "The triune nature of God is an essential part of Worldwide Church of God doctrine" (WCG 1994: 4), and by 1995 the Holy Spirit was "the third Person of the Godhead" (WCG 1995b: 2). A member of one offshoot

---

3. Shortly afterward this spokesman left the Worldwide Church of God and joined one of the major offshoots.

told me: "They went from 'hypostasis' to 'Person,' a process which took the Early Church a couple of hundred years, in just six months."[4]

Although the WCG had always denied that it taught salvation by works, critics pointed to statements like:

> We are not justified BY THE LAW—we are justified by the blood of Jesus Christ! But this justification will be given only on Condition that we REPENT of our transgressions of God's Law—and so it is, after all, only the DOERS of the Law that shall be JUSTIFIED. (H. W. Armstrong 1952b: 10)

Under the Tkachs the church changed to a more standard Christian theology, saying that it "teaches that salvation is the gift of God, by his grace, through faith in Jesus Christ, not earned by personal merit or good works" (WCG 1994: 10)

Larry Salyer, who was appointed to Joseph Tkach's former job of director of church administration in 1996, spoke of the irony of Armstrong's choice of Tkach:

> Mr. Armstrong personally told me one time why he would probably appoint Mr. Tkach, and this was in the summer of 1985, not too long before he died. He said, Mr. Tkach is a street fighter. Mr. Tkach will not let somebody come in and take over the Church. He specifically had in mind, believe it or not, Mr. Garner Ted Armstrong! And he said, I am fearful of what would happen if, after my death, GTA came back and got control over the Church! I'm fearful of the Church becoming very liberal, and unidentifiable as the Church of God.
>
> Now, I find that terribly ironic today, as Garner Ted Armstrong, who died just a couple of months ago, persisted in teaching most of the Truth, a great deal of the Truth, until the day of his death. But, there is no way his organization or congregation were in any sense, even a small percentage removed from the Truth as the Worldwide Church of God became. (Salyer 2003)

5.1.3   The Fallout

While mainstream Christians expressed an initially guarded delight that the Worldwide Church of God was coming closer to orthodox Christian doctrine, reaction within the church was more mixed. Some ministers resigned, and others were fired for refusing to teach the new doctrines. Some left one at a time; others in groups, the main ones leaving in 1989, 1992–93, and 1995 to form the Philadelphia, Global, and United Churches of God, respectively, as we shall examine in more detail below (6.2). Many, as they left, took their congregations with them.

---

4. "Hypostasis" has a number of closely related meanings, but in this context it meant "substantive reality" rather than "Person"—a subtle but significant distinction in the development of Trinitarian doctrine.

But some welcomed the changes in beliefs. Those who stayed had to learn a new terminology, and to teach the need to be "born again" in the Evangelical sense.

One of the characteristics of the Worldwide Church of God was its legalism, its insistence on obeying Old Testament Law; its members were not allowed to eat pork or shellfish; they had to observe the seven Jewish Festivals each year; they had to tithe a tenth of their gross income to the church; and they had to worship on the Sabbath, not on Sunday. Such were the marks of the true believer; those so-called Christians who talked about being "born again" and neglected God's clear commands were, Armstrong said, deceived by Satan: "Satan has deceived this world's churches into the belief that God's law was done away" (H. W. Armstrong 1985a: 225).

Now all these practices suddenly became unnecessary. Tithing, for example, "was commanded under the old covenant, but is a voluntary expression of worship and stewardship under the new covenant." As for the Sabbath, the absolutely essential mark of the true believer, by 1995 members were told:

> Though physical Sabbath keeping is not required for Christians, it is the tradition and practice of the Worldwide Church of God to hold its weekly worship service on the seventh-day Sabbath (Saturday). (WCG 1995b: 8–9)

To be told that the Law of God which they had taught for so many years was now only "voluntary" or a "tradition" was too much for many Worldwide ministers. Many of those who had struggled to accept, and even to teach others to accept the new teachings, and who had echoed the headquarters leadership's condemnation of those who had left, now walked out themselves.

In the words of Danny L. Jorgensen: "There is considerable agreement that dramatic sociocultural change is a necessary condition, if not a sufficient cause, of religious schism" (Jorgensen 1993: 37). It was inevitable that a sociocultural change as dramatic as the complete overturning of the social construction of reality of long-time ministers and members of the Worldwide Church of God would result in schism.

The leaders of the first two groups left in 1989 and 1992–93 because they refused to accept the doctrinal changes up to those dates. For the third and largest group to leave, the decisive moment came on Christmas Eve 1994, when Joseph W. Tkach preached a three-hour sermon. He had actually first preached this sermon on December 17 in Atlanta, but the December 24 version was in front of church members and, significantly, cameras, at the newly accredited Ambassador University in Big Sandy, Texas, the church's most important center after its headquarters in Pasadena, California. It is known as the Christmas Eve sermon.

Tkach's son later wrote of his father's sermon:

> In three hours he covered a wide assortment of topics. In some of his most important remarks he:

- affirmed that the church is no longer bound to the Old Covenant but is in fact a New Covenant organism;
- insisted that salvation is by grace through faith and is not gained in the least through law keeping;
- declared that members who needed to work on Saturday to care for their families were not committing sin;
- proclaimed that tithing is not a requirement for salvation but is a voluntary action performed in service and love to God. (Tkach 1997: 25)

The old Worldwide, with all its distinctive doctrines, was now officially dead, replaced by the new Worldwide, almost indistinguishable from standard Evangelical Christianity.

Many thousands left the church in the following months, forming the United Church of God. As the number of members remaining in Worldwide plummeted so, as a direct consequence, did the church's income. Many of those who stayed, now that they were told that tithing was voluntary, simply stopped tithing. With high expenditure commitments on its magazines and radio and TV programs, the church found itself having to lose hundreds of employees and to sell buildings to make ends meet. Joseph W. Tkach's letters to co-workers in early 1995 included increasingly frantic appeals for financial support. In 1995 the Worldwide Church of God withdrew funding for its proudest asset, Ambassador University (formerly Ambassador College), and in 1997 the university was forced to close. Joe Jr. describes the situation:

The Worldwide Church of God reached its peak attendance in 1988—two years after Mr. Armstrong's death—with 126,800 members and 150,000 in attendance. Those figures stayed relatively stable until 1992, when a slight dip was noted. By 1994 church attendance had slipped to 109,600...and then came the Christmas Eve sermon. In the year following that milestone message, attendance plummeted to 66,400 members and is now even less.[5]

Our membership losses have resulted in a corresponding drop in income. Receipts worldwide in 1990 amounted to more than $211 million. By 1994, the year immediately preceding "The Sermon," income stood at about $164.6 million. The following year income dropped to $103.4 million. In this past year our receipts totaled about $68.5 million. We expect a national income of $38 million in 1997.

With dramatically fewer members and greatly reduced income, expenses had to be cut as well. In 1986, our total expenses came to more than $131 million. By 1996 our total budgeted expenses fell to about $52.5 million. We were forced to lay off most of our headquarters staff, cut circulation of the magazine, sharply reduce subsidies to Ambassador University, end our acclaimed performing arts series at Ambassador Auditorium, and sell off many of our assets. In addition, we put up for sale our fifty-one-acre

5. These membership figures will be discussed in 5.2.

Pasadena world headquarters, and financial realities dictated that we do the same with our Ambassador University campus in Big Sandy, Texas. (Tkach 1997: 71–72)

In a remarkably short time almost the entire edifice of the Worldwide Church of God crumbled. An article about this in *New Times Los Angeles* was entitled "Honey, I Shrunk the Church" (Russell 1997).

Joseph W. Tkach died of cancer in September 1995, aged sixty-eight, and his son Joe Jr. (now known as Joseph Tkach) succeeded him as pastor general—an indication of how much of a power base had been created by a relatively young man (not yet forty-four at this point) who had been employed outside the church from 1976 to 1986 in youth work, social work, and with the chip manufacturer Intel, and who had never been pastor of a congregation. But according to a leading member of one offshoot church, speaking off the record, Joe Jr. had effectively been running WCG for some years, under the figurehead of his sick father—a close parallel to the Armstrong father and son in the 1960s and early 1970s. But where Garner Ted Armstrong had been ousted from the church by his father, largely for attempting to liberalize doctrines, Joe Jr. had successfully pushed through the doctrinal changes in the church and, on his father's death, gained his reward.

At his father's funeral Joe Jr. was photographed being embraced by Hank Hanegraaff, president of the Evangelical cult-watching organization the Christian Research Institute.[6] The photograph is in his own book, and has been widely reprinted in articles in Evangelical magazines, a powerful symbol of how much Worldwide had changed.

The offshoot churches point out an interesting progression over four or five years in the justification given by WCG for the changes they were making. In summary:

- Changes? What changes?
- We haven't changed any doctrines; we're simply clarifying the language in which we describe them.
- Mr. Armstrong, on his deathbed, asked Mr. Tkach to look into precisely this area/to correct the errors in this book. We're doing exactly what he wanted us to do.
- Although well-intentioned, Mr. Armstrong sometimes got a little carried away in his enthusiasm.
- Mr. Armstrong was wrong.[7]

One of the more conservative offshoots, the Restored Church of God, lists forty-three different ways in which "changes were described as 'non-changes.'" Many of

---

6. Founded by Walter R. Martin, author of the influential Evangelical cults study *The Kingdom of the Cults* (1965).

7. Paraphrased from conversations with leading members of two of the offshoots, and from G. Flurry 1994.

them fall broadly into the above five categories; it is worth quoting several of the others:

> 13. They say nothing and just change it.
>
> 14. They cloak it so deep in the language of scholarship that no one recognizes a change was made.
>
> 15. This change will not lead to that change.
>
> 16. The belief is still true poetically, or symbolically, or metaphorically, or analogically, or parabolically, or even theologically, just not literally.
>
> 24. Anyone who cannot accept the changes isn't satisfied with the leadership God has provided for His Church.
>
> 41. Anyone who resists these changes is only interested in glorifying the memory of a man (Pack 2008: 10–11).

Several former members of WCG have told me that when the Tkachs and their supporters changed their beliefs so radically from the beliefs of the church they belonged to, they should have left that church and gone off to join an Evangelical Protestant denomination. One made the analogy that if the archbishop of Canterbury converted to Catholicism, one would expect him to leave the Church of England, rather than to try to take the entire church with him into the Roman Catholic Church.

One former minister, who says, "I simply will not join another church again," wrote to the Worldwide leadership about being removed after serving the church in "five states, 14 congregations and 26 years":

> Frankly, those of you who "administer" the church should have left long ago and asked Benny Hinn, TBN and the Harvest Crock Church to take you in as spiritual refugees.
>
> I realize you could not continue to grant yourselves lifetime income and security by doing this, but it is what *you* should have done. You should have left alone the church whose perspective you scorned.
>
> If something is wrong for *you*, then leave it. Don't destroy it and drive many to despair, skepticism and, in some few cases, literal suicide.
>
> Instead you made everyone else leave. Now, that's power: stupid, self-serving and egocentric power. (Diehl 2008: 3, 6)

This "power" will be examined at 7.2.

The Tkachs and their supporters were, at least initially, very much the minority. It was they who had changed their beliefs. The majority of ministers and members still held to the teachings of Herbert W. Armstrong. The Tkachs rejected his teachings but, because of their position, were able effectively to hijack his church—an emotive term, perhaps, but one which several former members have used to me; that was how it felt to those who continued to hold to the old beliefs. If the Tkachs had left the church which Armstrong founded, they could have left the majority of members to remain true to those teachings within the organization which was founded on those teachings. That would have been, many felt, a more satisfactory and more honest resolution.

It would also have avoided what has been for many members the turmoil of the past few years, with loyalties, friends, and families split apart—and also the many problems over physical, financial and intellectual property rights: buildings, pensions, Armstrong's books and booklets, and his pride and joy, Ambassador University.

But from the viewpoint of the Tkachs, they had found the Truth, and had seen the error of their (and their church's) ways, and had an absolute duty to bring their church out of darkness into light. In 1997, Joseph Tkach Jr. published his own account of the changes in his church's beliefs. The front-cover splash reads: "The Worldwide Church of God rejects the teachings of founder Herbert W. Armstrong and embraces historic Christianity. This is the inside story." An appendix lists the "18 Truths Restored by Herbert W. Armstrong" in a chart, with a brief "Kernel of Truth" against each one and, in a third column, "Armstrong's Mistake." Every one of Armstrong's "18 Restored Truths" is dismissed (Tkach 1997: 212–13).

Just a decade earlier Joseph Tkach Jr.'s father had written, "Where would we be without these truths? Without them—without Herbert W. Armstrong's legacy of these 18 restored truths—there isn't much left" (Worldwide News 1986; see also 5.1.1).

That includes, for the victors, the reputation of Armstrong himself. At the 1998 Annual Conference of Evangelical Ministries to New Religions, one of the new Worldwide's most senior leaders, Greg Albrecht, said:

> I believe we have judged his teachings. I believe I have judged his teachings. Virtually all of his teachings are in error. I believe them to have been wrong. . . .
> He was a false prophet. He was a heretic. (Albrecht 1998)

On whether Armstrong taught his teachings in ignorance or in "willful deception," Albrecht said "I can't make that call." But he speaks plainly on his feelings about Armstrong:

> When you try to get a grip on Amstrongism it's kind of like trying to get a hold of a greasy pig in a barnyard. You're going everywhere, because there's nothing that always leads you back logically to one basis of reasoning. (Albrecht 1998)

And so not just the teachings but the founder of the Worldwide Church of God were dismissed with contempt by the church's new leaders.

5.2 MEMBERSHIP OF WORLDWIDE CHURCH OF GOD

As the doctrinal changes in Worldwide became more evident, an ever increasing number of ministers and members holding to Armstrong's teachings left to found new churches holding to slightly different versions of the old beliefs.

How many members did Worldwide lose? As with many religions it is difficult to ascertain the exact membership figures, both of Worldwide and of the offshoots (see 6.1.1). Some of the churches quote Feast of Tabernacles attendance figures, but as this is the major spiritual and social event of the year for churches in the Worldwide family, the attendance figures will include all family members there, and possibly their uncommitted friends, occasional church attendees who could be regarded as "peripheral" members, and also (in the case of the offshoots) members of other churches who have come to this Feast of Tabernacles site because it is more convenient than that of their own church. Other measures of membership could include total adult baptized membership, total number of tithe payers, or average total Sabbath service attendance; "members" might also loosely include "co-workers" who give financial support to the church but may not be baptized members. These figures might all be different.

For example, according to figures supplied to me by a Worldwide spokesman on behalf of Joe Jr., the church's peak festival attendance, in 1992, was about 133,000; its peak of baptized adult members, in the same year, was 99,000 (Michael Morrison, pers. comm.). However, Joe Jr. wrote in his account of the changes in Worldwide that the church's peak membership was in 1988, "with 126,800 members and 150,000 in attendance" (Tkach 1997: 71). It is difficult to ascertain which set of figures, if either, is accurate.

Strictly speaking, "membership" could be said to mean those (a) over the age of eighteen who (b) have been baptized in the church, and who (c) are regular attendees at services and also (d) actively choose still to be associated with the church. This last point is particularly important with churches (both Worldwide Church of God and most of the offshoots) which have a strong focus on literature and thus might use their mailing list as a measure of, if not active membership, at least strong interest.

Of the year when there was the greatest outflux of members, to the United Church of God, the Worldwide spokesman said:

> We began 1995 with 95,500 members and ended the year with 84,000 still on the list—
> but the actual membership was probably less. With the loss of many senior pastors and
> many employees, our record-keeping ability was severely compromised. We kept many
> people on our membership list because we didn't know whether they considered them-
> selves members—and some of them didn't know, either. We kept them on the list as
> long as there was any doubt, so we would continue mailing them the articles explaining
> the doctrinal changes. Membership—and attendance—continued to decline into 1999
> and seems to have leveled out. (Michael Morrison, pers. comm.)

By 2000, Worldwide officially estimated its membership as about 67,000 and gave its attendance as 51,000, though it is unclear whether this was Feast attendance or average church service attendance. As the membership figure almost certainly includes both inactive members and people who had not formally resigned from the church, it is a reasonable assumption that "meaningful" membership in 2000 was substantially less than the 67,000 claimed. According to Evangelical writer Ruth Tucker, membership had fallen to 49,000 as early as 1996 (Tucker 1996: 26–32). In 2001 independent COG observer Alan Ruth wrote to me of Worldwide's membership, "Peak was 120,000. Today easily less than 50,000, likely a lot less" (Alan Ruth, pers. comm.). In 2009 he told me:

> Inflated membership numbers are, shall we say, a Church of God tradition. Even today, as has been done for years, the number of members the WCG/GCI says it has is likely overstated.... It may include children and others who are not members, etc. (Alan Ruth, pers. comm.)

Because of the conflicting official figures for peak membership (126,800 in 1988 or 99,000 in 1992) and the variety of estimates, official and unofficial, of membership by 2000, it is not possible to give reliable figures for the fall in membership, but it is fair to say that by the turn of the century Worldwide's membership was probably less than half of what it had been a decade earlier.

5.3   THE WORLDWIDE CHURCH OF GOD TODAY

The Worldwide Church of God is now an Evangelical church, welcomed with open arms by the Christian cult watchers who had formerly condemned it. In the United States it was accepted as a member of the National Association of Evangelicals in May 1997. In the United Kingdom it joined the Evangelical Alliance in July 2000. Both organizations have strict doctrinal requirements; their acceptance of Worldwide demonstrates clearly the massive shift in its beliefs since the death of Herbert W. Armstrong.

Observance of the seven Jewish festivals has been downplayed; Christmas, Easter, and other such "pagan" festivals are now being observed; and, most telling of all, the church told individual congregations that it was up to them whether to worship on Saturday or Sunday. Initially many preferred to stay with Saturday, but after a few years Worldwide actively encouraged individual congregations to switch to Sunday.

Joseph Tkach Jr. openly reveled in the newfound freedom. In his account of the changes in Worldwide he describes a church colleague ordering a pepperoni pizza, and continues:

> I've had lunch or dinner with several others who have ordered similar items. I don't know if they're eating these things just to see how I react or if they really want to enjoy the new experience. One friend, a longtime church member, ordered a plate of mussels. Every insect in the ocean was on his plate. And you know what? It really didn't trouble me at all.
>
> I've tasted shrimp, I've tasted pork, I've tasted just about everything now. (Tkach 1997: 39)

After a lifetime of observing the Old Testament laws on "unclean foods" (Leviticus 11), such a change in attitude is revolutionary.

In personal conversations with several members of Worldwide in the United Kingdom around 2000 (with the obvious caveat that these might not be representative), I gained the strong impression that many were unhappy with the changes—or at least with the speed of the changes. One member said openly that the main reason she was staying with Worldwide, despite the new teachings, was that this was the church that God had called her to several decades before. Another, actually an employee of Worldwide, spoke of "pressure from Pasadena" (Worldwide's headquarters) to follow the new party line.

A more objective corroboration is that of the fifty or so Worldwide congregations in the United Kingdom in 2000, five years after the Christmas Eve sermon, only one met on Sunday; all the rest met on Saturday, as they always had done. Even nine years later the pressure from Pasadena had still not fully succeeded in Britain, according to the new UK director of the church:

> The choice of day for weekly meetings is congregationally driven. There [are] a number in the UK that still meet on Saturdays for various reasons. No, moving to a Sunday meeting is not mandatory.

On the matter of how happy members now were, he said:

> My view is that a degree of peace has been established. Of course there are still some individuals and small groups that have not fully embraced the changes. (James Henderson, pers. comm.)

This was nearly fifteen years after Joseph Tkach's Christmas Eve sermon.

There were some who still believed Armstrong's teachings, who did not accept the new teachings, and yet who remained in Worldwide because they believed that this was the church which God established though his End Time apostle, Herbert W. Armstrong, and that they had no right to leave it, even if its leaders had turned away from the truth (see 7.2).

According to John Jewell, first of United and later of the What Next broadcast, some stayed with Worldwide to fight from within, in a last-ditch attempt to save the church they had spent their lives working for from its apostasy.

Some of these attempted to form a separate group *within* Worldwide, called Worldwide Church of God Restored (WCGR); this was for "members who believed in traditional WCG doctrines as taught by the late Herbert W. Armstrong and who...felt they were not free to leave the WCG because of its status as God's church, even if the WCG had altered vital doctrines" (Overton 1999b: 28). In June 1999, led by minister Mardy Cobb, they agreed to recognize Joe Jr. as pastor general, and he agreed that they could hold meetings and that he would not disfellowship them for their beliefs—but within days he had disfellowshipped Cobb and others on the grounds that they were teaching what they believed (COGR 2011).

Only around thirty-five members left Worldwide in the United States, but according to Cobb, "In the international areas, we were communicating with over 20 countries. Our greatest impact was in mailing messages" (Mardy Cobb, pers. comm.). They changed their name to the Church of God, Restored,[8] and became one of a growing number of small independent churches (McCann 2002: 3, 10). By 2011 they had around 850 Sabbath-attending members in eight congregations worldwide.

This is a particularly clear example of what John Wilson, in his 1971 essay on schism, describes as "the part played by the attitudes taken by the parent church to the proposals and activities of dissidents" (J. Wilson 1971: 17); it was the actions of Joseph Tkach Jr. that created this schismatic group, which had not wanted to leave Worldwide.

Another group which has somehow managed to stay within Worldwide despite "holding fast to the faith once delivered through Herbert W. Armstrong" is known as Climb the Wall (see 7.2). Its members keep the Sabbath and all of Armstrong's teachings; their website hosts many of his books, articles, and recordings of his sermons (http://www.climbthewall.com/).

Undoubtedly the best known of the "old guard" who stayed in Worldwide was Herman L. Hoeh, one of Armstrong's first four students at Ambassador College in 1947, one of the first two graduates of the college in 1951, and the first person Armstrong ordained a minister, also in 1951. He was widely respected in Worldwide as one of the church's leading doctrinal experts; apparently he was one of the few people who Armstrong seriously considered for his successor, in the last months of his life (Havir 1999: 1, 10, 13). Either Hoeh had turned his back on everything he had studied, believed, and taught for over forty years, or he felt he could not leave the church that God had called him to—or perhaps he stayed because, as Jewell suggested to me, he felt "a duty to defend the people." Speaking of the offshoot churches, Hoeh told an acquaintance in United "that he would not be joining any of them—because the spirit of competition and jealousy was just too rampant among them and he did not wish to be part of that" (White 2005). Hoeh died in November 2004, aged seventy-five, without openly divulging his reasons for staying in Worldwide.

But there were certainly some who stayed in Worldwide because they approved of the changes:

> I am a twenty year member of the WCG and pleased with the change and believe it is upheld by the Bible. It is such a relief to be out from under the dictatorship of Mr. Armstrong's theories, which were very wrong and hard on people. While the people lived like rats trying to live up to his greed, the ministers lived like kings. Never again will

---

8. Not to be confused with David Pack's Restored Church of God (RCG).

any man get me brainwashed like that. I am very thankful to be free of his teachings. (Milks and Milks 1996: 14)

The "dictatorship of Mr. Armstrong's theories" will be explored in Chapter 7, "Authority in the Churches of God."

5.4 CONCLUSION

In this chapter we have seen how a heterodox Christian sect became an orthodox Christian sect as a consequence of two or three senior members beginning to question its most fundamental beliefs. From their viewpoint Worldwide had been "transformed by truth"—the title of Joe Jr.'s account of the revolution (Tkach 1997). Christian cult watchers, Evangelical associations, and the mainstream Christian press welcomed "the liberation of the Worldwide Church of God"—the title of a book by another of the architects of change (Feazell 2003).

But in changing their church the Tkachs not only destroyed much of its physical structure—its headquarters, its college, its magazine, its membership—but also deconstructed the social construction of reality which Armstrong, ministers, and members had spent their lives maintaining. Hundreds of ministers and over forty thousand members (see 6.1.1) elected to stick to their original beliefs, or to conserve their religious capital (Stark and Finke 2000: 121), and made the painful decision to leave the church they now saw as apostate, founding and joining new churches to uphold the old beliefs.

It is to their story that we now turn.

CHAPTER 6
Continuing Schism in the Offshoots

INTRODUCTION

The Worldwide Church of God had been denominationalized, becoming more-or-less a straightforward Evangelical church (see chapter 5). Bryan R. Wilson suggests that "in sects schism is often associated with denominational tendencies, which some members resist more than others" (B. Wilson 1961: 338); in the case of Worldwide this is something of an understatement. Many ministers resisted; many resigned, and their congregations followed them.

Roger Finke and Christopher P. Scheitle argue that each religion has its niche, appealing to a particular set of believers; both benefits and problems may ensue if a religion engages in niche shifting or niche stretching, i.e., either moving its niche in one direction or another or expanding it. "But if niche expansion offers the potential for growth," they say, "it also offers the threat of schism" (Finke and Scheitle 2009: 16).

After Armstrong's death Worldwide shifted its niche dramatically; the ensuing schisms were equally dramatic.

As we saw in chapter 4, there had been schisms in the Worldwide Church of God in the 1970s—for example, Raymond C. Cole left to found Church of God, the Eternal, because he believed that Worldwide was straying from the truth given to it by God (4.2.1 and 4.2.2)—but these were nothing on the scale of what happened in the years after Herbert W. Armstrong died.

The death of the founder of a religion changes everything, as we shall explore in some detail in chapter 8. To take an example from another religion, there were disputes and factions in the Mormon religion while its founder, Joseph Smith, was still alive. But as one writer says: "The death of the Prophet totally changed the picture for Mormonism's dissenting churches. Henceforth individual churches could and did claim to be not only the one true church but the legitimate inheritor of the Prophet's mantle" (Morgan 1953: 258).

In this chapter we shall see several such claimants for Armstrong's mantle.

The three major secessions from Worldwide, in 1989, 1992–93, and 1995, resulted in the formation of the Philadelphia, Global, and United Churches of God, respectively. All three churches have since had numerous schisms, as have their off-shoots.[1] Along with other churches, such as those which had left Worldwide in the 1970s (see 4.2), the total number of offshoots from Worldwide by 2001 was reckoned by several internal observers including Alan Ruth to be over three hundred. This figure continued to be quoted as a rough measure in succeeding years, but by the completion of the main part of this study in late 2009 Alan Ruth wrote to me of "the easily more than 400 splits from the WCG" (Alan Ruth, pers. comm.; but see appendix 6). These do not include "living-room churches" (see 6.4.3), which have been estimated by another internal observer to bring the total to over one thousand (Dixon Cartwright, pers. comm.).

The main body of this chapter explores the continuing process of schism and the wide range of offshoots from large to small and from hardline to relatively liberal (6.2). It also examines the continuing story of the GTA-originating churches (6.3) and the different types of offshoot movements (6.4).

The first section (6.1) begins with an overview of several aspects of the offshoot churches, including their membership and the problems in assessing it; it discusses what is meant by "the Work," explains the distinction between "hardline" and "liberal" churches, discusses complications with church literature when schisms occur, and describes a typical church service.

6.1   ASPECTS OF THE OFFSHOOT CHURCHES

6.1.1   Membership of the Major Churches

The largest mainstream offshoots are shown in Table 6.1, with estimated or claimed membership around 2004–5, and 2008–9. The last three churches in the table are the main offshoots from Garner Ted Armstrong's branch of the Worldwide family, not from the schisms following Herbert W. Armstrong's death.

The 2004–5 figures are mainly estimates by informed observers within the COGs, based on information from the churches. The 2008–9 figures are taken mainly from my correspondence with each of these churches.

It should be stressed that these figures may not all be measuring the same thing. In any religion "membership" can mean many things. In Britain, for example, is the membership of the Church of England everyone who has been baptized into it? Or everyone who says they are a member, perhaps when filling

---

1. As this book was being prepared for publication there was a major split in United Church of God, with a large number of its ministers and members forming a new church, the Church of God, a Worldwide Association (COGWA). Except where this split is being specifically discussed in 6.2.3.2 and a few other places, all references to United Church of God are to be taken to refer to that church from its founding in early 1995 up to December 2010/January 2011.

Table 6.1. MEMBERSHIP OF WORLDWIDE CHURCH OF GOD AND ITS MAIN OFFSHOOTS

	ca. 2004–5	2008–9
Worldwide Church of God	ca. 40,000–67,000[2]	ca. 43,000[3]
United Church of God	ca. 15,000–17,000	20,349[4]
Living Church of God	ca. 6,000[5]	ca. 7,000[6]
Philadelphia Church of God	5,000–5,500[7]	ca. 4,000[8]
Church of God, *an International Community*	ca. 2,500	2,645[9]
Restored Church of God	unknown	>1,000[10]
Intercontinental Church of God	<1,000	ca. 2,000[11]
Church of God, International	<1,000	ca. 1,500[12]
Churches of God Outreach Ministries (CGOM)	ca. 800–880[13]	ca. 750[14]

in a hospital form? Is it Christmas or Easter attendance? Or is it an average Sunday's attendance? The last is the most accurate figure of *active* membership, but the Church of England, like most religions, would normally include more passive members as well. (An extreme case of redefining "membership" comes with the Church of Scientology, which in 2008 was claiming 120,000 members in Britain and 10 million worldwide. But analysis of census figures and other studies shows that they actually had under 1,800 members in Britain in 2001, and that their worldwide membership must be below 100,000 [Barrett 2006]; some sources believe the true figure to be between 25,000 and 40,000 [Hawkins 2010; Barrett 2011: 366]. The massive disparity is partly because the Church of

2. See 5.2.

3. WCG website.

4. Peter Hawkins, pers. comm. After the split in United, in March 2011 COGWA claimed 8,000 members, which would leave United with ca. 12,000 if the figure of 20,000 was accurate.

5. "The combined Sabbath attendance worldwide for 2000 reached 5,957, an increase of 747 people over 1999" (*The Journal* 2001: 24). Losses over the next few years mean that membership is unlikely to have risen much above this figure, if at all, by 2004–5.

6. LCG, pers. comm.. In March 2011 Living claimed 8,000 members (Bob Thiel, pers. comm.).

7. Kuhne 2004.

8. This figure was given by a former PCG member on an internet forum (Gauthier 2008).

9. Thiel 2009.

10. Jeffrey R. Ambrose, pers. comm.

11. Chris Cumming, pers. comm.

12. Vance Stinson pers. comm.

13. "They have more than 40 independent fellowships that make up CGOM" (Alan Ruth, pers. comm.). Taking a rough average of twenty to twenty-two members per congregation (see main text), this gives 800–880.

14. James McBride, pers. comm.

Scientology claims as a member every single person who has ever taken even an introductory Scientology course since the church was founded in 1954—whether now alive or dead [Jentzsch 1992].)

As discussed at 5.2, with Worldwide family churches "membership" could mean a number of things. The offshoots often use Feast of Tabernacles (FoT) attendance, which tends to be higher than average Sabbath attendance because almost every member who is physically capable will attend the Feast, and sometimes nonmember friends or family may go with them for what is effectively an eight-day holiday in beautiful surroundings, with services each day. But in response to this point, a United Church of God spokesman argued that the FoT figure is a more accurate indication of true membership:

> Yes, simply because some of our elderly members can't make it to weekly Sabbath services every week, and some members live a long way from their closest congregation. But, these people do make a special effort for the Holy Days. Therefore, to get a good average of our overall membership number like you asked, the Feast of Tabernacles is a good figure to use. (UCG Information, pers. comm.)

For an example of the difference in numbers, in 2008 the Church of God, *an International Community* (COGaic) had 1,300 at their North American Feast sites, but 1,150 in regular attendance at their fifty-three churches in the United States and Canada (Thiel 2009).

Through examination of figures such as these from COGaic, or by dividing the total membership of a church by the number of congregations listed on its website, or even by counting the number of heads in photographs of individual congregations, I have found a consistent average of twenty to twenty-five members per congregation in a number of churches. This can serve as a useful guide to total membership. For example, a CGOM leader told me: "I don't know how many individuals we serve. Each congregation is independent and we don't solicit numbers, though each is relatively small" (James McBride, pers. comm.). The CGOM website listed thirty-six "associate" churches; when I multiplied this by twenty and suggested that they might have around 750 members in total, he was happy to accept both the figure and the reasoning behind it as valid.

Membership can be a sensitive issue. Following in the tradition of Armstrong's Worldwide, many churches are happy to publicize how many potential listeners their radio and TV programs might reach, or how many books and booklets they have distributed, or, nowadays, how many hits their websites receive. But not all will say how many members they have. Some of the churches interpret 1 Chronicles 21:1–17, in which God is angered by David numbering Israel, to be a prohibition on giving out their membership figures. But other observers have expressed privately to me that they believe some churches do not want to let the extended COG community ("the Worldwide family") know how small they really are.

A spokesman for the Restored Church of God told me:

> We generally do not discuss our size, as we wish to prevent the perception of our being either "too big" or "too small" from becoming a factor in an interested party's decision as to whether to join RCG. (Jeffrey R. Ambrose, pers. comm.)

After persistent questioning he eventually informed me:

> I will confirm—of course our membership is above 1,000. I am somewhat surprised that you would feel the need to ask this, as our online presence and overall productivity would seem to make it obvious. However, we realize that there are Internet critics who have spread misinformation in this regard. (One such individual went so far as to assert that our Headquarters staff is mostly comprised of workers from a "temp agency"!) While this regrettably has fostered misconceptions for some, it is so absurd that it is in a sense comical. (Jeffrey R. Ambrose, pers. comm.)

This leaves little doubt of the sensitivity of the issue.

6.1.2 "The Work"

One of the major divisions between the offshoot churches is whether "the Work" is over or continuing. By this they mean the task of telling the world about the coming (and literal) Kingdom of God on Earth. As outlined above (2.2.1), this is the Worldwide family "good news"; the mainstream Christian concept of preaching the gospel of salvation is not part of their teachings. Unlike Evangelical Protestantism, individual members have no responsibility for "witnessing" to non-believers; their role is to support the headquarters of their church financially, to pay for the magazines, booklets, and radio and TV programs which spread the message.

Philadelphia's explanation for why they do not have an "open door" policy at their services makes their attitude on members witnessing very clear.

> The sermons at our regular Church services—and at the annual festivals—are entirely too strong for the unconverted of the world! They would only prove a stumbling block....
>
> Therefore, the lay members should leave it to the ministers to know whom to invite to attend, and when. Never invite anyone not yet a member to attend either a Church service or an annual Festival or Holy Day....
>
> Now, finally, remember—never try to talk anyone into salvation, God's truth, Bible doctrines, or being converted. So far as non-member friends and neighbors are concerned, just try to avoid all mention of our church services. Try to keep the subject

from coming up. It is better if they do not even know about our services—then there is no embarrassment about not inviting them to attend. (Flurry 1992)

Some churches believe that with Herbert W. Armstrong's death the Work is over, and that their task now is to "feed the sheep," to give spiritual teaching to their existing members. United and Living COGs still maintain the Work; so do the GTA churches; so, in one way or another, do most of the more liberal smaller offshoots. But some of the more hardline churches see their mission as being to their former brethren, initially those still in Worldwide, and, as the years went on, those in other offshoots, rather than to the world. The Restored Church of God has a whole package of full-length books, booklets, and videos aimed at the other offshoots or "splinters."

Philadelphia changed its emphasis; for its first seven years it concentrated mainly on the Worldwide family; then it extended its focus to the wider Work of proclaiming the soon-to-come Kingdom.

A leading commentator, Living COG member Bob Thiel, who uses the online name COGwriter, is critical of Restored for what he sees as its ambiguous attitude to the Work. To emphasize his point he quotes from Herbert W. Armstrong's last letter before his death:

It may be that the Work that God has given me to do is complete, but not the Work of God's Church, which will be faithfully doing God's Work till Christ, the True Head of this Church, returns....

Each of you must commit yourself to support God's Work....God's work must push ahead as never before. (Thiel: HWA letter, January 10, 1986)

6.1.3   "Hardline" or "Liberal"

Throughout this book I refer to churches as being more or less hardline or liberal than each other. I had hoped to devise an objectively derived spectrum from hardline to liberal based on fifteen indicators, Yes/No answers to questions about specific beliefs and practices, but the lack of response from most of the churches to such direct questions made that impossible. The criteria included among others whether HWA was a type of Elijah; whether the church leader was considered an apostle or prophet; whether the church has hierarchical governance; the church's attitude to the use of medicines, to makeup, and to interracial romantic relationships; whether it has a members-only or an open-door policy for its services; and, as just discussed, whether the Work is finished or continuing.

Instead I am using the terms a little more loosely, based on my reading of the churches' literature; most of the above beliefs and practices are in fact mentioned within the magazines, booklets, and books of the churches. I believe that few,

Hardline	<<<		>>>	Liberal
Philadelphia		Living		United
Restored		COGaic		GTA Churches

Figure 6.1 A Spectrum from Hardline to Liberal

whether observers or leaders, ministers or members of the churches themselves, would disagree that, of the main churches, Philadelphia and Restored are at the hardline end of the spectrum, Living and COGaic somewhere in the middle, and United and the GTA churches at the liberal end.

However, GTA's comment should be noted:

> To most [i.e., in the outside world], I am viewed as being very conservative, far-to-the-right. But to some who had my father's ear unbeknownst to me, I was being subtly painted as a "liberal." (G. T. Armstrong 1992: 52)

In comparison with the other Worldwide family churches the GTA churches may well be liberal, but from an outsider's point of view, even the most "liberal" of the churches is very conservative in many ways. Generally within the Worldwide family "liberal" is a dirty word, as it was to Armstrong himself (see 4.4), and the churches I have labeled "liberal" might prefer I had used a different term.

When United split in two in December 2010, the editor of *The Journal*, Dixon Cartwright, distinguished between United and its major new offshoot, the Church of God, a Worldwide Association, as the "progressives" and the "conservatives," respectively, largely on the basis of their attitude to Herbert W. Armstrong (see 6.2.3.2).

The attitude of the Churches of God to Herbert W. Armstrong is complex. All the churches, including the most liberal, respect him and his teachings, but the more hardline churches show a reverence for him as God's End Time apostle, and for every word he spoke or wrote. In criticizing churches with "a seeming preoccupation or at times almost an obsession with Mr. Armstrong," a member of United—a church firmly at the liberal end of the spectrum—writes:

> God used Herbert Armstrong in a powerful way. We have all benefited directly or indirectly, from his labor for God. However, Mr Armstrong was just as human as any other member of God's church. He had his foibles, flaws, shortcomings and weaknesses. . . . His doctrinal understanding was very good, but not perfect. Mr Armstrong's words, no matter how highly we esteem them, are not Holy Writ of and by themselves. (Waite 2000: 221–22)

6.1.4 Complications with Church Literature

When a church splits, who owns its physical assets? The obvious answer is the original church from which the schismatic movement split away; and so when Philadelphia, Global, and United split from Worldwide, Worldwide continued to own, for example, its headquarters buildings, though it would end up having to sell them (see 5.1.3). It was the custom for individual church congregations, in Worldwide and in the offshoots, to meet in a rented room (see 6.1.5), so the ownership of church buildings was not usually a problem (but see 6.2.3.2). But there was one type of asset which would sometimes cause major complications: church literature.

The Worldwide family of churches has always been heavily literature-focused (see appendix 3.3). One of the first indications of the massive changes in Worldwide was its withdrawal of Armstrong's classic books and booklets (5.1.2). With this strong literature heritage, most of the major offshoots produce their own updated rewrites of Armstrong's works which were originally published by Worldwide. For example, one of Armstrong's best known booklets was *The Wonderful World Tomorrow: What It Will Be Like* (1966, 1973, 1979, 1982). Living's *The World Ahead: What Will It Be Like?* (2008), under Roderick Meredith's name, is a more succinct version of the same thing; Restored's *Tomorrow's Wonderful World: An Inside View!* (2002), by David C. Pack, is a much expanded version. Both have taken the opportunity to update references, statistics, and photographs. Similarly, most of the largest churches and some of the smaller ones have their own rewritten versions of Armstrong's core book *The United States and British Commonwealth in Prophecy* (see 2.2.3, note 22).

We shall see below (6.2.1) how instead of rewriting Armstrong's books and booklets, Philadelphia Church of God eventually bought the copyright to nineteen of his most significant works. They now publish Armstrong's final book, *Mystery of the Ages*, the 1982 version of *The Wonderful World Tomorrow: What it Will Be Like*, the 1980 version of *The United States and Britain in Prophecy*, and many more, in addition to their own booklets by their leader, Gerald Flurry.

But the problem of ownership of literature continues when the offshoot churches themselves split. In most cases the "parent" church will retain its literature and the "child" church will produce new booklets, often emphasizing the differences between them. But there was one unusual exception.

Roderick C. Meredith left his own church, Global, to found Living Church of God (see 6.2.2). His sermons, articles, and booklets were copyrighted by Global, a church he no longer belonged to. Legally he couldn't use them in Living, and Global would not want to use them with his name on them. There were negotiations about Global licensing Meredith's writings back to him for his own use, but it wasn't even as straightforward as that. As with any leader, much of what "he" writes is actually written (or either initially drafted or finally polished) by other people—and they might now be in different churches. Who, then, has the moral right to be considered the author, the originator?

This was not a new problem that faced the schisms following Armstrong's death. Garner Ted Armstrong, who had in fact written some of the WCG booklets of the 1970s, had to rewrite his own work as well as his father's when he founded the Church of God, International in 1978.

Many of the booklets written by (or attributed to) Herbert W. Armstrong continue to be circulated by the smaller offshoot churches, which do not have the resources to rewrite them. Most of them are also available on the internet or in CD libraries—which also include hundreds of articles and editorials under Armstrong's name from the *Plain Truth* and other WCG magazines and newsletters. For many in the Worldwide family, the original words of Armstrong still have a power that rewritten versions can never have.

Former Philadelphia and Church of God's Faithful member Daniel Cohran argues strongly that it is absolutely wrong for offshoots either to rewrite Armstrong's original books or to write new ones:

> Many of these are writing or re-writing books or booklets on topics that Mr. Armstrong ALREADY covered years ago. Many do this using their own names as the authors and mention very little or nothing about the original author—Mr. Armstrong. The question should be posed here: HOW CAN YOU MAKE THE PLAIN TRUTH ANY PLAINER?!...
>
> For example, WHY take a booklet called "Does God Exist?" and rewrite it into a long complicated dissertation when it has already been made plain? Or, why take the book "U.S. and Britain in Prophecy" and rewrite it into another book with the same information in it yet under another author's name? This is ludicrous, and an insult to Jesus Christ who used Mr. Armstrong to begin with, to make these subjects plain and clear!... Unfortunately the "egos" of many men are getting in the way. They want to do it their "own" way. This after all is the Laodicean way. (Cohran 2009a)

But despite his plea—noticeably written in Armstrong's own style—this is what most of the offshoot churches have done.

6.1.5 Worldwide Family Services

With a few exceptions Worldwide's larger offshoot churches follow the example of their parent: they have a glossy magazine, often a clone of *Plain Truth*; they have doctrinal booklets, sent free to enquirers; and they have radio and TV broadcasts spreading their message.

Their church services follow much the same pattern as well. Most congregations meet in a rented room in a community center or similar building. They may have a lectern for the speaker, and perhaps a vase of flowers, but there are no religious symbols in the room—no statues, no pictures, no cross (the Worldwide family of churches, like the Jehovah's Witnesses, believe that Jesus was executed on a stake, not a cross).

I attended Sabbath services of United and Living in or near London, England, having contacted their ministers beforehand. I also contacted the other main churches to see if I might attend. Philadelphia, Restored, COGaic, and Church of God's Faithful do not have an open-door policy and gave a firm but polite no; COG (UK), the small representatives of GTA's heritage in the United Kingdom, did not have a service near London.

A typical Worldwide family service begins with perhaps three hymns from that church's version of the old Worldwide hymn book, which largely consists of the words of psalms (taken from the Scottish Psalter and others) set to music by Dwight L. Armstrong, HWA's youngest brother; the piano music is usually recorded. A short extempore prayer is followed by either a live "sermonette" or a DVD video of the church leader; the latter might include church news or might be a TV program. After another hymn and announcements comes an hour-long sermon; many of the congregation follow the Bible references in their own Bibles and take notes. The service ends with another hymn and a closing prayer. The congregation stands for the hymns and prayers and sits for the remainder of the service.

At the services I attended I found both the style and the content of the main sermons to be little different from those in any Evangelical church, with the congregation following the preacher's movement from text to text in their own Bibles; if anything, there was a little less biblical exegesis than in many Evangelical sermons. A telecast by Roderick C. Meredith about Christ's imminent return, which I was told was "hard-hitting," could have been heard just as strongly if not more so, and with only slight doctrinal variations, in any Christian tent crusade. There is a tendency for millennial sects to give the impression that their message is unique, that they are the only ones preaching this warning of the End Times; but they are often less distinctive than they claim (Barrett 2001a: 186).

There were twenty-four attendees at the United service I attended and nearly sixty at the Living one, with a rough balance of males and females at both. A third to a half of the congregations were white;[15] the remainder, I picked up through conversation, had a variety of ethnic origins, though the majority appeared to be of Caribbean origin.[16] Although there were some aged fifty or more, and at the Living service several in their seventies, the majority were aged twenty-five to forty. There were a few teenagers, and several small children who were impeccably behaved throughout the hour-and-a-half to two-hour services. The age spread and the size of the Living service were quite different from what I had been led to expect by all my research into the offshoot churches; through conversation with members of the

15. This is not unusual in London, which has a large first-, second-, and third-generation immigrant population, whose members are proportionally more churchgoing than the indigenous population.

16. In Britain there has always been a strong correlation between Caribbean immigrants and Seventh-day Adventist Churches—to which the Worldwide family of churches is related (see 2.1.3). Several of the offshoot churches have a strong presence in the Caribbean.

congregation it seemed that this might simply be because the services were in or near such a major city as London.

The men, including the ministers, were smartly dressed in suits, or at least jackets and ties. Women are encouraged to "dress modestly," which generally meant a dress or skirt, though many were dressed stylishly and colorfully; very few covered their hair.

At both congregations I was greeted in a friendly manner by those running the services and by members of the congregation. I was open about why I was there, and over buffet snacks and coffee afterwards had interesting free-ranging conversations about the schisms and their leaders, and about the members' memories of their past in Worldwide.

6.2   THE MAJOR CHURCHES AND THEIR OWN OFFSHOOTS

6.2.1   1989: Philadelphia Church of God

The first group of any significant size to leave Worldwide in the transitional years of the Tkach era following Armstrong's death was the Philadelphia Church of God (PCG). This section is the most detailed of those on any of the offshoots for several reasons: because PCG was the first major offshoot; because of the long-running copyright dispute (see below); because PCG, perhaps more than any other COG offshoot, seeks to be seen as the direct continuation of WCG; because of its leader's controversial claims about himself and his church; and because of some of its own offshoots and the complex and sometimes contradictory views that these have of PCG and its leader.

Philadelphia Church of God is the most hardline conservative of the three major offshoots. It was founded by a previously almost unknown pastor, Gerald Flurry, in 1989, after he asked Joseph Tkach Jr. why the WCG had withdrawn Armstrong's final book, *Mystery of the Ages*, a book which Armstrong had said contained "important new biblical truths." Armstrong had written in a letter to co-workers dated September 12, 1985:

> I feel I myself did not write it. Rather, I believe God used me in writing it. I candidly feel it may be the most important book since the Bible....
>
> I am now in my 94th year and I feel that this book is the most valuable gift I could possibly give to you. (H. W. Armstrong 1987: 637, 640)

Joe Jr. told Flurry that the book "was riddled with error"; Flurry challenged this, and Joe Tkach "later changed that remark to 'many significant errors'" (G. Flurry 1994: 34). Flurry refused to accept this, and was sacked. He left to found his own church.

There has been some ironic comment on Armstrong's words, "I feel I myself did not write it." According to Garner Ted Armstrong, *Mystery of the Ages* was simply a rehash of earlier works, including portions of *The Wonderful World Tomorrow: What It Will Be Like*, which he had cowritten with his father in 1966.

How surprised I was to see page after page, major portions of whole chapters, of my father's book, *Mystery of the Ages*, containing word-for-word excerpts from my half of that booklet.

While millions had been told my father had written a new book; imagined him, as a ninety-one or ninety-two-year-old man sitting there pounding away on a typewriter, the truth was that his books were pieced together from dozens of his old co-worker and member letters, booklets and articles, with various inserts and new material added to tie it all together. While my name does not appear as co-author of *Mystery of the Ages*, I am, in fact, a co-author! (G. T. Armstrong 1992: 32–33)

This is not just the bitterness of an estranged son. Former Worldwide member Gary Scott, who is not in any of the offshoot churches, did a line-by-line comparison of sections of *Mystery of the Ages* with *The Wonderful World Tomorrow* and other earlier works, showing how much material was taken directly from earlier booklets (Gary Scott, pers. comm.).

But for Gerald Flurry and others in Worldwide, this book was Armstrong's most important work—in his words, perhaps "the most important book since the Bible." For Armstrong's own church to withdraw it and for his successor's son to say it was full of errors was unthinkable. In sociologist John Wilson's words, it was the reaction of the authorities which "fanned the flames of discontent and determination to secede" (J. Wilson 1971: 17).

In January 1997 Philadelphia began to advertise *Mystery of the Ages* in the *Philadelphia Trumpet*, sending copies free of charge to whoever requested it—despite the fact that its copyright was owned by Worldwide. Though Philadelphia was making no money from the book (in fact it was costing the church money to print and distribute it), and although Worldwide had no interest in publishing the book themselves now that they had abandoned the teachings in it, they sued Philadelphia for breach of copyright.

The ruling of Federal District judge J. Spencer Letts in the Federal District Court in Los Angeles, February 18, 1997, was profound:

This is admittedly a work by the founder of a religion who has died.... This [the Worldwide Church of God] is an entity that has a corporate structure and it also has a religious structure. The people who inherited the corporate structure are not all of the people who used to have religious position. Some of the people that had religious position have now either been taken out of the corporate structure, or they were never in it. The question is—and it is to me a new one—does the surviving corporation, through its board of directors and all such people, have the right to suppress the founder... the right to prevent there from being future printing of the religious founder's work?

The judge went on, albeit in a somewhat rambling way, to distinguish between a religion and a corporation:

I do think that if it is, as I suspect it is, that when you're dealing with the first generation after the founder, that you're dealing with very different religious issues. And you are dealing with a founder's work in the first generation after the founder's [death] and you've had a split in the religion, which was by definition different from the corporation.... The founder did not dream, I suspect...that by giving this corporation, which was his corporation that reflected his religion, that those who would come after him would use their corporate power to suppress his religion or to keep any prior practitioners of his religion, or keep any people that were vested with the authority of that religion, notwithstanding they don't have the corporate position, from making that book available on a continuous, freshly printed basis—I don't believe the founder dreamed that. (quoted in "Flurry Wins Big in Court," *Ambassador Report* 65)

This legal distinction between the corporate and the spiritual legacy of the founder of a religion was a landmark decision which could have had major implications in the future, not just for the Worldwide family of churches but for any schismatic religion, and perhaps most particularly new religious movements. However, Judge Letts's ruling was overturned by a court of appeals in September 2000.

In March 2003 Worldwide came to an out-of-court settlement with PCG, in which they sold them the copyright in *Mystery of the Ages* and eighteen of Armstrong's other books and booklets for a figure which a Philadelphia spokesman told me at the time was "an even $2 million" (Dennis Leap, pers. comm.). However, other sources put it at $3 million (WCG: MOA, n.d.; Gardner 2007) or $3 million plus $2 million court costs (Thiel 2007).

Very shortly after this settlement I asked the spokesman, one of Philadelphia's most senior writers:

> What will PCG's position be about any other ex-WCG Church that wants to use HWA's works, now that you own them? Will you be following the ruling of the original judge that the teachings "belong" to everyone who believes them? Or will you sub-license them to other Churches? Or, if anyone else used them, would you sue for breach of copyright, now that you own it? Or hasn't all of this been worked out yet?

He replied: "Let us ponder on this e-mail. I know these questions will be raised in the minds of many. We have not had much discussion on these issues to this point" (Dennis Leap, pers. comm.).

Despite repeated inquiries by myself and by other observers, over eight years later PCG had still not given an answer to these questions.

Philadelphia's struggle to gain control of *Mystery of the Ages* and the eighteen other works is documented in great detail in the 415-page hardback book *Raising the Ruins: The Fight to Revive the Legacy of Herbert W. Armstrong*, by Stephen Flurry, son of PCG's founder (S. Flurry 2006). Although, like most histories of any part of the Worldwide story, it is clearly a partisan account (see 3.1 and appendices 2.1 and 2.3), it is a fascinating insight into the beliefs and drives of the Philadelphia Church, and how far they were prepared to go (and how much they were prepared to spend) for what they believed.

While other churches produce their own rewritten and updated versions of the classic books and booklets of Worldwide's Armstrong years, Philadelphia reprints Armstrong's original books and booklets alongside their own.

The Philadelphia Church of God is based in Edmond, Oklahoma, not Philadelphia; its name is taken from the Book of Revelation, in which God says of the church in Philadelphia, "Thou hast a little strength, and hast kept my word, and hast not denied my name" (Rev. 3:8). (For the church eras see 2.2.1 and 3.2.2.) Armstrong had always described Worldwide as the Philadelphian church; Flurry's use of the name emphasizes his claim that his church is the only continuation of the true Church of God. Flurry describes the new "apostate" Worldwide as the Laodicean Church, which follows the Church in Philadelphia in order, and of which God says, "Because thou art lukewarm, and neither cold nor hot, I will spue thee out of my mouth" (Rev. 3:16).

Its public magazine, the *Philadelphia Trumpet*, is similar in tone to the *Plain Truth* at its most forceful, when Herbert W. Armstrong was proclaiming how current world events revealed the imminence of Christ's return. It preaches an uncompromising message tied in with a prophetic analysis of world political and economic events; the war in Kosovo, for example, was seen (through complex argument) to demonstrate how Germany was once again becoming a potentially imperialist world power.

In a very similar way to Armstrong, Flurry and his writers frequently indulge in, if not prophecy, then what Richard T. Ritenbaugh called "speculation" or "theories" (see 4.1), sometimes with similarly embarrassing results. For example, several articles in the *Philadelphia Trumpet* in 2010 suggested that the charismatic Baron Karl-Theodor zu Guttenberg was in line to become the new and very powerful leader of Germany, "Germany's new Charlemagne" (G. Flurry 2010: 1–7); in March 2011 a disgraced Guttenberg stepped down as defense minister after the University of Bayreuth stripped him of his PhD for plagiarizing other people's work in his thesis.

Philadelphia roundly condemns Worldwide for its apostasy, to the extent of identifying the "man of sin...the son of perdition, who opposeth and exalteth himself above all that is called God, or that is worshipped" (2 Thess. 2: 3–4) as Joseph Tkach:

THIS "MAN OF SIN" HAS REPLACED CHRIST AS THE HEAD OF THE WCG!
He exalts himself above Christ and what He taught through Mr. Armstrong. Like Judas, the "man of sin" proves to be a false apostle. (G. Flurry 1995b: 102–3)

It also argues strongly that the other major offshoots, although they have some of the truth, are not following God's will. God's true church, the Church of God, is only to be found in the Philadelphia Church of God (G. Flurry 1995b: 132).

Philadelphia sees Herbert W. Armstrong as the End Time Elijah, as God's true apostle to the twentieth century. It exemplifies what Bryan R. Wilson says of charismatic leadership—"In the strong instances we find the messiah-figure, the uniquely endowed guru, or the special vehicle transmitting to mankind a message from beyond" (B. Wilson 1990: 232):

> Herbert W. Armstrong fulfilled God's end-time covenant concerning the ministry.... God gave Mr. Armstrong the key of David....Only God's end-time Elijah was commissioned to restore the key of David (Matt. 17:10–11). That is why we print that same booklet by Mr. Armstrong. Nobody else was commissioned by God to produce their own version after he died [a criticism of the other offshoots which do this]. God is using the Philadelphia Church of God to build on the foundation which Mr. Armstrong laid....GOD ESTABLISHED HIS GOVERNMENT THROUGH MR. ARMSTRONG—ONE MAN....All of God's Laodicean churches today have rejected that government. That is why God reveals no new truth to them after Mr. Armstrong died. But God has deluged the PCG with new revelation, and it will continue to flow to God's very elect. (G. Flurry 1997: 5)

There is an inherent contradiction here, in that the Philadelphia Church of God claims to hold firmly to Armstrong's teachings (G. Flurry 1994: 89) yet has added to them. Philadelphia's claim to have been "deluged...with new revelation" is one of many reasons why, despite their very strong emphasis on Armstrong, the Restored Church of God condemns them, perhaps more than they do any other offshoot. Another is Gerald Flurry's claim that he, as well as Armstrong, is specifically foretold in the Bible (G. Flurry 2007: 96): although God's True Church, the Worldwide Church of God, would fall away from the truth, out of the ashes would arise the Philadelphia Church of God, led by Flurry himself. This is set out in Flurry's book *Malachi's Message to God's Church Today* (Flurry 1995b), which is itself the "little book" mentioned in Revelation 10:2 (Flurry 1995a: 4).

In another book, *Who Is "That Prophet"?* (G. Flurry 2007, first published 2001) Flurry starts by looking at John 1:21, when John the Baptist is asked "Art thou Elias? ... Art thou that prophet?" Elias (Elijah) and "that prophet" are two different people, Flurry argues, and "Herbert W. Armstrong fulfilled the end-time type of the office of Elijah" (G. Flurry 2007: 5)—so who is "that prophet"? The answer is Flurry himself. He also sees himself as God's Watchman, described in a prophecy in Jeremiah: "This prophecy does not apply to Mr. Armstrong as specifically as it does to me" (20). And he also finds a description of himself in Micah 4:9, as king and counselor (37).

Evidence that Philadelphia's members regard Flurry as someone special—more than just a church leader—comes in a long document written to him by a member shortly before he was disfellowshipped by Philadelphia; although in the document Gary Gauthier claims that there is corruption in the church he repeatedly addresses Flurry as "my king" (Gauthier, n.d.; see 6.2.1.1). Some of the others who have left Philadelphia are critical of Flurry not for his claims, as might perhaps be expected, but for missing the mark of what God had intended his role to be; in other words, he is right in the authority he claims, but wrong in his execution of it (see below).

The Philadelphia Church of God promotes itself as the true and direct continuation of Worldwide Church of God. It publishes Armstrong's original books; its magazine, *Philadelphia Trumpet*, shares its initials with *Plain Truth*; it has renamed its Imperial College as Herbert W. Armstrong College, abbreviated AC (the historic Worldwide had Ambassador College); similarly it has renamed its Philadelphia Foundation as the Armstrong International Cultural Foundation—AICF (Worldwide had the Ambassador International Cultural Foundation); it has built headquarters buildings that, while considerably smaller, reflect the style and grandeur of Worldwide's former headquarters in Pasadena, including the Armstrong Auditorium, an eight-hundred-seat concert hall (Worldwide had the fifteen-hundred-seat Ambassador Auditorium). In 2009 Flurry bought from Worldwide a bronze and steel sculpture of five stages of a swan taking flight, originally commissioned by Armstrong in the 1960s from English sculptor David Wynne (PCG 2009); the price was not revealed, but the sculpture was put up for sale in 2002 for $300,000. Flurry had previously bought from Worldwide a Steinway grand piano and two Baccarat 802-piece crystal candelabra from the Ambassador Auditorium for $100,000 (S. Flurry 2006: 358). This conspicuous expenditure is also in direct imitation of Herbert W. Armstrong (see 3.3).

Around 2003 PCG claimed some 7,500 members, with perhaps two hundred in the UK, though in 2004 a Worldwide family observer noted that its membership was actually only 5,000–5,500 (Kuhne 2004), and in late 2008 a former member stated that its membership "has again declined down to about 4000 members" (Gauthier 2008).

6.2.1.1 *Philadelphia Church of God Offshoots*

Philadelphia COG has suffered a number of schisms, as members have either left or been disfellowshipped. Several of them have founded churches or individual ministries; some have a large internet presence devoted to criticizing Philadelphia and/ or Flurry. Even the largest, the **Church of God's Faithful** (CGF), is quite small: "We are just a few hundred members and I would estimate that less than 50% are former PCG members" (John Durrad, pers. comm.). CGF was founded in 1997 by Robert G. Ardis. It believes that the Work ended at Armstrong's death (see 6.1.2); the many offshoots are wrong:

> Their "works" of attempting to take the Gospel to the World is an act of pious futility and utter disregard for the amazing accomplishments Christ performed through Herbert Armstrong—the man who taught these men the true Gospel.

Two paragraphs of CGF's Statement of Belief are specifically about Gerald Flurry:

We believe Gerald Flurry was the man God raised up to head the Seventh Candlestick—the Laodicean Work of Jesus Christ. Mr. Flurry fearlessly proclaimed the fact that a "man of sin" was sitting in the controlling position in the WCG—while most of the other ministers did nothing but compromise their beliefs....

He was not lukewarm at the beginning; he became that way. God began to remove the blessings from him because of the very abusive government Mr. Flurry adopted. Then Gerald Flurry changed his commission. He unlawfully seized *Mystery of the Ages* in January 1997 and went to the World—and God separated His Faithful Philadelphians as the CGF to warn Mr. Flurry and his PCG of their great error. (CGF 2010)

Like Philadelphia, the Church of God's Faithful has new truth, which "will set the True Church apart from all the other churches" (CGF website). It teaches that Christ has already returned, invisibly, on October 1, 1997, precisely six thousand years after the recreation of the world (Ardis 2006: 17)—a similar interpretation of the End Times to the Seventh-day Adventist belief that he returned in 1844 to cleanse the heavenly sanctuary (SDA 1988: 324) or to the Jehovah's Witness belief that he returned as God's presence in 1874 or 1914 (JWs 1993: 133, 144), but his physical return would be at a later time.

CGF's own secessions illustrate the intensity of the antipathy between the hardline offshoots. After disagreeing with CGF leader Robert Ardis on doctrinal matters, Glen Alspaugh left CGF and founded the **Church of God's Patience** in 1999. Citing Revelation 12:9 he wrote: "This great dragon is a man named Mr. Robert Ardis, the man of sin; Satan's agent to rule God's sons, the pillars of the Old Jerusalem temple." Alspaugh also finds himself specifically prophesied in the Bible:

I, Mr. Glen Alspaugh, am the "He" written about in [Revelation 3:12]....I will fulfill all the scriptures about me building this New Jerusalem temple who are converted sons led by Jesus' mind....

After two years Mr. Ardis from the C.G.F. went astray with Satan's lies in 1999. Jesus has anointed me to replace Mr. Ardis and to build the New Jerusalem temple in November 1999.

Jesus moved from the C.G.F. to the C.G.P. In 1999. (Alspaugh, n.d.)

In 2001 Alspaugh ordained two men as the Two Witnesses, important End Time figures (see 6.4.4). His website, which I accessed in 2003, no longer existed in 2009.

Other churches or ministries by former Philadelphia members include the **Church of God—Front Royal, VA,** founded by Daniel W. Dawson, whose website *A Voice Cried Out* is a tribute to Armstrong:

This news report [the Bible] plainly states, that during the twentieth century, God's greatest servant was Mr. Armstrong—not Mr. Churchill—not Mr. Roosevelt—nor any other human being. (D. Dawson, n.d.;)

Another church was founded by Daniel Cohran, whose website *Hold Fast to All Things* offers access to all of Armstrong's writings (and has Armstrong's voice on many pages). Cohran went from Worldwide to Philadelphia, then to Robert Ardis's Church of God's Faithful, then to Daniel Dawson's Church of God—Front Royal, VA, leaving each one because of doctrinal changes, "meaning departing or changing the truths and doctrines that Jesus Christ revealed and restored through His end time apostle, Mr. Herbert W. Armstrong" (Cohran 2009b).

This is a major distinction between mindsets, or socially constructed realities: the "new truth" which Flurry and Ardis claim proves that their churches are each the True Church is anathema to those who believe that God gave Armstrong *the* Truth, and that nothing should be added to or taken away from this.

> Many men or ministers have come along since the death of Mr. Armstrong, and have CHANGED basic doctrines and/or added so-called "new truth" to what was already given by Jesus Christ here in the end time through His chosen apostle. Some even try to continue on with work that only Mr. Armstrong was given to do, while neglecting what really needs to be done (preparing the Bride for example). (Cohran 2009b)

The **Elect Church of God** was founded by Gary Gauthier (not an ordained minister) after he handed a long document to Gerald Flurry in October 2006, in which he said that Satan had entered the Philadelphia Church of God, which had corrupt governance. The document, with annotations, is a 107-page account of Gauthier's struggle to come to terms with the idea that God's church, led by Flurry, who he calls "my king," could have been corrupted. Nearly three years later Gauthier wrote to me:

> Mr. Flurry is more concerned with sitting on Christ's throne than with the people in the PCG. . . .
>
> Mr. Flurry has stated that he is a king who sits on David's throne even today. I have his direct quote in writing. In respect I believed that Mr. Flurry was a type of king. I was wrong and have repented of this. (Gary Gauthier, pers. comm.)

Other former members have not founded churches but have active online campaigns against Flurry and his church. Robert S. Kuhne's very detailed websites argue that Flurry's book *Malachi's Message*, rather than being inspired of God, was plagiarized from a document entitled *The Letter To Laodicea*, sent by a former WCG member, Jules Dervaes, to Joseph W. Tkach in 1987, and copied to many Worldwide ministers, including Gerald Flurry and John Amos, who cofounded Philadelphia Church of God in 1989 (Kuhne 2003: 25; Dervaes, n.d.). Amos died in 1993.

From the above it can be seen that, for a number of reasons, including the status of its founder and the intensity of its offshoots, Philadelphia Church of God is arguably the most controversial of all the major churches in the Worldwide family.

6.2.2 1992–93: Global/Living Church of God and Offshoots

After Philadelphia the next of the major offshoots from Worldwide was the Global Church of God. Roderick C. Meredith was one of Worldwide's most prominent evangelists; ordained in 1952, he had been part of the third intake to Ambassador College (see 3.2.2). Meredith left Worldwide at the end of 1992. In an interview three years later he said:

> One young smart aleck…one of their leaders, he said, "Mr. Armstrong gave the whole Church a bucket of lies!"…When I realized that was their attitude, that those changes were heading in a total opposite direction from everything we had proved was the truth, then I knew it was time to leave. (Barnett and Pomicter 1995)

The last straw for Meredith was Worldwide's publication of the new *God Is…* booklet which, he said, in two editions within six months went from Armstrong's teaching of "the God family" to practically a full-blown Trinity. When Meredith refused to teach the new doctrine, the church he had been with since 1949 sacked him.

Meredith's split from Worldwide is described briefly in a Global Church of God booklet:

> In December 1992, 40 years after his original ordination, Evangelist Roderick C. Meredith was forced out of the Worldwide Church of God organization because of his refusal to compromise with the prevailing forces of apostasy. This marked the beginning of the Global Church of God. Soon joined by thousands of faithful brethren and scores of faithful ministers, Mr. Meredith and those with him have moved forward to revive the Work of God. (Ogwyn 1995: 71)

Meredith founded the Global Church of God, which quickly grew to around 8,500 members (less than two hundred in the United Kingdom), and claimed to be a conscious recreation of WCG: "All our major doctrines are the doctrines extant under Mr. Armstrong at his death in January, 1986" (Barnett and Pomicter 1995). Global's public magazine, *The World Ahead*, was very close to the classic *Plain Truth*, with articles about how world events show that Christ's return is imminent.

For the first few years the attitude within Global seemed relatively relaxed; and after the formation of the United Church of God in 1995 (see 6.2.3), individual members of the two churches had fairly cordial relations, the main difference being that Global members wanted strong leadership vested in one man.

But the issue of leadership became a problem. There began to be reports in both *The Journal* and *Ambassador Report* of criticism of Meredith within Global, particularly that he was holding the reins of power too tightly—for example, by not letting other, younger ministers in his church speak on his TV program. At first it appeared that Meredith responded positively to this criticism, but then things changed dramatically over the space of a few months.

Global, like any American church, was set up legally as a corporation; this meant, among other things, that there had to be a corporate structure. In November 1998 Meredith suddenly found that his decisions were being challenged by the governing body of his church. (This was a parallel with the situation in the Elim Pentecostal Church in the 1930s: "Here was the crisis in which the charismatic leader finds his leadership can be sustained only if he permits it to be circumscribed by the legal instrument of the bureaucratic administrator" [B. Wilson 1961: 52]. In that case too the charismatic leader was to leave his own church to found another.[17])

There was a proliferation of letters, some of them public, with each side accusing the other of obduracy, disloyalty, and worse. A letter from Meredith at the time begins (in language and style very reminiscent of Herbert W. Armstrong—see 4.5):

> In a very clever move to confuse and mislead God's people, the men on the "Board" of the Global Church recently sent out a MASSIVE attack against me personally. This is one of the biggest attacks and attempts at total character assassination in the modern history of God's Church! (Meredith 1998)

The half dozen men at the very top of Meredith's corporate structure had turned against him and removed him from the leadership of his own church.

> In November 1998 there was even an attempt, led by several Global Church of God board members, to stage a "corporate takeover" of that organization. Board members ousted Dr Meredith, against the wishes of a majority of the Church's Council of Elders, but soon found that the vast majority of GCG members and ministers continued to support the ousted leader, and those Council of Elders members who left after his ouster. (Ogwyn 2003: 56)

If Meredith wanted to retain control, there was only one solution. He left the church he had founded and of which he was until recently the head, Global Church of God, and established a new church, the **Living Church of God**. Some 70 to 80% of Global's members and ministers followed him (Introvigne 1999). They had joined Global in part because they believed in Meredith's strong, top-down leadership. If they had wanted government by committee they would have left Global to join United when it began.

Global was left with a name and a corporate structure, but with no charismatic leader, very few members, and (as when Worldwide started to disintegrate in the mid-1990s—see 5.1.3), a drastic reduction in income. We have seen the difficulty it faced over the authorship of its literature (6.1.4). But there was a far more serious problem.

Any organization needs start-up funding, especially if it has an ambitious and expensive publishing and broadcasting ministry. Once it was up and running it

---

17. Interestingly, George Jeffreys, the president of the Elim Church who left to found the Bible Pattern Fellowship in 1939, was a British Israelite.

could operate on the tithes of its members, but when it began, Global the corporation took loans from many of its better-off members. Now most of these had left Global and joined Living, and understandably asked for their loans to Global to be repaid. Global faced financial crisis. In September 1999 Global "voluntarily entered into a legal process called assignment for the benefit of creditors (similar to bankruptcy)" (Overton 1999a: 1). Global as a corporation and as a church was finished; its remaining members, only about a thousand worldwide, started up a new church, the **Church of God, a Christian Fellowship** (CGCF).

In June 2000 it was announced that CGCF and United had "begun a dialog to look for common ground and ways to cooperate with each other" (Overton 2000b: 1), and a year later most of CGCF merged with United. But in July 2000 there had been a further bizarre twist to the tale. The president of CGCF, Raymond McNair, stunned his church by resigning from it and applying to join Living, led by Roderick Meredith, from whom (as his second-in-command) he had split eighteen months earlier when he had effectively ousted Meredith from Global. Meredith accepted his application, but made it very clear that he would be coming in simply as an ordinary member, not as a minister (Overton 2000a: 1). (Apparently this is in character. According to David Robinson's account of Worldwide in the 1970s, *Herbert Armstrong's Tangled Web*, Meredith was renowned for demoting ministers from high positions to lowly roles.)

Raymond McNair—who had been in the second intake of Herbert W. Armstrong's fledgling Ambassador College in 1948, the year before Meredith (see 3.2.2)—later left Meredith's leadership for a second time to found his own church, the **Church of God—21st Century** (COG21), in 2004. He died in 2008—but apart from the addition of an "In Memoriam" page, the COG21 website was still, in 2011, maintained just as it was before his death, including a letter by him saying:

> Some have asked that I update them concerning the state of my health. I am happy to report that my health has greatly improved....
>
> Once again, brethren, I would very much appreciate your continued prayers that God will restore me to full health. (R. McNair, n.d.)

Email correspondence with Mrs. Eve McNair, Raymond McNair's widow, made it clear that COG21 had been, in a sense, a "virtual Church," similar to a service ministry (see 6.4.5), rather than a small denomination with physical congregations.

> No, the brethren who mainly belonged to the COG-21, were Sabbath keepers at home. Only a few met with brethren of the same mind on the Sabbath. But brethren from Australia, Canada, Ireland, Sri-Lanka, England, and many other countries abroad contacted us to support this Work and to be a part of the Church of God-21st Century.

The COG-21 will always continue as long as Jesus Christ wishes for it to. Whether through the COG-21 website or otherwise. It is His Work, His Church, they are His people.

I cannot tell you what may lie ahead for the COG-21, or the COG-21 website, or our part in the Church of God-21st Century. Only God knows this. The Church of God-21st Century will continue as long as Jesus Christ blesses this Work. (Eve McNair, pers. comm.)

See 8.2.2 for further comment on McNair and COG21.

Not all of the "rump Global" merged with United. The British branch of **Global Church of God**, being a legally separate entity from its American parent, continued separately under that name. The Canadian branch is still called the **Church of God, a Christian Fellowship**. A small CGCF group in the United States which chose not to merge with United took the name the **Church of the Eternal God**. These three differently named churches, which have the same literature and almost identical websites, are actually "one Church with different legal names in the USA, Canada and the UK, at present, due to legal reasons," according to Norbert Link, who is president of all three (Norbert Link, pers. comm.). Even seen as one entity, these three churches are very small. (The Church of the Eternal God should not be confused with either the Eternal Church of God, another Global offshoot founded by Art Braidic in 2000, or with the Church of God, the Eternal, founded by Raymond C. Cole in 1975 in protest against Herbert W. Armstrong's changes of doctrine on Pentecost and divorce; see 4.2.)

The foregoing paragraphs give an indication of the complexity of the relationships between different splinters of the Global/Living Churches of God and their leaders, made even more complicated by family members being in different churches, and by marriage connections; for example, Raymond McNair was Roderick Meredith's brother-in-law.

Meanwhile, the Living Church of God continued under Meredith's strong top-down leadership, a pattern of authority he had learned from his mentor, Herbert W. Armstrong. The style of church governance should place Living toward the hardline end of the spectrum, though doctrinally it is quite close to United at the more liberal end.

The seventy-eight-year-old Meredith suffered a mild stroke in September 2008, took some time away from work, and appointed another brother-in-law, Richard Ames, "to stand in for him as acting chief executive for the duration of his recovery" (*Journal* 2008: 24). This is one of the very few examples of a COG leader appointing a named deputy, and thus a potential successor (see 8.4).

When I met Meredith on his visit to Britain nearly two years later (May 2010) he was clearly infirm, walking on stage with a stick and giving his address seated, but his delivery was strong, if somewhat meandering. After his address, despite his obvious tiredness and deafness, he took the time to speak individually to several dozen people who wanted to meet him and be photographed with him.

6.2.2.1 *Restored Church of God*

The Restored Church of God (RCG) was founded by David C. Pack in May 1999, splitting from the "rump Global" very shortly after the Global-Living schism. Pack, who was also related to Meredith by marriage (Pack 2008: 27), was removed from Global's council of elders, then disfellowshipped, largely for complaining that Global was straying from the truths revealed by Herbert W. Armstrong.

One of his supporters wrote to the council; his letter is a damning criticism not just of Global but of much of Worldwide's troubled history:

> You are no doubt aware that there is a high level of suspicion and mistrust of the ministry. It is a widely held sentiment, if not belief, that the ministry—even in Global—cannot be trusted to tell the brethren the truth when it comes to matters of doctrinal aberration, finance and discipline of members and ministers. This suspicion has been nourished for decades, the brethren having witnessed a continual series of scandals at headquarters, beginning in the early 1970s with efforts to conceal the sexual immorality of church leaders, continuing with cover-ups of abuses of tithes in the late 1970s, and culminating with the introduction of heretical doctrines in the 1980s. (Medici 1999)

The church's website makes it clear that *only* the Restored Church of God has the full truth as taught by Herbert W. Armstrong. An article on the RCG website mentions the Tkach doctrinal changes.

> This caused several groups to separate from that church. But all groups that left had accepted some of the doctrinal changes taught by the new Worldwide Church of God leadership....
>
> Pastor General of the Church, David C. Pack, ordained in the Worldwide Church of God, and serving in the ministry since 1970, came to realize that no leader or organization was upholding all the original doctrines taught by Mr. Armstrong. Having been personally trained by Mr. Armstrong, Mr. Pack understood the need to continue the mission as he had been taught and to reach the entire world with the same gospel message. Under his leadership, The Restored Church of God was born....
>
> This reorganization of the Church of God began in May of 1999, established not as an offshoot of the Worldwide Church of God, but rather as the continuation of the Church as originally founded—carrying on the original apostles' ministry and teachings. (RCG website)

Versions of this last sentence are used by several offshoot churches on their websites, and in their literature, to establish the direct continuance of their church from the apostolic church, and so validate their authority (see 7.3).

Although the outside observer might see the doctrinal differences between the offshoot churches as slight, for the churches themselves, and particularly for their founders, they are crucial. Shortly after founding his church David Pack produced a 473-page book listing in great detail 280 doctrinal changes in Worldwide following Armstrong's death (Pack 2008), and a further list of 174 "false doctrines" found in the other offshoots (Pack 2001: 5–14). Only his church, he says, upholds every single teaching of Herbert W. Armstrong.

In the line quoted in the previous chapter (5.1.3), "Anyone who resists these changes [in Worldwide] is only interested in glorifying the memory of a man" (Pack 2008: 11), Pack is effectively describing not only the new Worldwide's view of himself but also how he is regarded by some of the other offshoots. One commentator within the Worldwide family wrote to me off the record:

> Groups like Dave Pack, PCG, etc. are, in my humble opinion, nuts. They are true believers. They worship every last sentence HWA ever said. Be careful of them—and take much of what they say with a grain of salt. (pers. comm.)

The Restored Church of God emphasizes the quantity of its output. It has produced more full-length books than any of the other offshoots, or even the Worldwide Church of God through its half-century under Armstrong—and most of them are written by David C. Pack, or at least under his name.

> In this regard, we provide more information about who and what we are than any other organization—far and away—on our websites and in our hardcopy literature! We are colossal in size, and simply unique. In terms of diversity of what we offer, we are the largest religious publishers on earth, and we maintain the world's largest biblically-based websites. We have vastly more material available than the Worldwide Church of God ever did, and more than the larger splinter groups combined. (Jeffrey R. Ambrose, pers. comm.)

Many long-established religious publishers would query the third sentence. Several of RCG's books and booklets are written in specific response to the schisms from Worldwide, and to show that all the other offshoots have altered Armstrong's teachings, but that the Restored Church of God is the only church maintaining his teachings and continuing his work. The boasts about size echo similar claims made by Armstrong in the heyday of Worldwide.

6.2.3   1995: United Church of God

The largest of all the offshoots, United Church of God, *An International Association*, was founded early in 1995, following Joseph W. Tkach's Christmas Eve 1994 sermon announcing that Worldwide was now an Evangelical church and that Armstrong had been wrong. It very quickly grew to around 15,000 members, with around 560 in the United Kingdom—though membership, as always, is open to question; according to its UK leader in 2009, "In 1995, several hundred ministers and nearly 20,000 members formed the United Church of God" (Peter Hawkins, pers. comm.). This is almost certainly an overstatement. Its public magazine, *The Good News*, is a rather milder version of the old *Plain Truth*.

Many individual congregations, whose ministers had already led them out of Worldwide before the mass exodus of 1995, now joined the new United Church of God, attracted by its promised collegiate governance and the belief that they could retain a great deal of local autonomy (see 7.3.1 for discussion on the significance of this).

Those who joined from Worldwide, both ministers and members, tended to be the more moderate adherents to Armstrong's teachings, those who accepted that the authoritarianism of the old Worldwide had been harmful, and that Armstrong might not have been 100 percent correct in the exact emphasis of every single one of his teachings.

They faced criticism from the start, initially from those in Philadelphia and Global who had left Worldwide before they did; they were perceived as having held on until the very last minute, accepting watered down beliefs, making accommodation with the Tkach leadership, hanging on to their jobs and salaries rather than having the courage of their convictions and leaving. Only when it became impossible for them to pretend any longer that the new Worldwide had anything at all to do with the church they had worked in all their lives, only when Tkach actually said that Armstrong had been wrong, did they leave.

Such criticism contained an element of truth. As ministers within WCG they had taught (willingly or unwillingly) the new doctrines, one by one, as they were introduced by the Tkachs. In 1989 and 1992–93, when members of their congregations had come to them with questions, worries, and fears about the new doctrines, wondering whether to follow Flurry or Meredith out of WCG, these ministers had persuaded them to stay under the authority of Worldwide, and had followed the Worldwide leadership's line in condemning those who did leave. But then, when the changes became too great to accept, and they themselves left and founded United, some members who joined United found themselves under the authority of the very ministers who had so recently been disciplining them for daring to question the authority of Worldwide's leaders (see 7.2). Letters and articles in *The Journal* several years later and responses to my questionnaire some fourteen years later revealed a considerable amount of lingering bad feeling over this.

In its first few years, from the evidence of its internal magazine, *New Beginnings*, United seemed to spend as much time organizing its structure, with checks and balances, boards of elders, doctrinal boards, and numerous committees and subcommittees, as in preaching its message. It was determined to get it right. It would have a collegiate structure of church government instead of the traditional Worldwide top-down authority (see 7.1), and instead of unquestioningly accepting every teaching of Herbert W. Armstrong, it would perform its own review of doctrines to prove the truth or otherwise of all its teachings.

Both reforming moves were to prove difficult.

Despite its committee structure, the new United was led largely by its chairman of elders, Robert Dick, and its president, David Hulme. Unusually, in a family of churches with such a strong American emphasis, Hulme is English. United's then UK leader, Peter Nathan (a New Zealander by birth), was also very senior in the organization, and on its council of elders.

United's name was soon to become somewhat ironic. The issue, as with the Global split, was over authority and governance.

United's selling point to many of its members was its initial determination to be collegiate in government—almost a voluntary federation of autonomous congregations—in marked contrast to the strict top-down government of the classic Worldwide Church of God. But either this was a misunderstanding, or the theory proved difficult to put into practice. During 1997 there were several disagreements between individual congregations and the "Home Office," causing some congregations to secede from United in protest against decisions from the top (see 6.4.2).

There was increasing talk of splits in United. In response to this, after a five-day meeting in November 1997, the council of elders issued a "Unity Statement" which included a declaration signed by each council member saying, in part, "I therefore renounce divisions and schisms as a means of solving our differences," and quoting Hebrews 13:17, "Obey them that have the rule over you, and submit yourselves" (Hulme 1998). This was to be read to each congregation on the following Sabbath. Many saw it as a disturbing response to their concerns about the increasing authoritarianism of their church hierarchy.

It was to get worse. Within two months United's council of elders removed David Hulme from his position as president for making decisions without their approval; although he was initially in favor of democratic government within the church, he came to believe that church government by a council did not work: "I could no longer support a governance structure that I believe has failed" (Hulme 1998).

Rather than taking the option of staying within United in a lesser role, Hulme founded his own church, the **Church of God, *an International Community*** (see 6.2.3.1).

Four or five years in, United's leaders were also being criticized for their lack of progress on the promised doctrinal review. Especially in view of their much greater resources, they had published far fewer booklets on aspects of their beliefs than either Philadelphia or Global.

United had started big, with well-defined intentions—and then seemed to give the impression that they didn't quite know what to do with them. There is of course a different view: John Jewell, who joined the United Council after Peter Nathan left (see 6.2.3.1), told me that they had poured a tremendous amount of effort into getting their new doctrinal booklets right; for example, their new booklet on British Israelism (Foster et al. 2001), eventually published early in 2001, apparently incorporated much new research and, according to Jewell, "will be seen as the definitive version" (John Jewell, pers. comm.).

Despite Jewell's explanation, it remains a fact that it took United over six years to produce a booklet on such a fundamental aspect of their doctrine. Rather than showing a hesitancy on doctrinal commitment, this might simply be a consequence of United's heavy bureaucratic structure; the booklet lists four authors, four contributors, and twenty editorial reviewers.

John Jewell is no longer a member of United Church of God. Following differences over doctrine and priorities between United's head office and United in the British Isles, he was removed from the council of elders in 2003. The following year he founded What Next Media International Ltd.:

> We are concerned that a message of warning and of hope be taken to all the world—and all nations. Most of the churches ORGANIZED don't seem to understand that. [They are] mainly concerned to gain members & build churches. (John Jewell, pers. comm.)

Jewell makes a weekly online broadcast, *Letter from London*, on Radio4Living.com, run by former Worldwide member Warren Zehrung (see 6.4.3).

There was to be another, far more serious split in 2010–11, which would slash United's membership from around 20,000 to 12,000 (see 6.2.3.2).

David C. Pack, founder of Restored, states that "it is a safe rule of thumb to say that the later individuals or groups left the WCG, the more doctrinal baggage they picked up" (Pack 2000: 15). United was the last of the major groups to leave. Doctrinally they are certainly not in any way Evangelical, as Worldwide had more or less become by the time they left; their major doctrines are still "Armstrongite," but they have little emphasis on Armstrong himself, even as the fount of their teachings, let alone as the Second Elijah (but see 6.2.3.2 for the ramifications of this). For example, in their booklet *The United States and Britain in Bible Prophecy*, Armstrong is mentioned only once, in a panel listing "advocates of British-Israelism"—and even then he is described as "founder and chancellor of Ambassador University" rather than as founder of the Worldwide Church of God (Foster et al. 2001: 38).

United are far removed from hardline churches such as Philadelphia and Restored. In some ways they could be seen as being closer to what Herbert W. Armstrong called the "liberal, watered-down" doctrines (H. W. Armstrong 1979: 25) of those who followed Garner Ted Armstrong out of his father's church in the late 1970s (see 6.3).

6.2.3.1 *Church of God*, an International Community

When United's president, David Hulme, was removed from this role, he left United and founded his own church, the Church of God, *an International Community* (COGaic), letting it be known that other disaffected United congregations were welcome to align themselves with him. In June 1998 the UK leader of United, Peter Nathan, led thirteen of the sixteen UK elders and most of his members, some four hundred of a total of around five hundred, into Hulme's church; the remainder stayed with United, with John Jewell taking over as CEO. United offered dialog with the UK church, but in a letter to Robert Dick, chairman of United's council of elders, Nathan wrote:

> We feel that such an invitation is very one sided. The purpose of such dialog would seem to be to help us reach your position, rather than for you to resolve and understand ours. Hence our concern over leadership appears to be misunderstood or evaded. (Cartwright 1998a: 14)

By May 2001 this new Church of God had around 2,500 members worldwide, under the top-down leadership of David Hulme (Peter Nathan, pers. comm.).

In its public face COGaic is unusual in two respects in comparison with the other churches in the Worldwide family. First, its publicly available magazine, *Vision*, is completely different in both appearance and content from all the *Plain Truth* clones of the other major COGs. Perfect-bound, with a more square shape (10.8 by 9 inches instead of the standard 10.4 or 10.8 by 8 inches) and with heavier stock and stiff covers, its distinctive "arty" style and layout make it appear more like a well-designed corporate magazine or an up-market in-flight magazine. Its articles take a measured, considered, almost intellectual approach to subjects, rather than the classic Armstrongite approach of preaching the coming End Times or against Easter or evolution with lots of capitals and italics. Many articles are on social topics and barely mention God, let alone strict Sabbatarian beliefs. The only mention of the magazine's connection with a church is hidden away in the masthead at the back.

Second, COGaic make it very difficult for nonmembers to find out anything at all about the church, its size, locations, and even its beliefs. There is a readily available website linked to the Vision magazine, www.vision.org, but the website of COGaic itself, www.church-of-god.org, is not advertised, and requires a member login, with username and password:

> This site has been created primarily to provide information and assistance for members and supporters of the Church of God, an International Community. If you are a member or supporter you will need to register so that you can logon and view this information. If you are a visitor who is interested in learning more about the Church of God, you can explore the public section of this site and if you have questions, please contact us by clicking on the "Contact Us" link at the top of this page.

However, there is nothing to stop a determined visitor from registering, as I did, and gaining access to the site, including the church's internal magazine, the *Church of God News*, which contains pastoral articles and news of church activities such as the Feast of Tabernacles, and of marriages and deaths of members. (This now-restricted online members' magazine used to be mailed to me in the earlier, more open years of COGaic.)

Even within the COGaic members' site, the section on the church's teachings, www.vision.org/foundations/, requires a separate login and password. Once again, strangely, it is possible simply to create this and gain immediate access; there is no verification procedure. But why make it so difficult to access the church's teachings? A COGaic member told me in 2009 that he was concerned about what he saw as the lack of doctrinal clarity in COGaic and indicated that there were currents of discontent over this at grassroots level; he himself was considering moving to a different church (pers. comm.).

This unease is echoed by John Meakin, a senior minister and former managing editor of *Vision*, who left COGaic in 2008 after passing on some of his members' concerns to David Hulme. Meakin became a minister in Living; he and two other former COGaic members now in Living told me they had several concerns. First, *Vision* is a very attractive and very expensive magazine—"But what is it *for?*" COGaic seems to be making little or no effort to preach the gospel, they told me; it is the only offshoot church of any size that does not have *any* booklets for enquirers. And yet David Hulme has made it clear to his members that it is the only church with the truth—which makes it even more confusing that members of the church are unclear as to exactly what that truth is (John Meakin, pers. comm.).

Despite the very modern styling of both *Vision* and the *Church of God News*, COGaic, like the majority of the Churches of God, remains socially conservative to the extent of seeming, to a British outside observer, almost quaintly old-fashioned. A report in *Church of God News* about a training session on biblical software at the 2008 Ministerial Conference reads:

> Although this training was primarily for the men, some of the wives sat in, too. Meanwhile, many of the rest of the ladies took advantage of a most enjoyable tour of beautiful Descanso Gardens in nearby La Cañada. (Orchard 2008: 6)

6.2.3.2 *Church of God, a Worldwide Association*

As we have seen (6.2.3), despite being the most avowedly democratic of the major churches, United had problems with its governance and authority since its beginning. Some individual churches which affiliated with it because of its collegiate structure found that they lost the independence they had believed they would be able to keep, and some later seceded from the church (see 6.4.2).

United also seemed to have problems establishing its direction, not particularly in doctrine but in its approach to the Work (see 6.1.2), and simply in the process of decision making. For fifteen years there were tensions in its governing body, the Council of Elders, as the people at the very top of the church came and went and jostled for influence. This finally came to a head at the end of 2010 when, with very little prior warning, a large number of ministers left to form the Church of God, a

Worldwide Association (COGWA).[18] This was formally founded on December 23, 2010 and held its founding conference in early January 2011.

The extent of the divisions at the highest level in United is highlighted by the remarkable fact that two of the church's former presidents have left United to set up a new church—first David Hulme with COGaic in 1998 (see 6.2.3.1), then Clyde Kilough with COGWA in 2010.

Kilough, the first president of COGWA, had been president of United from May 2005 until early 2010; he and another leading founder of COGWA, Richard Thompson, resigned from United's Council of Elders in July 2009.

In its first report on the split, *The Journal* quoted United's president Dennis Luker that "of 492 elders worldwide, 62 per cent, or about 307, stayed with the UCG. In the United States, 60, or about half the employed elders, left. In the United States overall, 68 per cent of the 381 ministers, or 259 men, remain with the UCG" (*Journal* 2011: 1). As Luker was speaking only a few days after COGWA's founding conference, these figures of a third to a half of United's ministry leaving to join COGWA show the severity of the split.

By the end of February 2011 COGWA was claiming 215 congregations, 108 in the United States and 107 elsewhere in the world (COGWA 2011), with five thousand members in the United States and a further three thousand elsewhere(Hawkins 2011). This would make it around the same size as Living Church of God.

Editor of *The Journal* and long-time Worldwide family observer Dixon Cartwright sees the difference between United and COGWA as an attitude that has divided United since its start: how Herbert W. Armstrong is viewed. "One direction leads away from the role and influence and memory of Herbert Armstrong. The other leads back toward Mr. Armstrong. That is a simplification to be sure. But I think it's a helpful one" (Cartwright 2011b: 3). Cartwright calls these two factions the "progressives" and the "conservatives," respectively (see 6.1.3).

Interestingly it is the "conservatives" who split away to found COGWA, leaving the "progressives" in a much-reduced United.

According to the blog *Banned by HWA!*, at the organizing conference five possible names for the new church were put forward for voting, out of 411 suggestions; these were Covenant Church of God; Church of God, Ambassadors for Christ; Church of God, a Worldwide Association; Faithful Church of God; and Church of God, a Christian Association (*Banned by HWA!* 2011).

The splitting of a church, as we saw with Global/Living (6.2.2) can have all sorts of consequences beyond the reaffiliation of ministers and members and the social realignments as family and friends end up in different churches (see 9.4). As mentioned above (6.1.5), most Worldwide family congregations meet in a rented

18. At the time of writing it remained to be seen whether this Church would become popularly known as COG Worldwide. This split in United occurred during the final editing of this book, and over a year after the final research for the thesis on which the book is based. It is therefore only possible to report the birth of the new Church. All other references to United, throughout, are from before this split.

room in a community center, school, or similar for their Sabbath services. Unusually, the United church in Big Sandy, Texas, formally known as the United Church of God East Texas to distinguish it from the earlier United church there, the Church of God Big Sandy (see 6.4.2), had its own building, where it had met since December 2007. Although the local congregation had raised over $250,000 to build the church, a year later it voted to transfer ownership to United's head-quarters. Two years after that its pastor led the majority of its members out of United into COGWA, and "they suddenly found themselves without a building to meet in" (Cartwright 2011a: 4).

This is not a new problem. Bryan R. Wilson referred to a similarly "extraordinary" situation when there was a split in the Elim Foursquare Gospel Church, a British Pentecostal denomination, in the early 1940s:

> Members of the secession churches were in the position of possessing and using churches and church properties over which they had no vestige of legal right, even though the congregation itself had paid for these buildings (B. Wilson 1961: 55).

The legal complications of schism, with regard to buildings, salaries and pensions of ministers, and intellectual property rights (see 6.1.4 and 6.2.1), have been touched on very briefly in this work, but are worthy of a full-length study in themselves.

6.3   GARNER TED ARMSTRONG'S LEGACY

The story of Worldwide's offshoots is further complicated by Garner Ted Armstrong's **Church of God, International** (CGI), founded in 1978 when he was expelled from Worldwide by his father. (His hurt and anger over this were still evident fourteen years later in his booklet *The Origin and History of the Church of God, International* [G. T. Armstrong 1992].) With teachings based on those of his father, but as modified by the Systematic Theology Project (STP) of the early 1970s (see 4.4), GTA built his church up to perhaps five thousand members, mainly in the United States; many of its members had joined him from WCG, either in 1978 or later, but as the church became established it took on many new members without a previous Worldwide background.

Leading members of other WCG offshoots have a complex attitude toward Garner Ted.[19] Many of them worked closely alongside him in Worldwide before 1978, and still regard him with friendship and respect, even over thirty years since they last saw him. But as one former colleague told me in 2001, "Ted is a great man, and great men tend to have great sins." GTA was embroiled in sexual scandals in the 1970s (see 4.3), and sex proved his downfall again in July 1995.

---

19. During the course of my research I have discussed Garner Ted Armstrong with members of several offshoots.

In brief, a masseuse released a video to the media showing a fully naked GTA in a highly compromising situation. Edited and pixelated extracts from this video were later shown on Geraldo Rivera's controversial TV talk show (Robertson 1997). In the interview the masseuse, Suerae Robertson, claims that GTA tried to push up her top and grab her breasts, and that in one scene where his back is to the camera, he is masturbating while telling her, in her words, that "his execution of the Lord's work was so vital that any transgression on his part would be overlooked by God" (Schultz 1995, quoted in "Ron Dart and Texas Whores Reject GTA—But True Fans Stand by Their Man," *Ambassador Report* 61; compare Herbert Armstrong's similar reported justification of his premarital sexual relations with his second wife, Ramona [4.3]).

Robertson pressed sexual assault charges against GTA and, initially, his church; three years later the case was concluded with an out-of-court settlement. According to the *Dallas Observer*, GTA's lawyer said that

> his client does not deny going to Suerae Robertson for a massage service for which he expected sexual contact, and for which he expected to pay. "Garner Ted Armstrong is an imperfect man," he says. "Unfortunately, he's done some stupid things, and this is one of them. He's never denied showing bad judgment in going there." (*Dallas Observer*, May 9–15, 1996, quoted in "GTA Porno Movie a Hit," *Ambassador Report* 62)

The masseuse said that GTA had behaved in a similar way in a previous session eleven days earlier, following which her ex-husband hid a video camera in the massage room. Although GTA's actions are incontrovertible, and appear to be his own fault, this incident does seem to have elements of entrapment (*Dallas Observer*, May 9–15, 1996).

The elders and ministers of the CGI asked GTA to step down as church president. When he refused, around two-thirds of them left CGI in February 1996, taking their congregations with them. Initially they intended to form completely independent churches, known individually as the Church of God (location), e.g., Churches of God (UK), but in May 1997 they set up an umbrella organization called **Churches of God Outreach Ministries (CGOM)** to help coordinate literature and other matters. Although CGOM is treated as one organization for the purposes of this study, it is still, at the time of writing fourteen years later, a loose confederation rather than a church. Its numbers had fallen to around 750 by 2009.

Garner Ted Armstrong continued with a slimmed-down CGI, publishing a newsprint magazine, *Twentieth Century Watch*, and issuing teaching tapes. However, this was only a temporary delay of the inevitable; at the end of 1997 the Council of CGI unanimously voted to remove GTA from all his positions in the church, including broadcasting and writing. GTA left the church he had founded and set up the Garner Ted Armstrong Evangelistic Association (GTAEA), and a new church, the **Intercontinental Church of God (ICG)**.

In personal terms, Garner Ted Armstrong's career as an evangelist was a down-hill path: from effective head and heir apparent of a thriving, truly worldwide church with around 100,000 baptized members at its height, to head of a church with at most five thousand members, to head of a church starting again with only a few hundred, with his moral lapses always on the record. It is perhaps a tribute to his skills as a preacher and his personal charisma that he continued to retain a band of loyal followers, and to build up his new church. Just over two years after it began, GTA wrote to me: "We are in the process of attempting to compile a membership list at the present time for ICG which I believe is around 2,000, but this is an approximate figure" (Garner Ted Armstrong, pers. comm.).

Garner Ted Armstrong died unexpectedly in September 2003 of complications from pneumonia. Though he is not an ordained minister, his son Mark took over the running of both ICG and GTAEA, together with his mother, GTA's widow, Shirley. This led to some ministers leaving ICG (see below).

The ICG and GTAEA websites still run video and audio sermons by GTA, and although in one place they say "Garner Ted Armstrong 1930–2003," their wording gives the impression that he is still alive:

> The Web Site Office, in simple terms, is the Internet arm of the Work Garner Ted Armstrong is conducting....
> The EA site is the gospel-spreading web site and specifically reflects everything Mr. Armstrong is doing. (ICG FAQ 2011)

One ICG website lists ninety-four local churches, seventy-seven of these in the United States (ICG Churches, n.d.). The church spokesman estimates that current membership is 2,000–2,500 (Chris Cumming, pers. comm.).

Without the charismatic leadership and preaching of GTA, the Church of God International lost out to ICG in terms of numbers. Its website and literature do not stress its history with HWA or GTA, though on CGI's Canadian website is this question:

> While I might agree with much of your teachings your past leaders had real character issues and yet your Church of God movement seems incredibly arrogant at times, so why should I consider your church any further?

The answer includes the following clear reference to GTA:

> It is amazing how God demonstrates in the Bible that he has worked through so many flawed individuals....
> We did deal appropriately with a known leader who sinned and was not willing to take correction. (CGI 2007)

CGI lists forty-eight churches in the United States, eight in Canada, and also churches in Jamaica and the Philippines. An article in the church's internal newspaper, *The*

International News, shows that CGI is doing particularly well in Jamaica, with a congregation of 220 in Kingston, far larger than the average COG assembly.

The article contrasts the ethos of this church with that prevalent in other churches in the Worldwide family:

> We strongly oppose and reject the mind-control, authoritarian, controlling tactics which have been used in the COG over the years and which have really stultified the growth of our brethren and rendered them incompetent to really give a reason for the hope that is within them. We have consciously and deliberately strategized against this evil practice in our history. Sadly, some of the corporate churches still practice these methods—not realizing that they are growth-inhibiting and spiritually destructive. (*Boyne* 2008)

The pastor makes the point that in Monday-night meetings members are free to disagree with him "and are encouraged to criticize any idea which they feel is not biblical. Even fundamental doctrines can be open for debate by members." This would be unheard of in almost any other Worldwide family church.

CGI was never prominent in the United Kingdom. James McBride, leader of COG (UK) and one of the leaders of CGOM, told me in 2000 that the remaining CGI "have about six UK members at present, with a European address in Oslo. COG (UK) are little bigger—we never had a huge following" (James McBride, pers. comm.). The numbers of both were little different by 2009. An indication of the historical importance of literature to the Worldwide family is that although COG (UK) has only about twenty-five members in all, in two congregations, its desktop-published magazine, *New Horizons*, has a mailing list of 1,750. CGOM publishes a slim pastoral magazine, *Fountain of Life*.

A small group of ministers led by George Trent, Tom Kerry, and Earl Timmons, who did not accept the new leadership of ICG under Mark Armstrong, split away early in 2004 to form **Church of God Worldwide Ministries** (COGWWM 2011).[20] This split in late 2005, with Kerry and other ministers founding the **Church of God Ministries International** (COGMI 2011), which by 2011 had five hundred members in twenty congregations, all but two in the United States (Tom Kerry, pers. comm.).

In 2006 COGWWM split again, with George Trent and other ministers setting up **Church of God New World Ministries** (COGNWM 2011). By 2011 this had eleven congregations, but only around one hundred members. "We are very small and most of our work is an outreach ministry via the internet" (George Trent, pers. comm.).

COGWWM itself became a small ministry providing internet sermons and literature to people who do not have a local church: "We are building a network of veteran Church of God members, made up of individuals and Independent Church

---

20. Not to be confused with the United offshoot, Church of God, a Worldwide Association (6.2.3.2).

of God groups to help bring fellowship back into the lives of isolated members who for whatever reason no longer have that available to them" (COGWWM 2011).

Of the post-Tkach schism churches, the churches with a GTA heritage are closest in doctrine, and perhaps even more in attitude, to United, and to the more liberal of the smaller independent churches. In July 1996 I asked Garner Ted Armstrong, when he was still with the remnant of CGI, whether there might be any possibility of merging with other churches. He replied with surprising openness:

> So far as any movement towards ecumenism or cooperation with any of those groups, I am afraid that the major obstacle to all of them would be me. I would imagine that the same thing might be said, however, of the leaders of every single one of them, for leaving me completely out of it, I have seen no moves toward any mergers among any of them, but, on the other hand, the desire on the part of each of the individual leaders (and I am astonished that you said that there are now about 75) to maintain a kind of fierce independence.[21] (Garner Ted Armstrong, pers. comm.)

This attitude applies to the GTA Churches as well as to the wider Worldwide family of COGs. It might be thought that the CGOM churches would have reunited with CGI once GTA was gone. They have much the same teachings, and the same heritage. But as with all the offshoots, the history of disputes makes organizational reunion difficult, though the two churches "have good relations," including joint Feast of Tabernacles locations (Eric P. Morris, pers. comm.).

6.4   THE VARIETY OF SMALLER OFFSHOOTS

In addition to the three original main offshoots, Philadelphia, Global/Living, and United, there are a few other offshoots of a thousand or more, as mentioned above, and some twenty to thirty smaller churches each with a few hundred members in several congregations (6.4.1).

There are at least four other types of group. Many of the offshoots are very small churches, often no more than one or two congregations, which for doctrinal or sometimes personal reasons prefer to be independent of any of the offshoots, large or small, or even of the looser "federations" such as CGOM (6.4.2).

Even smaller, there are "living-room churches" (6.4.3).

There are what might be called "special focus" groups, way outside the mainstream; most of these are also very small (6.4.4).

And there are ministries, which supply services of various kinds to the smaller churches and to individuals, whether members of Worldwide family churches or not (6.4.5).

---

21. Note how the number of offshoots has grown since then.

6.4.1 A Small Selection of Other Churches

Space precludes detailed description of many of the other churches, though a few will be mentioned briefly to illustrate their diversity.

The Christian Churches of God (unusually, an Australian-headquartered off-shoot) was founded by Wade Cox in 1994. It has several theological differences from traditional Worldwide beliefs, the most significant of which is its strict unitarianism. Only the Father is God; Jesus is not God, and Christians will not become part of the God family, a key Armstrong belief (see 2.2.1).

> What is important to note in regard to CCG is that we do NOT regard ourselves as an offshoot of WCG in the same way as these Armstrong worshipers. We only have a few hundred at most that come from WCG. (Wade Cox, pers. comm.)

CCG claims very large numbers of members in Africa.

> I can safely say that we are growing so fast that we would not know the actual numbers, even if we did number the church. The staff are flat out keeping up with it....
>
> We have more people in Africa for example than all of the Churches of God combined in Europe, Asia and Africa. (Wade Cox, pers. comm.)

It should be said that these claims in 2009 are not independently verified by any of my other sources.

The Church of God Fellowship (not to be confused with the Church of God, a Christian Fellowship) formed in the northwest US states when Global Church of God split in 1999. Its books, by founder Harold Smith, are mainly detailed commentaries on specific books of the Bible. It has several minor doctrinal differences from both the traditional Worldwide and the other offshoots, mainly involving details of the End Times. It claims over one thousand members in fifteen congregations, thirteen in the United States, and one each in Canada and England.

The Church of the Great God was founded by John Ritenbaugh in 1992 after he left Worldwide.

> I did not leave the WCG to start another church. I made no plans whatever and never once spoke about doing so. However, almost immediately that the news of my resignation and subsequent disfellowshipment got about people called asking me to pastor them. (John Ritenbaugh, pers. comm.)

Unlike many of the other offshoot churches CGG has a policy of not actively targeting the other offshoots, either with criticisms or with recruitment;

- The new church would not attack the WCG or its leaders.
- It would not proselytize the membership of other groups.

- It would function as a place of refuge, where members could be fed and grow toward God's Kingdom.
- It would not "ride Herbert Armstrong's coattails," as God's truth can and should stand on its own.
- It would preach the truths the church had learned through Herbert Armstrong, the apostle God had used to reveal His way in our time. (CGG website)

CGG is small: "about 400 attend services every week" in around fifty small groups mainly in the United States and Canada, with around 1,500 on its mailing list. Its website disarmingly notes: "The church's ground rules and its emphasis on feeding the flock have almost guaranteed little numerical and financial growth." Despite the low membership the CGG's magazine, *Forerunner*, has a circulation of 25,000.

The Eternal Church of God, founded by Art Braidic when he left Global in 2000, is one of the smaller COGs. He wrote to me in 2008:

> We had about 50 people meet at the Feast this year, I generally don't count because it doesn't matter.
>
> We do not have a magazine, do have about 26 booklets and 4 books plus tons of HWA materials on the site.
>
> We do a bi-weekly tv show. (Art Braidic, pers. comm.)

Even with so few members, this level of productivity is typical of a Worldwide family church. However, Braidic's church is atypical in two ways. First, its books are not rewrites of the Worldwide standard texts, but are on the 144,000 (Revelation 7:4, 14:1–3), church eras, the Sabbath, and biblical prophecy in the light of 9/11. Secondly, in distinguishing itself from other COGs it consciously accepts a mixture of conservative and liberal approaches—and, unusually, uses those words:

> The Eternal Church of God agrees with the core beliefs of most of the splinter groups. However, we differ from the larger and more established groups in two primary ways.
>
> First we are more conservative in doctrine. For example, we teach that Christians are not to do business on the Sabbath, including eating out at restaurants. . . .
>
> Secondly, the Eternal Church of God is generally more liberal when it comes to people. We realize that each person is at a different level in his spiritual growth and we therefore do not condemn those who are weak in the faith, but rather encourage them to study the Scriptures and to grow in grace and knowledge. We host a question and answer session after each weekly Sabbath service in which members can comment on the sermon and question the speaker without fear of repercussion. (ECG website)

This last point, shared by the CGI church in Jamaica (see 6.3), is rare in the Worldwide family.

Many other offshoots, sometimes with very similar names, include the Church of God in Peace and Truth (a Global/Living offshoot), the Church of God in Truth (see 6.4.4), the Stedfast (*sic*) Church of God (a Restored offshoot), the Church of God's Faithful (a Philadelphia offshoot), the Church of God Faithful Flock (a Global offshoot), a Congregation of the Church of God (a Church of the Great God offshoot), the Church of God Worldwide Ministries and the Church of God, New World Ministries (both ICG offshoots)—a small but illustrative selection.

6.4.2 Unaffiliated Churches

The four hundred–plus offshoots include a number of unaffiliated individual churches. One example is a church in Big Sandy, in eastern Texas, historically a major Worldwide center because of the Ambassador College campus there. The **Church of God Big Sandy** was founded, with Dave Havir as pastor and a board to run it, in 1995, a few weeks before United Church of God was formed; it soon affiliated with the newly formed UCG. Three years later, in May 1998, United decided to move Havir elsewhere. Most of the congregation wanted him to stay, and the board asked him to stay on, telling United that they would pay him directly instead of through the UCG organization, but United imposed a new pastor. The Big Sandy church informed UCG that they would need to find a new meeting place for their new pastor and his church.

According to *Journal* editor Dixon Cartwright, who played piano for both congregations at the time of the split, the stance of the Church of God Big Sandy was based on

> statements made loud and clear at Indy [UCG's founding conference in Indianapolis] in 1995 that the new church corporation would be simply a home office, not a HQ, and that the congregations would retain their autonomy; that is, their independence. (Dixon Cartwright, pers. comm.)

This meant there were two "United-style" churches in Big Sandy, the original Church of God Big Sandy under Dave Havir and the **United Church of God East Texas**—most of whose members would later leave United to join the new Church of God, a Worldwide Association at the end of 2010 (see 6.2.3.2).

The Church of God Big Sandy is just one example of many churches which have not set themselves up as new church organizations but are simply individual unaffiliated congregations, the equivalent within the Worldwide family of independent Evangelical churches (see appendix 4). Some of these congregations were led out of Worldwide by their pastor, and never joined an organized body. Others were members of United or another church, then decided to break their affiliation. Some have a website; many do not. Some are loosely linked with a handful of other congregations; others are not. Most tend to be on the more liberal wing of the spectrum, closer to United and the GTA churches in their beliefs and practices than to Philadelphia or Restored. Many, because they do not have their own resources, make use of literature and teaching material from the ministries (see 6.4.5), and are happy to have visiting preachers from other churches in the Worldwide family.

6.4.3 Living-room Churches

There are believers within the Worldwide family who have chosen for one reason or another not to belong to any of the churches. They worship as families (sometimes with friends) at home, often making use of teaching tapes and booklets from teaching ministries, and they go to whichever Feast of Tabernacles sites most appeal to them. By 2008, according to Dixon Cartwright:

> I figure if you count the living-room churches there are more than 1,000 [churches in total]. There are probably 18 or 20 in the area that includes Big Sandy, Gladewater, Hawkins, Tyler and Longview [a small area of East Texas]. (pers. comm.)

The living-room churches (option 6 in my list at 1.1) are outside the scope of this study, though I have received comments from some individuals. However, there is at least one church which exists specifically to provide a service to them, the **Sabbath Church of God**, led by Warren Zehrung, which is effectively an internet church ministering to scattered members in twelve countries.

> We are very small. Though we have had over 50 attendees at our Feast of Tabernacles site, our primary ministry is to a widely (international) scattered internet congregation by way of live services. We have chosen to primarily serve those who are aged and incarcerated. We have had approximately 28 funerals in our short existence. We do not fit the profile of most local congregations. (Warren Zehrung, pers. comm.)

6.4.4 Special Focus Organizations

A few groups, whether churches or ministries, have a specific focus which marks them out from the rest. Some, for example, stress the Hebrew "Sacred Names" by which they believe God the Father and Jesus should be known. Several focus on their own interpretation of the Hebrew calendar, claiming that only they hold the feasts on the correct days; one of these, the **Church of God in Truth**,

> is dedicated to the task of enlightening the brethren in God's Church of the error to which God's people have been introduced. When following the Jewish calendar, sometime referred to as "God's Sacred Calendar," we have failed to meet with our God on His appointed Feast, 60% of the time. (CGT website)

A few in America have latched on to the right-wing conspiracy theories which are shared by both extreme Fundamentalist survivalists and certain New Age believers. William F. Dankenbring founded **Triumph Prophetic Ministries** when he left Worldwide in 1987. A former associate editor of *Plain Truth*, he produces the bimonthly *Prophecy Flash!* magazine, containing long articles by Dankenbring himself and reprinting pieces from Christian conspiracy theorists, mainly David J. Meyer of Last Trumpet Ministries Online. Like other COGs he finds indications in the daily news that these are the End Times; unlike most other COGs he often makes specific dated predictions. But unlike most End Time prophets he is willing to admit when he gets it wrong. For example, he thought Saddam Hussein would put up stiff resistance to US forces. "I admit that I was mistaken. This, however, was speculation on my part—not anything I claimed was 'direct revelation' from God!" (Dankenbring, n.d.)

Just before the US presidential election in 2008, his front-page headline read: "The Dynamic Duo—John McCain and Sarah Palin *Revolutionize* the American Political Arena! What Does It Mean for Bible Prophecy?" In the next issue, with Obama elected President, he wrote a very negative article, concluding:

> Could the FINAL, age-ending world emperor of the earth also be a "black man," yet also be related to British royalty, and therefore a descendant of king David? Could Obama be the "stern-faced king" prophesied by Daniel? Could he become the end-time Antichrist, prophesied in the Scriptures? Time will tell the tale. (Dankenbring 2008: 9)

In a long article in the following issue he spends some time on the "number of the beast," 666, giving calculations to show that "William Jefferson Clinton" in Hebrew adds up to 666, that "William J. Clinton" in Greek adds up to 666 (with a couple of tweaks), and that the new secretary of state, "Hillary Rodham Clinton," in Hebrew adds up to 666. But what of President Obama? He has already referred to Obama as a king, so he adds the Hebrew word for "king," *melek*, to Obama's name—and "Melek (King) Barack Hussein Obama" in Hebrew adds up to 666 (Dankenbring 2009a: 22–26).

Having previously suggested 1998, 2004, and 2007 as likely dates for the End, Dankenbring joined many others in turning his focus on 2012:

> 2012 could very likely be the year when the final "war in heaven" breaks out and Satan the devil and his angels will be "cast out upon the earth" (Rev. 12:7–9). (Dankenbring 2009b: 74)

Dankenbring's uncritical quoting of right-wing conspiracy theorists and the titles of some of his booklets (e.g., the eighty-five-page *Angels, Women, Sex, Giants, UFOs, Alien Abductions & the Occult: What on Earth is Going On?*) cause him to stand out as something of a maverick, and he appears to have little support or respect in the Worldwide family.

Several other small groups focus on the work of one man. Most of these are in America, but one small British group, **Midnight Ministries**, is run by Malcolm B. Heap, a member of Worldwide for over twenty years before falling out with his local ministers over alternative health therapies; he was disfellowshipped in 1990 and set up Midnight Ministries in 1992. Since then he has devoted much of his time to a prophetic ministry and to criticizing Armstrong and Worldwide for their teachings and alleged abuses.

Midnight Ministries is effectively a family business; for some years one of Heap's daughters desktop-published his newsletters and booklets while, unusually, much of his teaching is based on his interpretation of his own and his wife Helena's dreams. His booklets include not just *God Speaks to the WCG* (2000) but also *Dreams From God About the WCG* (2002): a ramshackle house with "ancient rusty guttering … depicts the present spiritual state of the Worldwide Church of God"; "a fat, ugly, spoiled baby" which "slobbered all over the place … depicts the Worldwide Church of God in its present state. Doctrinally, it slobbers everywhere." One of the more unusual interpretations was of "a woman who was naked from the waist up. Her upper torso was tattooed all over with a map of Britain! … They used her bare torso as a screen for the weather forecast on TV." A friend revealed to the Heaps that "it portrayed the vile, lewd spiritual state of affairs in the WCG" (Heap 2002: 6, 12–13, 25).

A defining characteristic of the churches in the Worldwide family is their strong emphasis on End-Time prophecy. Usually, though not always, they avoid setting precise dates or calling their leaders prophets. Ronald Weinland, a former Worldwide and (for two years) United minister, founded the **Church of God—Preparing for the Kingdom of God** and calls himself "a prophet for this end-time" (Weinland 2004: cover flap). In his books *The Prophesied End-Time* (2004) and *2008: God's Final Witness* (2006) he describes the very-soon-to-come events, and states that he is one of the Two Witnesses of Revelation 11 and Zechariah 4:14 (Weinland 2006: 16); he later announced that his wife is the other one (Weinland 2008).

Many of the hardline churches believe that they are the One True Church and all the others are wrong; Weinland takes this a heavy step further. He has petitioned God that the leaders of the other churches will die:

> The most notable among them will be those who die towards the beginning. However, every minister who was scattered, who fails to repent early on and return to God (with me, as God's minister, teaching them) will die during the final three and one-half years of great tribulation.

In the next paragraph he removes any doubt about who he means:

> The most notable deaths early on, which are yet to come to pass, will be the two remaining television presenters in the Living Church Of God. The sound of this thunder will be intensified by the early deaths of the leaders of the Philadelphia Church of God, the Restored Church of God and the Church of the Great God. (Weinland 2006: 107–8)

And after that, "the deaths of many in the United Church of God will begin."

The failure of any of his specific prophecies for 2008 to occur does not appear to have fazed him, despite his writing, "If the things written in the book do not shortly come to pass, then what is written here is false, and I am false" (Weinland 2004: 145). Instead he castigates those who criticize him:

> Foolishly there are those who are quick to find fault by saying we are wrong or that I am a false prophet since physical destruction did not come at a time I had previously stated. (Weinland 2009)

Coping strategies for failed prophecies are nothing new (Festinger, Riecken, and Schachter 1956). In previous books I have summarized the usual explanations (Barrett 2001a: 79; Barrett 2011: 115–16), two of which are "It occurred, but on an invisible plane" and "The Lord was merciful and stayed his hand." Weinland uses versions of both:

> The reality is that the Seventh Seal of Revelation was opened on November 14, 2008, and then 30 days later the First Trumpet sounded....
>
> Thank God that these massive powers of end-time destruction have not yet been unleashed. The kind of suffering that will finally come to pass is horrific beyond comprehension. God is being merciful by temporarily holding back the day when the Second Trumpet sounds and massive physical destruction begins....
>
> This "holding back" is in large part due to the result of God answering the prayers of His people who set aside a time of fasting. (Weinland 2009)

Weinland went on to set a specific date, May 27, 2012, and stuck to it till the last. In a sermon the day before he pronounced, "We're there! We're at the end of 6,000 years of human history. That's what we believe. We are hours away from Christ returning in the atmosphere of this earth" (Weinland 2012c). Three days later he wrote,

> May 27th has come and gone, so how can I say *this is still the day of Christ's return*? The answer is a matter of God's revelation which is spiritual in nature, but having a definite physical outcome. It is prophetic. I did not know that when I stated this was the "day" of Christ's coming. I viewed it in a physical manner until God revealed that it was spiritual. (Weinland 2012c)

A few weeks later he was able to be more explicit, using two further common coping strategies: redefining terms and shifting the date. "Yes, the 'Day of the Lord' is a year in actual length. May 27, 2012, was the beginning of the 'Day of the Lord' when Jesus Christ will return on the final day of Pentecost 2013" (Weinland 2012c).

Several other former Worldwide members claim to be one of the Two Witnesses (one minister told me he has met five of the Two Witnesses), but Weinland is by far the most prominent—though he does not appear to have many followers.

6.4.5 Ministries

Since the major schisms of 1989–95 several new organizations have formed which are not churches but which have set themselves up to provide teaching materials—booklets, tapes, CDs, radio programs—for whoever wants them. Some provide copies of books, booklets, magazines, articles, and sermons from the original Worldwide Church of God, either in printed form, or online, or as PDF downloads, or on CD or DVD. Some of these organizations hold closely to Armstrong's classic teachings, but most of the teaching ministries are more liberal, some providing criticism of Armstrong's teachings or even personal criticism of Armstrong himself. Generally these latter organizations are closer to the revised teachings of the GTA churches and the more relaxed attitudes of United and of many of the independent churches.

One of the most prominent of these ministries, **Christian Educational Ministries**, was founded in 1995 by Ronald L. Dart, formerly in the Church of God, International and before that a board member, vice president, and director of church administration in Worldwide. CEM has a radio program, *Born to Win*, and a newsletter, *Living to Win*; publishes a number of booklets; and has "correspondents comprising a mailing list of 7000 or so." Dart told me he does not see himself as being in competition with any other Worldwide family church:

> Frankly, I have moved so far away from that universe that I am having a hard time relating to it. Our ministry is primarily to individuals of any stripe, and only through those individuals to any church. I have little doubt that I have made a lot of Baptists better Baptists.
>
> We have a hard and fast rule that we make no overt effort to divide anyone from his church. Thus we can claim to be non-competitive with any church/organization. We do make a few of them uncomfortable, but that is life. (Ronald L. Dart, pers. comm.)

He founded CEM because, he says, "I felt there was a need for an independent voice to teach and support individuals and churches. It was compatible with my belief in congregationally governed churches" (Ronald L. Dart, pers. comm.). That last statement in itself separates him clearly from the more hardline churches with their top-down governance (see 7.3.1).

The nonprofit mail-order bookstore **Giving and Sharing** was founded in 1978 by former Worldwide member Richard C. Nickels (1947–2006), who was also president of the nondenominational Bible Sabbath Association in 1996–99 and 2004–6. Nickels left Worldwide in 1975 and was a founder member of Raymond Cole's Church of God, the Eternal (see 4.2.2), which he left in 1978. He wrote a number of historical works including the two-volume *History of the Seventh Day Church of God*, and compiled the collection *Early Writings of Herbert W. Armstrong*; both are quoted in this book. Giving and Sharing still has a website, but no longer appears to be an active ministry since Nickels's death.

Servants' News is a bimonthly magazine edited and published by Norman S. Edwards of the Church Bible Teaching Ministry since April 1995. It contains both teaching articles and news of the assorted Churches of God. Norman Edwards also runs the Port Austin Bible Campus in Michigan, a small residential teaching center for Sabbatarian young adults.

6.4.5.1 The Journal

In the midst of all the turmoil following the largest exodus from Worldwide in 1995, a group of former members produced a monthly newspaper for nearly two years, *In Transition: News of the Churches of God*. It was published by John Robinson, son of David Robinson, who wrote the book *Herbert Armstrong's Tangled Web* (1980). Its writers were closest to United and the more liberal churches in their attitude, though the paper was not linked to any church and gave fair news coverage to all the churches, liberal and hardline, and to their teachings.

When *In Transition* closed in January 1997, its editor, Dixon Cartwright, continued with a similar newspaper, *The Journal: News of the Churches of God*, with broadly the same attitudes. These papers kept and still keep many former members of Worldwide, whether or not they belong to any of the offshoots, in touch with the wider picture.

They have also, for the first time in the history of the Worldwide family, enabled differing beliefs and viewpoints to be aired in detail and in public. Articles and letters in any one issue might hold up Armstrong as a revered teacher and prophet, God's apostle, or the second Elijah; or they might criticize him for his authoritarianism, inconsistencies, false prophecies, and other failings. Hotly debated issues—such as the precise calendar to be followed to set the dates of the Holy Days each year, or the importance or otherwise of using the Sacred Names Yahweh and Yeshua (or similar), or (a perennial favorite; see chapter 7) exactly how God's Church on Earth should be governed—are set out and argued from many different sides.

There is a considerable amount of in-depth theological debate—far more so than is normally readily available to members of *any* religion, alternative or mainstream. For example, in the years immediately following the United mass exodus from Worldwide, there were articles on whether the Old Testament requirement for tithing applies to Christians today (five articles, April–August 1999), while the long and complex arguments of the first few centuries of Christianity were revisited in a series of articles of divergent opinions on the balance of divinity and humanity in Jesus (three articles, July–September 1998).

The letters pages show how valuable individual members find this free exchange, and also reflect a range of stances from the absolute intransigence of "We alone have the Truth; all the rest of you are wrong" to "Why can't we accept the 99 percent we all hold in common, and agree to differ on the 1 percent?" (paraphrased comments).

Not only former members of Worldwide and current members of the offshoot churches are given space in *The Journal*. A radical Seventh-day Adventist (SDA) scholar, Dr. Samuele Bacchiocchi (1938–2008), wrote a number of articles for *The Journal* emphasizing doctrinal links between the Worldwide family and the SDA. As an outside and objective scholarly observer I have been invited to write three articles for the newspaper, including my thoughts on the death of Garner Ted Armstrong.

6.5   CONCLUSION

By 2009 it was estimated that there were over four hundred offshoot churches, most of them offshoots of offshoots, and the majority consisting of only a few congregations. Former WCG members can now "shop around" for the right church for themselves within the Worldwide family. In Bryan R. Wilson's words, schismatic groups "compete for the same public, and frequently appeal to the same sources and authorities in legitimation of their position, thus engendering a competitive struggle to prove the purity of their doctrine and social practice" (B. Wilson 1967: 36). Chapter 9 will explore some of the factors affecting ministers' and members' choice between the range of offshoots, large or small, hardline or liberal.

More than one church leader has suggested to me that the three largest churches are images of Worldwide as it was in different decades: the 1950s can be seen in Philadelphia, the 1960s in Global/Living, and the 1970s in United. Most of the smaller churches fit somewhere into this same general pattern.

A sizable number of former members have left Worldwide but have not joined any of the offshoots. Several of the leaders I have spoken to have added up their estimates of the current membership figures of all the churches including the new Worldwide, compared them with the old Worldwide at its height, and concluded sadly that thousands, perhaps as many as twenty thousand, cannot be accounted for. Even allowing for the problems in assessing membership mentioned above (6.1.1), the likelihood is that some thousands of former Worldwide members have severed all connection with the Worldwide family of churches.

Some of these may have accepted the doctrinal changes, become orthodox Christian believers, and started attending a geographically more convenient church of a mainstream denomination without all the historical baggage of the Worldwide Church of God—why travel fifty miles to your nearest Worldwide church if the Baptist church on your street corner has the same beliefs? Others may have turned to other varieties of Christianity. Some former members have dropped out of any form of Christianity at all; some of their voices are heard, often bitterly, on the blogs that are heavily critical of both the historical and the current Worldwide and of today's offshoots. It is not possible to quantify these last three groups (options 2, 7, and 8 in my list at 1.1); beyond my noting their existence, they form no part of this study.

PART TWO

The Analysis

CHAPTER 7

Authority in the Churches of God

INTRODUCTION

Throughout this study two related concepts have been mentioned repeatedly: authority and government/governance. We have seen Herbert W. Armstrong imposing his authority, diminishing his son's authority, having his authority challenged, using his authority to change long-held doctrines, and being accused of authoritarianism. We have seen Joseph W. Tkach and Joe Jr. making use of the strong ethos of obedience to top-down authority in the Worldwide Church of God to revolutionize its teachings, thus precipitating the three major schismatic moves of 1989, 1992–93, and 1995. We have seen various attitudes to authority in the offshoot churches, from the hardline position of Philadelphia, Restored, and others to the more liberal attitudes found in United and its smaller offshoots and in the GTA group of churches.

As for church government or governance, for some churches in the Worldwide family this is a crucial part of their beliefs; differing attitudes to governance are a major distinguishing factor between the hardline and the more liberal churches.

This chapter draws together these threads to focus on the inseparable elements of authority and governance and their importance to the Worldwide family. First it examines the legitimation of Herbert W. Armstrong's authority in the light of Weber's well-known typology. Then it shows how Joseph Tkach used his authority as Armstrong's successor to change the church's doctrines.

The third section looks at authority in the offshoot churches, and how it is viewed by ministers and members. This section includes comments from respondents to my questionnaire, who were invited to add any observations they wished; many of these touched on authority, both institutional and personal. The anonymity of respondents was guaranteed, so these quotations are not attributed. Although these comments cannot necessarily be taken as representative of former members of Worldwide Church of God (see 9.1), they clearly display the thoughts and feelings of *some* former members.

Finally I look at Herbert W. Armstrong as a guru, in the context of two recent psychological models.

7.1   ARMSTRONG'S AUTHORITY

In his *Basic Concepts in Sociology*, written shortly before his death in 1920 and published in 1925, Max Weber describes four ways that authority is validated, rather than the three usually ascribed to him.[1] These are:

> by tradition...
> by virtue of emotional attachment...
> by virtue of a rational belief in its absolute value...
> because of a form of positive proclamation whose legality is recognized as being beyond questioning...(M. Weber 1993: 81)

These are ideal types, and are not mutually exclusive. It will be demonstrated that Armstrong validated his authority by all four means—but first and foremost by the fourth of them, legality. They will be discussed in reverse order.

Legalism was a hallmark of Armstrong's Worldwide, and later of the more hardline offshoots: "But once the *knowledge of the truth* comes, they must OBEY" (H. .W. Armstrong 1985a: 55). Although early in his ministry he did not believe in hierarchical church governance (see 7.3.3), as his organization grew, top-down governance became a point of doctrine—so important that it was number one on the list of the "18 Restored Truths" posthumously ascribed to Armstrong that he and his church had brought to the world (see 2.4.4):

> **1. The government of God.** When Christ comes, He will restore God's government to the whole earth. So you can be sure the one to come in the spirit and power of Elijah would restore God's government in his church....
>
> Today, the government of God has been restored to His Church. (Worldwide News 1986)

This was a glimpse, a foreshadowing, of God's own government on Earth in the Millennium, with Armstrong ("the one to come in the spirit and power of Elijah") at its head. This model of governance is followed by the more hardline offshoot churches, but not by the more liberal churches (see below).

One of the teachings of Worldwide was that in the soon-to-come Millennium members of the church would be rulers over all mankind (see 2.2.1 and 2.2.3). This had implications for the rule of God's church today—and Armstrong warned

---

1. The last two types are usually combined as rational-legal or legal-rational, but their separation in this work by Weber adds to their relevance to the current study.

church members that any of them who objected to the strict top-down governance of the Worldwide Church of God were being deceived by Satan:

> Brethren, CAN YOUR MIND COMPREHEND THE TRANSCENDENT *MAGNITUDE* OF THAT SUPREME *PURPOSE*? The entire UNIVERSE to be put under subjection to you? That means you are to *RULE* over it all—IF you are submissive, obedient to God and his government over you NOW!
>
> Do you want to let resentment against God's government over you NOW disqualify you—snatch you from God's GRACE and PURPOSE for you, and cast you into a lake of fire?
>
> God's PURPOSE for us is SO GREAT, we need to FEAR lest Satan divert our minds from that GOAL! Satan is subtle! (H. .W. Armstrong 1974c)

The concept of restored truths, lost by the early church but now recovered by Armstrong, is crucial to his authority; Weber comments on the difficulty of imposing new authority "unless the new system of authority was not really looked upon as new but was regarded instead as a truth that had already been valid but temporarily obscured and was now being restored to its rightful place" (M. Weber 1993: 82).

Weber describes the third of his four means of validating authority as "by virtue of a rational belief in its absolute value: what has been revealed as being absolutely valid *is* valid" (M. Weber 1993: 81). This absolute reliance on the *rationality* of their beliefs and practices provided meaningful order in the worldview of Worldwide members, the social construction of their reality; to paraphrase Peter Berger, the most important function of the legalism and authority in their church was nomization, the establishment and maintenance of *nomos* or meaningful order in their lives (Berger 1969: 28, 31).

The second ideal type Weber lists is "by virtue of emotional attachment, legitimizing the validity of what has been newly proclaimed or is considered worthy of imitation" (M. Weber 1993: 81). This can be seen as similar to the more usually cited "charismatic authority," by which power rests in or stems from the man as much as his role. It was Armstrong whom God had used to restore his truths (including hierarchical governance); Armstrong was thus God's Anointed—or rather, God's Ambassador. Issue after issue of the *Plain Truth* in the 1970s showed photographs of Armstrong's travels—truly worldwide—to meet world leaders as if their equal. More than twenty years after his death the magazines, booklets, and websites of dozens of offshoot churches extol Armstrong as God's End Time Apostle, the type of Elijah returned for the Last Days.

One small but telling indication of the reverence accorded to both Herbert W. Armstrong and (before his "ouster") his son and heir apparent Garner Ted can be found in the files of a former member of Worldwide. In the notes he took from sermons and lectures by the Armstrongs, father and son, when he was a student at the

Bricket Wood campus of Ambassador College in the mid-1960s, the young man always referred to "Mr. Herbert W. Armstrong" and "Mr. Garner Ted Armstrong": always the title, and never just the surname (INFORM confidential files). Respect for the Armstrongs was very deeply instilled.

The first means of validating authority in Weber's list is tradition. "A system of authority can legitimately assume validity in the eyes of those subject to it...by tradition; that which has always existed is valid" (M. Weber 1993: 81). I would suggest that the last seven words are unnecessary; "tradition" can be established quickly in new religions, as in other areas of life. Indeed, once Armstrong had cemented his authority in the strict top-down governance of Worldwide through the rational establishment of obedience to God's law (as interpreted by Armstrong), respect for his authority would itself become a tradition—as would the "emotional attachment" of members to him.

So all four of Weber's types, interacting with each other, can be seen to apply to Armstrong.

In a later section in the same work Weber writes on power, domination, and discipline, which he defines in this context as "the opportunity to obtain prompt and automatic obedience in a predictable form from a given group of persons because of their practiced orientation toward a command" (M. Weber 1993: 117). Such obedience was concomitant to the requirement to obey God's law. Weber describes "psychic coercion," "the granting or withholding of religious benefits" to safeguard authority (M. Weber 1993: 119). Richard C. Nickels of the Giving and Sharing ministry (see 6.4.4) wrote of Armstrong:

> The important thing seemed to be obedience to him as "God's Apostle" no matter what. Those who refused to toe the line on any issue, no matter how small, were summarily removed. (Nickels 1996d: 215)

But many saw this in a different way from Nickels: that Armstrong truly was God's chosen servant and so his authority was from God—*and not from himself.* Raymond C. Cole left Worldwide to found the Church of God, the Eternal in 1975 because Armstrong had changed doctrines given to him by God (see 4.2.2).

> What makes this remnant group truly different from the 300+ splinter groups of our parent organization? No one else believes what Mr. Armstrong *originally* taught about Truth—that it comes only by revelation to a chosen servant, and even that servant has *no authority* to change what Christ gave! (Cole 1999a)

So Cole could no longer accept Armstrong's authority, because all the authority he had came from God, and he had turned his back on the divine revelation given to him.

The "prompt and automatic obedience" became enshrined as "hierocratic coercion" (M. Weber 1993: 119)[2] in the very organization of the Worldwide Church of God, not just in the leader Herbert W. Armstrong. It had consequences which Armstrong could hardly have foreseen.

How did Joseph W. Tkach, Joe Jr., Michael Feazell, and the other "revolution-aries" turn the Worldwide Church of God around? Betty R. Scharf, commenting on H. Richard Niebuhr's belief that "a pure sect-type religion is always transient," says: "The original leader dies, and his successor may not be able to evoke the same personal loyalty (if he does so among part of the following, there is likely to be a further split in the sect)" (Scharf 1970: 105). Further splits in the sect were certainly the result with Worldwide, though not always for the reason Scharf suggests. However, Tkach did not engender anything like the personal loyalty which Armstrong had attracted, except amongst his own lieutenants. He had little charis-matic appeal; he was almost unknown to most Worldwide members; he was regarded as an efficient administrator but not as an inspiring preacher. COG historian Richard C. Nickels wrote: "Tkach was not a good speaker, not a good writer, but he was a personable man who knew how to utilize political power" (Nickels 1999: 318). Even Worldwide's own website says of him: "He did not have the magnetic personality that Armstrong did, and he assigned other people to pre-sent the television program and write the articles" (WCG: History, n.d.). His loyal assistant and sermon-writer Michael Feazell says: "Tkach Sr. did not possess the same facility of written and oral expression as Armstrong" (Feazell 2003: 138).

So far as authority is concerned the Armstrong-Tkach succession is more com-plicated than the "pure" type which Scharf describes.

Armstrong had inspired strong personal loyalty and, since his death, still does among many of the former WCG ministers and members. When there had been changes in beliefs and practices (and there were several over the years; see 4.2), Armstrong spoke and his followers (mostly) followed. Although Garner Ted Armstrong had much support, and his Systematic Theology Project doctrinal review was popular with many ministers, when the senior Armstrong repudiated the STP it was utterly quashed (see 4.4).

Scharf lays the emphasis on the person of the leader, and this is undoubtedly true, but this is only part of the story. Although Joseph Tkach had been appointed his suc-cessor by Armstrong, the continuing power of the leadership in WCG did not rest on the succession of personal loyalty alone. The strict top-down form of church government which Armstrong had enforced continued after his death. Despite Tkach's

2. "Corporate domination will be called 'hierocratic' if, and insofar as, it employs, in order to safeguard its authority, 'psychic coercion' by means of the granting or withholding of religious benefits ('hierocratic coercion')."

personal shortcomings, Michael Feazell accepts that "as Armstrong's successor, Joseph Tkach Sr. held the same church authority as had Armstrong" (Feazell 2003: 138). The church leadership had its authority directly from God, and must be obeyed even if it was wrong: "Servants, be subject to your masters with all fear: not only to the good and gentle, but also to the froward [RSV: overbearing]" (1 Pet. 2:18). This was why so many loyal ministers struggled with their consciences for so long to teach what they were told they must now teach, even if they personally still believed the old teachings. The church hierarchy led; they must follow. It spoke; they must obey.

Although the authoritarianism of the Armstrong era was one of the things the Tkach era said was most harmful, and must go, they made use of this same authoritarianism in order to impose the new beliefs on an (at least partly) unwilling church. One former member commented in his questionnaire response:

> The legacy of HWA is to me the most interesting and conflicted of the COG saga. His teachings were undoubtedly powerful and attractive to so many, including me. Yet the authoritarianism which he developed over time marred and negated so much of what he did. *It was this very powerful hierarchy which allowed the Tkachs to do what they did, while the members sat in frustrated and helpless silence.* So many members had not been taught, or allowed, to think for themselves. (my emphasis)

Remarkably, John Halford, who was UK leader of the "reformed" Worldwide for some years after the Tkach revolution, agrees with this analysis, telling me in a 2001 interview that Joseph Tkach was able to use the very authoritarian structure he criticized to force through the changes.

> *Halford:* Sociologically, because our church was governed from the top down, we had the extraordinary situation of leaders being able to hold enough of it together until the rationale of the changes was essentially accepted by the body politic....And so therefore, in a sense, the man at the top was able to rule by decree even though he was undecreeing what had happened. That can only happen in an organization which is hierarchical....
>
> Now we are seriously looking at the question of how the church should be governed. Cynically you could say, Yeah, okay, so you make your changes, then you say how you're going to govern the church. And my answer is, Exactly, because [otherwise] we wouldn't have made the changes, so it's a circular argument: we wouldn't be where we were unless we'd been where we were....
>
> *Barrett:* And *now* we can become democratic....
>
> *Halford:* Now we can become democratic. And there's a tremendous feeling that we need to become...not democratic, exactly; we call it modified Episcopalian, or something—that the Worldwide Church, if it's to stay together, must become more than a set of missions controlled by the USA, particularly since mother has run out of money. So if the WCG will survive—I'd say since, but realistically, if—we have got to do something about our representation and our governance. Joe Tkach wants to be the last autocratic pastor general. And he is taking active steps....

You've got to be very careful before you make steps, that you're still able to function. So Joe's being careful. But we are having active discussions, very active discussions, about what weight should the USA carry, what weight should smaller parts of the group, what should be the governance structure. And cynics say, Yeah, it's because they made the changes they won. (John Halford, pers. comm.)

Joseph Tkach was clearly well aware of the authority he could wield as pastor general of Worldwide, the position Armstrong had appointed him to; but there was another title with a more spiritual authority that Armstrong had not conferred on him.

Yet, ironically, in the very documents Mr. Armstrong approved for the sake of *establishing* Tkach's godly authority, what stands out most is the one office he did *not* transfer to his successor. Tkach would assume all the titles and offices Mr. Armstrong held *except the spiritual rank of apostle*. So Mr. Armstrong never laid hands on him. He never ordained him as an apostle. What he did that January 7 was *appoint* Joseph Tkach to succeed him as pastor general. That's it. (S. Flurry 2006: 36–37)

Apparently this was not an oversight. According to Aaron Dean, Armstrong's personal aide in his last years, Tkach specifically wanted the title.

"He asked for it and Mr. Armstrong refused," Dean says. "In fact, he asked several times." Mr. Armstrong then took the extraordinary step of clearly stating in the final resolutions and directives he left the church that Joseph W. Tkach would succeed him in all his offices and titles, *except* the spiritual rank of apostle. (S. Flurry 2006: 42)

But just ten months after succeeding Armstrong as pastor general Tkach announced to senior staff that he had also succeeded Armstrong as apostle, and a few months later the church's newspaper, the *Worldwide News*, was referring to Tkach as "Christ's apostle" in front page headlines (S. Flurry 2006: 40–41).

It was not just with his authority as pastor general of the church but also with the authority he claimed to himself as apostle that Joseph Tkach was able to make the dramatic doctrinal changes in Worldwide in the years to come.

In 5.3 we saw that some members who still followed the teachings of Herbert W. Armstrong remained in Worldwide because they believed that this was the church which God established through him; God had called them to his church and they had no right to leave it, even if its leaders had embraced heresy and abjured Armstrong's teachings and God's Truth. Furthermore, they found scriptural support for submitting to the authority of Joseph W. Tkach, Joe Jr., and other leaders of the new regime, quoting 1 Peter 2:18 (see above). The writer of one article in the newspaper *In Transition* explained:

Without question, Herbert Armstrong taught, preached and wrote more zealously on the subject of government than on any other topic....

Do you realize that the ultimate test is not our willingness to submit to a righteous government? No, that would be too easy. Rather, our acid test involves the proper response to a corrupt government. Are we willing to be under authority to a wicked leader? Will we see God's authority behind the office of that unrighteous leadership?...

Our calling is to involve suffering at the hands of froward (wicked) leaders....

This is exactly what the trial on God's church for the last 10 years has been all about: being under a froward government... (Neal 1996: 4)

A respondent to my questionnaire wrote:

I was patient with changes in WCG, hoping God would cause a reversal and I would not have to leave WCG. I wanted to respect authority, and as long as they did not require that I believe and practice the changes, I wanted to stay. But the straw that upset me emotionally was an article, I think around February 1996, in the Worldwide News that was very disrespectful to HWA on a personal level. It poked fun at him, implied that he was lazy, etc. That had never happened before.

This comment is remarkable in several ways. The respondent hoped for God's intervention to put things back the way they had been, but he would have stayed in Worldwide, even disagreeing with the new beliefs. He "wanted to respect authority," but in the end the personal authority of Armstrong outweighed the institutional authority of the church.

There is still a sizable group of adherents to the old beliefs in Worldwide—and it is the issue of authority that keeps them there.

We are not a splinter group, a church, or an organization—in fact, we're not really a "group" at all. We are simply active members (or, in some cases, former members) of the Worldwide Church of God who are holding fast to the faith once delivered through Herbert W. Armstrong.

Most assuredly, we do not agree with the false teachings today coming out of the WCG. But we also feel that leaving the WCG—that starting another church organization— is not the answer to this trial on God's people. There is a better way—one that truly reflects the mind of Christ.

We take the unique position that God has only one church—that scripturally there can be no mother church with many daughter churches. And, we believe that God's one church is still the WCG. As corrupt as it has become, it is still the only place where God Himself has established authority. (Climb the Wall website)

Gavin Rumney of Ambassador Watch quotes from an email about this supposedly non-group:

They have their own services, holy days, mailing lists, literature, pastors, etc. but refuse to incorporate into a "church" because somehow they think that act of putting a name to their organization would make it a sin because God doesn't want them to start a new "church". (Rumney 2008)

His source adds: "I know they attract about 600 to their feast site." That is a significant number of people who, despite the "false teachings," believe that the Worldwide Church of God is "still the only place where God Himself has established authority." And that must surely be the ultimate authority.

7.3   AUTHORITY IN THE OFFSHOOTS

7.3.1   Authority and Governance in the Larger Offshoots

Breaking away from a church which holds—or at least, under Armstrong, held—the ultimate authority is a huge move, a massive disjunction from everything that ministers and members had steadfastly held firm to for decades. According to Danny L. Jorgensen, "The crucial feature of fissiparousness is the ability of potential leaders to secure authority for legitimating separation" (Jorgensen 1993: 21). How, then, did the leaders of the three initial schismatic groups, and to some extent the hundreds that followed, legitimate their own authority to break away and set up new churches?

For charismatic authority, Philadelphia's Gerald Flurry simply reflected Armstrong's; Living's Roderick Meredith had plenty of his own; while United, which had stayed in Worldwide the longest while Tkach chipped away at Armstrong's authority bit by bit until he finally demolished it altogether, decided they would do without it.

But charisma, as Roy Wallis points out, is not the only bulwark of authority. "On some occasions traditional authority may provide a legitimation for schism from a group or movement experiencing innovation" (Wallis 1979: 186). This was certainly the case with those who broke away from Worldwide.

The new schismatic leaders were able to appeal, to a greater or a lesser extent, to much the same Weberian means of validating authority as Herbert W. Armstrong had (see 7.1), all bound up together: the long tradition of their beliefs and practices, a strong emotional attachment to them, a rational belief in their absolute validity, and the unyielding legalism that underlay Worldwide's teachings before Tkach changed everything. The reestablishment and maintenance of the *nomos*, the meaningful order that came from their social construction of reality under Armstrong but which had been destroyed by Tkach, was paramount. Ministers and members yearned for the traditional authority—even the *tradition*—of the old Worldwide; their new leaders were willing and able to offer this to them. The legitimation of their authority was readily assured.

As for the exercise of their authority, even the "collegiate" United soon found itself flexing its muscles (see 6.2.3 and 6.4.2). Indivisibly bound up with the practical application of authority is the issue of governance.

While the contention that "Without question, Herbert Armstrong taught, preached and wrote more zealously on the subject of government than on any other topic" (Neal 1996: 4) may be overstating the case, it was certainly an important doctrine of Worldwide during his life. As mentioned above (see 2.2.4, 5.1.1 and 7.1) it was the first of the "18 Restored Truths." In his last book Armstrong wrote:

> The very fact of law presupposes GOVERNMENT. Government is the administration and enforcement of law by one in authority. This necessitates authoritative leadership— one in command....
>
> The government of God is of necessity government from the top down. It cannot be "government by the consent of the governed". (H. .W. Armstrong 1985a: 40)

The same principle must, he taught, be applied to church government.

Yet John Jewell, at the time of interview in 2001 the CEO of United Church of God in Britain (see 6.2.3), recalled it differently. Criticizing the largest offshoot from United he told me firmly: "David Hulme's group have made church government a doctrine. Which it never was. Never has been." Later he repeated it: "They had made church government a doctrine, which it never has been and never was" (John Jewell, pers. comm.).

Was Jewell's memory at fault, or was there a reason for this markedly different interpretation of the past? It may be linked to United's choice of a different form of church government. This would not be democratic, Jewell hastened to point out— like John Halford (see 7.2) he still shied away from the D-word—but would be consensus or collegiate in place of top-down, hierarchical, pyramidal, authoritarian. With this decided, it became necessary to deal with the fact that for many of the other offshoots, church government *is* such a fundamentally important doctrinal point. One solution would be, by fiat, to make it not so: "It never was. Never has been."

Later in the interview Jewell returned to the matter of church government:

> And the Bible does not give one particular form of government. Now, there are some people, and I've heard them do this in meetings, [who] speak very strongly and say that there was a form of church government which Christ gave to HWA, and that is absolute rubbish, absolute nonsense, there is no one form of biblical government. There is a different form of government depending on times and circumstances.

Whether or not he is correct on this is not relevant to this study; but he is speaking directly against what Armstrong taught. He is not the only senior minister to do so.

When United began in 1995 (see 6.2.3) it was with the stated intention of having a more collegiate approach to church governance, rather than top-down.

According to Dixon Cartwright, editor of *The Journal* (see 6.4.4.1), they quickly lost this vision. Writing about "more progressive" members joining the Board of United in 2008 he said:

> "Progressive", in this case refers to an outlook that tends to promote forward-looking views of church governance such as the founders of the UCG espoused at the first conference, in Indianapolis in 1995.
>
> At that time the founding elders heard from church organizers that the UCG would assist individual congregations and members in preaching the gospel and feeding the flock, not the other way around.
>
> But in fact, especially beginning in December 1995, the council for the next decade steadily consolidated more and more responsibility and influence in itself and the administration and also, to significant degree, in elders as opposed to lay members.
>
> This development, the consolidation of governmental power and authority with the council at the top, contrasts with the stated intentions of the church as explained to the founding elders (and others in attendance) at the conference in the spring of 1995. At that conference the church organization was promoted as a way to assist lay members and congregations in their efforts rather than members and congregations assisting the church organization. (Cartwright 2008: 1)

Whatever the original intentions of the founders of United, the top-down mentality appears to be hard to leave behind; the effects of the "consolidation of governmental power and authority" on individual congregations were described above (6.2.3 and 6.4.1). The always niggling conflict between the "progressives" and the "conservatives" in United finally came to a head in December 2010 with the secession of the conservatives, around a third of all United's ministers, into COGWA (see 6.2.3.2).

When David Hulme left United in 1998 to found the Church of God, *an International Community*, the main reason he gave was governance:

> I resigned from the Council of Elders for reasons of conscience. I could no longer support a governance structure that I believe has failed. I have had to admit that Herbert W. Armstrong was right in *Mystery of the Ages*, especially chapter six, where he describes a proven form of government for the Church.... It was also increasingly difficult to participate with men with whom I had less and less in common about how the job of president should be done. A council cannot run the day to day affairs of a church very successfully, and two cannot walk together unless they are agreed. (Hulme 1998)

The Philadelphia, Restored, and Living Churches of God all strongly uphold the traditional Worldwide position on authority. Philadelphia's leader Gerald Flurry writes:

> The *most important doctrine* in God's Church IS GOD'S GOVERNMENT—or the Head. If you lose a doctrine equal to the hand or the foot, you continue living. But if you lose the doctrine of government—or the Head—the body dies unless God can somehow

awaken you before it is too late! As Herbert Armstrong said, "GOVERNMENT IS EVERYTHING!" Yes, YOU CAN COMPARE IT TO NO OTHER DOCTRINE. No doctrine is even close to being as important! (G. Flurry 1993: 9–10)

Flurry castigates the then–Global leader Roderick C. Meredith for his "Protestant" attitude toward government. He quotes from a booklet by Meredith, *Church Government and Church Unity*: "In fact VERY SELDOM in its 2000 year history has God's Church ever had one administration, with one man in charge" (p. 8), and "the right church government should be 'collegial.' That is, it should include a broad representation of all the elders and ministers of the Church..." (p. 29; cited in G. Flurry 1993: 36, 41). This was, of course, some years before Meredith fell out with the board of Global (see 6.2.2) and left to found a new church, Living, without the complications of collegial government and a powerful board.

Meredith's own authority is validated in large part by his seniority and longevity, and so, in a sense, by tradition: "That which has always existed is valid" (M. Weber 1993: 81). In a remarkably frank interview in 1995 Meredith was asked outright, "By what authority did you start a church yourself?"

> I started the church because I had been taught for over 40 years by Mr. Armstrong and certainly others and by Jesus Christ through example, through teaching of the Bible, that we are to go into all the world and preach the gospel. I felt the one that Mr. Armstrong handed the torch to had not merely dropped it but had deliberately thrown it to the ground. It was my responsibility, as one of the three senior evangelists who had been left in the work up to that time, to carry on the work Christ began through Mr. Armstrong. I would have felt guilty had I not done so. (Barnett and Pomicter 1995)

Meredith was in the third intake of students to Ambassador College in 1949 (see 3.2.2). In 1952 he was ordained as an evangelist, the highest spiritual level in the Worldwide Church of God below Armstrong. Over the decades he held numerous very senior positions in the church, including deputy chancellor of two of the campuses of Ambassador College, associate editor of *Plain Truth* magazine, superintendent of US ministry, and director of pastoral administration worldwide.

Yet this same long history with the church also has some strongly negative aspects. During one of the several power struggles within the church Armstrong exiled Meredith to Hawaii for around six months in 1979–80. In March 1980 Armstrong wrote an extremely scolding letter to Meredith:

> But as time went on I began to realize very deeply that God has not prepared ANYONE to take my place. You, Rod, could never take it. I know that is 100% contrary to your own estimate of yourself. You have a WILL to lead, but not the qualifications.

Meredith had established a reputation for harshness when he had responsibility for ministers in America. Armstrong himself refers to this very bluntly in his letter:

> You were a harsh task-master over the ministers. You, yourself, find it difficult and perhaps impossible to TAKE what you dished out. Dozens of ministers would testify to that. You rubbed the fur the wrong way! That has been your life-style!...
>
> Rod, in frankest candor, JESUS CHRIST will NEVER put any one at the head of His Work on earth who is competitive, covetous of power and status, and [self-righteous]. In brutal frankness, you lack the charisma to lead God's work. You do not attract—as I said before, you REP[EL]—people. You are a harsh taskmaster over those under you. THAT IS YOUR RECORD! (H. .W. Armstrong 1980b; brackets in original)

Armstrong ensured that Meredith would not succeed him in Worldwide (see 5.1.1). And yet he became the leader, and the charismatic leader, of the second largest offshoot.

Armstrong was not alone in his assessment of Meredith. An article ten months before Armstrong's death, speculating on possible successors, says of him:

> Roderick Meredith, although ambitious, has little support on the WCG board. His years of harsh rule over the WCG ministry have left him with few important supporters for any major power role. Thus his name can be eliminated.

Interestingly, the same article, imagining the scenario that Armstrong would not have named a successor by the time of his death and that the church would have to choose a new leader, said of Joseph Tkach:

> Joe Tkach, another lightweight, also bears the onus of being indiscreet about his personal life, as well as overbearing in his administration of the WCG ministry (he is currently the WCG ministry's top administrator). He maintains his current administrative position solely at the pleasure of Aaron Dean, HWA's personal aide. Thus Tkach is not a true contender. (Trechak 1985)

And yet Armstrong, to everyone's surprise, appointed him.

Looking now at one of the most hardline churches, the Restored Church of God, its communications director was clearly aware of the validation of authority when he wrote to me: "We do not consider ourselves a splinter at all—but rather, the true Church of God, and the legitimate continuation of Mr. Armstrong's ministry." Their Ambassador Training Center is "continuing in the tradition and spirit of the original Ambassador College founded by Mr. Herbert Armstrong in 1947," while:

> We believe it can be proven that RCG is the only group that retains and actively teaches all of the doctrines restored to the Church of God by Mr. Armstrong. We also continue in the traditions he established, and follow the pattern of the Work done through him,

while using cutting-edge technology and the phenomenally powerful medium that is the Internet. (Jeffrey R. Ambrose, pers. comm.)

The Restored Church of God leaves it in no doubt that "the doctrines restored to the Church of God by Mr. Armstrong" include the hierarchical governance of the church; one of the many books by Restored leader David C. Pack is the 339-page *The Government of God: Understanding Offices and Duties*, which opens with the quotation from Armstrong that "we need to FEAR lest Satan divert our minds" (see 7.1, p. 153).

7.3.2 Offshoot Members' Views on Authority and Governance

Quotations from some of the respondents to my questionnaire add to the impression of authoritarianism of Meredith and other leaders. One wrote:

> I was initially an advocate of joining the Global Church of God ... but I now see that as a mistake. My reasoning then was that we shouldn't reinvent the wheel. But unfortunately, Dr. Meredith just wants to be in charge too much and was too harsh to his ministerial subordinates in the general c. 1960–1972 period. That largely made sure the elders leaving the WCG in 1995 mostly went to and created the UCG, instead of joining the already existing GCG.

A female respondent wrote:

> The reason I did not attend churches led by Meredith, Flurry, Dankenbrink, etc. was those members were very angry and self-righteous. I did not see an attitude of peace.

Another respondent was critical of Armstrong, Meredith, and, by implication, many of the other leaders:

> HWA did do some of God's work, but was so mistrusting and distanced from the common people that he did not see the pain that he also caused. As long as people like Dr. Meredith are going to insist on religious titles, such as "Mr. and Dr.", there is always going to be this us and them mentality that puts people in their place and elevates them to whatever that place is that they are elevated to.

Another criticized United:

> We went with United for a few years but it slid back into the authoritarian WCG ways. Too often it did one thing and claimed another. In the end we simply grew up: we grew wise to the ways of human church organizations and departed from them.

Another respondent linked Armstrong's "God-given authority" to Worldwide's doctrine, particularly on prophecy:

> It is sad that many of the extremes of WCG continue to live on in COGs, but that is hardly a unique consequence. HWA/WCG leaders believed that they were once on a "short leash" when it came to being divinely influenced, a claim many non-WCG others have made. Without checks and balances, autocratic authority can obviously produce devastating hurt. Most WCG prophecy teachings were borrowed or rubbish—when you recall that young men barely removed from teenage hormones in the 1940s and 1950s cooked up much of this end-time "theology" (Ernest Martin/Hoeh/etc.) heavily influenced by WW II and the Great Depression aftermath, or worse, furnished the "groupthink" mentality that reinforced HWA's belief that he was speaking *ex cathedra*, it's not very surprising that it all blew up in the end.

One former Worldwide headquarters employee points out how individual members with grievances were kept in line:

> I was also sick of the misuse of authority and spiritual abuse that continued to be thrown at members. When I worked for the Personal Correspondence Dept. [see 8.3.2] we received letters from members asking for help. But superiors told us to report them to their pastors and tell them to shut up.

Another paints a dire picture of the relationship between members and their ministers:

> The excessive authoritarianism seems to be a reaction to all the liberalism. They want to "protect the church" and this causes some to be too suspicious of members and too hard nosed. When problems arise some people blame others (who then get in trouble) because they are too chicken to take the blame themselves. Of course nobody will speak up and put any blame on the minister because they are afraid to get in trouble, so if you stand up to the minister you are the odd man out.
>
> A few ministers seem to think that hammering people into line is the right kind of government.

A member of the Intercontinental Church of God, the remnant that remained loyal to Garner Ted Armstrong, was harshly critical of the old Worldwide's style of authority:

> While not the only true church organization, ICG shuns authoritarianism and is not operated as a fascist organization, as the old WCG was.

One respondent discussed the nature of hierarchy and its apparently inevitable outcome in the offshoots:

> In practice (not what is written, stated or believed to be true) 90%+ of the splits still operate based on the concept of hierarchical church government. Some are very much

a hierarchy (e.g. PCG, LCG, etc.) while others practice a "kinder, gentler" form of hierarchy (e.g. UCG). But it is hierarchy nevertheless where in the end the leadership/ordained, not the members, are the final authority (even in spite of what the majority of their members think about something).

Most members are "pay, pray, stay and obey".

Another drew attention to the gulf between Herbert W. Armstrong's "natural authority"—or charismatic authority—and his subordinates' inability to carry the same authority:

> Herbert Armstrong, by the way, could be a lovely and warm personality. Aaron Dean still regards him highly, and he was closer to HWA than anyone else. Armstrong could roar, but he could also hear disagreements. He had a natural authority that many of his students tried to emulate but could not, due both to their youth and to their own very different personalities. The church government theory too-often required men of lesser gifts to carry the Armstrong authority forward. It couldn't work. Not always but too often it produced little tyrants, insecure and suspicious of their congregants yet forced by "church authority" to emulate HWA while lacking his gifts (and possessing his doctrinal errors).

We shall see a very similar problem in a very different religion, the International Society for Krishna Consciousness, in the next chapter (8.2.1).

7.3.3 Other Offshoots on Authority and Governance

From the many writings on governance by the offshoot churches, and from what several ministers in offshoot churches have said or written to me, it appears that the great majority of church members and ministers, and perhaps even some church leaders, are unaware that in 1939 Herbert W. Armstrong wrote a long article arguing for local church autonomy rather than hierarchical government (Nickels 1996c: 32–41; see also 205–9; see 3.2.2). In it he denounces centralized governance:

> All authority and power to rule is limited solely to each LOCAL congregation. But there is NO BIBLE AUTHORITY for any super-government, or organization with authority over the local congregations!...

> What has split and divided up the saints in the Church of God? Nothing but ORGANIZATION—which has led to politics, ministers lusting for rule and for power—striving against each other, lining up the brethren on THEIR side, against the other! It is SUCH PREACHERS who have split up and divided our brethren!...
>
> Organization and church GOVERNMENT has brought us only strife, jealousies, divisions, bitterness! It is not of God, and it can bear no other fruit. (H. .W. Armstrong 1939, cited in Nickels 1996c: 38, 41)

According to Wade Cox, founder of the Christian Churches of God (see 6.4), "What he said in 1939 he abrogated later" (Wade Cox, pers. comm.). However, an article on Worldwide's governmental history quotes a private conversation between Armstrong and a newly ordained minister in 1975:

> [Armstrong] said the New Testament reflected a collegial approach to church government and that what he wrote in 1939 was the ideal. Mr. Courtenay said Mr. Armstrong added that if he had had more faith he would have continued that practice, but he "was afraid of losing control." (J. Robinson 1997: 24)

As we have seen the Worldwide Church of God under Armstrong was characterized by strong, authoritarian, top-down governance. Today many of the smaller independent churches, especially those with a background in United or in the GTA churches, consciously avoid anything smacking of the old-style Worldwide authority. Homer Kizer is the leader—or perhaps the coordinator—of a handful of independent groups under the overall name of the Philadelphia Church (unconnected to Gerald Flurry's Philadelphia Church of God). He wrote to me:

> Philadelphia is an association of fully autonomous fellowships united only by a common reading strategy. In the usual sense of the word "founder" I am the founder and leader but there is really no "leader" when there are no followers....I have written nearly every word on all of the websites....But I have no "authority" over anyone but myself. My authority comes entirely from what I write. (Homer Kizer, pers. comm.)

It is difficult to fit that into Weber's ideal types; perhaps the closest is the subset of legality—"because it has been agreed to voluntarily by all those concerned" (M. Weber 1993: 81).

Warren Zehrung, leader of the Sabbath Church of God (see 6.4.3), wrote to me:

> All of us various "splinter groups" are trying to re-establish what we individually believe that the Church of God should be. The problem arises in the fact that many of the ministers, if not most, who left Worldwide are trying to recreate organizations which embrace some of the wrong components and aspects of Worldwide. You mentioned "loyalty to the authority of your Church" organization. That single teaching was probably the most abused concept in Worldwide, and is still grossly misused by many groups at this time. Ministers teach people to "look to headquarters" rather than to God. (Warren Zehrung, pers. comm.)

Zehrung also said:

> We do not believe that "ministerial rank" gives one authority over another's faith....
>
> We emphasize serving, caring for, and defending the weak, over the politics of organizations. The easiest way to understand this is by our definition of the ministry.

In Worldwide (especially at the end) and in many of the splinter groups today, the minister rules and dominates those under him. Jesus came as a servant—washing the feet of His students. To minister means—to nurse, to serve, to help, to lift up, even as in the duties of a slave—like a waiter or janitor.

In contrast, he wrote, there were always ministers in Worldwide who "abused God's people":

Many of the ministers of old WCG who ended up in United, Living, Philadelphia, etc., also sought to control the brethren. They do not like for the brethren to think for themselves or ask questions. Many are elitists and politicians like the Pharisees of Jesus' day. They will continue to split and hemorrhage members until they realize that Jesus came to save all mankind. They are going to have to learn to always put God's principles ahead of their petty politics, and self-serving concerns.

Art Braidic, founder of the Eternal Church of God (see 6.4.1), told me:

In the case of the Pack, Flurry and Meredith churches, we are in disagreement with their heavy handed dictatorial fear approach to church government. We recommend that people attend United when they can't attend with us, but see that church as really not united, and some pretty weird things are taught or accepted there. (Art Braidic, pers. comm.)

Dave Havir, founder of the Church of God Big Sandy (see 6.4.2), told me simply: "A group of us started together with me as pastor—we as a group did not want to be a part of the old government structure."

I asked church leaders, on the record, some of the same questions that were in the questionnaire. One asked them to identify the most disagreeable aspect of the old Worldwide Church of God and the biggest improvement of their current church over the old Worldwide. Havir said "HWA's government structure" and "not HWA's government structure," respectively (Dave Havir, pers. comm.).

Havir's stark statements confirm the impression from the more liberal offshoots that it was the government structure of Worldwide that allowed the abuses of authority over the decades—and that, as stated at the beginning of this chapter, the issues of Armstrong's authority and church governance are inseparable.

In response to the same two questions Ronald L. Dart, founder of Christian Educational Ministries (see 6.4.5), said "authoritarianism" and "freedom of thought and teaching." When I asked if his organization had changed any teaching from the old Worldwide, he said, "Church government, individual freedom of conscience."

When asked which one person he felt had caused most harm to Worldwide in the 1970s, Dart replied, "HWA. Captain of the ship is responsible for everything" (Ronald L. Dart, pers. comm.).

Dart was not alone in this opinion. This was a write-in answer in my questionnaire rather than a multiple-choice one, so responses were completely free. I had expected the responses to be split between GTA and his nemesis, Armstrong's attorney, Stanley R. Rader, who was greatly disliked throughout the church. In fact HWA had the dubious distinction of coming in first with seventy-four respondents choosing him, a little above GTA with sixty-eight.[3] Rader was a long way behind with twenty-nine, and, interestingly, eleven people named Roderick C. Meredith.

The reasons given for the choices offer a great deal of insight into what ministers and members thought of the people in charge of their church. Many of those who chose Armstrong gave broadly similar reasons to Ronald Dart's: "The buck stopped there"; others wrote "Harsh dictatorial rulership creating fear," "He allowed himself to be idolized," and "He felt he was never wrong, ruled with iron fist." Most of the reasons for choosing GTA focused on his sexual behavior, though several were critical of his liberal doctrinal attitude and one, poignantly, said, "Had potential power to reform—selfishly wasted." The criticisms of Stanley Rader were largely to do with power and money, and also his influence over Armstrong: "Con man who hoodwinked HWA into wasting money," "Herbert Armstrong was controlled by him," and several comments along the lines of "Pitting the Armstrongs against each other." Some of the criticisms of Roderick Meredith are potentially libelous, showing that he is still a divisive figure; most are variations on "His legalistic influence on the ministry" and "He was in charge of the ministry and set the tone."

There is little doubt from these and many other comments of ministers and members that the exercise of authority in Worldwide, particularly in the 1970s, often shaded into authoritarianism.

Not all COG leaders seek the mantle of authority. Jon W. Brisby, who took over the leadership of the Church of God, the Eternal, after Raymond C. Cole's death in 2001, says on the church's website:

Neither Mr. Cole nor the current Pastor (this writer, ordained by Mr. Cole in 1997) has ever claimed authority as an apostle, and has never advanced "new doctrines" to repudiate our former beliefs. We do not claim to have prophetic gifts, and we do not attempt to entice brethren to look to us for their salvation. We have no pride of ownership in anything we are teaching. God did not use us as an instrument to reveal that Truth—the work of an apostle. No, Mr. Cole learned all of those doctrines from Mr. Armstrong, the same as did the entire church. We have nothing new to offer to draw attention to ourselves. After Mr. Cole's death, rather than disintegrate as many other groups have done, we have not only remained strong, but increased in stability and viability, proving that our members were never here to participate in a personality cult. We are a continuing

3. The number of people naming GTA shows that, although the questionnaire respondents tended to come largely from the more liberal offshoots (see 9.1), a sizable number still saw the strongest liberal influence in Worldwide in the 1970s (see 4.4) as at least partly responsible for the problems in the church in that troublesome decade.

body because we all share a sincere belief in the truth God gave the Church by divine revelation through Herbert Armstrong. (Brisby 2008)

(Interestingly, one respondent wrote that C. Wayne Cole, younger brother of Raymond C. Cole and most recently a member of United Church of God, would have been the best successor to Herbert W. Armstrong because "he didn't have an ego fit—'I'm the boss, you're not.'")

Although the Church of God, the Eternal, abjures "a personality cult," it emphasizes that its teachings came from God through Herbert W. Armstrong. In an Eastern religion that would make Armstrong a guru.

7.4 HERBERT W. ARMSTRONG AS A GURU

Almost from the time it became an organization rather than just an individual church, the Worldwide Church of God has been very authoritarian, very "top-down." Roy Wallis puts it clearly:

> This centralization of authority will be legitimized by a claim to a unique revelation which locates some source or sources of authority concerning doctrinal innovation and interpretation beyond the individual member or practitioner, typically the revelator himself. (Wallis 1975: 43)

There are many accounts of abuse of leadership during the 1960s and 1970s, and right up to Armstrong's death, which were still unforgotten and unforgiven by former members decades later. As senior leaders—powerful, ambitious men—constantly jockeyed for position in the hierarchy, they would suddenly find themselves demoted or even disfellowshipped for what often seem trivial reasons. Six months or a year later they might be back in favor, and the person who had fired them might himself be in the wilderness. Armstrong's treatment of Roderick C. Meredith (see 7.3.1) was replicated in senior ministers' treatment of more junior ministers. We shall explore later whether one reason for all the many variant offshoots might be the unresolved grievances and lack of trust between people who had worked together for decades (see 9.7–9.9).

Armstrong himself has sometimes been portrayed as authoritarian and arrogant. John Jewell, formerly of United, disagrees. "That was not so. He was a very nice man, very humble" (John Jewell, pers. comm.). He would take the time, says Jewell, to sit down and chat with his staff, unlike some of his chief lieutenants. But others have written or spoken of Armstrong's sometimes explosive anger if things did not go his way. His own writings show clearly that he had a tendency to overreact (see 4.5 for one of many examples).

While this is a sociological rather than a psychological study, two recent psychological examinations of modern prophets, gurus, or "cult" leaders offer models which are worth considering with regard to Armstrong.

1. Betty Bates and Herman Hoeh, the first two students to graduate from Ambassador College, 1951 (© Doris Cole)

2. Herbert W. Armstrong radio broadcast, late-1950s/early-1960s (© Robert Macdonald)

3. Herbert W. Armstrong and Loma Armstrong arriving at Sydney International Airport, 1966 (© Doris Cole)

4. Garner Ted Armstrong singing, late–1950s/early–1960s (© Robert Macdonald)

5. Garner Ted Armstrong, ca. 2001 (© Dixon Cartwright)

6. Roderick C. Meredith and Sheryl Meredith, ca. 1992, around the time he left Worldwide Church of God to found Global Church of God (© Dixon Cartwright)

7. Gerald Flurry, founder of Philadelphia Church of God, 1997 (© Dixon Cartwright)

8. David C. Pack, founder of The Restored Church of God (© The Restored Church of God)

9. The former Hall of Administration, Ambassador College (© Dixon Cartwright)

10. The former Ambassador Hall and the Italian Sunken Gardens, Ambassador College (© Dixon Cartwright)

In his introduction to *Feet of Clay: A Study of Gurus*, Anthony Storr sets out "some characteristics of gurus." He says that "a person becoming a guru usually claims to have been granted a special, spiritual insight which has transformed his own life. This revelation is sometimes believed to come direct from God..." (Storr 1996: xii). Armstrong claimed this, though as we have seen (chapter 2), the elements which made up his "true gospel," which was supposedly being preached for the first time in 1,900 years, were largely drawn, without attribution, from existing religious traditions.

"Many gurus appear to have been rather isolated as children, and to have remained so. They seldom have close friends," says Storr (xiii). I have seen no evidence of the first premise, and the second and third are likely to apply to anyone in a position of supreme authority, almost by definition a state of isolation.

In his early days with the Church of God (Seventh Day) in the 1930s, other ministers apparently found Armstrong difficult to work with. Commenting on the withdrawal of Armstrong's ministerial credentials in 1938, Elder John Kiesz said, "The real reason seems to have been because of his uncooperative attitude....Nobody can work with him." Three other ministers who worked with Armstrong at the time commented on him: Brother Helms said, "Herbert was always the big man and everybody else was the little man"; Elder Haber said, "He [HWA] said that he didn't have to pay any attention to anybody"; and Elder Straub said, "He wasn't willing to study with the ministers, and what the Church of God was teaching....There was no way of reasoning with the man....He had his way, he ordered the people" (Gerringer 1977).

Storr continues: "Gurus tend to be intolerant of any kind of criticism, believing that anything less than total agreement is equivalent to hostility" (Storr 1996: xiii). This was certainly the case throughout Armstrong's long life and ministry, where his letters to co-workers frequently showed his anger toward perceived opponents (see 4.4 and 4.5).

"Gurus tend to be élitist and anti-democratic, even if they pay lip service to democracy" (Storr 1996, xiii). We saw above (3.2.2 and 7.3.3) how in 1939 Armstrong was prepared to pay at least lip service to democracy, but that later he inveighed against it as a form of church governance (see 2.2.4).

"It is frequently the case," says Storr, "that the guru's new insight follows a period of mental distress or physical illness" (xiv). In Armstrong's case, with his businesses repeatedly collapsing (see 3.2.1), this was perhaps more the case of a "mid-life crisis" that Storr mentions rather than a "creative illness" or a "dark night of the soul."

Although physically Armstrong was a small man, and no Adonis, there is no question but that he was charismatic in the classic Weberian sense. In his model of a guru (Storr 1996: xv) Storr quotes Eileen Barker (Barker 1992: 13) that "almost by definition, charismatic leaders are unpredictable, for they are bound by neither tradition nor rules; they are not answerable to other human beings"; both statements apply strongly to Armstrong. His controversial reversals of doctrine on the date of Pentecost and on divorce and remarriage (see 4.2) and his troubled relationship with his son, including countermanding his executive decisions, rejecting the Systematic Theology Project, and finally ousting him (see 4.4), are examples of his volatility. He also tended to describe any criticism of or attacks on his church in the most extreme language, as when the state of California put the church into receivership in 1979: "this most monstrous and outrageous travesty of justice ever heard of by any state government!" (see 4.5).

Most of Storr's other characteristics of a guru also apply: Armstrong very clearly displayed "intensity of conviction" about both his beliefs and his own role. Though he did not "invent a background of mystery" (Storr 1996: xv) as some gurus do,[4] he had a tendency to rewrite his past (see 3.2.1 and 3.2.2), especially in his autobiography:

> His autobiography is highly subjective and heavily slanted in his favor. Those who still survive from his days in Oregon have a far different story to tell. His own son reports his dad's autobiographic account is at least 30% false. One is immediately suspicious when there is almost no faulting of himself in his writings about himself. (D. Robinson 1980: 10)

On the negative side, Storr's model paints a clear picture of some of Armstrong's attributes that we have seen demonstrated in earlier chapters: for example, "Gurus risk becoming corrupted by power" (Storr 1996: xvi).

> As HWA began to proclaim the Petrine doctrine ["the primacy of Peter," i.e., the apostle Peter's—and his successors'—supremacy over all others], soon after the removal of his son Ted, he told church members "they had learned everything they knew from him." He alone set doctrine, and he was "the only apostle of the twentieth century." He was a father to them. It takes only a small step to proclaim himself the "Holy Father." (Robinson 1980: 107)

That might be overstating the case—but from many accounts of Armstrong's "primacy" as the "apostle," perhaps only by a little.

"If a man comes to believe that he has special insights, and that he has been selected by God to pass on these insights to others," Storr writes, "he is likely to conclude that he is entitled to special privileges" (Storr 1996: xvi). This could apply to Armstrong's love for surrounding himself with the good things in life, including hugely expensive architecture, artwork, wristwatches, and tableware (see 3.3).

Storr gives specific examples: a guru feels "entitled to demand and make use of any money which his followers can raise" (see 3.3); gurus "often engage in sexual behavior which would be condemned as irresponsible in an ordinary person"—or at least are accused of this (see 4.3); and gurus "not infrequently exploit their followers in other ways" (xvi). We have seen that all of these could be applied to Armstrong. The leader of one ministry wrote to me about Armstrong: "Too often

---

4. See Barrett 2000: 40–44 for a discussion on foundation myths of new religions.

he didn't practice what he preached and he did not live up to the standards God sets in his word for leaders to lead by righteous example in their own life."

Could Armstrong be described as having suffered any form of "definable mental illness," as Storr says some gurus have? Probably not in the sense of being psychotic; it is more the case that he was one of those gurus who "remain socially competent and reasonably well-balanced throughout their lives" (Storr 1996: xvii)—at least until his old age. Former Worldwide member David Robinson relates a story about someone presenting Armstrong with a mock-up newspaper about his card-playing success:

> You never saw such beaming in your life! He loved it! And he continued to mention his making the front page in Wisconsin Dells around the remainder of the preaching circuit. Of course, Bill was appealing to his great, massive vanity, and we all knew it. But it worked. That is the way people had to continually deal with HWA. He was never quite normal, and Christian virtues were hard to find in him by the year 1972. (D. Robinson 1980: 37)

Indeed, in his later years especially, Armstrong displayed an increasingly mercurial temperament, according to the same author:

> He can present himself as the kindliest and most benevolent of men before an audience— radiating a real grandfather image. He can come across as having only love in his heart and put on the most charming smile. He can laud and praise a man above all others and then turn and destroy the very man whom he has so lavishly praised. He can brag powerfully about a man before an audience, then turn privately, almost immediately, and lacerate the same man unimaginably. As Sherwin McMichael [director of Festival Operations in the late 1970s] said once to me, "Mr. Armstrong's back trail is literally strewn with the wreckage of men who have faithfully served him." (D. Robinson 1980: 114)

Armstrong's vanity, his combination of affability and explosive anger, and the deception or self-deception about his past might perhaps hint at schizophrenic tendencies, according to criteria outlined in another psychological study of religious leaders, by Anthony Stevens and John Price. Although their *Prophets, Cults and Madness* argues within what they themselves admit is the "inherently untestable" new field of evolutionary psychology (Stevens and Price 2000: 200) and shows little scholarly knowledge of new religious movements and their leaders (Barrett 2001b), it does discuss some concepts which could perhaps, with great care, be argued to apply to Armstrong.

The Stevens and Price model of a guru is of someone who is not fully schizophrenic but schizotypal, i.e., displaying some of the characteristics of schizophrenia in a milder form. Citing the *Diagnostic and Statistical Manual of Mental Disorders* of the American Psychiatric Association, they describe the schizotypal personality disorder as "a pervasive pattern of social and interpersonal deficits marked by acute discomfort with, and reduced capacity for, close relationships as well as cognitive or perceptual distortions and eccentricities of behavior" (*DSM-IV*, quoted in Stevens and Price 2000: 209). The criteria for diagnosis are that five or more out of a list of nine features are present. In the case of Armstrong, as a nonpsychologist I can identify four features which might well be applicable—

(1) ideas of reference (i.e. incorrect interpretations of external events as having a particular meaning specifically for the person concerned)

(4) odd thinking and speech (e.g. vague, circumstantial, metaphorical, over-elaborate, or stereotyped)

(5) suspiciousness or paranoid ideas

(9) excessive social anxiety that does not diminish with familiarity and tends to be associated with paranoid fears rather than negative judgments about the self (Stevens and Price 2000: 210)

—with the caveat that these are likely features of many fundamentalist millenarians.

Other features such as "(2) odd beliefs or magical thinking…superstitiousness, belief in clairvoyance" and "(3) unusual perceptual experience, including bodily illusions" clearly do not apply to Armstrong, while two other features are so vague, subjective, or commonplace that they could apply to many people: "(7) behavior or appearance that is odd, eccentric or peculiar" and "(8) lack of close friends or confidants other than first-degree relatives." The remaining feature, "(6) inappropriate or constricted affect," is variously defined as appearing "cold and aloof" (http://www.mentalhelp.net), or "an incongruity between the content of what the person is saying and his or her vocal inflections and facial expression" (First et al. 1997: 20); to my knowledge neither description applies to Armstrong.

The four possibly applicable features quoted here can also be seen more clearly among the leaders of the more hardline Worldwide offshoots than those of the more liberal offshoots. But with only four rather than five such features, it would appear that neither Armstrong nor the vast majority of other Worldwide family leaders can be diagnosed as schizotypal according to the *DSM-IV* criteria.

Stevens and Price also discuss "two fundamental biosocial complexes" with different modes of functioning: one is "concerned with rank, status, discipline, law and order, territory and possessions" and the other "with attachment, affiliation, care-giving, care-receiving and altruism." To label these two "fundamental systems" and "the contrasting forms of social organization they give rise to," they borrow terms from studies by Michael Chance (Chance 1988; Chance and Jolly 1970) of social competition amongst chimpanzees—"the *agonic mode* is characteristic of hierarchically organized groups," and "the *hedonic mode* is associated with affiliative behavior in more egalitarian social organizations"—distinctions which they find "of interest for our discussion of charismatic leaders" (Stevens and Price 2000: 168, 169).

It is clear that the Worldwide Church of God under Armstrong fits the *agonic* model rather than the *hedonic*; this is quite similar to the distinction between groups for which nomization is crucial and antinomian groups, as we saw in the introduction to chapter 2.

Stevens and Price paraphrase Storr on a guru feeling "that he is entitled to special privileges" (Storr 1996: xvi)—which certainly seems true of Armstrong; but this is at the head of their section titled "The Prophet as Stud," which begins with the rather sweeping statement "Though some cult leaders advocate celibacy among their followers, few of them apply this injunction to themselves" (Stevens and Price 2000: 116). Although we have seen that—at least according to informed critics—Armstrong did not practice what he preached so vehemently (see 4.3), it is reckless and entirely unsupported for Stevens and Price to assert as a general statement that "examples could be multiplied to illustrate the truth that...charismatic prophets are notoriously, and one might almost say heroically, promiscuous" (Stevens and Price 2000: 119). This displays what might be called a tabloid understanding of "cult leaders" (Barrett 2001a: 19–23).

Neither psychological study, by Storr or by Stevens and Price, includes Armstrong among the gurus discussed, but it is interesting and instructive to consider him in the context of their categorizations.

7.5 CONCLUSION

Throughout this chapter we have seen how authority and governance are inseparable issues in Worldwide (under both Armstrong and Tkach) and in the offshoots.

We saw that Herbert W. Armstrong in one way or another embodied all of Weber's ways of legitimizing authority (see 7.1). His successor, Joseph W. Tkach, and the leaders of the offshoot churches draw, in some ways apparently deliberately, on different combinations of Weber's ideal types.

Traditional authority, "based upon hereditary leadership and the appeal to tradition" (H. P. Secher, introduction to M. Weber 1993: 20), is clearly visible in many of the offshoots, as it was in Worldwide before Garner Ted Armstrong's "ouster" in 1978 (see 4.4). If the Armstrongs, father and son, had not fallen out, Garner Ted would undoubtedly have succeeded to the leadership on his father's death. Ronald L. Dart, founder of Christian Educational Ministries, told me that GTA would have been the best successor to his father: "Obviously, the logical successor, who, if not cannibalized would have retained the loyalty of the membership and who would not have trashed the doctrinal structure" (Ronald L. Dart, pers. comm.). Joseph W. Tkach passed on the new Worldwide to his son Joe Jr., who wrote about their remaking of the church in *Transformed by Truth*. On Garner Ted Armstrong's death the practical leadership of the Intercontinental Church of God passed to his son Mark, despite him not being an ordained minister (see 6.3).

A number of other offshoots are effectively "family businesses." Stephen Flurry is often the spokesman for Philadelphia instead of his father, Gerald Flurry, and wrote the book *Raising the Ruins*; Gerald Flurry's son-in-law Wayne Turgeon is also very senior in the church (see 6.2.1). Leader Robert Ardis's sons Gerry and Jon are senior in the Church of God's Faithful (see 6.2.1.1). Richard T. Ritenbaugh is an elder in his father John W. Ritenbaugh's Church of the Great God, and managing editor of the church's magazine *Forerunner* (see 6.4.1). A similar pattern can be seen in several other offshoots. Perhaps the ultimate case of keeping it in the family is Ronald Weinland; some months after he named himself one of the Two Witnesses of Revelation 11, he named his wife as the other (see 6.4.4).

The fact that he was Herbert W. Armstrong's appointed successor overcame any lack of personal charisma for Joseph W. Tkach, who was able to make use of the strict top-down authority instituted by Armstrong to overturn all of his teachings (see 5.1.2 and 7.2).

Reflected charisma is a useful aid to legitimation for leaders like Roderick C. Meredith, who are able to point to their long history with and closeness to Armstrong (see 6.2.2 and 7.3.1). Others, who like Gerald Flurry were fairly low down the hierarchy under Armstrong, claim (like him) a special commission from God, even to the extent of being prophesied in the Bible. By naming his church's college after Armstrong and purchasing sculptures and candelabra commissioned by him for Worldwide, Flurry is effectively stepping into Armstrong's shoes (see 6.2.1 and 7.3.1). David C. Pack is doing much the same, visibly outdoing Armstrong and Worldwide with his very traditional TV studio and the number of books he has written (see 6.2.2.1); even his 565-page biography (Vol. 1) is slightly larger than Volume 1 of Armstrong's autobiography at 510 pages (1967 ed.) or 540 pages (1973 ed.).

Flurry, Pack, and other leaders of churches at the hardline end of the spectrum are strong, visible, *personal* leaders, with authority and power resting in them as charismatic individuals; Meredith's problem in his original Global Church was that he had allowed the board to have too much power (see 6.2.2). The interesting question of what will happen to their churches when these leaders eventually die will be explored briefly in 8.4.

In contrast, the more liberal churches, mainly from the United and GTA church families, lay far less stress on the leader as the individual figure of authority. They argue that the top-down governance espoused by Armstrong is not found in the Bible; they elect their leaders and govern by committee. Indeed, in its early years United was renowned for its setting up of committees and subcommittees and systems of checks and balances (see 6.2.3)—"an increasing tendency in modern society to displace the rule of law by a more bureaucratized system of administration" (H. P. Secher, introduction to M. Weber 1993: 21).

The difference between the leaders of the hardline and the more liberal offshoots could also be described more simply as the difference between prophets (charismatic and traditional validation of authority) and pastors (rational and legal validation).

CHAPTER 8

After the Founder Dies

How Movements Change

INTRODUCTION

In 1980 an article in the American news magazine *The Atlantic* came to a prophetic conclusion:

> What does Herbert Armstrong want? A year ago, he told Wayne Cole he wanted to appoint a board of directors that would take control after his death, working as an administrative team until a clear leader emerged. Though susceptible of deteriorating into a power struggle, this approach would probably have the best chance of accomplishing, in a more or less orderly fashion, what Max Weber called "the routinization of charisma." In fact, however, the elder Armstrong has moved in precisely the opposite direction, restructuring the ministry to transform what was once an elaborate hierarchy into a system in which each local minister is answerable directly to, and only to, Herbert W. Armstrong, Pastor General. As has been his custom for almost half a century, he legitimates the arrangement by proclaiming it to be the purest form of the Government of God. Those who continue to regard Mr. Armstrong as God's Only Apostle for our Time will accept his claim and follow him to the end. But when the end comes, as it must, the WCG is certain to experience devastating trauma. (William Martin 1980: 65)

What happens when the founder of a religion dies?

In most organizational structures, when the person at the top of the hierarchy leaves, whether through resignation, retirement, or death, there is an established procedure for his or her replacement. In the corporate world a new chairman or managing director is appointed, usually following a formal selection process.

In the more rarefied areas of monarchy and religion, procedures have developed over centuries. When a monarch dies the next in line will be ready to step forward:

"The King is dead!" "Long live the King!" The role of monarch continues, independent of the person. In the past there might sometimes have been confusion over who the next incumbent should be, possibly with a war of succession between the followers of rival claimants. But the position of monarch remains.

The head of the Roman Catholic Church remains in post until his death, at which point there is a conclave to elect his successor. Inconclusive ballots result in black smoke issuing from the chimney over the Sistine Chapel; the final conclusive ballot results in white smoke and the announcement "Habemus papam" (Greeley 1979: 156, 221).

The spiritual head of Tibetan Buddhism, the Dalai Lama, also continues in post until his death—after which there is a search for his reincarnation in a young boy (Smart 1989: 92).

There is always a monarch; there is always a pope; there is always a Dalai Lama. The role is not dependent on the incumbent. These institutions have continuity built in.

The same does not apply to the founder of a religion. It cannot; the founder of a new religion, a prophet figure or guru, is almost by definition outside the normal rules of society. And once he or she has died, the successor cannot also be founder, but must simply be leader.

The Worldwide Church of God is by no means unique in having a problematic succession, or in suffering schism following the death of the founder and the appointment of his successor. Roy Wallis mentions "the impressionistically well-founded observations that (1) schisms tend to be characteristic of the early stages of a movement's life cycle, and that (2) schism occurs disproportionately often on the death of a charismatic leader.... They relate to periods when the authority structure of a movement is, or becomes, unstable" (Wallis 1979: 187). Worldwide was well-established by the time of Armstrong's death, so Wallis's first observation is not relevant; but his second is the subject of this entire study.

This chapter presents a typological model for the different directions a religious movement can move in after the death of its founder (8.1). It offers examples of the ideal types from a number of religions, old, nineteenth-century, and new (8.2), and examines Worldwide after the death of Herbert W. Armstrong in the context of the model, exploring the many complex changes within both Worldwide itself and some of the offshoots.[1] It then considers a number of factors which might affect a movement after the death of its founder (8.3). Because many changes in a movement result from the (perhaps changing) attitude to the founder himself after his death, and this depends partly on his authority and the legitimation of his authority, this discussion follows naturally from chapter 7.

1. Some parts of this chapter first appeared in a less developed form in chapter 6, "After the Prophet Dies," of my book *The New Believers: A Survey of Sects, Cults and Alternative Religions* (Barrett 2001a), written at the beginning of my research for this study. I have included some references here to more detailed information on other religious movements in that book and in my more recent *A Brief Guide to Secret Religions* (Barrett 2011) where relevant.

8.1 A MODEL OF HOW MOVEMENTS CAN CHANGE AFTER THEIR FOUNDER'S DEATH

It could be argued that the most crucial point in the development of any religion is not its foundation, nor the initial revelation of its founder; it is the founder's death.

The death of the founder precipitates the inevitable change from charismatic to rational-legal authority (M. Weber 1948: 295–301),[2] from personal to organizational power, from a prophetic to a pastoral type of leadership (see 7.5). What happens to a movement after its founder dies is to a large extent bound up with how successfully it manages this transition. While the founder remains alive, he or she is the focal point of the movement;[3] as "a group with a very strong focus on one person" (see appendix 1), it could be labeled a cult, or at least a personality cult. After his death, if it does not fade away completely with the loss of its charismatic leader, does it remain focused on him, or does it move on, mature, and "graduate" from that earlier state to being a religion? It could become something quite different from what its founder had ever intended, or it could fragment into a dozen or more competing sects; in the case of Worldwide it did both.

Wise founders, aware of the inevitability of their death and desiring that their teachings should continue, may plan with their senior followers for how their movement will continue to function after their death. Sometimes this works well; in other cases it seems to add to the eventual confusion.

The model outlined in this chapter is an attempt to map the main directions in which a new religion can move following the death of its founder. It looks at the conjunction of two variables (see Figure 8.1). First, movements can stay broadly as they are (stasis) or they can change. Second, in each case the outcome can be either stable or unstable. Stable stasis leads to continuation (A); unstable stasis to dissolution (B).

	STASIS	CHANGE
STABILITY	A. Continuation (Stays essentially the same)	C. Reform/Revolution (New leader, new directions)
INSTABILITY	B. Dissolution (Fades and dies)	D. Schism (Competing offshoots)

Figure 8.1 After the Founder Dies: A Model

2. If this has not already occurred while the leader is still alive—see the unusual case of Elizabeth Clare Prophet at 8.2.1.
3. Some new religions are founded by women; the male pronouns used for simplicity in this discussion should be taken to include female founders as well.

Stable change leads to reform, which may be seen as revolution (C); unstable change to schism or fragmentation (D).

- There may be a transitional period, short or long, of uncertainty, even confusion, before the movement begins to settle in one direction or another.
- These four outcomes are not mutually exclusive. For example, schisms (D) may occur under the circumstances of (A), (B), or (C), or combinations of these.
- Type (A) accepts that some changes will be inevitable, such as an end to new teachings from the founder and changes in the hierarchy, and also allows for gradual change through evolution over the years.
- Type (B) may be relatively quick (a few months, or a year or two) or relatively slow (for example, until the death of the last member alive at the founder's death).
- It is possible for the original movement either to continue as before (A) or to fade and die (B) while a splinter group (D) under a powerful new leader (C) thrives.

8.1.1 Convergence and Divergence

Another dimension could be added to this model: convergence with (E) or divergence from (F) more mainstream society and religious beliefs and practices (see Figure 8.2). Such convergence in Christian sects has been called "denominationalization" (B. Wilson 1990: 109). Convergence and divergence are movements toward greater orthodoxy or greater heterodoxy, respectively (see appendix 1).

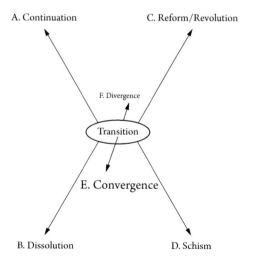

Figure 8.2 Convergence and Divergence

After his death a movement might choose to downplay the person of their founder in favor of his teachings; there might be some embarrassment at some of his excesses, and now that he is gone there is the opportunity for some of his more idiosyncratic ideas or practices to be quietly dropped. And once that has happened, it might turn out that the underlying doctrines of the movement are not so far removed from the mainstream after all.

In contrast, a movement might, at least in the short term, move further away from the mainstream after its founder's death. With the founder gone a new leader, or the members in general, in seeking to maintain their identity, their social construction of reality (Berger and Luckmann 1966), might increase the emphasis on unusual aspects of his teachings that previously were relatively minor.

But if the movement has moved closer to the mainstream, as the Worldwide Church of God did under Joseph W. Tkach, this in itself can be a trigger for schism:

> As religious groups move into range of the largest niches and abandon their original market niche(s), they tend to suffer schisms as sect movements break away to serve members with higher-tension preferences. (Stark and Finke 2000: 205)

The processes of convergence and divergence of movements used in this model are also broadly comparable to Roy Wallis's types of world-affirming and world-rejecting groups, respectively (Wallis 2003).

8.2   THE MODEL APPLIED TO VARIOUS NEW RELIGIONS

Models such as this can be useful for both analysis and prediction. On the basis of this model it could be possible both to explore reasons why different movements have reacted in different ways and to project possible outcomes for movements whose founders are still alive. In this study the model is used descriptively, to categorize religious organizational change using ideal types.

The four categories will be illustrated briefly by examples from several new religious movements, before the model is applied to the Worldwide Church of God.

8.2.1   A: Continuation

In several new religious movements the founder sought to set up a safe-continuation scheme, with various degrees of success.

The exact details of the transition from founder L. Ron Hubbard to David Miscavige as the power behind the Church of Scientology may never be known. Miscavige was certainly a favorite of Hubbard, and was one of the few to spend time with him during his last years, but we cannot know for sure whether his taking over the reins of power was planned between them as the church asserts (Church of Scientology International 1994: 31) or was a palace coup, as some critics have claimed (Atack 1990: 286–88, 320; Lamont 1986: 94–98).

Before Hubbard's death in 1986 two external organizations were set up, the Religious Technology Center (RTC), to have control over the church's doctrine to ensure its purity, and Author Services Incorporated (ASI), to control the publication of all of Hubbard's written works, fiction and nonfiction. Both were ultimately in the hands of Miscavige. With the structure set up, the changes began in 1982–83 with the weeding out of the old guard; Hubbard's well-accepted heir-apparent, David Mayo, was declared a Suppressive Person (someone perceived as an enemy of Scientology) and left the church. Immediately after Hubbard's death, his close confidant Pat Broeker said Hubbard had appointed him "first loyal officer"; within a year he too had been ousted (Duignan and Tallant 2008: 102, 147; Atack 1990: 354, 362). By removing credible opposition and by maintaining complete control over the purity of the "Tech," the practical application of the teachings, through RTC and ASI, Hubbard's successor at the head of the religion could ensure that Scientology, as set up by its founder, is protected against change (Barrett 2001a: 468–70).

Three movements which planned for what would happen after their leaders' deaths have successfully managed change, through evolution rather than revolution. Long before David Berg, founder of The Family (formerly the Children of God), died in 1994, his wife Maria had been accepted as the next prophet and leader. The running of the movement had also been democratized through the setting up of a Charter for all Family homes. "Maria (Karen Zerby) and Peter (Steve Kelly) are the co-spiritual leaders and administrative overseers of The Family International" (pers. comm.), but authority is actually vested in a structured group of people, World Services. "It may be argued that the ability of the Children of God/ The Family to adapt to change over time has contributed significantly to its survival into the 1990s" (S. Wright 1994: 123)—and beyond.

Richard Lawrence, British leader of one of the oldest UFO religions, the Aetherius Society, told me that as their founder, George King, grew older, they deliberately planned for the future: "We looked at other groups when their leader died, and learnt from it" (Barrett 2001a: 387). They already had an ecclesiastical structure in place, and so far as the society's leadership and organization is concerned, this has simply continued, though Lawrence admitted, "It's probably more democratic since he died." Since King's death in 1997 the teachings and practice have continued much the same, with perhaps a slightly stronger emphasis on spiritual healing. As there will be no more Cosmic Transmissions from Ascended Masters in the postprophetic phase of the movement, the balance between the Theosophical roots and the New Age aspects of the Aetherius Society has swung more toward the latter; Lawrence has become a regular speaker at Mind, Body, Spirit events. (See Barrett 2011: 119–26 for further details.)

Elizabeth Clare Prophet (1939–2009) took over the Theosophy-inspired Summit Lighthouse after her husband's death in 1973, turning it into the publishing house of a new movement, Church Universal and Triumphant, with herself as the Messenger, receiving communications from Ascended Masters. This was a smooth transition from husband to wife, leading to a greatly expanded and more publicly visible religion under her leadership. Diagnosed with Alzheimer's disease in the mid-1990s, Prophet retired from active leadership, appointing a management consultant as president of the church to handle the transition from charismatic prophetic leadership to rational-legal leadership under a board of directors, with the stated intention that the church would move safely and smoothly (A: continuation) into a new phase of its existence (Kelley 1998; Steinman 1999). The church had thus already been in a postprophetic phase for some years when she died in 2009. Although there are means by which the Council of Elders can "recognize ongoing revelation through a new Messenger or Vicar of Christ, should the Ascended Masters choose to anoint an individual to one of these offices in the future" (pers. comm.), over a year after her death they had not done so—though a few very small splinter groups have formed around people claiming to be new Messengers (D: schism; see Barrett 2011: 70–81 for further details).

But two other movements had very different outcomes from their founders' attempts to "fix the future."

Christian Science has been cited as "a sociological model for routinization of charisma" (Simmons 1991: 109). Perhaps because of the number of New Thought schisms during her life, founder Mary Baker Eddy wanted to protect the church she established in 1879 against change. She set up a board of directors to run the church after her passing, and spent fifteen years working and reworking *The Manual of the Mother Church* (published in 1895), setting firmly in stone how the church should be run—the order of services, disciplinary procedures, and so on. She wrote to the board in 1903, seven years before her death:

> Never abandon the By-laws nor the denominational government of the Mother Church. If I am not personally with you, the Word of God, and my instructions in the By-laws have led you hitherto and will remain to guide you safely on. (quoted in Peel 1977: 228)

There was a schism at her death, following a court case establishing the authority of the self-perpetuating board, and several offshoot movements have broken away since, mainly in rebellion against the strict rule of the church leaders, or out of a desire for modernization (Barrett 2001a: 180, 185). But for the church itself, one result of Mrs. Eddy's strictures is that for the last century Christian Science has been constitutionally unable to modify itself to adapt to changes in society. The religion still exists, but it now has the appearance of a nineteenth-century relic out of its time, and its numbers are falling; it survived the twentieth century, but it remains to be seen how far it can make it through the twenty-first century without accepting change; a nonevolving type A could become a moribund type B.

In the case of the Hare Krishna devotees' movement ISKCON (International Society for Krishna Consciousness), despite the best intentions of the founder, there was a greatly extended period of chaotic transition following his death before things settled down in the form of reformed continuation. Before his death in 1977 the founder of ISKCON, A. C. Bhaktivedanta Swami Prabhupada, appointed a twenty-strong international Governing Body Commission (GBC) to be the management group running the movement after his death, including eleven initiating gurus, or sanyassins, to have spiritual authority. In the event, immature and ambitious gurus took too much power, claiming supremacy over the non-guru members of the GBC, and the whole movement degenerated into chaos for several years before a reform group began, in 1984, to sort out the mess. ISKCON's then UK communications manager, Bhagavat Dharma, told me in 1995, "That was really an error, to do that.... Looking back, we can see now that Prabhupada wanted the governing body to have authority, without anyone above them" (Barrett 2001a: 284). The problem stemmed from a confusion and conflict between the charismatic authority of guru-like sanyassins, and a committee-led management structure—the rational-legal authority type necessary for postprophetic continuity.

> This problem concerned the way in which the position of initiating guru had become institutionalized in ISKCON after Prabhupada. The problem arose when the conception of guru was implicitly based on a traditional model of an inspired, charismatic spiritual autocrat, an absolute and autonomously decisive authority, around whom an institution takes shape as the natural extension and embodiment of his charisma. Indeed, Srila Prabhupada himself was such a guru. Yet starting in 1970, Srila Prabhupada had worked diligently to establish a quite different sort of leadership structure in ISKCON, a structure he repeatedly emphasized that would continue after him. (Svarupa dasa 1994: 25)

The moral, whose irony would not have been lost on Herbert W. Armstrong, is that however careful the founder is to set up a safe succession, the reliability of one's successors cannot be guaranteed.

8.2.2 B: Dissolution

Some movements fade away and die, for various reasons, as we shall see in two very different examples.

After the death of the millenarian prophetess Joanna Southcott (1750–1814) after failing to give birth to the new Christ Child, her followers continued to make claims about her for some years; but without her inspiration and prophecies there was no real substance to any of her successors, and eventually interest faded away—though not quite entirely. Today, though as more of a historical curiosity than a religion, the Panacea Society in Bedford, UK, guards Joanna Southcott's box, which contains, they claim, her prophecies and the secret of world peace; the box may only be opened in the presence of twenty-four bishops of the Church of England (Katz and Popkin 1999: 115–18; Sladek 1978: 318–19). But the fervent devotion to Southcott and her millenarian teachings died with her immediate followers; the society today is simply a small charity owning and administering some property.

The Catholic Apostolic Church failed less because of the death of its founders—there were several—than because it set up a one-off system of twelve apostles in expectation of the return of Christ in 1855, with no means of appointing new apostles. The church kept going, but after the last apostle died in 1901 no further priests could be ordained; the last active priest died in 1970, and the few remaining members merged into the Church of England. However, the German church broke away in 1863 (D: schism), appointing new apostles, and today the New Apostolic Church claims to be the fourth largest church in Germany (David Middleton, pers. comm.). (See Barrett 2011: 70–81 for further details.)

Some of the smallest offshoots from Worldwide have already died away with the deaths of their leaders, though in the Information Age they have left sometimes eerie echoes behind. In March 2011 the website of the Church of God 21st Century still had a message from founder Raymond F. McNair reading: "I am happy to report that my health has greatly improved." McNair died in October 2008 (see 6.2.2).

McNair's widow told me, "The COG-21 will always continue as long as Jesus Christ wishes for it to" (Eve McNair, pers. comm.), but as its ministry was largely the distribution of newsletters by McNair, which had obviously now ceased, all that really remained were the archive of his old articles and the memories of those who knew him. COG21 is not alone; the untended websites of several other small churches and ministries in the Worldwide family also give the impression that their founders are still alive and their work is still active, when the sites have clearly not been updated for several years and emails to the sites are not responded to. In other cases websites of small offshoots which I accessed early in my research had vanished by the end of it, the only trace remaining of those churches being in old lists of offshoots.

Larger offshoots have survived the deaths of their founders (see 6.3 and 7.3.3)—though a casual visitor to the websites for the Intercontinental Church of God and the Garner Ted Armstrong Evangelistic Association would almost certainly leave with the impression that GTA was still alive and well and preaching regularly on TV programs.

8.2.3 C: Reform/Revolution

Sometimes the change in a movement after the founder's death is such a revolution that the successor could almost be seen as the true founder of what follows, with the original founder effectively relegated to the role of forerunner.

There was a huge power struggle within the Church of Jesus Christ of Latter-day Saints after Joseph Smith was shot and killed in 1844, partly because over the years Smith had not made it clear who should succeed him, and had also given too many conflicting instructions about choosing his successor. In the decade before his death he "had by word or action established precedents or authority for eight possible methods of succession" (Quinn 1976: 187). (Until just before his death Herbert W. Armstrong had been similarly unclear.) There were at least half a dozen main leaders and groups, including one under "the youthful and charismatic James Strang" (Abanes 2002: 210), who was apparently named as Smith's successor in a letter just nine days before Smith's death, and whose faction attracted a number of leading elders and bishops (Strangite Mormons, n.d.), and another group under Smith's son Joseph Smith III, which is still the second biggest Mormon group, the Reorganized LDS (RLDS);[4] but the main battle for succession, between Sidney Rigdon and Brigham Young, was won by the latter (Abanes 2002: 206–10). After Strang was shot in 1856, having not appointed a successor, most of his followers joined what became the RLDS, though a small Strangite Church still exists today (see 2.3)—along with dozens of other small Mormon offshoots. (One can only speculate on how many churches in the Worldwide family will exist in 150 years' time; see appendix 6.)

Another problem for the Mormons was that different groups held Smith's teachings from different periods as the most authentic version of the religion; a similar phenomenon is currently happening in the Worldwide offshoots (see 6.5). Brigham Young emphasized certain doctrines and practices which some other groups dropped, including polygamy; he was a fiery and charismatic leader who effectively remade the Mormon Church, turning it in his own direction rather than Smith's.

The founder of the Jehovah's Witnesses, Charles Taze Russell, died in 1916. A very bitter power struggle was won by Joseph Franklin "Judge" Rutherford, who deemphasized Russell's role so much that around four thousand members left to form other churches based firmly on Russell's teachings;[5] the remaining church under Rutherford for some years did not acknowledge any connection with Russell. Russell has now been reinstated in the official Jehovah's Witness history, and Rutherford's stormy succession to the leadership has been smoothed over. (See Barrett 2011: 119–26 for further details.)

There is an interesting parallel between Rutherford and Roderick C. Meredith's problems with the board of Global (see 6.2.2), though with a different outcome. The legal authority of the society that would become the Jehovah's Witnesses belonged to seven directors.

> [Rutherford] was dissatisfied with the Board of Directors, over which he adopted total control. This culminated in open rebellion, after which several disaffected leaders were

4. Renamed the Community of Christ in 2000.
5. These include the Pastoral Bible Institute and the Laymen's Home Missionary Movement among others.

dismissed from their official positions. This led to the formation of small schismatic groups. (Holden 2002: 19)

It is the job of the successor to the founder to take the personality cult of a living mouthpiece of God and turn it into a functioning and continuing religion—to adapt it from charismatic authority to rational-legal authority—and in doing so perhaps to change it out of all recognition, as Joseph W. Tkach and Joe Jr. did with the Worldwide Church of God. This is nothing new; it has often been argued by New Testament scholars that Christianity as a religion was the creation of Paul of Tarsus rather than Jesus of Nazareth—and that Paul changed it markedly from the Jewish sect led by the Jerusalem Christians under James, the brother of Jesus. "It would be easy to argue that after Jesus himself, Paul was the most important figure in the history of Christianity," writes Bart D. Ehrman (Ehrman 2006: 122; see also Tabor 2006: 237–45; Bütz 2005: 100 passim, etc.).

In the case of Worldwide it is worth considering the words of Federal District judge J. Spencer Letts in the court case over the copyright of Herbert W. Armstrong's last book *Mystery of the Ages* (see 6.2.1): "The founder did not dream, I suspect ... that those who would come after him would use their corporate power to suppress his religion" (Letts 1997). The successors to the founders of Mormonism and the Jehovah's Witnesses changed emphases within those religions; the Tkachs, father and son, changed their religion fundamentally. It was the extent of that change, and how the Tkachs achieved it, that created such shock, anger, and distrust among the ministry and membership of Worldwide, as has been evident throughout this book.

It was, of course, very different from the viewpoint of the Tkachs, as we saw in 5.1.3: having found the Truth, it was their spiritual duty to transform their church, as reflected in the very title of Joe Jr.'s book, *Transformed by Truth* (Tkach 1997).

8.2.4   D: Schism

Social science models can be useful tools, but they are not images of reality. Like many other religions, the Seventh-day Adventist Church (SDA) is "a special case," in this case with a significant schism occurring long *before* the founder's death. It was when Ellen G. White introduced the name Seventh-day Adventist Church at a major conference at Battle Creek, Michigan, in 1860, that some congregations splintered away, such as the Church of God (Seventh Day) and other variants (see 2.1.3).

During the twentieth century the SDA has moved closer to the mainstream (E: convergence), while the schismatic offshoots have continued to fragment— with one of those offshoots of offshoots, the Worldwide Church of God, currently spawning over four hundred offshoots of its own. Some of these, as we have seen

(6.4.4), have moved even further away from the mainstream (F: divergence). Another offshoot of an offshoot of the Adventist Sabbatarian movement, and another example of divergence, was the ill-fated Branch Davidian sect, a distant cousin of Worldwide.[6]

Schism following the death of the founder is particularly commonplace in esoteric and some Eastern movements, especially those such as Eckankar and other Sant Mat–derived religions which lay emphasis on the interpretation of dreams, or on meetings on another plane with Secret Chiefs or Hidden Masters, as I have written elsewhere:

> In the West, these are constantly splintering to form new movements, each one claiming to be the true successor to one of the others....
>
> From an outsider's point of view, such constant splits in this type of religion are almost inevitable because of the essentially subjective nature of the spiritual experience; when the leader of a movement dies, it is quite possible that more than one senior member of the movement, in their individual Soul Travels, will be "told" by the Masters that they have been appointed to take over. (Barrett 2001a: 320)

Christianity was used as an example of change under a new leader in the previous section. It has also been prone to many schisms, major and minor, over the last two thousand years—but instead, let us briefly consider Islam.

The religion of Islam split within a few years of the death of Muhammad (632 CE). As with Mormonism 1,200 years later, some believed the leader should come from the Prophet's family. The first two caliphs had been close associates of Mohammed; the first nominated his successor, but the second was assassinated before doing the same. A six-man council, the Shura, choosing between two main candidates, offered the leadership to Mohammed's son-in-law Ali on the condition that he would not declare a dynasty; Ali refused, and the other candidate was appointed. When he was killed, Ali became caliph and almost immediately declared a dynasty; he was briefly followed by his son, before a "nonfamily" leader took control (Horrie and Chippindale 1991: 65–68). Out of this very early conflict, stemming mainly from family and tribal loyalty, arose the two main divisions of Islam which still exist today, Sunni and Shi'ite.

---

6. The tragedy that happened at Waco could quite possibly have been averted if the FBI had allowed two scholars with both a theological and a sociological comprehension of David Koresh, his teachings, and his movement, Philip Arnold and James D. Tabor, both with a background in the Worldwide Church of God, to advise them and to speak directly with Koresh, who wanted to communicate with them.

> The Waco situation cried out for an expert to think and then communicate in terms that the Davidians could comprehend. The expert would have helped control the situation by talking David Koresh's language and understanding his world view. (Cartwright 1998b: 11; see also Edwards 1996: 24–25; Barrett 2001a: 87–88, 93–94)

But the FBI had their own ideas on how to end the siege—with tanks—with the horrific consequences that millions watched live on television.

Family has clearly been an important factor in leadership succession within the Worldwide offshoots, as well as in Worldwide itself (see 7.5); so too, perhaps, are what might be called more "tribal" loyalties of shared history, and both friendship and enmity (see 9.7 and 9.8).

8.2.5 Future Successions

It is not the purpose of this study to use the model in this chapter for predicting the future regarding movements whose leaders are still alive at the time of writing. But we shall look briefly at two movements to ponder their future in terms of the model.

Born in 1946, Claude Vorilhon, or Raël, founder of the Raelian Movement, is still relatively young and could live for several more decades. The Raelian Movement, a UFO religion, anticipates no problems when he eventually dies. Its hierarchy is organized as levels of Guides, with the Guide of Guides (currently Raël) elected by the Guides every seven years; if anything happens to Raël, someone else will simply take the position (Eric Bolou, pers. comm.). This might be helped by the fact that Raël has had no further extraterrestrial experiences since 1975; effectively they are already operating in a postprophetic phase. On the other hand, because their mythology, teachings, and practices stem wholly from the reported experiences of one man, when that man and his charismatic authority are gone, there may not be sufficient glue to hold the movement together, as several other "flying saucer movements" have found in recent decades (Lewis 1995; Lewis 2003; Partridge 2003).

Any of the four ideal types of the model could come into play when Raël dies, but two outcomes are likely. First, the election of a new Guide of Guides could easily involve the sort of battle for succession familiar from some other religions, with the possibility of schisms (D); secondly, even if the leadership succession is smooth, without Raël's charismatic leadership many of the movement's members may well drift away (B). (See Barrett 2011: 119–26 for further details.)

Now known as Prem Rawat, the Guru Maharaji (b. 1957) was only thirteen when he sprang to prominence as leader of the Divine Light Mission, now Elan Vital, in 1971. Like other gurus before him he brought an adapted version of an Eastern spiritual message to the West; he "made it increasingly clear that the Knowledge was not an Indian teaching, but universal" (Glen Whittaker, pers. comm.). He is still actively involved in the movement, but he has changed the focus, stepped back from the traditional Hindu position of guru, and dropped many if not all of the Hindu trappings. Although he came from a line of Perfect Masters, "this is not where the authority comes from, not the recognition of Maharaji as the master by his student; this comes rather from the nature of the teaching and the benefit to the individual" (Heather Evans, pers. comm.).

Because the founder himself has made such sweeping changes during the life-time of the movement so far, because the organization is decentralized, and because the Knowledge is now often transmitted by video rather than personally by Maharaji, the movement is less strongly focused on him than it previously was, and thus is perhaps more likely to continue relatively unchanged (A) after his death.

8.2.6   The Worldwide Church of God: A Complex Combination of Types

When using models, in a sense every religion could be argued to be a special case, partly because we are dealing with human beings and human institutions, and partly because the ideal types of any model are theoretical constructs, not representations of reality. It is clear that the Worldwide Church of God does not fit neatly into any one of the ideal types of the model. They are not mutually exclusive. Just as Herbert W. Armstrong validated his authority by all four means described by Weber (see 7.1), so what happened to his church in the aftermath of his death can be seen to encom-pass all of the ideal types of this model.

Briefly, since the death of its founder the Worldwide Church of God itself has continued (A) at least in name (until April 2009, when even that changed), with a major reform/revolution (C) under a new leader, taking it into far closer conver-gence with the mainstream (E); as a result many schisms (D) occurred, some fol-lowing a path of greater divergence (F) than before. Dissolution (B) has also occurred to a small extent within the offshoots, both in the collapse of Global due to conflicts of authority and in the fading away of small groups such as COG21 after the death of their founders (see 6.2.2).

8.3   SOME FACTORS AFFECTING A MOVEMENT AFTER THE DEATH OF ITS FOUNDER

J. Gordon Melton says that "the problem of succession is not the determinative trauma it has often been considered to be" (Melton 1991: 11–12). The examples given above demonstrate clearly that in some cases, however, it is exactly that. The death of the founder is, at least potentially, a major crisis point. At the two extremes the religion could fade and die or it could mature from a "cult" into a "religion," with a range of other possibilities, as we have seen. To avoid confusion and chaos after his or her death, a founder needs to set up an unambiguous system for succession of leadership.

The sections that follow explore some of the factors to be considered in the con-tinuance of a movement after the founder's death. These are illustrated by reference to both the Worldwide Church of God succession itself and the various successors to Herbert W. Armstrong in the leaders of the offshoots, and also by examples in a number of other new religions.

8.3.1 The Second Leader

There is a strong case for arguing that the second leader of a movement is crucial to its continuance, largely because it is in his or (more rarely) her term of office that the movement has to make the transition from charismatic to rational-legal authority, in Weber's terminology. (This is not specifically the focus of the current study, but it would make a worthwhile research project in itself.)

Indeed, some of the most successful new religions really only took off after their founders' death, under a strong new leader—for example, Brigham Young with the Mormons and "Judge" Rutherford with the Jehovah's Witnesses (see 8.2.3). If, as in these cases, the second leader also has charismatic authority, it is vital that he formalize the leadership procedure and the governance structure before he too dies, or the potential problems of succession are simply shifted by a generation.

In the case of the accessions of both Young and Rutherford there were bruising battles resulting in the losing candidates taking their supporters into breakaway organizations. It is possible that those schisms might have been avoided if the founder in each case had named his successor.

Herbert W. Armstrong *did* name his successor, though only at the last moment—and according to those close to him in his last months he considered a number of other people before naming Joseph Tkach. His main concern, it seems, was that his church should not fall into the hands of either of two particularly charismatic men, his disfellowshipped son, Garner Ted Armstrong, and Roderick C. Meredith, who, he told his close aide Aaron Dean, "should never, ever be over the church" (S. Flurry 2006: 35), or his legal advisor Stanley R. Rader (see 5.1.1).

Armstrong's choice of Tkach could be argued to be a very sensible decision, considering the role of the second leader in changing the leadership of a movement from charismatic to rational-legal. Tkach was not charismatic, he was no scholar, he was not even a great preacher—but he was a good administrator. He was the ideal person to oversee that difficult transition. No one could have foreseen what would happen, that Tkach's son and a friend would begin to question their church's teachings, and carry the new leader with them. But again, according to Aaron Dean, Armstrong had stipulated that Tkach should not bring his own staff with him when he took on his new role: "If you bring your staff up, they'll lead you astray," he is reported to have said (S. Flurry 2006: 36)—one of Armstrong's prophecies that *did* come to pass.

If Armstrong had appointed one of his more charismatic evangelists as his successor, instead of a supposedly safe administrator, things might have worked out very differently for the Worldwide Church of God. Garner Ted had once been the heir apparent and, in the early 1970s, was effectively running the church while his father spent much of each year on his "ambassadorial" visits around the world. But GTA had major difficulties with his father, with executive decisions being overturned, even before the doctrinal differences over the Systematic Theology Project (see 4.4 and 6.3)—let alone the sex scandals (4.3). By the time Armstrong died the rift between them was probably too great to be overcome.

If Armstrong had died from his heart failure in August 1977 and his son had taken over, there is little doubt that GTA would have made changes to doctrine in line with the Systematic Theology Project (see 4.4); Worldwide would almost certainly have become more liberal under his leadership, similar in beliefs and style to CGI and ICG, the churches he actually founded and led. Hardliners such as Raymond C. Cole had already left over the date of Pentecost and the divorce and remarriage issues (see 4.2.1 and 4.2.2). Others may have left over other doctrinal changes, or over GTA's personal morality. One of the first to go would almost certainly have been Stanley Rader, the éminence grise who helped cement GTA's "ouster" (see 4.4 and 4.5). Rader would not have been missed by many; but other, more charismatic figures in the church such as Roderick C. Meredith might have clashed with GTA, leading to their resignation or dismissal, and to schism.

To continue the speculation for a moment longer, if Garner Ted Armstrong had succeeded his father, there might have been a generally smooth transition, with Worldwide continuing largely in one piece; on the other hand, there could have been a struggle for succession between supporters of GTA and supporters of Meredith. In the questionnaire I asked who from a list of names, with the benefit of hindsight, would have been the best successor to HWA. Only 174 gave a name (127 actively stated "No opinion/prefer not to say"); of these, GTA with 27 came only a little ahead of Meredith (23), followed by Roy Holladay, later chairman of United (17), Herman Hoeh (10), and David Hulme, later leader of COGaic (8). Only three named Gerald Flurry (Philadelphia), and one David Pack (Restored). Write-in names, mainly scoring 1 or 2 apiece, totaled 85.

Herman L. Hoeh, the elderly, quiet, and well-respected theologian of the church, was one of the other names Armstrong actively considered; but he did not, as we have seen, consider Roderick C. Meredith a suitable successor (see his March 1980 letter to Meredith in 7.3.1).

Armstrong did not name his successor until a few days before he died. For an ailing founder to appoint a charismatic successor is actually a huge personal risk, because it creates a leader-in-waiting while the founder is still alive, a potential rival, like a younger lion or stag awaiting its chance to supplant the weakening old leader.

Christian Science founder Mary Baker Eddy would certainly not have accepted the possibility of announcing an heir. "Verifiable statements from Mrs. Eddy make clear that she did not envisage that the future continuity of her church would rest upon a charismatic, personal leadership," a Christian Science official told me (David Vaughan, pers. comm.). Indeed, according to one writer, "Mrs. Eddy regularly sacked anyone who shined forth with the slightest glint of leadership ability" (Simmons 1991: 113).

If things had worked out differently in the 1970s, it is most likely that Garner Ted Armstrong would have succeeded his father. Joseph Tkach Jr. succeeded Joseph W. Tkach. We have seen that the hereditary principle of succession, or at least of the placing of sons into positions of authority under their fathers' leadership, is quite widespread in the Worldwide family (see 7.5). If things don't go wrong, as they did between Herbert W. Armstrong and his son, hereditary succession can avoid much of the "determinative trauma" which, contra Melton (see 8.3), does afflict many new religions on the death of the founder.

When Garner Ted Armstrong died unexpectedly in 2003, his son Mark, operations director of the Intercontinental Church of God, became CEO and thus the new leader with the active support of his mother, GTA's widow, Shirley. Although it was obviously a traumatic time on a personal level for those close to GTA, the Work of the church was able to continue.

There are many other factors affecting the continuation of a movement after the founder's death; it is worth looking briefly at a few of them.

8.3.2   The Continuing Organization

One important element is the organizational structure that is already in place in a movement. If this is well established, the transition from personal to organizational authority is likely to be easier. Some founders, by the time of their deaths, have already delegated most of the running of their movement to others; the founder might still be the source of teaching or, in Eastern religions, the guru, but he or she has perhaps become more of a figurehead than a hands-on leader. The larger the movement, the more likely it is to have "department heads" running different aspects of it, such as finance, publishing, training, recruitment, and ministerial deployment. It is relatively easy for this situation to continue with only the slightest of modifications after the founder's death.

This was the case with the Worldwide Church of God, which had among much else a massive printing and publishing department for its books, booklets, magazines, and newsletters, and a very long-established correspondence department, which sent stock answers to enquirers' questions. It had a hierarchically structured ministerial department which administered placement and discipline of ministers. It had teams of experienced people who would organize, set up, and run the annual eight-day Feast of Tabernacles, sometimes catering for thousands of people on one site.

So long as the organization has a sound legal and financial basis—effectively, as an established business corporation—then it doesn't actually need a *living* figurehead in order to continue its "business." It has a product to sell, and often in actual terms as well as figurative; this might include books, CDs or DVDs of the founder and other preachers or teachers, as well as ongoing and well-established magazines, radio and TV broadcasts featuring other leaders within the movement, evangelistic rallies, cultural events, and so on, in addition to the normal day-to-day aspects of a religion such as regular and special services, study groups, nurturing existing members, and recruiting new ones. Worldwide was unusual in providing all its books and magazines free; many religious movements make a significant part of their income from selling their books, magazines, DVDs, and CDs.

In the case of some esoteric movements such as Rosicrucian organizations and most personal development movements (whether or not they classify themselves as religions) such as the Church of Scientology, Insight, and Neuro-Linguistic Programming, there are lucrative courses to be marketed and sold.

A well-structured, well-organized religion of reasonable size is able to keep going with little interruption after its founder's death simply because it has the machinery and the momentum to continue operating just as it did before his death. But even then the introduction of a new leader might eventually bring sweeping changes, as it did with Joseph W. Tkach.

8.3.3   Demography

The interaction between doctrinal and demographic factors is an important factor. The Catholic Apostolic Church, for example, had a doctrinal principle that no new apostles would be appointed; they weren't needed, because Christ was returning. But without apostles to ordain them there could be no new clergy; when the clergy grew old and died, no one replaced them, and the church, in that form, died too (see 8.2.2).

A movement which stresses celibacy must have a strong recruitment program if it is to survive into another generation. The Shaker community in America adopted orphans; some of the children grew up into the community, thus maintaining the numbers. When the state took over such social provisions, the Shakers began to decline in numbers. A movement with a strong male or female bias in membership must also consider carefully how it will continue by natural growth without its charismatic founder to draw new members in. If at the founder's death most of the members are elderly, what inducements can they offer to recruit the young? If the membership is predominantly young, are there any older members in positions of authority, to offer teaching, guidance, continuity, stability? An immature leadership was one of the main problems faced by ISKCON—see 8.2.1.

And how large is the membership? It is certainly possible for a movement only a few hundred strong to grow and prosper; Garner Ted Armstrong twice began from scratch to build medium-sized churches. But when the founder dies, as a general observation, the larger the membership, the more likely that continuance is assured, and vice versa: GTA's Intercontinental Church of God has survived his death in 2003 with 2,000–2,500 members in ninety-four local churches in 2009 (see 6.3), but Raymond F. McNair's tiny COG21 effectively died with its founder (see 6.2.2 and 8.2.2).

8.3.4   Doctrine

If a movement's focus is primarily on the figure of its founder, then his death will cause major problems; once the center is removed, what is left? This is especially problematic if, as in a number of Eastern and esoteric movements, he had claimed some form of divinity himself, or special revelation or a personal hotline to higher powers, whether God, Hidden Masters, or aliens. If the focus is on the founder's teachings, and these were from some form of revelation, is his death an end to new teachings, as with the Aetherius Society (see 8.2.1)? Or can somebody else take on the prophetic mantle of the founder, stepping into his or her shoes as the channel for further revelations? The Mormons, for example, have continuing revelation, though this is reserved for the president of the church (see 8.2.3).

Crucially, is the doctrine of the founder fixed in stone forever, or may it be adapted to fit better with changing circumstances, to avoid conflict with the civil authorities, or simply to drop possibly embarrassing beliefs or practices? One of the leaders of the Church of God, International, told me quite bluntly how his church had changed since parting with Garner Ted Armstrong as its leader (see 6.3):

> There have been no *doctrinal* changes, but there has been a change of *emphasis* since GTA's departure from CGI. The STP remains the foundational document....
>
> GTA put far more emphasis on prophetic speculation—relating current events to biblical prophecies—than we do. That's the only change of emphasis. Soon after the separation, we published an article on the meaning of Jesus' command to "Watch." We pointed out it did not mean "Watch world events!" as GTA and the old WCG seemed to think, but that it simply means to be vigilant at all times (in a continual state of preparedness), *regardless* what is going on around you. We also wrote and spoke of the errors that have come out of "headline theology." GTA ridiculed us for this, claiming that we were no longer "watching world events." He began putting emphasis on the word "headlines" in his many highly speculative articles about world events and biblical prophecy. He thought he was God's anointed "watchman." (He actually made such a claim.) To him, that meant that he was supposed to keep his eye on world events and analyze them "in light of Bible prophecy" while "warning" modern Israel (USA, etc.) and the world of what was coming. That was the one area we sharply disagreed with him on. (Vance Stinson, pers. comm.)

If the founder's teachings are adapted, then by whose authority? This is perhaps one of the prime causes of schisms in churches after the death of the founder: if the new leadership accommodates itself more to the world, doctrinal purists will leave and set up their own church—in their view, to quote Paul, "Therefore, brethren, stand fast, and hold the traditions which ye have been taught" (2 Thess. 2:15). This was the case with Worldwide when Joseph W. Tkach changed its doctrines; several leaders of offshoots made it clear to me that they did not leave Worldwide so much as Worldwide had left them. They "stood fast"; it was their church which had departed from the Truth.

Much depends on the doctrines themselves, whether concerning salvation, purity, the End Times, church government, understanding of history, and much else.

How unusual are these? How close are they to the doctrines of mainstream Christianity, Hinduism, Buddhism, or other world religions? Are the differences great enough to invite condemnation from the "establishment" of those religions? Are the similarities close enough that dialogue is possible, now that the (perhaps awkward and inflexible) founder is out of the way? Or are the teachings so precise, so tightly focused, that members couldn't conceive of any change without risking their salvation? All of these are factors which have a bearing on how a new religion may develop under new leadership after its founder's death.

In the case of Worldwide the architects of change, Joe Jr. and Michael Feazell, changed the doctrines slowly and carefully, one at a time, until they were in a position where they could turn to organizations of the Evangelical Christian establishment and be welcomed by them (see 5.3); the process is documented (as history written by the victors) in their books (Tkach 1997; Feazell 2003). The ultimate seal of approval came with Worldwide's acceptance into the true Christian fold by Evangelical counter-cult writer Hank Hanegraaf, photographed hugging Joe Jr. at his father's funeral (see 5.1.3).

But for those who left to found and join the offshoots, the package of beliefs put together by Herbert W. Armstrong (see the list at 2.2.1) had to be taken as a whole; changing any one of them threatened them all—and threatened the believers' place as rulers in God's kingdom on Earth.

Rodney Stark and William Sims Bainbridge developed a theory of religion based on costs and rewards (Stark and Bainbridge 1985: 6–7; Bainbridge 1997: 9–12). Sometimes the promised rewards are so great, and perhaps unique to a movement, that nothing, not even the death of the founder, will sway members from their chosen path. But in other cases the rewards are much the same as those found in many other movements, including mainstream churches; if it turns out that the most significant difference was simply the personality or style of the founder, then after his death members might seek the same rewards from a more conventional religion with fewer "costs" attached; they may hold happy memories of their founder, but now that he or she has gone they will find somewhere more socially acceptable for their fellowship and their salvation; and so the movement will fade into memory with its founder. This has not yet happened with Worldwide, though thousands of members who accepted the new teachings and initially stayed with the church are believed to have left it for other more convenient churches without the historical baggage of Worldwide's name (see 6.5).

This could have been part of the reasoning behind the decision of the leaders of the Worldwide Church of God in April 2009 to change its name to the uncontroversial, even anonymous, Grace Communion International. "Denominational leaders believe the new name better describes what the church has become and will serve it more effectively in the future," says the church's website, quoting Joe Jr.: "We are a church that God radically transformed. Our new name is consistent with that transformation and aptly describes what God has made of our fellowship" (WCG 2009).

8.3.5 Inward- or Outward-Looking

The relationships of new religious movements (NRMs) with outside society are also important. Do they get on well with their neighbors, or are they at war with them? Some alternative religions deliberately foster good relations with local schools, hospitals, social centers, and charities; others constantly face their meetings being banned from community halls. Is the movement respected for its charitable works, or is it feared as a menace to decent, clean-living society? Is it well-integrated with its surrounding world nationally, even internationally? Some movements, such as the Unification Church, sponsor international conferences on peace or science; others, such as Subud and the Bahá'í Faith, have health, education, social work, or emergency relief bodies which are recognized as United Nations Non-Governmental Organizations (NGOs).

Other movements are more inward-looking, closed societies, even if they live in the world rather than separating themselves in communities like the Rajneesh ashrams of the 1970s and 1980s, or the Amish communities in North America. Such movements have an inward focus, seeing themselves as God's Elect, or as the "Small Remnant" of Romans 11:5; they keep themselves withdrawn from the world, with a strong aversion to any possible corruption from contact with outsiders; in Roy Wallis's term, these are extreme "world-rejecting" groups. Sects like the Exclusive Brethren deliberately separate themselves from the society that surrounds them, as Bryan R. Wilson explains:

> The principle of separating from evil as the essential basis for true Christian unity was taken to apply to separation from all forms of human association which did not have Christ as their head, and also from those who were at all involved in worldly practices, and who were therefore considered to "dishonor God." (B. Wilson 2000: 2)

Such separation precludes natural growth through recruitment by evangelizing in any social context.

As with many movements, the Exclusive Brethren have suffered schisms both over strict adherence to doctrine (including separation) and over personality clashes; interestingly, their largest branch was led for two-thirds of the twentieth century by a father and son, both named James Taylor. Earlier I commented that Christian Science has the appearance of a nineteenth-century relic out of its time (see 8.2.1); so do, in a different way, the Exclusive Brethren. Some of the tracts they still distribute are actually from the nineteenth century, some written by their founder John Nelson Darby (1800–1882); but even those which are more recent are grounded firmly in a bygone age. One, for example, still being distributed around 2000, inveighs against the computer: "The electronic hulk that rules him distances him from the law of God."

> Should computers be part of our young people's education? I would say unhesitatingly, "NO!" No enlightened Christian would embrace computerization for himself or for his children. (P. MacGregor, n.d.)

This emphasizes the view explained in an academic paper on the Brethren that

> the computer is thus seen as an immensely anti-Christian force, an agent so to speak, of the Devil himself. Therefore, "Exclusive" Brethren do not use computers in any form, and do not wish their children to learn how to use them in school. (Bigger 1990)

But by the early years of the twenty-first century the children of Exclusive Brethren parents were allowed to use computers, so long as they are not connected to the internet—and there is now an Australian Exclusive Brethren website.

> Today, Brethren do utilize equipment as we deem it to be appropriate and particular care is taken to ensure that access to corrupt and defiling material is limited. The stance taken on technology has generally been in reference to its potential applications rather than the device itself. Brethren don't normally have computers in their homes except where required to carry out work on not for profit matters and charitable causes. (Brethren FAQ 2007)

8.3.6   The Internet

The rapidly spreading availability of the internet in the past decade has been of massive importance to alternative religions—and something of a double-edged sword. Many new religious movements have designed attractive websites setting out their beliefs, in a new form of preaching in the marketplace. The churches in the Worldwide family, with their heritage of providing free literature, have placed their booklets online; some now only offer them online in PDF format, which is considerably less expensive than printing and distributing them around the world.

Most of the Worldwide offshoots' websites have a "Who we are" page and give a doctrinal statement (David Hulme's COGaic is unusual in not doing so; see 6.2.3.1), and some offer information about their congregations, though as we have seen some prefer not to. Some of the churches—usually the more hardline ones—also use their websites as a platform to criticize other offshoot churches. Several churches broadcast sermons online; a few, such as Warren Zehrung's Radio4Living.com, are basically internet churches (see 6.2.3).

But the internet can cause problems for religious movements as well. Some NRMs had exercised strict control over their members' access to information about both their own and other movements, or even about the outside world; now they can no longer do so without banning access to computers altogether. Members, and perhaps as important, potential members, now have access to vast amounts of material that is not just uncontrolled but uncontrollable, and uncensored by their religious leaders. In some cases they might find that their religion is not, as they had been taught, the only one which believes certain doctrines essential for their salvation, or they could discover trenchant criticisms of their movement by ex-members, or by outsiders, providing them with information of which they were formerly completely unaware. Through the medium of forums and blogs members with questions, doubts, and problems may now contact others with similar questions, and with the safety of anonymity; they are no longer isolated.

Over the decades, while Herbert W. Armstrong was still the leader of Worldwide, there were a number of critical books and booklets both by former members and by anticultists and Christian counter-cultists. Among the books, *Armstrongism: Religion or Rip-off?*, by Marion J. McNair (brother of Raymond F. McNair of Global, CGCF, Living, and finally COG21) was published in 1977; *Herbert Armstrong's Tangled Web*, by David Robinson, father of the original publisher of *In Transition: News of the Churches of God* (see 6.4.5.1), was published in 1980; and John Tuit's *The Truth Shall Make You Free: Herbert Armstrong's Empire Exposed* was published in 1981. All were by people who had been close to the center of Worldwide for many years. But although insiders were aware of them, most ordinary members were probably not, because all their information *about* their church came *from* their church.

Another former member, John Trechak, published the critical newsletter *Ambassador Report* from 1976 until his death in 1999. Again, although it caused a lot of ripples among ministers and Ambassador College alumni, most ordinary scattered members of Worldwide were probably not even aware of its existence. But even for those who were, few would want to risk such things being found in their homes; at times in the church's history, evangelists and senior ministers (including Joseph W. Tkach) would make unannounced house calls on ministers and members, looking in kitchen cupboards for white sugar and white flour (disapproved of by the church)—and looking for "dissident literature" (Gardner 2008). Possession of books critical of the church or its founder would be a serious offense.

But with the internet access to such material is both easy and safe in Worldwide and its hundreds of offshoots. Several former members of Worldwide or the offshoots run blogs or forums; some are humorous, almost exasperated observations of the ongoing Worldwide family saga, while others such as *Exit and Support Network* are support groups, but most of them are excellent information sources, accepting their inevitable bias (as with all literature and comment in this study). Anticult websites and Christian websites also provide information—sometimes accurate, sometimes not—that is critical of the historical Worldwide and the present-day offshoots.

It is a similar situation for many other new religions, especially those which received negative attention in the 1960s and 1970s, and those which are still controversial today, perhaps most of all the Church of Scientology. Unless a religious movement is able to forbid its members access to computers altogether, it can no longer control what they read.

A sign of how much things have changed with ready access to the internet is the fact that in 2011 there was a Facebook group (now discontinued), "United Church of God—Resolving Issues," described as "a place where people supportive of UCG are free to post concerning issues in the United Church of God"—and all content was public. This is a far cry from the ministerial house visits of 1960s Worldwide.

8.3.7   Personality of New Leaders

Attitudes to the internet or other new technology, the movement's stance on interaction with the world and even aspects of doctrine may all change with a new leader, who will bring his own ideas and interests, perhaps kept quietly suppressed under the previous leadership, to bear on the movement. A new broom has the opportunity to sweep clean—which brings us back to the crucial importance of the second leader to the development of a movement (see 8.3.1).

Societal attitudes can easily change with a new leader, either because he is of a different generation or because of emphasis on different aspects of the movement (as we saw with Worldwide offshoots' different views on "the Work"—see 6.1.2), or simply because of a difference in personality.

The impact of a new leader can be seen from the top down or at a more local level; it can be as shattering as an earthquake, like the effect of Joseph W. Tkach's changes to Worldwide, or it can take the form of a quite simple change which nevertheless affects the movement's relationship with the outside world. For one example of the latter, the small UK branch of the Raelian Movement used to have a monthly two-page newsletter, the *Raelian Gazette*, for members and enquirers, including interested scholars. When a new person took over the UK leadership in 1998, that stopped abruptly. He told me firmly that there would be "no more newsletters" (Eric Bolou, pers. comm.); he was also more difficult for outsiders to contact than his two immediate predecessors had been. His own successor since 2002, actor and singer Glenn Carter, reintroduced a newsletter, available online to any interested enquirers.

One new leader of a New Age movement was so different in personality from his predecessor—his father—that he eventually left his own movement. Michael Cecil, the Marquess of Exeter, took over the leadership of the Emissaries when his father, Martin Cecil, died in 1988. Martin Cecil had favored a centralized leadership of several geographically scattered communities; for example, each community would read a transcript of a talk by him at their Sunday services. Michael Cecil decentralized the leadership, making each community effectively self-governing, though without his father's strong charismatic centralized leadership membership fell by over two-thirds. But Cecil was clearly out of sympathy with the attitudes of the hardcore membership; he left the Emissaries in 1996, saying that he believed they had become too introverted—"an enclave separate from the world" (Todd 2003). (See Barrett 2011: 70–81 for further details.)

Each leader of a new Worldwide offshoot is both the founder of a new organization and, in effect, a new leader in a succession from Herbert W. Armstrong, through Joseph W. Tkach, through any number of intermediary leaders of different churches, each splintering from its predecessor. Each, in terms of pop psychology, could probably be termed an "alpha male"—ambitious, competitive, go-getting, and convinced of his own rightness, in terms of both doctrine (the right beliefs) and rightness for the job.

The leaders I contacted in the course of this research displayed a wide range of attitudes toward me. Some simply did not reply. Some were offhand in their responses, and some quite curt and dismissive; some were firm but polite; and others were friendly and helpful, appearing genuinely interested in my inquiries. One might perhaps have expected a correlation between how "liberal" a church is and its degree of helpfulness, but this was not always the case; at times I had quite friendly correspondence with representatives of hardline churches, while some of the more liberal churches were far less cooperative. It really did seem to be a matter of personal attitude.

For just one example, early in my research I had personal correspondence with Garner Ted Armstrong, who was very cooperative and gave frank and open answers to my questions. Early in 2009 I tried to make contact with his son Mark, now in charge of GTA's last church, but he chose not to respond to me. An ICG minister wrote to me in successive emails:

> Mr. Armstrong generally does not respond to these types of inquiries, I am finding out.

and

> The differences you are experiencing are nothing more than a difference in personality and that from life experience. Nothing more than personal preference. GTA did not mind apparently but Mark does. No big deal. (Chris Cumming, pers. comm.)

The personality of a new church leader, whether he be bombastic like the Mormons' Brigham Young or uncharismatic and quietly uncontrolling like the Emissaries' Michael Cecil, can make a crucial difference to the development of a movement after its founder's death.

8.4 AFTER THE OFFSHOOT LEADERS DIE

There is some speculation amongst COG watchers about what will happen to the larger offshoots when their founder-leaders die.

Of the largest offshoots, the Living Church of God is perhaps most likely to have to meet this problem first; its founder, Roderick C. Meredith, was born in 1930. When he suffered a mild stroke in 2008, he appointed one of his main preachers, Richard F. Ames, to stand in for him briefly (see 6.2.2). Unlike Philadelphia and other COGs (see 7.5) he has not placed a son in a position of authority, though Ames is Meredith's brother-in-law, so leadership would be kept in the family, at least for Ames's lifetime—he is in his seventies, not much younger than Meredith.

When I saw Meredith address a packed lecture hall in London in 2010 he joked about his own death, saying that his ministers claimed he would want to die in the middle of preaching—"Repen-n-n-nt!"—and falling over sideways.

One COG watcher states bluntly:

> Meredith isn't going to be around much longer. He is the center of gravity for his LCG sect, and when he "passes on" the rubber bands will snap and his sect will disintegrate under pressure. (Rumney 2009)

With falling church income, and with the number of family ties across the churches, Rumney suggests that it would make sense for United to "conduct a mop-up operation when LCG self-destructs," pointing out that "a significant number of Global Church of God refugees, both ministers and members," went to United after Global split in 1998—those in CGCF. Doctrinally, Living and United are close; their main point of difference is their style of governance (see 6.2.2). It is unlikely that there would be a merger between the churches, but there could be some crossover of members between Living and not United, perhaps, but its more conservative offshoot, Church of God, a Worldwide Association (6.2.3.2). Depending how Living changed with a new leader, other churches such as Restored might also hope to recruit members.

But a Living minister I asked about this scenario seemed comfortable about both Ames's succession and the succession after him, naming two or three well-respected people in the church as possible future leaders: "There is a great deal of unity at the moment around Dr. Meredith; I think he has set up a container which will carry on without a beat" (John Meakin, pers. comm.).

A church perhaps more in danger of splitting apart is Philadelphia. Gerald Flurry, born in 1935, is only five years younger than Meredith. His son Stephen is clearly in place to succeed him (see 7.5), but Flurry has created a Bible-foretold identity as "that prophet" of John 1:21 (G. Flurry 2007: 5), as well as watchman, king, and counselor (see 6.2.1). Will his son assume those divinely appointed roles, or will he routinize the charisma of Philadelphia's leadership (M. Weber 1964: 363–86)? Philadelphia's numbers appear to have fallen considerably over the years (see 6.1.1), and it already has several offshoots challenging Flurry's handling of the roles God has given him (see 6.2.1.1); of all the large churches its future could be the least certain.

Such speculations will be answered in the fullness of time. Many of the offshoot church leaders are elderly; several leading figures in the Worldwide family died during the course of my research (see appendix 3.4, note 4).

8.5 CONCLUSION

There are clearly many factors which, singly or in combination with each other, can affect what happens to a movement after its founder dies. Because there are so many variables, it would be difficult, if not impossible, to foretell what might happen in the case of any individual movement; any such attempt is likely to be no more accurate than any other prophecy.

But as many of the new religious movements of the 1960s and 1970s have either already negotiated the difficult transition to the postcharismatic phase of leadership or are likely to do so in the next few years, an awareness of these factors, illustrated here with the Worldwide family of churches and with other new religions, can perhaps help us understand the sometimes traumatic changes which these movements may go through.

The simple theoretical model which began this chapter could be of value when studying the complex process of what happens after the founder of a religion dies. The four ideal types of continuation, dissolution, reform/revolution, and schism, singly or in combination, offer a useful framework within which the almost inevitable changes to a religion, of one sort or another, may be explored systematically. The model could also be applicable to other, nonreligious, personality-led organizations.

CHAPTER 9
Who Went Where and Why

INTRODUCTION

Who went where and why? This is the question I posed at the beginning of this study. What makes someone join one offshoot in preference to all the others—and then perhaps change to a different one? So far I have examined the writings of the churches, interviewed and corresponded with a number of church leaders and ministers, and made use of a variety of other sources. It has been clear from the very start that all sources have their own bias. I have aimed to write as factual an account as possible, but I know from exchanges I have had with church leaders and ministers that some of what I have recounted here is likely to be challenged by those who actually lived through the events. They have their own versions, not just of interpretation but of the events themselves—and those versions often disagree with each other.

Part of my aim in this study has been to let a variety of conflicting voices be heard. In phenomenological terms I have made as much use as possible of emic accounts, the individual voices of those involved in the story, in order to help me compose my etic account, the overview of the objective observer (see appendix 2). I have tried throughout, both in my dialogue with leaders, ministers, members, and other observers and in this study, to make clear the importance of personal perception.

In this chapter I investigate which doctrinal changes in particular caused members to leave Worldwide (9.3), I look at the importance of social ties—family and friends—for members of the offshoots (9.4) and I look at offshoot members' attitudes to church governance and leadership (9.5). Building on these, I examine why and how individual people make religious choices, specifically reaffiliation between one group and another, on the theoretical basis of Rodney Stark and Roger Finke's rational choice concepts of "social capital" and "religious capital" (Stark and Finke 2000: 114–24; 9.6). From my study of ministers' and members' movement from Worldwide to a schismatic offshoot, and then sometimes from one offshoot to another, these two factors did not seem sufficient in providing an explanation. In 9.7 and 9.8 I introduce a third factor, "moral capital," which covers in this instance people's past experience, good and bad, with church leaders; I then test the relative strengths of these three factors.

This chapter is largely based on responses to my questionnaire for ministers and members; first, then, it is necessary to discuss the strengths and limitations of the questionnaire responses.

9.1   QUESTIONNAIRE CAVEATS

I have already made some use of comments made by respondents to my questionnaire, some in response to individual questions and some from the large "any additional comments" space at the end. In this chapter I include tables summarizing data from the responses to a number of questions.

The questionnaire was publicized in an article in the monthly newspaper *The Journal: News of the Churches of God* (Barrett 2008) and on its website, and also on possibly the best known blog by a former member, Gavin Rumney's *Ambassador Watch*. Both websites provided a direct link to the questionnaire, which was online for just over three months, from October 20, 2008, to February 2, 2009. Access to the questionnaire was protected by a password (Eugene1934) which was published in *The Journal* but was not given out online except as a clue which would deter any casual approaches but which any former Worldwide member would easily work out: "The password is the name of the city where HWA began his radio ministry on KORE, followed by the year" (see 3.2.2).

Asked how they had first heard of the questionnaire, 60 respondents (of the 307 who answered the question) said *The Journal* newspaper and a further 78 *The Journal* website; 102 said the *Ambassador Watch* website, and 42 heard of it from family or friends. Of the remainder, 14 heard of it from other websites, 5 directly from me, 3 from a church newsletter or website, and 3 via a Churches of God singles email group.

I knew in advance that there would be difficulties with the questionnaire. The respondents were self-selected, though it is difficult to see how this could have been avoided; with the lack of cooperation I received from the major churches on my formal questioning it is inconceivable that I could have gone to each of the churches and asked them for a proportionately numbered and randomly selected group of members to fill out the questionnaire.

In addition, the number of respondents (317) was lower than I had hoped, and less than 1% of the total number of members of the main offshoot churches (see 6.1.1). Knowing that some respondents might be sensitive about certain questions, I wrote on the first page:

> The events of the last few years have clearly caused a lot of disruption and distress for many ministers and members. It is not my intention to add to this. Please excuse me if any of these questions cause you offense. Feel free to ignore any questions you wish, or

which are not applicable to you. Please add additional comments or reasons for your answers if you wish.

This had the inevitable effect that different numbers of respondents answered each question; the lowest total used was 219, but for most questions there were over 250 respondents.

I was never under the misapprehension that my respondents would be a representative sample of ministers and members across the entire range of offshoots. It was not likely that many members of the more hardline churches such as Philadelphia and Restored would respond to it—if, indeed, they even knew of it; it was promoted in a newspaper that few of them would read and a website that most of them would actively avoid. If the leaders of hardline churches were not prepared to answer any of my questions to them, it was unlikely that they would encourage their ministers and members to fill in my questionnaire, though I asked every church I contacted if they would do so.

I was therefore expecting the survey to have a built-in bias toward the liberal end of the spectrum of churches—broadly speaking, members of United and its offshoots, and of the GTA churches. It came as no surprise, then, that only two respondents were currently members of Philadelphia, and that there were none from Restored, though on first leaving Worldwide eleven of the respondents had joined Philadelphia, and one Restored (see table A.4.1).

However, although the respondents cannot be taken as representing all the off-shoots proportionally, some of the attitudes that emerged in response to questions on doctrine, governance and leadership, and the problems of the 1970s, for example, show that respondents actually cover the entire spectrum from liberal to hardline (see 7.3.2, 7.3.3, 9.3, and 9.5). Although, for the reasons given, these questionnaire results cannot be claimed to be a statistically valid sample of former Worldwide members, I am therefore more comfortable than I expected to be in presenting them here, and in drawing (albeit tentative) conclusions from them.

In order not to overburden this chapter with tables and statistics, the detailed questionnaire results on the church affiliation and demographics of the respondents have been placed in appendices 4 and 5.

In brief, around a quarter of respondents belong to United,[1] 5% to Living, and the remainder to a variety of churches, mainly quite small ones, or to none. However, when they first left Worldwide, 38% of the respondents joined United and 13% joined Global/Living. Though just over half said they had belonged to only one church after leaving Worldwide, many members have changed from one offshoot church to another. Just over a quarter said they had belonged to two churches, 12% to three, 5% to four, 0.9% to five, 1.4% to six, while one person claimed seven churches. Obviously the last three figures, with such low numbers, cannot be taken as reliable percentages, but they do at least show that some members have changed church several times.

1. Note that the questionnaire was disseminated two years before United split in two.

Four-fifths of the respondents had been in the Worldwide family of churches since the 1970s or before.

As might be expected, the majority of respondents were American: between 63% and 73% (some answers were ambiguous). A further 20% were from Canada, Britain, Australia, or New Zealand. Seven out of ten were male, and around the same proportion of both sexes were aged over fifty. Many were in middle-class professions and well educated; half of all respondents were university graduates.

9.2 MEMBERS OR MINISTERS

Around 9% of the respondents who answered the question (28 out of 308) said they were ordained COG ministers. In addition to those, a further 23 said they were deacons or deaconesses; 8 were local church elders, local ministers, or sermon givers; 7 were song leaders/choral directors; and 2 described themselves as ministers' wives. There were two Ambassador College/University professors, two lecturers and a member of the Ambassador University board of directors. A further eight were writers or editors on church magazines or programs. In all, 97 (31%) held or had held some position either in Worldwide or another COG.

When I originally asked the question "Who went where and why?" I was thinking of individual members: why they chose to join one offshoot over another. But in a family of churches where top-down authority has always been the norm, and where the touchstone of the path toward the Kingdom of God was obedience, members were expected to follow their ministers. In the course of my research, in conversation and in comments in literature, on websites, in personal correspondence, and in questionnaire responses, I found that in the schisms, from the earliest to the most recent, it is primarily *ministers* who have actively left one church to join or to found another, and in many cases they took their members with them.

In Bryan R. Wilson's study of three Christian sects, he said of Christian Science that schism "has almost invariably been among the teachers of the movement" (B. Wilson 1961: 340). For teachers, read ministers.

Top-down authority works right down the line from top to bottom. Members were used to following the teaching of their own minister and obeying his instructions—in more spiritual language, the pastors tended their flocks—and so when their ministers left Worldwide for Global, for example, or left Global for the Church of God, a Christian Fellowship, and then did or did not merge with United, their members, on the whole, followed them. It was not just a matter of obedience and familiarity, but also of practicality; if an individual member left his congregation he might easily have to travel dozens if not hundreds of miles to find another suitable one.

Wilson takes as a given that "it is a feature of established sects that schism comes only from the divisions among the influential elite within each movement; no other person is sufficiently influential to cause division, no other person, perhaps, has sufficient motivation." Indeed, there is a close parallel between his comments on the Elim Church and what has been apparent within the Worldwide family: "Schism must thus be from the ministerial ranks, and in particular from those at the center of the organization; the laity are too receptive and docile to initiate schisms, and have no opportunity to preach heresy, or to challenge organizational arrangement" (B. Wilson 1961: 339). For "docile" read "accustomed to obedience."

The transition of ministers and members from Worldwide to an offshoot, or from one offshoot to another, is in itself a social movement. The Worldwide family of churches exemplifies Stark and Bainbridge's statement that "the rank and file do not produce social movements; they merely support them" (Stark and Bainbridge 1985: 104).

For example, when David Hulme was removed as leader of United in 1998 and founded what was to become the Church of God, *an International Community*, he invited any other United ministers who agreed with his stance to join his new group. The head of United in the United Kingdom, Peter Nathan, decided to join Hulme. Thirteen of the sixteen United elders in Britain followed Nathan, and their members went with them in the same proportion—around four hundred out of the total UK membership of five hundred (see 6.2.3.1).

So the question of *Who went where and why?* is not so much about the members as about ministers: why individual ministers would join an offshoot, leave it for another, then perhaps another, before (in some cases) founding yet another.

The newspaper *In Transition: News of the Churches of God* reported in June 1995, around the time that United Church of God was being founded, that

> nearly **40 percent** of the Worldwide Church of God pastors in the United States have resigned or otherwise been separated from employment in the past year, most within the past three months.
>
> Shortly prior to WCG Pastor General Joseph Tkach's Dec. 24, 1994, sermon announcing sweeping doctrinal changes, the WCG listed 463 congregations. All were pastored by elders paid by the WCG. Some pastors handled only one congregation, but many handled two or more congregations.
>
> Therefore, even though there were 465 congregations, there were only 267 elders who held the title pastor. Of this 267, 100 or 37 percent, are no longer in the employ of the WCG. The vast majority of those separated from WCG employment left or were terminated over doctrinal matters. (*In Transition* 1995)

United provided further information to me:

> United began in Indianapolis in May of 1995 with 155 elders present. All of these were from WCG. By December when we met in Cincinnati there were 350 elders, with all coming from WCG. Since that time there has been a gradual movement of elders from WCG to UCG. Currently we have 470 elders in United. Many of the additional elders since December of 1995 were ordained by United and did not come from WCG. (pers. comm.)

According to Michael Feazell, one of the architects of the doctrinal changes in Worldwide, between 1989 and 2000 "the number of career pastors [in Worldwide in the United States] declined from 458 to 120" (Feazell 2003: 185)—i.e., 74% of the paid ministers in the United States left the church. The disparity in numbers from the three sources here is probably largely due to the different time periods they apply to.

The huge outflow from Worldwide to United, following the previous secessions to Philadelphia and Global, is despite the assertion by Roger Finke and Christopher P. Scheitle that

> a congregation's dependency on the larger denomination deters schism. When clergy rely on the denomination for job placement, seminary training, annuity accounts, and professional networks, splitting from the denomination becomes increasingly more costly for the clergy and their denominations. Rather than leading a call for schism, they are more likely to call for reforms from within. (Finke and Scheitle 2009: 26–27).

Despite this the ministers left in their hundreds, giving up their paid jobs and their hard-fought-for positions in the church hierarchy. They did this because they had found there was no point in calling for reforms; as Gerald Flurry and Roderick Meredith had discovered before them (see 6.2.1 and 6.2.2), their pleas for discussion and debate were rejected—precisely because Worldwide was a strongly centralized church. The reality of their situation was the exact opposite of what Finke and Scheitle put forward as theory, that the more centralized a religion, the less prone it is to schism (Finke and Scheitle 2009: 20).

9.3   THE FINAL DOCTRINAL STRAW

Rational choice theory posits that when making life choices, people select the most rational or reasonable option, the best overall outcome, bearing in mind the variety of potential costs and rewards associated with any choice, and in light of their personal preferences (Stark and Finke 2000: 36–38).

In their discussion of rational choice theory, specifically regarding conversion and reaffiliation—joining a new group within one's existing religious tradition—Rodney Stark and Roger Finke discuss the factors which affect people's choices of, broadly, whether to move or to stay put (Stark and Finke 2000: 114–24). Inertia is a powerful factor: "Under normal circumstances," they say, "most people will neither convert nor reaffiliate" (Stark and Finke 2000: 119: proposition 30).

As we have seen (7.2), many people hung on in Worldwide, hoping that somehow things would improve. One person wrote:

> I was patient with changes in WCG, hoping God would cause a reversal and I would not have to leave WCG. I wanted to respect authority, and as long as they did not require that I believe and practice the changes, I wanted to stay.

Many stayed until a particular doctrinal change made it impossible for them to compromise any longer, even though they had been troubled by earlier changes (see 6.2.3). I asked ministers and members, "At what stage did the changes in WCG first cause you to feel seriously troubled?" and "Which was the final doctrinal straw which caused you to leave WCG?," with the same list of seven options from which they could choose one or write in their own (see table 9.1).

The change of teaching on the Trinity was listed by most respondents as the change that first caused them to feel seriously troubled (30%, 88 out of 289), with very nearly twice as many as the next change, abandoning the Sabbath requirement (16%, 45); reducing the requirement to obey Law was in third place (11%, 33). The same three changes were listed by most respondents as the final straw which caused them to leave Worldwide, but in a different order. First was abandoning the Sabbath requirement (32%, 89/282), with almost exactly twice as many as reducing the requirement to obey Law (16%, 45), and the change of teaching on the Trinity in third place (10%, 29).

It must be noted that most of the doctrinal changes came quite close together in time, that different accounts give the dropping of British Israelism, the change in teaching on healing or the Trinity, or downplaying the importance of Sabbath keeping as the first change (see 5.1.2), and that I was asking these questions fourteen years after Joseph W. Tkach's Christmas Eve sermon (see 5.1.3), a long time in which to keep the order of events clear. Accepting these caveats, these three doctrinal changes clearly had the most effect on members.

Of the many write-in responses, four people wrote "Trinity, obey Law, Sabbath," further emphasizing the significance of these three changes. Fifteen write-in responses to "seriously troubled" and thirteen to "last straw" wrote "all of the above," "all that is listed," "acceptance of Protestantism," "embrace of Evangelical-isms," "clear path to mainstream" or something similar. One showed both awareness and acceptance of the nomization of the pre-Tkach church (Berger

Table 9.1. AT WHAT STAGE DID THE CHANGES IN WCG FIRST CAUSE YOU TO FEEL SERIOUSLY TROUBLED? WHICH WAS THE FINAL DOCTRINAL STRAW WHICH CAUSED YOU TO LEAVE WCG?

Changes in WCG	First Troubled	Final Straw
Withdrawal of *Mystery of the Ages*	13	2
Change of teaching on healing	16	2
Change of teaching on the Trinity	88	29
Change of teaching on British Israelism	8	1
Acceptance of Evangelical "born again" doctrine	20	7
Reducing the requirement to obey Law	33	45
Abandoning the Sabbath requirement	45	89
Other	66	107
Total	289	282

1969: 31) (see appendix 2 and chapter 2: Introduction) by stating that the last straw for him was "anti-nomianism in general."

Few respondents listed the withdrawal of *Mystery of the Ages* as the first change to seriously trouble them, and only two as the last straw—the second lowest after the change of teaching on British Israelism. (The leader of one medium-sized off-shoot admitted to me off the record, "I *personally* consider Anglo-Israelism to be highly speculative, but as long as it does not become a central doctrinal matter... it is essentially harmless.") Despite the great importance placed on the withdrawal of *Mystery of the Ages* by Gerald and Stephen Flurry (see 6.2.1 and S. Flurry 2006), only four of the eleven respondents who said they joined Philadelphia Church of God on leaving Worldwide gave this as the first change to cause them to feel seriously troubled, and none said it was the final doctrinal straw which caused them to leave. Again, it must be stressed that these eleven (only one of whom was still a member of Philadelphia at the time of the questionnaire) can obviously not be taken as a representative sample of all Philadelphia members.

9.4   FAMILY AND FRIENDS

Commenting on the Worldwide schisms, new religions scholar J. Gordon Melton told the local newspaper in Eugene, Oregon, where Herbert W. Armstrong began his work in 1934, that

> the fallout, with almost as many members leaving the church as staying, follows a pattern found in any organizational split.
> "People with the highest dedication to the old beliefs move out to the schism groups," he says. "And the ones for whom social ties are most important, they stay." (J. Wright 1998: 6A)

We looked at dedication to the old beliefs in the last section; here we shall briefly examine the importance of social ties for members of the Worldwide family of churches.

Respondents were asked how many members of their immediate family (parents, siblings, spouse, children) and how many members of their extended family (in-laws, uncles and aunts, cousins, nephews and nieces, etc.) were currently in the same church as themselves, in a different Worldwide family church, still in Worldwide, or not connected with any Worldwide family churches at all (see table 9.2).

Even though I had encountered several cases of brothers, or fathers and sons, being in different churches, I had expected that families would largely tend to stick together. But only 7.6% (21/278) said that all the members of their immediate family were in the same church that they were in, and a surprisingly high 46% (127/278) said that *none* of their immediate family were in their church. Even fewer respondents said that the various proportions of their immediate family were in

Table 9.2. IMMEDIATE FAMILY AND EXTENDED FAMILY IN THE CHURCHES

	All	Most	Some	Few	None	Total
Immediate Family						
In the same church	21	36	35	59	127	278
In different Worldwide family church	4	9	26	38	201	278
Still in Worldwide	1	2	8	24	243	278
Not connected with Worldwide family	92	42	43	42	62	281
Extended Family						
In the same church	4	8	23	27	210	272
In different Worldwide family church	1	3	34	41	198	277
Still in Worldwide	0	0	6	28	242	276
Not connected with Worldwide family	112	52	31	25	58	278

other offshoots, and a massive 72% (201/278) said that none of their immediate family were in other offshoots. Fewer still said that any, from "all" down to "few," were still in Worldwide; 87% (243/278) said that none of their immediate family were. A third of respondents (33%, 92/281) said none of their immediate family were connected to the Worldwide family of churches; at the other extreme 22% (62/281) said that none of their immediate family were outside Worldwide.

As might be expected, when it came to respondents' extended families, the numbers in the same church were far lower, only 1.5% (4/272) saying that all their extended family were in their own church, a total of only 23% (62/272) having any at all in their church, and 77% (210/272) saying that none of them were. The figures were not much higher for members of their extended families in other offshoots: only 29% (79/277) having any at all, while 71% (198/277) said they had none. Once more, large numbers reported that none of their extended family had any connection with the Worldwide group of churches—40% (112/278)—while 21% (58/278) said that none of their extended family were outside Worldwide, a very similar proportion to the immediate family.

As a general observation, then, for the respondents to this questionnaire, family ties are not a major influence on church affiliation.

Respondents were also asked to say how many of their five closest friends were currently in their own church, another offshoot, still in Worldwide, or not connected with the Worldwide churches at all (see table 9.3). A high-seeming 14% (37/274) said that all five of their closest friends were in their own church; a further 22% (59) said that three or four of them were. But 37% (101) said that *none* of their closest friends were in their church. The numbers were lower for close friends in other offshoots: only 8.5% (23/272) said that all of their five closest friends were in other offshoots, while a further 16% (44) said that three or four of them were. This time 47% (128/272) said that none of their five closest friends were in other offshoots. The distribution of figures is relatively close: between 9% and 14% of respondents

Table 9.3. FIVE CLOSEST FRIENDS IN THE CHURCHES

Five Closest Friends	Five	Four	Three	Two	One	None	Total
In the same church	37	24	35	39	38	101	274
In different Worldwide family church	23	20	22	43	36	128	272
Still in Worldwide	6	2	3	22	25	206	264
Not connected with Worldwide family	55	10	27	31	54	88	265

have either one, two, three, four, or five friends in their own church, with a mean of 12.6%, while between 7% and 16% have either one, two, three, four or five friends in other offshoots, with a mean of 10.6%.

Very few said that the majority of their five closest friends were still in Worldwide, but 18% (47/264) had either one or two friends there. Most, though, had broken or lost their significant friendship ties with Worldwide; 78% (206) said that none of their five closest friends were still in Worldwide.

Far more respondents had close friends completely outside the Worldwide family of churches; a surprisingly high 21% (55/265) said that *all* of their five closest friends were not connected with Worldwide or its offshoots. This number is perhaps suspicious, as the numbers for one to four friends decrease from 54 to 31 to 27 to 10; to then leap to 55 seems unlikely. Having said that, it is clear from the responses to this question that a large majority of the respondents have a number of close friends with no connection to the Worldwide family of churches; only a third (33%, 88) said that none of their five closest friends were outside the churches.

For the respondents to this questionnaire, close friendships are clearly not limited to those in their own church or related churches. Even though the beliefs and practices of the Worldwide family of churches are quite distinctive, and the offshoot churches, like many other sectarian churches, are in tension with society (B. Wilson 1990: 46–68; Stark and Bainbridge 1985: 48–50; etc.) with a social construction of reality at odds with wider society (see chapter 2: Introduction and 7.1), and are world-rejecting in that they view the outside world "as having departed substantially from God's prescriptions and plan" (Wallis 2003: 36), yet their members are very much *in* the world; like churchgoers in most denominations, they live and work and shop and socialize among people with no connection with their church.

From the responses on family and friends it is safe to say that—for these respondents, at least—social ties are not a major influence on church affiliation.

9.5   CHURCH GOVERNANCE AND LEADERSHIP

Respondents were asked two questions about church governance and leadership. First they were asked to rate six statements about governance from Strongly Agree through Agree, No opinion/Unsure, and Disagree, to Strongly Disagree (see table 9.4). Note

Table 9.4. QUESTIONS ABOUT GOVERNANCE

	SA	A	N	D	SD	Total
The correct form of church government is hierarchical.	41	39	37	65	96	278
Local congregations should always follow "Home Office" directives.	16	46	29	91	95	277
Individual members should follow the instructions of their church leaders.	13	102	54	68	41	259
Democracy is beneficial to church government.	33	102	48	55	41	279
Local congregations should be able to choose their own minister.	63	64	49	64	43	283
Individual members should be able to disagree with their church leader or local minister and still stay in their church.	140	110	15	8	6	279

that even in a survey which has a built-in bias toward the liberal end of the spectrum (see 9.1), considerable numbers of respondents took a conservative stance on most of these questions. For example, 29% (80/278) said they agreed or strongly agreed that the correct form of church government is hierarchical, though twice as many, 58% (161), disagreed or strongly disagreed. However, far fewer believed that local congregations should always follow "Home Office" (church headquarters) directives (22%, 62/277) than disagreed with this (67%, 186).

On three other questions the conservative and liberal responses were more evenly split, with significantly large numbers stating "No opinion/Unsure." A very small majority took the more conservative stance that individual members should follow the instructions of their church leaders (44%, 115/259) against those who disagreed (42%, 109), with a fifth of respondents (21%, 54) saying "No opinion/ Unsure." A somewhat larger majority agreed with the general concept that democracy is beneficial to church government, 48% (135/279), against 34% (96) who disagreed, with 15% (41) abstaining. On whether local congregations should be able to choose their own minister, the margin was narrower: 45% (127/283) agreed and 38% (107) disagreed, with 17% (49) abstaining.

The final statement had overwhelming support: 90% (250/279) agreed or strongly agreed that individual members should be able to disagree with their church leader or local minister and still stay in their church; those who disagreed or strongly disagreed with this (5%, 14) were about the same as those who abstained (5%, 15).

This last question led naturally to the next: I offered a number of options for what members should do if they believe their church leader is wrong; they had to choose the one statement closest to their view.

Very nearly half (49%, 138/281) said they should discuss their doubts privately with their minister or a senior person in their church; a fifth (21%, 59) said they thought they should quietly try to convince the leader of his error. In contrast, very few thought they should openly challenge their leader (7%, 20) or discuss their doubts with friends in their church (6%, 16); just as few thought they should ignore him but stay in his church (6%, 17). Almost no respondents took what might be called the "blind obedience" option, "Follow him because he is the leader" (1%, 3). A tenth of all respondents said they should leave his church and find one whose leader they agreed with.

The following question stemmed from frequent comments on blogs and in personal correspondence about individual offshoot leaders' fitness to be leaders. I asked: "Without naming them, are there any leaders of 'Worldwide family' churches today who you consider unfit for their position because of …" and listed seven negative qualities, each with a Yes/No answer (see table 9.6).

The response to this question was generally lower than for most of the other questions, perhaps because it was a negative question. However, it is worth noting that the highest-scoring qualities attracted the most responses (i.e., whether yes or no), and so were more representative of all the respondents to the questionnaire. For this question, then, I am giving not only the percentage of respondents saying yes to each individual question, which varies from 95% down to 72% of respondents to the individual questions, but also the percentage of all 317 respondents,

Table 9.5. OPTIONS IF MEMBERS BELIEVE THEIR CHURCH LEADER IS WRONG

	No.	%
Follow him because he is the leader	3	1
Quietly try to convince him of his error	59	21
Discuss your doubts privately with your minister or a senior person in your church	138	49
Discuss your doubts with friends in your church	16	6
Openly challenge him	20	7
Ignore him but stay in his church	17	6
Leave his church and find one whose leader you agree with	28	10
Total	281	100

Table 9.6. LEADERS CONSIDERED UNFIT FOR THEIR POSITION

Leaders Considered Unfit Because of:	Yes	No	Total	Yes (% Total)	Yes (% All 317 Respondents)
Pride or arrogance	267	13	280	95	84
Authoritarianism	261	14	275	95	82
Poor understanding of doctrine	235	29	264	89	74
Poor leadership skills	219	32	251	87	69
Personal morality	189	54	243	78	60
Poor teaching/preaching ability	181	63	244	74	57
Weakness	164	64	228	72	52

varying from 84% down to 52%, in order to demonstrate more clearly the relative strength of feeling for each quality. This is apparent in table 9.6. (Note that the seven qualities are here listed in order of their score, not in the order they were listed in the questionnaire.)

The two highest qualities which respondents felt rendered one or more leaders unfit for their position were pride or arrogance (267/280, 95% of those who answered this question, and 84% of all respondents to the questionnaire) and authoritarianism (261/275, 95% of respondents to this question, and 82% of all respondents). Although it is perhaps unsurprising that these topped the list, the very high figures demonstrate that in this survey at least, there is considerable feeling about these particular negative characteristics.

(When asked to give their reasons for who they thought would have been the best successor to HWA (see 8.3.1), and who would be the best person to lead a reunited church, several respondents wrote strongly worded comments such as "The ones I know are all control freaks," "He's not a maniac, and more sincere than others," "Not a nut case," "Example of someone with no desire for power," "HUMILITY!," "Least authoritarian," "Power crazy," "Someone not power-hungry," "Less of a dictator," "Not a control freak or a maniac.")[2]

Some way behind pride or arrogance and authoritarianism came poor under-standing of doctrine (235/264, 89%, or 74% of all respondents) and poor leader-ship skills (219/251, 87%—69% of all). Then came, in order, personal morality (189/243, 78%—60% of all), poor teaching/preaching ability (181/244, 74%—57% of all) and weakness (164/228, 72%, or just 52% of the whole).

9.6 RELIGIOUS CHOICES: SOCIAL CAPITAL AND RELIGIOUS CAPITAL

People left Worldwide at different times, most joining, initially, Philadelphia, Global, and United. Over the following years many of them left these three churches to join another, and sometimes another, and yet another. Glen Alspaugh went from Worldwide to Philadelphia to the Church of God's Faithful to the Church of God's Patience (see 6.2.1.1); Raymond McNair went from Worldwide to Global to Church of God, a Christian Fellowship, back to Living, and then founded Church of God, 21st Century (see 6.2.2). Others, both ministers and probably to a lesser extent non-minister members, have followed similar journeys. While about half the questionnaire respondents were still in the church they had joined on leaving Worldwide, and a quarter had belonged to two, 26 (12% of those who answered the question) said they had belonged to three offshoots, while 17 (7.8%) said they had belonged to four, five, six, or even seven offshoots (see appendix 4).[3]

---

2. The number of respondents to these two questions was small, so the results are not being used; but here the write-in comments are of more interest than the tabulated results.

3. With the splitting in two of United in December 2010/January 2011, thousands more mem-bers increased the number of offshoot Churches they had belonged to.

Bearing in mind Stark and Finke's proposition 30, "Under normal circumstances most people will neither convert nor reaffiliate" (see 9.3), what causes these people to go through the disruption of reaffiliating, whether just once, or twice, or three or more times? Stark and Finke discuss two factors, social capital, which "consists of interpersonal attachments" (Stark and Finke 2000: 118), and religious capital, a term borrowed from Laurence R. Iannaccone (Iannaccone 1990), which they define as "the degree of mastery of and attachment to a particular religious culture" (Stark and Finke 2000: 120). Their stance is the other way around from Melton's quotation above (see 9.4): "To the extent that people have or develop stronger attachments to those committed to a different version of their traditional religion, they will reaffiliate" (119: proposition 31), but "the greater their religious capital, the less likely people are either to reaffiliate or to convert" (121: proposition 34).

To paraphrase both Melton and Stark and Finke, it's a balance between family and friends on the one hand and faith on the other. In Stark and Finke's classification, if your faith is the more important of the two, you'll stay where you are, but if your attachment to your family and friends is stronger, you'll go and join them. But in the case of Worldwide the religious capital that people had spent their lives investing in was the beliefs and practices of *Armstrong's* Worldwide, not Tkach's. Meredith B. McGuire captures well the motivation of those who founded Philadelphia, Global, and United: "Rarely do schismatic groups consider themselves to be *leaving* their faith; rather, they view their exit from the group as keeping the true faith" (McGuire 2002: 94–95)—a point made very clearly by Gerald Flurry, founder of Philadelphia, who wrote with deliberate emphasis: "WE ARE NOT REBELLING—WE ARE TAKING A STAND AGAINST THOSE WHO ARE!" (G. Flurry 1995b: 151). This accounts for Melton's reversal of Stark and Finke: those who put their beliefs before their family and friends were the ones who left Worldwide for the three main offshoots; those with less investment in their beliefs than in their social attachments, says Melton, took the less stressful option of staying where they were.

The 1998 newspaper article which quoted Melton (see 9.4) also quoted members and former members of the Eugene congregation of Worldwide who had made different choices. One, sixty-four-year-old Glenn Harmon, expressed the ideas of religious capital and social capital in his own words. He said the seventh-day Sabbath was "a pivotal point because it's one of God's commandments."

> "It's been a key point in my mind ever since."
> So when Worldwide leaders began backpedaling on the issue, Harmon says he had little choice but to leave.
> "These are the things I have built my life on," he says. "They are more important than (belonging to) a social club." (Wright 1998)

This is clear so far as it goes. But the evidence of this study suggests that in the complex case of the Worldwide family of churches the concepts of religious capital and social capital are not sufficient to account for the choices that ministers and members have made. Even from the beginning it was never simply a case of "Should I stay or should I go?" That choice was presented to ministers and members of the post-Armstrong Worldwide three times—in 1989, 1992–93, and 1995: to stay within the social setting of the church they had committed themselves to, in many cases for decades, which was now at various stages of overthrowing its belief system, or to leave behind their social attachments in order to maintain their attachment to their religious culture, in the three quite different expressions of it in Philadelphia, Global, and United.

Hundreds of ministers and tens of thousands of members left. "When people reaffiliate, they will tend to select an option that maximizes their conservation of religious capital" (Stark and Finke 2000: 123).

Having made that choice, to leave Worldwide for Philadelphia, or to stay but then leave for Global, or to stay but then leave for United, in each case favoring their religious capital over their social capital, the logical next step would be for people to rebuild new social capital within their new church, or, in human terms rather than theoretical language, to settle down, make new friends, and build up a new spiritual "home." Religious reaffiliation is an upheaval, and especially if you leave family and friends behind—or if they left you behind, if they had gone to a previous schismatic church. So why go through all the upheaval of changing again? Yet this is what many ministers and members have done in the years since the first three splits.

The question is, why? Is there a sociological means of exploring this continuing process of schism and reaffiliation, of analyzing who went where and why? And if religious capital and social capital are not sufficient to account for these choices, should we consider a further factor?

9.7 EXPERIENCE OF LEADERSHIP AS A FACTOR IN REAFFILIATION

We saw in chapter 7 the great importance of authority and governance in the Worldwide family of churches. When these are such major issues in the worldview of a religion, leadership and the people who are leaders become hugely important. The comments from questionnaire respondents (see 7.3.2 and 9.5) give an indication of this; for example:

> A few ministers seem to think that hammering people into line is the right kind of government.

and:

> But it is hierarchy nevertheless where in the end the leadership/ordained, not the members, are the final authority.

When ministers and members are considering leaving their church and reaffiliating with another, might their past experience of leadership be another factor to be considered? If the importance of beliefs and practices and of family and friends are labeled religious capital and social capital, then past experience could be labeled moral capital.

The concept of three factors rather than two is borne out by the responses to my asking why people first joined the church they did on leaving Worldwide. I did not provide any options but left space for a free response. There was, as might be expected, a wide variety of answers, but many of them fell into three main categories. Two of these fitted well with the concepts of religious capital and social capital: doctrinal (e.g., "It was still holding to what I had been taught," "Holding to the original doctrines taught by HWA," "Most in line with doctrinal accuracy"), and the importance of family and friends or location ("In-laws were attending—close to home," "Family members attended," "Friends were there"). Counting them up, these groups of comments were made by 43 and 35 respondents, respectively.

The largest group of write-in comments (52 respondents) did not fit into either religious capital or social capital; they were, instead, based on the respondents' personal experience of leadership and individual leaders (e.g., "Least authoritarian in my community," "UCG was not formed as a personal power grab," "Had my favorite ministers," "Was familiar with leader's background," "Personal association with Ron Dart," "RCM [Meredith] pledged to teach the truth"). It is these memories, thoughts, and feelings of past experience, with their obvious emotional intensity, that I am labeling moral capital.

In a religious milieu like the Worldwide family of churches, ministers and members get to know who the church leaders, evangelists, and senior ministers are. They meet them and hear them at the annual Feast of Tabernacles, or as visiting preachers at their services; they see or hear them on TV or radio programs or on the internet; those who in the past were employed at Worldwide's headquarters in Pasadena, or who worked or studied at any of the three Ambassador College campuses, or who worked in any other way in the ministry or administration, will have encountered many of them over the years. And over those years, especially in an authoritarian church where those in senior posts were constantly jostling for position, and people were moved or demoted because of the changing winds of who was in favor at any moment, injustices and abuses occurred or are perceived to have occurred. Memories are long.

With this in mind I stated in the questionnaire:

There are many accounts from the history of Worldwide, particularly from the difficult decade of the 1970s, of ministers and members believing that they were badly treated by people above them in the church hierarchy.

I asked the specific questions:

a. Do you have such memories in your own personal experience?
b. Would you be prepared to belong to a church now whose leader treated you badly in the past?

Table 9.7. EFFECTS OF PAST BAD TREATMENT BY LEADERS

Do you have memories of bad treatment?	Total	Would you belong to a church whose leader had treated you badly?				
		Yes	%	No	%	Unstated
Yes	163 (55%)	36	22	123	75	4
No	132 (45%)	33	25	85	64	14
Totals	295 (100%)	69		208		18

Both were straightforward yes/no questions (see table 9.7).

Just over half of those who answered the first question, 55% (163/295), had personal memories of being badly treated by people above them in the church hierarchy. Of those, 22% (36) said they would be prepared to belong to a church whose leader had treated them badly in the past; 75% (123) said they would not; 2.5% (4) did not answer.

Of the 45% (132) who did not have personal memories of poor treatment in the past, 25% (33) said hypothetically they would join such a church, 64% (85) said they would not, and a much larger percentage, 11% (14), did not say.

First of all, it is noteworthy that over half of the respondents had personal experience of being badly treated by those in authority over them. As well as underlining the perhaps obvious observation that in a church with strong authority, authoritarianism and abuse of authority are likely to occur, this also confirms that I was right to pursue this line of investigation.

Secondly, it is probably significant that while just under two-thirds of respondents who did *not* have personal experience of bad treatment said they would not be prepared to belong to a church whose leader treated them badly in the past, this rose to three-quarters of those who *did* have such personal experience. The actuality of bad treatment in the past strengthened the response compared to what was a hypothetical question for those with no such memories.

Thirdly, those who had memories of past bad treatment were far more decisive in their response, with only one in forty not declaring yes or no, while over a tenth of those who did not have such memories failed to give an answer.

9.8 AN EXTENSION OF STARK AND FINKE: MORAL CAPITAL

So far these comments and answers offer strong anecdotal and some quantitative evidence that personal memories of past experiences with people who are now leaders of offshoot churches have some effect on members' choices of churches. But can this moral capital be balanced with social capital and religious capital as factors governing reaffiliation?

I asked two questions to assess how these three factors could be measured against each other, one based on the respondents' most recent reaffiliation and one hypothetical. The first set out seven statements beginning "I left my previous church to join my current church because…" and asked the respondents to rate each statement separately on a scale from Strongly Agree through Agree, No opinion/Unsure, and Disagree, to Strongly Disagree (see table 9.8). The results (here ordered by response) were extraordinarily clear-cut.

It is immediately apparent that the two strongest responses by far were "I had problems with the leadership of my previous church" (75%, 181/242, strongly agreed or agreed) and "I disagreed with the teachings of my previous church" (72%, 174/241). At the other extreme were "Friends or family were already in my current church" (21%, 48/233), and, even lower, "My current church was more convenient to get to" (14%, 33/237).

In the middle were people who thought their previous church was too hardline (35%, 82/237) or too liberal (27%, 64/237). Over half (54%, 130/239) said they agreed or strongly agreed with the statement "I left my previous church to join my current church because I believe God wanted me to move to my current church"; it is perhaps more surprising that 20% (47/239) said they disagreed or strongly disagreed with this statement.

When asked to assess their reasons for reaffiliation, then, problems with leadership (moral capital) and disagreement with teachings (religious capital) were shown to have been far more influential than friends, family, or convenience (social capital).

The experience of "problems with the leadership of my previous church" is clearly a negative experience, but moral capital itself may be negative or positive; in the case of leadership one can dislike or like a leader.

Table 9.8. REASONS FOR REAFFILIATION

"I left my previous church to join my current church because…"	SA	A	N	D	SD	Total
I had problems with the leadership of my previous church.	119	62	17	25	19	242
I disagreed with the teachings of my previous church.	107	67	23	32	12	241
I believe God wanted me to move to my current church.	77	53	62	26	21	239
My previous church was too hardline.	43	39	41	52	62	237
My previous church was too liberal.	32	32	50	52	71	237
Friends or family were already in my current church.	11	37	47	56	82	233
My current church was more convenient to get to.	11	20	56	63	87	237

I designed a question specifically to test the hypothesis stated as Starke and Finke's proposition 36: "When people reaffiliate, they will tend to select an option that maximizes their conservation of religious capital" (Stark and Finke 2000: 123). The question proposes and tests an extension of the rational choice concepts of social capital and religious capital to include the third factor of moral capital (whether positive or negative) when people make religious choices, specifically involving reaffiliation.

I posed a hypothetical situation which would test the relative strength of these three factors:

Please imagine that you are choosing between two offshoot churches to join, and that there are three factors which might affect your choice of church. These are:

- Doctrine (teachings and practices)—either exactly the same as you believe, or different on two or three points (e.g., day of Pentecost, tithing policy, makeup).
- Your family and close friends—either most of them are in the church, or few of them are.
- The leader of the church—either you like and trust him or you don't, perhaps because of good or bad memories of him in the past, or because of what you know about his character.

Ideally you would like to join a church with all three of these as you prefer, but this isn't an ideal world, and you have to make a difficult choice. In each scenario below, one of these factors is assumed to be exactly as you prefer in both of the churches, and so is ignored for the purpose of the question; I want you to consider the relative importance of the remaining two, and say which of the two churches you would join in each case.

Scenario 1. (Doctrine the same in both churches, so ignored.)
   Church A: Most of your family and close friends are in the church, but you don't like or trust the church's leader.
   Church B: Few of your family and close friends are in the church, but you do like and trust the church's leader.
Would you choose church A or church B?

Scenario 2. (Family and close friends the same in both churches, so ignored.)
   Church C: The church's doctrine is exactly what you believe, but you don't like or trust the church's leader.
   Church D: The church's doctrine is different from what you believe on two or three points, but you do like and trust the church's leader.
Would you choose church C or church D?

Scenario 3. (Your opinion of church leader the same in both churches, so ignored.)
   Church E: The church's doctrine is different from what you believe on two or three points, but most of your family and close friends are in the church.
   Church F: The church's doctrine is exactly what you believe, but few of your family and close friends are in the church.
Would you choose church E or church F?

Between 267 and 272 respondents answered these questions, around 85% of all respondents to the survey (see table 9.9). In tables 9.9, 9.10, and 9.13, "+" indicates a favorable factor and "−" an unfavorable one; for example, "A. Family + Leader −" is shorthand for "Church A: Most of your family and close friends are in the church, but you don't like or trust the church's leader."

Following Stark and Finke's proposition 36, one might predict the two options emphasizing the church's doctrine (C and F) to come out on top and those favoring family and friends (A and E) to be at the bottom, with no prediction for those which were positive about the leader (B and D). My own expectation was that the results for the three options would be broadly even, with religious capital, social capital, and moral capital at more or less the same level of importance. I was wrong, and for the two factors they consider, Stark and Finke were right. But what of the third factor?

It was striking that in the two scenarios (1 and 3) which balanced the importance of family and friends against either the importance of doctrine or liking and

Table 9.9. HYPOTHETICAL CHOICE OF CHURCHES

Positive (+) and Negative (−) Factors	No.	%
Scenario 1		
A. Family + Leader −	49	18
B. Family − Leader +	221	82
Totals	270	100
Scenario 2		
C. Doctrine + Leader −	140	52
D. Doctrine − Leader +	127	48
Totals	267	100
Scenario 3		
E. Family + Doctrine −	65	24
F. Family − Doctrine +	207	76
Totals	272	100

Table 9.10. HYPOTHETICAL CHOICE OF CHURCHES BY GENDER

Positive (+) and Negative (−) Factors	M	M%	F	F%	?	Total	Total %
A. Family + Leader −	39	21	10	12	0	49	18
B. Family − Leader +	144	79	72	88	5	221	82
Totals	183	100	82	100	5	270	100
C. Doctrine + Leader −	94	51	42	55	4	140	52
D. Doctrine − Leader +	91	49	35	45	1	127	48
Totals	185	100	77	100	5	267	100
E. Family + Doctrine −	54	29	11	14	0	65	24
F. Family − Doctrine +	133	71	69	86	5	207	76
Totals	187	100	80	100	5	272	100

trusting the leader (or not), family and friends were markedly less important. Only 24% (65/272) rated family and friends above doctrine (76%, 207/272), while, if given the choice between a church leader they liked and trusted but few family and friends or being with most of their family and friends but having a leader they did not like or trust, a huge 82% (221/270) said they would choose the former and only 18% (49/270) the latter.

In scenario 2, when family and friends were taken out of the picture, there was a very even balance between the importance of the church's doctrine and having a leader they liked and trusted, with the former (52%, 140/267) coming out just ahead of the latter (48%, 127/267).

Table 9.10 expands table 9.9 to include the gender of the respondents. Around 68–69% were male and 29–30% female (five respondents did not say)—broadly the proportions of all respondents. Would men and women make different choices? Might women, for example, follow a gender stereotype and place a higher emphasis on family and friends? The answer to that was no; in fact, the opposite was the case. In this survey more women rated the importance of the leader over family and friends (88% to 12%) compared to men (79% to 21%), and substantially more women rated the importance of doctrine over family and friends (86% to 14%) compared to men (71% to 29%). On the question of the relative importance of correct doctrine and liking and trusting the leader, a higher proportion of women (55%) than men (51%) rated doctrine more highly.

I next looked at whether the age of the respondents might have an effect on their choices in these three scenarios (see Table 9.11).

Because of the relative proportions of each age group of respondents, it is not possible to come to any conclusion from the straightforward numbers; instead I calculated the percentage of those in each age group who made each choice from each scenario (see table 9.12)—e.g., 12 out of 48 respondents in their forties chose

Table 9.11. HYPOTHETICAL CHOICE OF CHURCHES BY AGE

Scenario	20s	30s	40s	50s	60s	70s	No Age	Totals[4]
A	0	11	11	15	9	1	2	49
B	5	17	35	86	51	15	12	221
								270
C	3	15	20	57	33	6	6	140
D	2	14	25	41	28	9	8	127
								267
E	1	10	12	24	12	1	5	65
F	4	17	36	76	49	16	9	207
								272
Totals[4]	5	27–29	45–48	98–101	60–61	15–17	14	

4. Because slightly different numbers of respondents answered each question, the totals do not work out the same, but this is not of great significance.

option E, and 36 chose option F, being 25% and 75%, respectively—and plotted these on a graph (see figure 9.1).

It is striking how on the graph the six choices fall into three groups: in order down the left-hand side of the graph, the high selection of scenarios B and F, which rate leader and doctrine, respectively, over family and friends, the roughly equal selection of scenarios C and D, where respondents had to choose between doctrine and leader, respectively, and the relatively low selection of scenarios E and A, putting family and friends above doctrine and leader, respectively.

The other very clear observation that can be made from this graph is that as age increases from the thirties to the seventies, the importance of both doctrine and leader rises substantially and the importance of family and friends falls just as substantially. (Note that as there were only five respondents in their twenties, their results cannot be counted as significant.) Without further data any explanations for this phenomenon must be speculative, but I would suggest two possibilities. First, respondents in their thirties with young families are perhaps more likely than older respondents to rate social ties as important. Second, the older respondents are, the

Table 9.12. PERCENTAGE OF EACH AGE GROUP CHOOSING EACH SCENARIO

Scenario	20s	30s	40s	50s	60s	70s
A	0	39	24	15	15	6
B	100	61	76	85	85	94
C	60	52	44	58	54	40
D	40	48	56	42	46	60
E	20	37	25	24	20	6
F	80	63	75	76	80	94

Figure 9.1 Percentage of Each Age Group Choosing Each Scenario

more years they spent in Worldwide; thus the doctrines are more deeply in their blood, and they will have had more years' personal experience of the offshoot leaders, for good and for bad.

The responses to these three scenario questions can be manipulated and displayed in several ways. Table 9.9 summarizes the results succinctly: doctrine and liking and trusting the leader far outweigh how many family and friends are in a church. Table 9.10 breaks this down by the gender of the respondents, and tables 9.11 and 9.12 and figure 9.1 by their age.

Table 9.13 summarizes the responses of *individual* respondents, i.e., how many people voted for exactly the same combinations of scenarios. The table shows all those who answered all three questions, excluding those who answered only one or two of them.

This table shows the eight possible combinations of choices in three ways: the scenarios A through F; a shorthand of what each of those means in the choices column (as with tables 9.9 and 9.10 "+" shows a favorable factor and "−" an unfavorable one); and a summary which shows simply the combination of the three factors.

Once again the results are striking. Two-fifths of all those who answered all three questions (40%, 102/257) made exactly the same choices: for the leader over family and friends, for doctrine over the leader and for doctrine over family and friends—in summary, doctrine 2, leader 1, family and friends 0. A quarter (26%, 66) chose the leader over family and friends, the leader over doctrine, and doctrine over family and friends: leader 2, doctrine 1, family and friends 0. Of the next two combinations, 14% (37) chose leader 2, family and friends 1, doctrine 0, while 9% (23) chose doctrine 2, family and friends 1, leader 0. The remaining four combinations, of the eight possible, were selected by only 10% of the respondents in total, with only 2% (6) of individual respondents choosing equally among the three factors.

Looking at these choices another way, a total of 49% (125) of these 257 respondents chose doctrine twice, 40% (103) chose leader twice, and 9% (23) chose family and friends twice.

Table 9.13. SUMMARY OF INDIVIDUAL RESPONDENTS'
HYPOTHETICAL CHOICES

Scenario	Choices	Summary	No.	%
B + C + F	Ldr + Fam −/Doc + Ldr −/Doc + Fam −	Doc 2 Ldr 1	102	40
B + D + F	Ldr + Fam −/Ldr + Doc −/Doc + Fam −	Ldr 2 Doc 1	66	26
B + D + E	Ldr + Fam −/Ldr + Doc −/Fam + Doc −	Ldr 2 Fam 1	37	14
A + C + F	Fam + Ldr −/Doc + Ldr −/Doc + Fam −	Doc 2 Fam 1	23	9
A + D + E	Fam + Ldr −/Ldr + Doc −/Fam + Doc −	Fam 2 Ldr 1	16	6
A + C + E	Fam + Ldr −/Doc + Ldr −/Fam + Doc −	Fam 2 Doc 1	7	3
A + D + F	Fam + Ldr −/Ldr + Doc −/Doc + Fam −	Fam 1 Ldr 1 Doc 1	3	1
B + C + E	Ldr + Fam −/Doc + Ldr −/Fam + Doc −	Fam 1 Ldr 1 Doc 1	3	1
			257	100

It is also worth looking at what proportions of these respondents did *not* choose each factor. A huge two-thirds (66%, 168) did not choose family and friends in *any* scenario; 20% (53) did not choose doctrine at all, while only 12% (30) did not choose leader at all. The last two are a reversal of what one might have expected, considering the small lead of doctrine over leader in the other breakdowns. This is probably because although in a straight choice between doctrine and leader (scenario 2), doctrine is rated as a little more important (52% to 48%), in the choice of either of these over family and friends, consideration of the leader (scenario 1: 82% against 18%) rates more highly in comparison to consideration of doctrine (scenario 3: 76% against 24%)—see table 9.9.

With the caveats noted above (9.1), the preceding tables show clearly that in both the actual situation of their last reaffiliation and a carefully considered hypothetical reaffiliation, moral capital—in this case whether or not members like and trust the leaders of churches—is of broadly equal importance (within a few percentage points) to religious capital for members of the Worldwide family of churches when changing from one offshoot to another, and that social capital is of far less importance.

9.9 CONCLUSION

In this chapter we saw that, for the respondents to my questionnaire, the final doctrinal straws causing most people to leave the Worldwide Church of God were, in order, the abandoning of the Sabbath requirement, reducing the requirement to obey Law, and the change of teaching on the Trinity (9.3). The first two are vital components of the socially constructed reality of Armstrong's Worldwide, based on obedience to God (see 2.2.2 and 3.2.1); the third is one of the most fundamental doctrines separating the old Worldwide from mainstream Christianity (see 2.2.1 and appendix 1).

Questions on family and friends showed clearly that social ties are not a major influence on church affiliation (9.4).

When asked if there were any church leaders they thought unfit for a variety of reasons, pride or arrogance and authoritarianism topped the list of disqualifying traits (9.5). Over half the respondents had personal memories of bad treatment from people above them in the church hierarchy, and three-quarters of these said they would not belong to a church led by such a person (9.7). When asked to rate the reasons they had left their last church, problems with the leadership and disagreement with the teachings were overwhelmingly the most significant; by far the least important reasons were social issues such as family and friends and convenience (9.8).

Believing that Rodney Stark and Roger Finke's rational choice concepts of social capital and religious capital (Stark and Finke 2000: 114–24) did not offer sufficient explanation for the religious choices people made in reality, I designed a question to test an extension of their theoretical construct by including a third factor, moral capital, in this case past experience of leadership (9.8). This confirmed in a readily quantifiable way my previous finding that, in this group of churches, doctrine and leadership issues—religious capital and moral capital—far outweighed family and friends—social capital—in people's decisions on reaffiliation. This extension of rational choice theory is a significant development in the analysis and understanding of the complex issue of religious choice.

CHAPTER 10

The Fragmentation of a Sect

A Conclusion

This study has told the extraordinary story of a Christian sect with its own heterodox doctrines and its distinctive worldview based on the fundamental importance of order and obedience, and of its fragmentation following the death of its founder.

The earlier chapters described the origins and development of the Worldwide Church of God, focusing on its doctrine and its social construction of reality, on the vital importance of founder Herbert W. Armstrong, and on the significance of leadership, authority, and governance in the church (chapters 2 to 4)—and how everything changed after Armstrong's death (chapter 5).

At the beginning I asked who went where and why. In chapter 6 we saw *where* former members of Worldwide went, both in the three initial exits of 1989, 1992–93, and 1995 and into some four hundred different churches in the years since—an astonishing story of fragmentation which is clearly not finished yet (see appendix 6).

The later chapters explored and analyzed the process of schism and the schismatic churches in the Worldwide family in several ways.

Chapter 7 examined the validation of authority of Armstrong, his successor Joseph W. Tkach, and offshoot leaders both in relation to classic sociological typology and in other ways, and the effect of this on their attitudes to governance in their churches. The complex range of attitudes toward Herbert W. Armstrong is crucial to the consideration of authority and leadership in both the historical Worldwide and all its offspring in the Worldwide family of churches even a quarter of a century after Armstrong's death (consider the fissioning of United at the end of 2010: see 6.2.3.2).

In chapter 8 I looked in some detail, with the use of an original typological model, at what can happen to a religion after the death of its founder, and explored many of the factors which can affect this. The model uses two variables, whether a movement stays much the same or changes, and whether in each case this is stable or unstable, to determine four ideal types of outcome: continuation, dissolution, reform/revolution, and schism. It also considers convergence with and divergence from more mainstream religious beliefs and practices. What happened with the Worldwide Church of God is quite an exceptional case, but examining it in the context of other religious movements after the deaths of their founders is a reminder that while every religion has its own combination of characteristics, no religion is uniquely distinct.

Finally in chapter 9 I examined *why* former members of this doctrinally heterodox and authoritarian sect chose to go in different directions, and found that their religious choice is by no means as straightforward as a simple preference for more hardline or more liberal versions of the church they all came from, as might have been inferred from the list of options presented in 1.1, and also from some of the views expressed on authority in chapters 6 and 7.

Neither is it a balance between just two factors, social capital (ties with family and friends, and convenience) and religious capital (belief in and adherence to certain doctrines); by introducing a third factor, moral capital (in this specific case members liking and trusting the various church leaders or not) I have shown that the reality of choice in religious reaffiliation is substantially more complex than Stark and Finke proposed in their theoretical propositions. In other religious choices—or in political or other worldview choices—the factor of moral capital might well be something quite different from liking and trusting a leader; but here I believe I have shown the need for extending the theory of religious choice to enable it to fit reality better, so overcoming some of the limitations of this area of rational choice theory.

I hope that others will find these two original contributions to sociological theory of practical use.

This has been a complex story. Ultimately, when we ask why people take the momentous step of leaving the religion to which they have devoted much of their lives to go off to join a new one, and then perhaps leave that to join (or even to found) another, and then maybe another, each person's reasons are his or her own. No one, insider or outsider, could possibly recount everything that happened, and how and why, from every possible perspective. There have been numerous personal accounts by ministers and members, from a few hundred words to a few hundred pages long; each, quite naturally, has its own bias, as it is the story of an individual's experience and, crucially, his interpretation of that experience.

But this study, in examining who went where and why in the fragmentation of this particular Christian movement, has attempted to paint a wider picture.

By using a largely phenomenological approach I have allowed a number of very different former members of Worldwide to tell their own tales, and have accepted the validity of each person's *perception* of events, though not necessarily the *factuality* of their accounts. As an outsider, as I told ministers and members of the offshoot churches both in personal communication and in the article introducing my questionnaire, I had no ax to grind. I did not share the worldview of either the old or the new Worldwide. I did not share the doctrinal beliefs of the members of the offshoots, or their social ties, or their memories of past authoritarian excesses. Neither did I share their shock and their sense of betrayal at the doctrinal changes which first caused them to leave Worldwide. But nor did I rejoice with the Tkach reformers, or with the Evangelical Christians who welcomed them into their fold, at the transformation of Worldwide. With none of this doctrinal, social, and emotional baggage from any side, I was free to watch, to listen, to read, to ask questions—to be a detached professional observer.

And as such, I could write the first major sociological study of the Worldwide Church of God after the death of its founder, including of necessity its beliefs, origins, and development up to that point, and then its doctrinal revolution and its ensuing fragmentation, and analyze in depth the processes of schism and reaffiliation.

John Wilson's definition of a schismatic group sums up the main Worldwide offshoots neatly: "A movement which has its origins in a dispute over norms and allegations that the main group has departed from those implicated in the values of the original movement" (J. Wilson 1971: 5). This applies clearly to the three major initial schisms from the Worldwide Church of God, which had departed radically from the norms and values—the teachings—of its founder, Herbert W. Armstrong.

This study of the complicated reality of the Worldwide schisms has, I believe, demonstrated that some earlier sociological approaches to schism are lacking. For just one example, while Danny L. Jorgensen states categorically that "the intuitively pleasing idea that schism is caused by doctrinal disputes has been substantially rejected by conventional theories of religion in preference of social differentiation" (Jorgensen 1993: 18), this study has shown clearly that this is simply not so. In the case of the Worldwide Church of God, the initial schisms in the years after Herbert W. Armstrong's death were incontrovertibly caused by doctrinal disputes.

Two decades before Jorgensen's statement, John Wilson wrote that sociological observation of schisms "as the expression of social differences rather than the doctrinal and liturgical disputes they ostensibly represent" is "informative" but "does not tell the full story, for it does not tell us why social conflict should lead to religious separation, simply because it does not look inside the schism-rent group to examine the tensions and strains found within" (J. Wilson 1971: 1). It is my hope that the present detailed study of the tensions and strains within the schism-rent Worldwide family of churches has done just this.

APPENDIX 1
Sect, Cult, New Religious Movement

The historical Worldwide Church of God is normally thought of as a Christian sect. Detractors have called it a cult—Christian counter-cultists because of its deviation in beliefs from mainstream Christianity, and ex-members because of alleged instances of authoritarianism and abuse.[1] Sociologists of religion would be more likely to refer to it as a new religious movement (NRM), though the founding of the work that would become Worldwide in 1934 puts it before the arbitrary cutoff point of World War II proposed by Eileen Barker (Barker 1992: 145).

Only a brief summary is necessary of the many sociological typologies of religious movements.

Weber distinguished between church and sect (M. Weber 1965); Troeltsch developed this into a more formal dichotomy between the church, which maintained the accepted social order, and the sect, which appealed to the socially marginalized (Troeltsch 1931). Niebuhr proposed that sects are transient; they either die or evolve into denominations (Niebuhr 1957). Other sociologists, including both Becker and Yinger, expanded the typology with reference to ecclesia and denominations; Yinger in particular distinguished between established sects, transient sects, and cults (Yinger 1970). Berger distinguished between enthusiastic, prophetic, and gnostic sects (Berger 1954).

More recent typologies, of greater relevance to the present study, include the idea that a cult is a culturally innovative new group, different from its surrounding culture—or, in Stark's phrase, a *novel* religious movement (quoted in Bainbridge 1997: 23–24); Stark and Bainbridge's work on tension with society (Stark and Bainbridge 1985: passim); Wallis's two axes of unique or pluralistic legitimacy and

---

1. Just as this study remains agnostic or value-free on the spiritual truth of the doctrines of the Worldwide family, so it must on the objective validity of alleged authoritarian abuse; again, I am seeking to understand, not to judge. However, the *perception* of abuse is of major importance, as seen particularly in chapters 7 and 9.

respectability or deviance, to distinguish between church, denomination, sect, and cult (Wallis 1975: 40–41); Wallis's later proposal of a threefold typology of world-rejecting, world-accommodating, and world-affirming movements (Wallis 2003); and Wilson's original fourfold typology of sects, which was later expanded into a more complex sevenfold typology (B. Wilson 1970: 37–40).

All of these (and the many other typologies which have been proposed) have their worth, but for the purposes of this book I treat a sect as a schismatic movement and/or a religiously intense movement, within the traditions of a more mainstream religious culture (Bainbridge 1997: 23); and a cult (though I avoid the word wherever possible) as a group with a very strong focus on one person, place, or idea (this is more the standard Roman Catholic usage—the cult of Mary or the cult of Lourdes—than a sociological definition). By these definitions both the historical Worldwide Church of God and its offshoots could be classified as sects and (in some cases) as cults, without the pejorative connotations of the popular usage of that word.

Many typologies are based on the relationship between movements and the society in which they exist (Stark and Bainbridge 1985; Stark and Bainbridge 1987; Wallis 2003, etc). Although this is useful, I find it limiting in the present case. Within Christianity, for example, it makes little distinction between two groups of movements. On the one hand there are Methodist, Baptist, Pentecostal, Brethren, independent Evangelical churches, and others which, while they have their differences in doctrine and practice, share large portions of their core beliefs and are regarded as theologically "acceptable" within the broad spread of mainstream Christianity both by individuals and churches and by ecumenical organizations such as the World Council of Churches and Churches Together in Britain and Ireland (CTBI).[2] On the other hand there are movements such as the Mormons, Jehovah's Witnesses, Unitarians, Christadelphians, Unification Church, and others, which have such substantial theological differences from the core beliefs of mainstream Christianity that they are regarded as unacceptable, if not heretical, by mainstream ecumenical organizations; Christian counter-cult organizations target this group because of their "false" beliefs.[3]

The most fundamental theological divergence is on the nature of the Godhead, and such movements' dismissal or radical reinterpretation of the doctrine of the Trinity. Thus, however respected Unitarians might be as individuals, or for their social and humanitarian work, because they are by definition not Trinitarian, they are not granted even observer status in CTBI (Barrett 2001a: 148; Smith 1967).

The term "Christian sect," then, can embrace a wide variety of movements, and actually includes two quite different groups of movements in theological terms.

2. Successor to the British Council of Churches.
3. Books such as Walter R. Martin's influential *The Kingdom of the Cults* carefully compare the beliefs of such movements with the standard beliefs of Evangelical Christianity to demonstrate that the movements' beliefs are unbiblical and therefore false.

This is a difficulty in traditional sociological typology, which does not usually concern itself with the theological content of beliefs. (It is irrelevant to the argument that movements such as the Methodists and Baptists are now regarded as denominations rather than sects; following Niebuhr, a denomination is effectively an evolved or mature or even an accepted sect.)

I do not intend to formulate a new typology of religious movements beyond noting a substantive difference between these two groups of movements *as perceived by a general consensus within mainstream Christianity* and ascribing the labels of *orthodox sects* to those which fit broadly within mainstream Christianity and *heterodox sects* to those which mainstream Christians would regard as heretical. It should be understood that these two terms mark two ends of a continuum. Some movements are doctrinally substantially orthodox but have been criticized by counter-cultists for specific practices (e.g., authoritarianism in the Jesus Fellowship/Jesus Army and the International Churches of Christ); others accept all the major doctrines of mainstream Christianity with one or two alterations or additions (e.g., The Family, with their "Law of Love" and their acceptance of David and Maria Berg as inspired prophets).[4]

As we see in chapter 2, the historical Worldwide Church of God and its offshoots are effectively Binitarian rather than Trinitarian, and also have several other substantial theological differences from mainstream Christian beliefs. For the purposes of this study, the current Worldwide is treated as (more or less) an orthodox Christian sect, and the historical Worldwide and the offshoot Churches are treated as heterodox sects not just of Christianity but, more specifically, of the Sabbatarian millenarian movement.

---

4. In *The Kingdom of the Cults* Walter Martin accepts this difficulty when discussing the Seventh-day Adventist Church, whose doctrinal changes over the last few decades have brought it almost "acceptably" close, from his viewpoint, to mainstream Christian beliefs (see 2.2.1).

APPENDIX 2
Theoretical Basis and Methodology

Although this is a sociological study, it should not be seen as limited to just that one academic discipline. Its phenomenological approach should make it of interest to scholars and students of religious studies in general, history of religion, theology, anthropology, psychology of religion and, because of its subject matter, the religious subset of American studies.

In some ways this is a basic ethnographic study, though based largely on literary sources, interviews and correspondence rather than traditional participant observation. It is a study of groups of people who have left their parent group to create or join other groups in order to preserve their social construction of reality, and an examination of the methods by which they produce and maintain a shared sense of social order (Garfinkel 2002: 117). But it is within the sociological phenomenology of religion that it best fits.

In seeking to answer the question "Who went where and why?" I have been aware from the beginning that there are many answers, and that they frequently contradict one another. Part of my aim in this book has been to let a variety of disparate voices be heard. In terms taken from cultural anthropology, *emic* and *etic*, coined by linguist Kenneth L. Pike in 1954 and used in a variety of different ways in different disciplines over the past half century (Headland 1990), I utilize both the conflicting self-descriptions of the churches and individuals (the emic approach) and my external critical analysis of these and other descriptions (the etic approach). Both are vital.

Both are also essential components of the phenomenology of religion, which I first studied at undergraduate level in the 1970s.[1] Ninian Smart coined the term

---

1. I studied at Charlotte Mason College in Ambleside, UK, which then came under the University of Lancaster, where Professor Ninian Smart had founded the first religious studies course in Britain in 1967. My Phenomenology of Religion course, taught by Gordon Aldrick, was based largely on Smart's work, especially *The Religious Experience of Mankind* (Smart 1969), and also on *The Sociological Study of Religion* (Scharf 1970) by Betty R. Scharf, who, in a further connection, taught for many years at LSE. I was privileged to meet both Smart and Scharf many years later, albeit briefly, through my doctoral supervisor at LSE.

"informed empathy" to describe the approach: a combination of *epoché* (suspension of judgment or belief) and "the use of empathy in entering into the experiences and intentions of religious participants" (Smart 1987: chap. 1; Smart 1996: 2). These are the qualities I sought to bring to bear on the people who form my subject matter: those ministers and members of Worldwide who left that church to found or join another, and then in many cases left that for yet another.

It is essentially a value-free approach. I have had several years of correspondence with deeply believing members of various Churches of God who took for granted many beliefs which I do not share. Sometimes they assumed that I believed in them too, or occasionally tried to persuade me of their truth, though most seemed to understand the concept of a disinterested scholarly observer. The spiritual truth of the beliefs of the Worldwide family of churches, both those they all share and those they disagree on, is of no relevance to this study. I have stressed to ministers and members that "I don't have a position on the various doctrinal and organizational differences between United and its offshoots, or between, say, Living and Philadelphia and Restored. I am seeking to understand, not to judge" (Barrett 2008: 23).

This, to me, is the essence of phenomenological sociology.

The religious legitimation of the Worldwide Church of God was dependent on the founder, ministers, and members sharing a particular mindset, or worldview, or *Weltanschauung*, or, in the terminology of Peter Berger and Thomas Luckman, social construction of reality (Berger and Luckmann 1966). They were complicit in the creation, acceptance, and maintenance of a very specific social construct in which "meaningful order, or *nomos*, is imposed upon the discrete experiences and meanings of individuals" (Berger 1969: 28). It was the destruction of this carefully constructed reality in the doctrinal changes in the years after the founder's death—the threat to the plausibility structure underlying their religious world (Berger 1969: 54)—that was to cause the initial schisms, as ministers and members tried to maintain this meaningful order of their lives.

I have sought to examine and explore this worldview—in all its variations—and how it affected the personal choices of ministers and members in their reaffiliation with other groups, through a number of means.

First, as a fundamental basis for all my research, came the literature of Worldwide and its many offshoot churches, in books, booklets, magazines, and websites (see appendix 3.3). As I examine in some detail (see 2.2.1), both the historical Worldwide and its offshoots have always been open and upfront about their beliefs. These include not only theological doctrine but, essentially, how this should impact on the lives of believers, from worshiping on the seventh-day Sabbath to observing the Hebrew holy days and not celebrating "pagan" festivals like Christmas and Easter, to managing their finances, to what to eat, to how to adorn oneself. Without a thorough grounding in and understanding of the Worldwide family beliefs, there is no chance of comprehending their socially constructed reality—or why it mattered so much when it was forcibly changed.

Other written works about Worldwide and the schisms are described in appendix 3.

Next, over the years of this research I have had personal communications with a wide assortment of Worldwide family members, ministers, church leaders, and internal observers, and also a number of critical former members. These have included letters and emails, tape-recorded interviews, and more informal conversations, both face-to-face and by telephone, all of which have provided a wealth of, in most cases, attributable quotations which appear throughout this book. Through this personal contact I have gained a far deeper understanding of the issues at the heart of this book, such as beliefs, authority, leadership, and personalities, and how they affected the choices of individual ministers and members.

What I learned from these personal communications, building on the grounding of the churches' literature, enabled me to compose a questionnaire (see chapter 9 and appendices 3.6, 4, and 5) to elicit further information from members I had had no previous contact with, and to test a number of ideas concerning the basic questions of who went where and why.

It was not feasible for me to undertake much traditional participant observation during my research. The overwhelming majority of the many offshoot churches are based in the United States, as are most of their congregations, and for a number of practical reasons, including other responsibilities, family and health issues, and lack of funding, it was not possible for me to go there. I was, however, able to meet several church leaders and spokesmen and to attend services of the United and Living Churches of God in Britain.

Literature and Other Sources

APPENDIX 3.1 BOOKS ABOUT WORLDWIDE CHURCH OF GOD

Numerous books were published about the Worldwide Church of God during its heyday, when Herbert W. Armstrong was still alive. A few were written by outsiders, and some by former members, including two scathing attacks on the church, and specifically on Armstrong himself, by former senior ministers. The author of *Armstrongism: Religion or Rip-off?* (M. McNair 1977) joined the then Radio Church of God in 1948 and rose to the highest ministerial rank of evangelist before Armstrong suspended him as a minister. The author of *Herbert Armstrong's Tangled Web: An Insider's View of the Worldwide Church of God* (D. Robinson 1980) worked mainly in senior administrative roles in the church; his book documents many of the alleged abuses and scandals of the 1970s. Two other internal books give very different views of a major event in Worldwide's history, when the state of California put the church into receivership in 1979 (see 4.5). One, *The Truth Shall Make You Free: Herbert Armstrong's Empire Exposed* (Tuit 1981), was by the man who initiated the lawsuit against the church which caused the receivership; the other, *Against the Gates of Hell: The Threat to Religious Freedom in America* (Rader 1980), was by Armstrong's own attorney, who fought the case on behalf of the church. These two books, which might almost be describing different events, exemplify a point which is apparent throughout this book: the very strong personal bias of my internal sources.

The same applies to books written about the changes in Worldwide since 1995. Three are very positive about the changes. *Transformed by Truth* (Tkach 1997) is by Joseph Tkach Jr., the current pastor general of WCG, who, with his father, was largely responsible for the changes. *The Liberation of the Worldwide Church of God* (Feazell 2003) is by another of the architects of change. The third, *Discovering the Plain Truth: How the Worldwide Church of God Encountered the Gospel of Grace* (Nichols and Mather 1998), is by two Lutheran ministers and tells the story from an Evangelical Christian viewpoint. The titles of these books give a clear indication of their stance. None of them spends much time on the offshoot churches, but they are useful in presenting the viewpoint of those at the top of the new Worldwide.

Taking a diametrically opposed stance to these three is *Raising the Ruins: The Fight to Revive the Legacy of Herbert W. Armstrong* (S. Flurry 2006), by the son of the leader of the Philadelphia Church of God, the first of the three major offshoots. This details the doctrinal changes in Worldwide, the first schism from it, and the legal battles over the ownership of Armstrong's books (see 6.2.1).

Other books are more scholarly.

APPENDIX 3.2 ACADEMIC WORK ON WORLDWIDE CHURCH OF GOD

Although this study is mainly of the events after Armstrong's death in 1986, I have also made some use of two earlier critical studies of the historical WCG. *The Armstrong Empire: A Look at the Worldwide Church of God* (Hopkins 1974) is by Professor Joseph Hopkins, formerly of the Department of Religion and Philosophy at Westminster College, New Wilmington, Pennsylvania. *Ambassadors of Armstrongism: An Analysis of the History and Teachings of the Worldwide Church of God* (Benware 1977) was a doctoral thesis written by Paul N. Benware, a student at Grace Theological Seminary, Winona Lake, Indiana. Both authors are Evangelical Christians, and their books are written from that perspective, but both are scrupulously fair in their accounts of Worldwide and its teachings.

Two previous doctoral theses have been written about the doctrinal changes in Worldwide. One, by Cornelius A. O'Connor at St. David's College, University of Wales, Lampeter, was completed in 1993 during the transitional years between Armstrong's death and Tkach's declaration of Evangelical orthodoxy in 1995: *A Comprehensive Analysis of the History and Doctrines of the Worldwide Church of God (Armstrongism), Together with an Exegetical Commentary and a Discussion of Some of the Radical Doctrinal Changes in the Post-Armstrong Era of the Church* (O'Connor 1993). Much of this thesis was on doctrine—392 of its 662 pages—but some of the author's closing discussion was relevant to my own research. Under the name Neil O'Connor he also has a chapter, "'Take One, It's FREE!': The Story behind the Worldwide Church of God and the Plain Truth Magazine" (O'Connor 1997), in a 1997 book on millennial themes in world religions (Bowie 1997).

Johannes Lothar Felix Buchner, a psychology student at the University of Western Sydney, was kind enough to send me a copy of his 2006 doctoral thesis, *The Worldwide Church of God: A Study of Its Transformation in Terms of K. Helmut Reich's Theory of Relational and Contextual Reasoning* (Buchner 2006). Although this is specifically about the changes in Worldwide, its approach makes it of only peripheral usefulness to the present study. Buchner has been researching Worldwide for many years; he has also written the detailed and useful (though obviously now very outdated) *Armstrong Bibliography* (Buchner 1983) and the report *Armstrongism in Britain* (Buchner 1985).

A much shorter psychological study of Herbert W. Armstrong was written by a pastor of the current Worldwide Church of God, Neil Earle, as part of his MA at the Fuller Theological Seminary, Pasadena, California (Earle 2004).

In addition, though its subject matter predates the Worldwide Church of God, the MA dissertation "The Political Influence of the British-Israel Movement in the Nineteenth Century" by Richard Simpson (Birkbeck College, London; Simpson 2002) provided useful background information.

APPENDIX 3.3 "WORLDWIDE FAMILY" WORKS

It is a truism that history is written by the victors, and in the case of books about the changes in Worldwide (Tkach 1997, Feazell 2003, etc.) this is at least partly valid. But to quote the historian John Callow, "History is actually written by the literate" (Callow 2008). Since its beginning as the Radio Church of God in the 1930s, Worldwide was characterized largely by its literature, and this trait has been inherited by most of the offspring of the Worldwide family. Nearly all of the largest and medium-sized offshoots[1] and even some of the smallest have produced their own books and booklets.[2] Even those churches which would not assist my research by answering formal questions were prepared to send their literature; their books, booklets, and magazines have been invaluable source material, both for direct quotation and for background.

Most of the books and booklets are doctrinal or exegetical, often setting out ways in which Worldwide family teachings are different from mainstream Christianity, for example *Sunset to Sunset—God's Sabbath Rest* (United), *Which Day is the Christian Sabbath?* (Global), *God is a Family* (Philadelphia), *The Trinity—Is God Three-in-One?* (Restored), *When I Die, What Happens Next?* (GTA Evangelistic Association). Many of these are in one way or another rewrites of Herbert W. Armstrong's booklets from the original Worldwide (see 6.1.4), including at least half a dozen variants on Armstrong's British Israelite work *The United States and Britain in Prophecy* (see 2.2.3), ranging from the 44-page *What's Ahead for America and Britain?* from Living (Ogwyn 1999) to the mammoth 448-page A4-sized *America and Great Britain—Our Identity Revealed!* from Triumph Prophetic Ministries (Dankenbring 2005; see 2.2.3 note 17).

Some literature deals with the changes in Worldwide that precipitated the schisms; for example, the leader of the Restored Church of God produced a 425-page book, *There Came a Falling Away* (Pack 2008), detailing 280 doctrinal changes in Worldwide (see 6.2.2.1); the leader of the Philadelphia Church of God produced the slimmer 89-page *Worldwide Church of God Doctrinal Changes and the Tragic*

1. COGaic is the most notable exception (see 6.2.3.1).
2. For this study I am arbitrarily defining books as more than one hundred pages and booklets as fewer than one hundred pages.

Results (G. Flurry 1994). A member of United, Roger Waite, provided a copy of his 323-page unpublished book, "An Analysis of the WCG Doctrinal Changes and Crisis in the Church of God" (Waite 2000).

Some books, more often from individuals or from small organizations rather than from the larger churches, are presented as scholarship, such as *Restoring the Original Bible*, by Ernest L. Martin of Associates for Scriptural Knowledge (E. Martin 1994); a series of books by Art Mokarow with titles like *God's Puzzle Solved* (Mokarow 2004); and several very substantial hardback books by Fred R. Coulter of the Christian Biblical Church of God including a 482-page volume on the meaning of the Christian Passover and on what day it should be observed (Coulter 1999), a harmony of the gospels (Coulter 2001) and new translations of the New Testament (Coulter 2003) and the whole Bible (Coulter 2007).

Other books set out to prove that their authors themselves fulfill Bible prophecy, whether Gerald Flurry, founder of the Philadelphia Church of God (G. Flurry 1995a; G. Flurry 1995b; G. Flurry 2007; see 6.2.1), or Ronald Weinland, who believes that he and his wife are the Two Witnesses of the End Times (Weinland 2004; Weinland 2006; see 6.4.4).

I have also made use of books, CDs, and DVDs produced by ministries rather than churches in the Worldwide family (see 6.4.5), providing archive material, including all the books, booklets, and Bible correspondence courses from the historical Worldwide, Armstrong's articles and letters to church members and co-workers, and many articles from *Plain Truth* and other Worldwide magazines.[3] Richard C. Nickels, of Giving and Sharing, had a particular interest in the history of the Seventh-day movement and the origins and early days of Worldwide, and most usefully provided me with a copy of his collection *Early Writings of Herbert W. Armstrong*, which contains articles from 1928 to 1953 (Nickels 1996c).

In addition to these and other books, there are vast numbers of booklets, reprint articles, and magazines—and, of course, websites—from churches, ministries, and individuals. All of these have provided invaluable source material.

I have tried wherever possible to use print sources for quotations, but have on a number of occasions quoted from the websites of churches or individuals; these are often undated citations. The URLs are given in the bibliography, but are inevitably subject to change; in a few cases websites I accessed early in my research had disappeared completely by the end of it.

The factual reliability of all such sources is discussed in 3.1. The many internal sources are a valuable record of how their history was and is seen by those involved in it. They often present very different viewpoints of the old Worldwide and the new, and of the offshoots; it is such *perceptions* that form the setting for this book: "Our phenomenological approach gives some status to perceived history as one of the causative factors at work in a given context" (Smart 1996: 17).

---

3. All copies of *Plain Truth* magazine from 1934 to 1986 are archived in PDF form at http://www.herbertarmstrong.org/Plain%20Truth.html.

APPENDIX 3.4 OTHER SOURCES

One of the most useful resources for ongoing news about churches in the Worldwide family is the monthly newspaper *The Journal: News of the Churches of God* (see 6.4.5.1). This succeeded a similar newspaper, *In Transition: News of the Churches of God*, which ran from May 1995 to February 1997. Both papers were run by members from the more liberal end of the spectrum of churches (see 6.1.3) but published factual news of events, publications, and changes in the whole range of churches, and also provided a platform for doctrinal debate. *The Journal*'s website allowed for more timely news of, for example, the deaths of several major personalities in the Worldwide family.[4]

Another source for news of the churches, *Ambassador Watch,* changed from being an online news website to a personal blog during my research, but even as a blog it provided some useful information, and was at times very helpful for tracking down a piece of information. Although its creator, New Zealander Gavin Rumney, a former member of Worldwide, is roundly critical of both the old Worldwide and the offshoots, and also of the new Worldwide, he seems to be regarded with a certain amount of respect by some members of the more liberal offshoots, and appears to have a number of informants on the "inside." I also consulted several other critical websites and blogs by former members.

For older material I was able to make use of a number of issues of an occasional newsletter, *Ambassador Report*, which was set up in 1976 (initially as *Ambassador Review*) by John Trechak and other former graduates of Ambassador College, to turn a critical, sometimes humorous, often investigative, but usually fair eye on the Worldwide Church of God.[5]

APPENDIX 3.5 PERSONAL COMMUNICATIONS

All quotations not otherwise sourced are taken from my personal communications with leaders, ministers, and members of the churches.

A few of the quotations and paraphrased comments in this book are off the record or anonymous. These include all the comments by questionnaire respondents, who were guaranteed anonymity. In a few other cases the people concerned asked not to be identified with their comments; sometimes this was when they were expressing a slightly cynical view which might not be quite in line with the official stance of their church. On one occasion it was the spokesman for a church,

---

4. During the course of my research a number of leading individuals who had been of help to me died, including John Trechak (1999), Ernest L. Martin (2002), Garner Ted Armstrong (2003), Richard C. Nickels (2006), and Raymond F. McNair (2008); others who died before I was able to contact them include Raymond C. Cole (2001) and Herman L. Hoeh (2004).

5. This has now been archived online in its entirety at http://www.hwarmstrong.com/ar/.

who was about to leave that church to join another. (Several individuals I quote changed their church, sometimes more than once, during the course of my research. In some cases I make this clear, but in all cases personal quotations are a snapshot of when they were spoken or written, irrespective of where the person may later have gone.)

The anthropologist H. Russell Bernard notes that some of the best informants are those who are "observant, reflective and articulate." This applies to most of those I spoke to. Bernard suggests that, while "solid insiders...they claim to feel somewhat marginal to their culture by virtue of their intellectualizing of and disenchantment with their culture" (Bernard 1988: 179). Again, this applies to some of those I communicated with personally; their "disenchantment" with the changes in Worldwide seemed to have caused them to cast a more critical eye over the ongoing story, even within their own churches. They were also responding, to a greater or lesser extent, to my line of questioning as an outside commentator.

Just as I had to be wary of the objectivity of my written sources, I also found that I could not necessarily rely on the factual accuracy of my informants (see 7.3.1). Their rewriting of history, ranging from subtle to occasionally blatant, did not just show that one source might be more (or less) historically reliable than another; it also reminded me constantly that each person I dealt with had his (or rarely her) own agenda. I became aware that in a sense even holding a conversation or having an exchange of emails is a form of participant observation; all the time I had to observe, objectively, the conversations in which I was participating—or to put it another way, maintain the balance of emic and etic (see appendix 2).

APPENDIX 3.6 QUESTIONNAIRE

I designed a questionnaire for three main reasons: to reach more members than I had been able to with individual contact; to gather information about who went where and why; and to test a specific hypothesis. I was given valuable criticism before I launched it by two Worldwide watchers, one internal and one external, and technical assistance in encoding it and putting it online by a software consultant. The main analysis of its results is in chapter 9, which begins with my comments on the usefulness and value of the responses.

Because there was no way of anticipating the volume of response, I deliberately took the opportunity to gather comments through numerous write-in answers to questions in addition to the box-checking and ranking questions; I also offered a large space at the end with the heading "If you wish to make any additional comments..." Most of the respondents made good use of this, providing me with a wealth of comments from which I could select representative quotations, especially for chapter 7.

APPENDIX 4

Church Affiliation of Respondents

The questionnaire asked which church respondents had first joined when they left Worldwide, and which church they now (2008–9) belonged to.

Of the 293 who gave a valid year, 31 left Worldwide before Armstrong's death, 13 of those in 1978–79 (of whom 8 joined Garner Ted Armstrong's CGI). In the nine years between Armstrong's death and the founding of United, 63 left, 32 of them in 1993–94 (17 of those to Global). In 1995, the year United was founded, 110 respondents say they left Worldwide (75 of those to United), followed by 30 in 1996 and a further 32 in the following three years. People continued to leave Worldwide over the years, 27 respondents saying they left from 2000 to 2008.

Table A.4.1 shows which churches respondents first joined on leaving Worldwide and which church they belonged to at the time of the questionnaire, late 2008.

Of those who identified their current church, 76 of 291 (26%) belonged to United, 15 (5%) to Living, and a surprisingly low 5 (1.7%) to GTA churches, though it is possible that some of those who said Church of God (location) were referring to member churches of CGOM. Many more had originally joined all of these churches when they left Worldwide—114 of 298 (38%) joined United, 38 (13%) joined Living, and 23 (8%) joined GTA's Church of God, International— but some had since left them for other churches or none.

What is perhaps of most interest is how many of the respondents, in ones and twos, are members of medium to small churches, some of these with several congregations (those listed alphabetically in table A.4.1 from Christian Biblical Church of God through to Triumph Prophetic Ministries) and some with apparently just one ("Church of God" with no further identification, COG with a location, and COG Big Sandy). Whether the fourteen listed as Independent are independent churches in the Worldwide family (see 6.4.2) or independent Evangelical or other churches cannot be known.

The category "Other (Worldwide-Related)" includes a wide variety of small churches in the Worldwide family and also a number of nonmainstream churches with a special emphasis on Sabbatarianism, Adventism, Sacred Names, Jewish Messianic theology, etc. A few members left not just Worldwide but the Worldwide family altogether; "Other (Mainstream Churches)" includes Baptist, Roman Catholic, Orthodox, etc.

Table A.4.1. CHURCH MEMBERSHIP ON LEAVING WCG AND IN LATE 2008

Church	On Leaving WCG	Late 2008
United	114	76
Global/Living	38	15
CGI, ICG, CGOM	23	5
Philadelphia	11	2
Christian Biblical COG	1	6
COGaic (Hulme)		3
COG Eternal	4	2
COG Faithful Flock		3
Church of God's Faithful		1
Enduring COG		2
Great Commission COG		2
Maranatha COG		2
Restored COG	1	
Triumph Prophetic Ministries	1	3
Church of God		3
Church of God (location)	9	14
COG Big Sandy	5	2
Independent	2	14
Home Church/Living-Room	2	13
Other (Worldwide-Related)	18	43
Other (Mainstream Churches)	15	12
None	52	66
Total	298	291

As well as all the small churches, the thirteen who said "Home Church" or "Living-Room Church" should be noted. From their comments many of these, while maintaining their beliefs, have decided that they no longer want to belong to an organized church with a leader and a hierarchy.

Some of the fifty-two who put "None" as their church on first leaving Worldwide said they fellowshipped with others. Of those who gave reasons for not joining a church, one wrote "I was done with churches," and another, "I could no longer trust any church or church leader."

I asked respondents how many Worldwide family churches they had belonged to since leaving Worldwide, not counting Worldwide itself. To avoid ambiguity I specified that if their leader stayed the same but their organization changed, e.g., Global and Living, or CGI and ICG, they should count these as two churches.

Just over half of the 219 who answered this question (116, 53%) said they had belonged to only one church after leaving Worldwide, just over a quarter (60, 27%) said they had belonged to two churches, 26 (12%) to three, 11 (5%) to four, 2 (0.9%) to five, 3 (1.4%) to six, and 1 (0.5%) claimed seven churches.

APPENDIX 5
Demographics of Respondents

The demographics of the respondents to the questionnaire are of interest, though it must be stressed that they cannot be taken as a proportionate sample of the whole population of Worldwide family members.

Of the 292 respondents who gave their nationality (see table A.5.1), 184 (63%) were American; it is likely that most of the 29 who wrote "Caucasian" or "White" as their nationality were also American, which could raise the American total as high as 213 (73%). The large proportion of Americans, followed by Canadians, British, and Australasians in reasonable numbers, is what would be expected from an American-based British Israelite religion. At least 244 (or 273 if the Caucasians and whites are added in)—84% or 93%—are from English-speaking countries.

Of the 294 respondents who gave their age, 206 (70%) were over fifty. Of the 308 who gave their gender 218 (71%) were male and 90 (29%) female (see table A.5.2). Twelve respondents had joined Worldwide in the 1950s, 86 in the 1960s, 135 in the 1970s, 63 in the 1980s, and 3 in the 1990s. Eighty-eight said they had grown up in Worldwide, i.e., their parents were members when the respondents were young.

Many of the respondents were middle-class and well educated. Those in employment were very largely professional: around 20 each in education, management and accountancy, engineering, and information technology; 12 in healthcare; and 10 in writing and editing; while 8 described themselves as self-employed. Sixty said they were retired; 20 described themselves as homemakers or housewives.

Exactly half of those who gave their academic qualifications (see table A.5.3) said they had at least one accredited university degree. These included 52% of male and 40% of female respondents.

Just over a quarter (27%) of the male respondents who answered the question (57/209) and 20% of the female respondents (18/89) had attended Ambassador College or Ambassador University. Of these, 46 male and 7 female respondents were awarded a bachelor's degree; these were unaccredited for nearly all of the time Ambassador College/University was in existence (see 3.2.2).

Table A.5.1. NATIONALITY OF RESPONDENTS

Nationality	
American	184
Canadian	25
British	21
Australian	9
New Zealand	4
Dutch	4
German	3
Hispanic	3
Filipino	2
Columbian	1
Fiji Islander	1
Italian	1
Jamaican	1
Puerto Rican	1
South African	1
Swedish	1
Anglo-Israelite	1
Caucasian/White	29
Total	292

Table A.5.2. AGE AND SEX OF RESPONDENTS

Age	M	F	Unstated	Total
Under 21	0	0	0	0
21–30	4	1	0	5
31–40	20	12	0	32
41–50	35	15	1	51
51–60	76	33	2	111
61–70	51	21	3	75
71–80	15	4	0	19
Over 80	0	1	0	1
Total	201	86	6	294

Table A.5.3. ACADEMIC QUALIFICATIONS OF RESPONDENTS

Highest Qualifications	M	F	Unstated	Total
None	9	3	0	12
High School	87	48	2	137
Bachelor's	66	27	1	94
Master's	34	7	2	43
Doctorate	13	2	0	15
Total	209	87	5	301

APPENDIX 6

The Future State of Schism

When I first began taking notice of the offshoot organizations with some familial link to the Worldwide Church of God in 1996 there were around 75 of them. By July 1999 there were said to be 237, and by April 2001 there were at least 305. By the completion of the major part of this study in September 2009 there were reckoned to be over four hundred (see Figure A.6.1).[1]

The rate of increase was clearly slowing, but from the experience of the last few years the number perhaps seems more likely to continue to increase rather than to decrease, at least for the next few years. Even as I was editing my thesis into this book, the largest offshoot church, United, split in two, with the formation of Church of God, a Worldwide Association (6.2.3.2).

Mergers have so far proved very few, and far outnumbered by schisms. Schisms are likely to continue, for all the reasons discussed in chapters 8 and 9, including when the strongly top-down leaders of some of the churches eventually die (see 8.4); there may well be struggles for succession (and hence schisms) in some churches as ministers decide, on the grounds of doctrine or of experience (religious capital or moral capital—see 9.8), that they cannot work under a particular new leader (Alan Ruth, pers. comm.).

But the likelihood is that, as has already happened in a number of cases, some of the smaller churches and ministries may end with the death of their leaders (many of whom are elderly), with any remaining members dispersing to other churches. Others may just become too small to be viable; I was once told of a split in a church which had just twelve members (John Jewell, pers. comm.).

Indeed, the fading away of small churches may already be beginning to happen. In March 2011 I contacted Alan Ruth of Barnabas Ministries. In December 2008 he had written to me of "the easily more than 400 splits from the WCG"; what was the figure now? Ruth surprised me by saying:

---

1. The figures come from Alan Ruth of Barnabas Ministries, accepted by many in the offshoots as a reliable source.

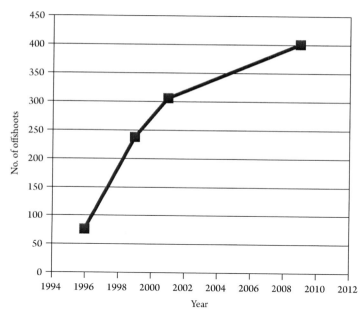

Figure A.6.1 Number of Offshoots

> Splits from the COGs come and go. Many have just stopped operating or maintaining an address or office. Some of the smaller fellowships no longer exist for a variety of reasons. But, some new splits have also formed in recent years. Sticking with the 300 splits number is likely more accurate. (Alan Ruth, pers. comm.)

So was it now four hundred or three hundred?

A list of online links to groups (ministries as well as churches) on *The Journal's* website in 2011 totaled 360, but some groups had two links, for their church and their magazine; others, such as the eight local Church of God (7th/Seventh Day) sites, were related churches rather than Worldwide offshoots—and, as is inevitable in a list of this length, some links were dead (*The Journal* website). But against that, not every small independent local church with roots in Worldwide will have its own website.

For an accurate list, Ruth says, "It would be a monumental task to pin down existing COG splits"; any total number can only be "the roughest of estimates."

Looking to the future, the demographics of the survey (see appendix 5) should also be recalled: 70% of the respondents who gave their age were over fifty, 32% over sixty, and 7% over seventy. Anecdotal evidence suggests that these figures are a broadly accurate reflection of an aging church membership. Although some younger members are joining the churches, and some children of members are becoming adult members themselves, as the years pass it is likely that the overall numbers of members will fall.

I asked respondents to the questionnaire whether they thought in five, ten, and twenty years' time there would be many fewer, fewer, about the same, more, or many more offshoots than there are today (see table A.6.1 and figure A.6.2).

Table A.6.1. HOW MANY OFFSHOOTS IN 5, 10, 20 YEARS FROM 2008–9

	5 Years		10 Years		20 Years	
Many Fewer	20	96	63	173	157	207
Fewer	76		110		50	
About the Same	77		30		11	
More	110	120	67	84	43	69
Many More	10		17		26	
Total	293		287		287	

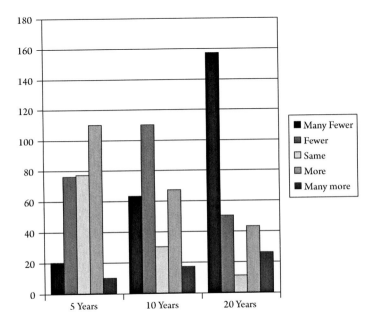

Figure A.6.2 How Many Offshoots in 5, 10, 20 Years from 2008–9

Those who thought there would be about the same number decreased from 77 to 30 to 11 over the three time periods; those who thought there would be fewer or many fewer increased from 96 to 173 to 207; while those who thought there would be more or many more decreased from 120 to 84 to a surprisingly high 69 twenty years on. The biggest change in forecast, many fewer offshoots, went from 20 to 63 to 157 for five, ten, and twenty years ahead. However, although by a much smaller margin, a greater number of respondents thought there would be more offshoots rather than fewer (120 to 96) five years on. If these responses in any way reflect reality, the number of offshoot churches may increase slightly in the five years following the survey, but then the numbers will begin to fall away.

But for now, at least, the story of fragmentation in the Worldwide family of churches continues.

REFERENCES

All of Herbert W. Armstrong's books and booklets, all copies of the *Plain Truth*, *Good News*, and *Tomorrow's World* magazines, and many more Worldwide Church of God publications are archived in PDF format at http://www.herbert-armstrong.org/.

The *Ambassador Report* newsletter is archived at www.hwarmstrong.com/ar/.

Selected news stories and articles from *The Journal: News of the Churches of God* are archived at http://www.thejournal.org/back-issues-of-the-journal-newspaper.html.

When dates are given for websites, this is usually the date of access, unless the date of origin is stated on the relevant page. URLs are subject to change, and in a few cases websites listed here no longer exist.

Abanes, Richard. 2002. *One Nation Under Gods: A History of the Mormon Church*. New York: Four Walls Eight Windows.

Albrecht, Greg. 1998. Recording from Annual Conference of Evangelical Ministries to New Religions. CD. *Compendium of Literature and Audio Material for the Church of God*, disc 1. October 3.

Alexander, Pat, and David Alexander. 1999. *The Lion Handbook to the Bible*. 3rd ed. Oxford: Lion.

Allen, J. H. 1917. *Judah's Sceptre and Joseph's Birthright*. 18th ed. Boston: A. A. Beauchamp.

Alspaugh, Glen. 2003. Church of God's Patience website (no longer active).

Altholz, Josef L. 1989. *The Religious Press in Britain, 1760–1900*. New York: Greenwood.

Ambassador College. 1972a. *How To Understand Prophecy*. Pasadena, CA: Ambassador College.

——— . 1972b. *This Is the Worldwide Church of God*. Pasadena, CA: Ambassador College.

——— . 1973a. *Are We Living in the Last Days?* Pasadena, CA: Ambassador College.

——— . 1973b. *Is This the End Time?* Pasadena, CA: Ambassador College.

——— . 1974. *This Is Ambassador College*. Pasadena, CA: Ambassador College Press.

Anglo-Israelism. 1880. *Church Quarterly Review* 10: 318–39.

Antion, David, and Al Carrozzo. 1974. Letter to HWA & GTA. February 28. Available online at http://hwarmstrong.com/history-spiritual-abuses.htm.

Ardis, Robert G. 2006. *The Day of the Lord*. Eutawville, SC: Church of God's Faithful. Available online at http://www.setapartbytruth.org/en/literature/pdf/dayoflord.pdf.

Armstrong, Garner Ted. 1967a. *The Amazing Archer Fish Disproves Evolution!* Pasadena, CA: Ambassador College.

——— . 1967b. *The Fable of the First Fatal Flight*. Pasadena, CA: Ambassador College.

——— . 1969. *Some Fishy Stories about Evolution*. Pasadena, CA: Ambassador College.

——— . 1992. *The Origin and History of the Church of God, International*. Tyler, TX: Church of God, International.

——— . 1994. *Europe and America in Prophecy*. Tyler, TX: Church of God, International.

Armstrong, Garner Ted, and Paul W Kroll. 1968. *A Whale of a Tale, or The Dilemma of Dolphins and Duckbills*. Pasadena, CA: Ambassador College.

Armstrong, Herbert W. 1939. Did Christ Reorganize the Church? *The Good News of the Kingdom*, April. Available in Nickels 1996: 32–41.

———. 1941. Hitler. *Plain Truth*, October.

———. 1945. *The United States and Britain in Prophecy*. Edmond, OK: Philadelphia Church of God. Slightly amended reprint, ca. 2002.

———. 1952a. *Easter Is Pagan!* St. Albans, UK: Radio Church of God.

———. 1952b. *The Plain Truth About Christmas!* London: Ambassador College.

———. 1952c. *The Resurrection Was Not on Sunday!* Pasadena, CA: Radio Church of God.

———. 1952d. *What Kind of Faith Is Required for Salvation?* St. Albans, UK: Ambassador College.

———. 1954. *The British Commonwealth and the United States in Prophecy*. London: Ambassador College.

———. 1956. *1975 in Prophecy*. Pasadena, CA: Radio Church of God.

———. 1958a. Is All Animal Flesh Good Food? Ambassador College reprint, 1980.

———. 1958b. *The Proof of the Bible*. Pasadena, CA: Ambassador College.

———. 1959. *Ending Your Financial Worries*. Pasadena, CA: Radio Church of God.

———. 1962. *Just What Do You Mean ... Kingdom of God?* St. Albans, UK: Radio Church of God.

———. 1963. The Real CAUSE of the RACE CRISIS! *Plain Truth*, October.

———. 1967a. *Autobiography of Herbert W. Armstrong*, vol. 1. Paperback ed. Pasadena, CA: Ambassador College Press.

———. 1967b. *The United States and British Commonwealth in Prophecy*. Pasadena, CA: Ambassador College Press.

———. 1968. *The Truth about Makeup*. Pasadena, CA: Ambassador College Press.

———. 1969. *What Will You Be Doing in the Next Life?* Pasadena, CA: Worldwide Church of God.

———. 1972a. *The Resurrection was not on Sunday*. Pasadena, CA: Worldwide Church of God.

———. 1972b. Personal from Herbert W. Armstrong. *Tomorrow's World*, February.

———. 1973a. *Autobiography of Herbert W. Armstrong*, vol. 1. Paperback ed. Pasadena, CA: Ambassador College Press.

———. 1973b. *Marriage and Divorce*. Pasadena, CA: Ambassador College Press.

———. 1974a. May 14, 1974 HWA Divorce and Remarriage Letter. Available online at http://climbthewall.com/hwa/ra1/BA/HWA_D&R_MAY74.HTM.

———. 1974b. Ministerial Conference May 1974. Quoted in Gerringer 1977.

———. 1974c. 1974 Letter to the Membership. May 2. http://www.cgca.net/pabco/cog-gov74.htm.

———. 1974d. *The Plain Truth about Christmas*. Pasadena, CA: Ambassador College Press.

———. 1976a. *Which Day Is the Christian Sabbath?* Pasadena, CA: Worldwide Church of God.

———. 1976b. Sermon July 24. Quoted in Gerringer 1977.

———. 1977. Co-worker letter. January 20. Available online at http://www.friendsofsabbath.org/ABC/Coworker%20Ltrs%201930s-80s/.

———. 1978. Co-worker letter. June 28. Available online at http://www.cogiw.org/coworker/780628.htm.

———. 1979. Why My Son No Longer Stands "Back to Back" with Me. *The Good News*, April.

———. 1980a. Letter to Roderick C. Meredith from Herbert Armstrong. March 14. Available online at http://www.servantsnews.com/docs/merlet02.htm.

———. 1980b. *The United States and Britain in Prophecy*. Pasadena, CA: Worldwide Church of God.

———. 1981a. How Subtly Satan Used MAKEUP to Start the Church off the Track: How Satan Began Injecting Liberalism into God's Church. *Worldwide News*, November 16. Available online at http://www.hwarmstrong.com/history/history-back-on-track.htm.

———. 1981b. *The Missing Dimension in Sex*. Pasadena, CA: Worldwide Church of God.

———. 1981c. Stanley R Rader Resigns Executive Responsibilities. *Worldwide News*, March 6. Available online at http://www.herbert-armstrong.org/Worldwide%20News%201980s/WWN%201981%20%28Prelim%20No%2004s%29%200306.pdf.

———. 1985a. *Mystery of the Ages*. Pasadena, CA: Worldwide Church of God. Page numbers refer to the PCG reprint: New York: Dodd, Mead, 1985.

———. 1985b. Recent History of the Philadelphia Era of the Worldwide Church of God. *Worldwide News*, June 24. Available online at http://www.hwacompendium.com/BA/WN850624.HTM.

———. 1986. *Autobiography of Herbert W. Armstrong*, vol. 1. Hardback ed. Pasadena, CA: Worldwide Church of God.

———. 1987. *Autobiography of Herbert W. Armstrong*, vol. 2. Hardback ed. Pasadena, CA: Worldwide Church of God.

Armstrong, Herbert W., and Garner Ted Armstrong. 1966. *The Wonderful World Tomorrow: What It Will Be Like*. Pasadena, CA: Ambassador College Press.

Armstrong, Karen. 1993. *A History of God: From Abraham to the Present; The 4000-Year Quest for God*. London: William Heinemann.

Atack, Jon. 1990. *A Piece of Blue Sky: Scientology, Dianetics, and L. Ron Hubbard Exposed*. New York: Lyle Stuart.

Bainbridge, William Sims. 1997. *The Sociology of Religious Movements*. New York: Routledge.

Banned by HWA! (blog). 2011. Balloting to Start for New COGaWA Church Name: 411 Different Names Suggested. January 10. http://armstrongismlibrary.blogspot.com/2011/01/balloting-to-start-for-new-cogawa.html.

Barker, Eileen. 1992. *New Religious Movements: A Practical Introduction*. London: HMSO.

Barnett, Ewin H., and Sue Ann Pomicter. 1995. Interview with Roderick C. Meredith. *In Transition*, December 18. Available online at http://www.thejournal.org/in-transition/v1issue9/interview-with-roderick-meredith.html.

Barnstone, Willis. 1984. *The Other Bible*. San Francisco: Harper & Row.

Barrett, David V. 2000. Eastern Promise: Foundation Myths in Religions. *Fortean Times* 141 (December): 40–44.

———. 2001a. *The New Believers: A Survey of Sects, Cults and Alternative Religions*. London: Cassell.

———. 2001b. Review of *Prophets, Cults and Madness*, by Anthony Stevens and John Price. *Catholic Herald*, January 12.

———. 2006. How Many Members Do They Really Have? *Church Times*, December 1.

———. 2008. Author Requests Help with His Study of the Worldwide Church of God Offshoots. *The Journal: News of the Churches of God*, July 31.

———. 2011. *A Brief Guide to Secret Religions*. London: Constable & Robinson.

Benjamin, Marina. 1998. *Living at the End of the World*. London: Picador.

Benware, Paul N. 1977. *Ambassadors of Armstrongism: An Analysis of the History and Teachings of the Worldwide Church of God*. Nutley, NJ: Presbyterian and Reformed Publishing.

Berger, Peter L. 1954. The Sociological Study of Sectarianism. *Social Research* 21:467–85.

———. 1969. *The Social Reality of Religion*. London: Faber. Pagination refers to 1973 Penguin reprint.

Berger, Peter L., and Thomas Luckmann. 1966. *The Social Construction of Reality*. London: Allen Lane.

Berkhof, Louis. 1938. *A Summary of Christian Doctrine*. London: Banner of Truth Trust.

Bernard, H. Russell. 1988. *Research Methods in Cultural Anthropology*. Newbury Park, CA: SAGE.

Bigger, Stephen. 1990. "Exclusive" Brethren: An Educational Dilemma. *Journal of Beliefs and Values* 11.1: 13–15.

BIWF Canada (British-Israel-World Federation [Canada]) website. http://www.british-israel-world-fed.ca/.

BIWF (British-Israel-World Federation) website. http://www.britishisrael.co.uk/.

Bowden, John. 1973. *Herbert W. Armstrong and His Worldwide Church of God: An Exposure and an Indictment*. Chippendale, Australia: Rationalist Association.

Bowie, Fiona, ed. 1997. *The Coming Deliverer: Millennial Themes in World Religions*. Cardiff: University of Wales Press.

Boyne, Ian. 2000. Why Will Man Become God? *The Journal: News of the Churches of God*, August 31.

———. 2008. The Jamaican CGI Story: How to Grow a Church. http://www.cgijamaica.org/localnews/20080703/20080703_cgija-story.php (no longer active).

Brethren FAQ. 2007. The Exclusive Brethren Christian Fellowship: Frequently Asked Questions. http://www.theexclusivebrethren.com/update/faq.htm.

Brisby, Jon W. 2008. By What Authority Do We Exist as a Group? http://www.cogeternal.org/2000s/01094_1008authorityforexistencejwb.htm.

Buchner, Johannes Lothar Felix. 1983. *Armstrongism Bibliography*. Sydney: privately published.

———. 1985. *Armstrongism in Britain*. Gordon, Australia: Ambassador Research International.

———. 2006. The Worldwide Church of God: A Study of Its Transformation in Terms of K. Helmut Reich's Theory of Relational and Contextual Reasoning. PhD thesis, University of West Sydney.

Bushman, Richard L. 1984. *Joseph Smith and the Beginnings of Mormonism*. Urbana: University of Illinois Press.

Bütz, Jeffrey J. 2005. *The Brother of Jesus and the Lost Teachings of Christianity*. Rochester, VT: Inner Traditions.

Butler, Samuel. 1901. *Erewhon Revisited*. London: Grant Richards.

Callow, John. 2008. Infidelity, Impotence and Innocence Lost: Robert Devereux's Encounter with Jacobean Witchcraft. Paper presented at the Moot With No Name, London, July 16.

Campbell, Roger F. 1962. *Herbert W. Armstrong: Mr. Confusion*. Lincoln, NE: Back to the Bible Broadcast.

Carrozzo, Al. 1977. The Profligate Son. *Ambassador Report* 2. Available online at http://www.hwarmstrong.com/ar/Profligate.html.

Cartwright, Dixon. 1998a. It's Official: Much of UCG-UK Leaves, Joins New Affiliation. *The Journal: News of the Churches of God*, June 30.

———. 1998b. Waco Eyewitness Claims 1993 Holocaust Avoidable. *The Journal: News of the Churches of God*, November 30.

———. 2008. Vote Changes Complexion of United Church of God Council of Elders. *The Journal: News of the Churches of God*, April 30.

———. 2011a. 2008 Deed Transfer Means UCGIA Owns Big Sandy Building. *The Journal: News of the Churches of God*, January.

———. 2011b. What's the Difference in the Warring Sides? *The Journal: News of the Churches of God*, January.

CGF (Church of God's Faithful). 2010. Statement of Belief. http://www.setapartbytruth.org/en/statement/index.htm.

CGF (Church of God's Faithful) website. http://www.setapartbytruth.org/en/greeting.htm.

CGG (Church of the Great God) website. History of the Church of the Great God. http://cgg.org/index.cfm/fuseaction/About.history.

CGI (Church of God International Canada). 2007. Why Consider the CGI? http://www.cgicanada.org/why-consider-the-cgi-article-2007/.

CGT (Church of God, In Truth) website. http://www.postponements.com/.

Chadwick, Henry. 1967. *The Early Church*. The Pelican History of the Church 1. Harmondsworth, UK: Penguin.

Chance, Michael R. A., ed. 1988. *Social Fabrics of the Mind*. Hove, UK: Lawrence Erlbaum.

Chance, Michael R. A., and Clifford J. Jolly. 1970. *Social Groups of Monkeys, Apes and Men*. New York: E. P. Dutton.

Chandler, Russell. 1982. Church Founder to Divorce Wife. *Los Angeles Times*, April 22.

Church of Scientology International. 1994. *Reference Guide to the Scientology Religion*. Los Angeles: Church of Scientology International.

Climb the Wall website. Who Are We? http://climbthewall.com/htm/whoarewe.htm.

Cline, Eric H. 2007. *From Eden to Exile: Unraveling Mysteries of the Bible*. Washington, DC: National Geographic.

COGMI (Church of God, Ministries International). 2011. Church of God, Ministries International website. http://www.thecogmi.org/.

COGNWM (Church of God, New World Ministries). 2011. Church of God, New World Ministries website. http://www.cognwm.org/.

COGR (Church of God Restored). 2011. The Church of God Restored: Summary of Our Story. http://www.cogrestored.org/about.htm.

COGWA (Church of God, a Worldwide Association). 2011. COGWA Congregations. February 27. http://cogwa.org/congregations.

COGWWM (Church of God Worldwide Ministries). 2011. Church of God Worldwide Ministries website. http://www.thechurchofgodworldwideministries.org/.

Cohn, Norman. 1970. *The Pursuit of the Millennium: Revolutionary Millenarians and Mystical Anarchists of the Middle Ages*. Rev. ed. London: Paladin.

———. 1993. *Cosmos, Chaos, and the World to Come: The Ancient Roots of Apocalyptic Faith*. New Haven, CT: Yale University Press.

Cohran, Daniel. 2009a. Books and Booklets! *Hold Fast to All Things* (blog). http://www.hold-fast2allthings.org/id17.html.

———. 2009b. My Testimony. *Hold Fast to All Things* (blog). http://www.holdfast2allthings.org/id1.html.

Cole, Raymond C. 1999a. Church of God, The Eternal Homepage. http://www.cogeternal.org/.

———. 1999b. An Open Letter From Raymond C. Cole. December. http://www.cogeternal.org/whoweare2.html.

Coulter, Fred R. 1979. Call to Repentance & Resignation: Part 2. Sermon, October 1. Available online at http://www.cbcg.org/resignation_part2.htm.

———. 1999. *The Christian Passover: What Does It Mean? When Should It Be Observed—the 14th or the 15th?* 2nd ed. Hollister, CA: York.

———. 2001. *A Harmony of the Gospels in Modern English: The Life of Jesus Christ*. Hollister, CA: York.

———. 2003. *The New Testament in Its Original Order: A Faithful Version with Commentary*. Hollister, CA: York.

———. 2007. *The Holy Bible in Its Original Order: A New English Translation: A Faithful Version with Commentary*. Hollister, CA: York.

Cowper, B. Harris. 1867. *The Apocryphal Gospels and Other Documents Relating to the History of Christ*. London: Williams & Norgate.

Crim, Keith, ed. 1981. *The Perennial Dictionary of World Religions*. New York: Harper & Row.

Dankenbring, William F. 2005. *America and Great Britain—Our Identity Revealed!* Omak, WA: Triumph Publishing.

———. 2008. Coming Soon—Obama—King of the World? *Prophecy Flash!*, December.

———. 2009a. A New Look at Barack Obama. *Prophecy Flash!*, February.

———. 2009b. The Man of "Change"! *Prophecy Flash!*, April.

———. n.d. Who Are You? The True Story Behind Triumph Ministries! http://www.triumph-pro.com/triumph-story-updated.htm.

Davies, Horton. 1954. *Christian Deviations: The Challenge of the Sects*. London: SCM.

Dawson, Daniel. n.d. A Voice Cried Out—The Church of God. http://dawson55.u102.swhdns.com/dawson/.

Dawson, Lorne L. 2002. Crises of Charismatic Legitimacy and Violent Behavior in New Religious Movements. In *Cults, Religion and Violence*, ed. David G. Bromley and J. Gordon Melton, 80–101. Cambridge, UK: Cambridge University Press.

Dean, Aaron. 1996. Accepting God's Way. Sermon presented at the Feast of Tabernacles, Mount Pocono, PA, October.

———. 2009. HWA Succession. *Elijah Forum*. September 8. http://groups.yahoo.com/group/elijahforum/.

Dervaes, Jules. n.d. Do You Believe That Gerald Flurry Took Your Message The LETTER TO LAODICEA and Used It as His Own? Sword of Joshua. http://swordofjoshua.org/faqs/do-you-believe-that-gerald-flurry-took-your-message-the-letter-to-laodicea-and-used-it-as-his-own/.

Dewey, Pam. 2001. History and Overview of the Ministry of Herbert W. Armstrong. Field Guide to the Wild World of Religion, http://www.isitso.org/guide/hwahist.html.

Diehl, Dennis. 2008. When Is a Church Like a Game You Don't Want to Play? *The Journal: News of the Churches of God*, June 30.

Douglas, J. D., ed. 1962. *The New Bible Dictionary*. London: Inter-Varsity Fellowship.

Duignan, John, and Nicola Tallant. 2008. *The Complex: An Insider Exposes the Covert World of the Church of Scientology*. Dublin: Merlin.

Earle, Neil. 2004. A Developmental Study. http://www.glendorachurch.org/bio.htm.

ECG (Eternal Church of God) website. Questions and Answers about the Eternal Church of God. http://www.eternalcog.org/ecgarticles/ecg.html.

Edwards, Norman S. 1996. Far-Reaching Insights at Friends of the Sabbath Conference. *Servants' News*, August.

———. 1997. Changes Continue in WCG. *Servants' News*, June. Available online at http://www.servantsnews.com/sn9706/s70605.htm.

———. 1998. Has Time Been Lost? & Found. *Servants' News*, November. Available online at http://www.servantsnews.com/sn9811/s981123.htm.

———. 1999. Church of God 7th Day Old Documents about Herbert Armstrong. *Servants' News*.

Ehrman, Bart D., ed. 2003a. *Lost Christianities: The Battles for Scripture and the Faiths We Never Knew*. Oxford: Oxford University Press.

———. 2003b. *Lost Scriptures: Books That Did Not Make It into the New Testament*. Oxford: Oxford University Press.

———. 2006. *Peter, Paul and Mary Magdalene: The Followers of Jesus in History and Legend*. New York: Oxford University Press.

Exclusive Brethren website. Exclusive Brethren Christian Fellowship website. http://www.the-exclusivebrethren.com/.

Feazell, J. Michael. 2003. *The Liberation of the Worldwide Church of God: The Remarkable Story of a Cult's Journey from Deception to Truth*. Grand Rapids, MI: Zondervan.

Ferguson, Everett, ed. 1990. *Encyclopedia of Early Christianity*. London: St. James.

Festinger, Leon. 1957. *A Theory of Cognitive Dissonance*. Evanston, IL: Row, Peterson.

Festinger, Leon, Henry W. Riecken, and Stanley Schachter. 1956. *When Prophecy Fails*. New York: Harper & Row.

Finke, Roger, and Christopher P. Scheitle. 2009. Understanding Schisms: Theoretical Explanations for Their Origins. In Lewis and Lewis 2009: 11–34.

First, Michael B., Miriam Gibbon, Robert L. Spitzer, Janet B.W. Williams, and Lorna Smith Benjamin. 1997. *Structured Clinical Interview for DSM-IV Axis II Personality Disorders (SCID-II)*. Washington, DC: American Psychiatric Publishing.

Flurry, Gerald. 1992. Open Door Policy. *Philadelphia Trumpet*, November.

———. 1993. *God's Family Government*. Edmond, OK: Philadelphia Church of God.

———. 1994. *Worldwide Church of God Doctrinal Changes and the Tragic Results*. 4th ed. Edmond, OK: Philadelphia Church of God.

———. 1995b. *Malachi's Message to God's Church Today*. 2nd ed. Edmond, OK: Philadelphia Church of God.

———. 1995a. *The Little Book*. Edmond, OK: Philadelphia Church of God.

———. 1997. Jeremiah and the Greatest Vision in the Bible #9. *Philadelphia Trumpet*, October.

———. 2007. *Who Is "That Prophet"*? 2nd ed. Edmond, OK: Philadelphia Church of God.

———. 2010. The Holy Roman Empire Is Back! *Philadelphia Trumpet*, February.

Flurry, Stephen. 2006. *Raising the Ruins: The Fight to Revive the Legacy of Herbert W. Armstrong.* Edmond, OK: Philadelphia Church of God.

Foster, Roger, Jeff Patton, John Ross Schroeder, and David Treybig. 2001. *The United States and Britain in Bible Prophecy.* Cincinnati, OH: United Church of God.

Gardner, Stan. 2007. Philadelphia—Freedom through "The Work"? *Ambassador Reports* (blog), July 28. http://ambassdorreports.blogspot.com/2007/07/philadelphia-freedom-through-work.html.

———. 2008. Spanky's "Canons of Evangelistic Discipline of the Living Church of God." *Ambassador Reports* (blog), September 18. http://ambassadorreports.blogspot.com/2008/09/now-is-timexxxxxxxxxxxxxxxx.html.

Garfinkel, Harold. 2002. *Ethnomethodology's Program: Working out Durkheim's Aphorism.* Lanham, MD: Rowman & Littlefield.

Gauthier, Gary. 2008. Where Can I Find Current Information on the Philadelphia Church of God? December 3. http://community.cnhi.com/eve/forums/a/tpc/f/41310611/m/5531083661 (no longer active).

———. n.d. The Elect Church of God. http://www.theelectchurchofgod.org/page/page/5627168.htm.

GCSDA (General Conference of Seventh-day Adventists). 1988. *Seventh-day Adventists Believe . . . : A Biblical Exposition of 27 Fundamental Doctrines.* Hagerstown, MD: Review and Herald.

George, Andrew, trans. 1999. *The Epic of Gilgamesh: The Babylonian Epic Poem and Other Texts in Akkadian and Sumerian.* London: Allen Lane.

Gerringer, Robert. 1977. Herbert Armstrong's Religious Roots. *Ambassador Report* 2. Available online at http://hwarmstrong.com/ar/Roots.html.

Glock, Charles Y., and Rodney Stark. 1965. *Religion and Society in Tension.* Chicago: Rand McNally.

Greeley, Andrew. 1979. *The Making of the Popes: The Politics of Intrigue in the Vatican.* London: Futura.

Greer, John Michael. 2012. *Apocalypse: A History of the End of Time.* London: Quercus.

Greer, Nick. 1997. British-Israelism and the Revival Centres. Available online at http://www.preteristarchive.com/dEmEnTiA/British-Israelism/1997_greer_revival-center.html.

Haggith, David. 1999. *End-Time Prophecies of the Bible.* New York: Putnam.

Hammond, T. C., and David F. Wright. 1968. *In Understanding Be Men: A Handbook of Christian Doctrine.* 6th ed. Leicester, UK: Inter-Varsity Press.

Hansen, Klaus J. 1981. *Mormonism and the American Experience.* Chicago: University of Chicago Press.

Harrison, Shirley. 1990. *Cults: The Battle for God.* London: Christopher Helm.

Havir, Dave. 1999. HWA Considered Several Men Besides Mr. Tkach. *The Journal: News of the Churches of God*, June 30.

Hawkins, Jefferson. 2010. So How Big Is the Church of Scientology Really? *Leaving Scientology* (blog), March 27. http://leavingscientology.wordpress.com/2010/03/27/so-how-big-is-the-church-of-scientology-really/.

Headland, Thomas N., ed. 1990. *Emics and Etics: The Insider/Outsider Debate.* Newbury Park, CA: SAGE.

Heap, Malcolm B. 2002. *Dreams from God about the WCG.* Aylesbury, UK: Midnight Ministries.

Hinnells, John R., ed. 1984. *The Penguin Dictionary of Religions.* Harmondsworth, UK: Penguin.

Hoeh, Herman L. 1956. Did the "Thief on the Cross" Enter Paradise Immediately? *Plain Truth*, August.

———. 1959a. *The Crucifixion Was Not on Friday!* Pasadena, CA: Ambassador College.

———. 1959b. *A True History of the True Church*. Pasadena, CA: Radio Church of God.

———. 1959c. What You Should Know About Tithing. *Good News*, July.

Hoekema, A. A. 1973. *Mormonism*. Exeter, UK: Paternoster.

Holden, Andrew. 2002. *Jehovah's Witnesses: Portrait of a Contemporary Religious Movement*. London: Routledge.

Hooke, S. H. 1963. *Middle Eastern Mythology*. London: Penguin.

Hopkins, Joseph. 1974. *The Armstrong Empire: A Look at the Worldwide Church of God*. Grand Rapids, MI: William B. Eerdmans.

Horrie, Chris, and Peter Chippindale. 1991. *What Is Islam?: A Comprehensive Introduction*. London: Virgin.

Howlett, Thomas R. 1892. *Anglo-Israel and the Jewish Problem*. Philadelphia: Spangler & Davis.

Hulme, David. 1998. David Hulme Letter about His New Organization. *Servants' News*, April 15. Available online at http://www.servantsnews.com/sn9803/s980326.htm.

Iannaccone, Laurence R. 1990. Religious Practice: A Human Capital Approach. *Journal for the Scientific Study of Religion* 29: 297–314.

ICG (Intercontinental Church of God) Churches. n.d. Church Towns of the ICG. http://www.intercontinentalcog.org/icgchurchtowns.php.

ICG (Intercontinental Church of God) Doctrines. n.d. STP-01 Primary Doctrines. http://www.intercontinentalcog.org/STP/stp01.htm (no longer active).

ICG (Intercontinental Church of God) FAQ. 2011. http://www.intercontinentalcog.org/faq2.shtml.

INFORM confidential files. London School of Economics and Political Science.

Ingersoll, E. P. 1886. *Lost Israel Found*. Topeka: Kansas Publishing House.

In Transition. 1995. Worldwide Church of God Loses Almost 40 Percent of its Ministers, June.

Introvigne, Massimo. 1999. Schism in the Global Church of God, Birth of The Living Church of God. CESNUR. http://www.cesnur.org/testi/Living.htm.

Irvine, William C. 1980. *Heresies Exposed*. New York: Loizeaux Brothers. First published 1917.

Jentzsch, Heber. 1992. Church of Scientology Definition of "Membership." ABC Nightline, February 14. Quoted on *Operation Clambake* (website), http://www.xenu.net/archive/COS_members.html.

Jorgensen, Danny L. 1993. Dissent and Schism in the Early Church: Explaining Mormon Fissiparousness. *Dialogue: A Journal of Mormon Thought* 28.3 (Fall): 15–39.

The Journal. 2001. LCG Reports 2000 Growth. *The Journal: News of the Churches of God*, January 31.

———. 2008. Living Head, Recovering from Stroke, Appoints Acting Head. *The Journal: News of the Churches of God*, July 31.

———. 2011. UCG Goes Forward with Two Thirds of Its Elders. *The Journal: News of the Churches of God*, January.

The Journal website. Church of God Web Site Links. http://www.thejournal.org/church-of-god-reference-desk/links/cglinksc.html.

JWs (Jehovah's Witnesses). 1993. *Jehovah's Witnesses: Proclaimers of God's Kingdom*. Brooklyn, NY: Watch Tower Bible and Tract Society.

Katz, David S., and Richard H. Popkin. 1999. *Messianic Revolution: Radical Religious Politics to the End of the Second Millennium*. London: Allen Lane.

Kee, Alistair. 1982. *Constantine versus Christ: The Triumph of Ideology*. London: SCM.

Kellett, Arnold. 1965. *Isms and Ologies: A Guide to Unorthodox and Non-Christian Beliefs*. London: Epworth.

Kelley, Chris. 1998. CUT Spiritual Leader Gets By with a Little Help from Her Friend. *Church Universal and Triumphant*, September 3.

Kessler, W. Jack. 1981. Letter to the Board of WCG. December 30. Available online at http://gavinru.tripod.com/kessler.htm.

Kuhne, Robert. 2003. The Plain Truth about Malachi's Message and That Prophet. http://www.pcog.info/Frames.htm.

———. 2004. Philadelphia Church of God Membership. Cited in Teachings Unique to the Philadelphia Church of God, http://www.cogwriter.com/pcg.htm.

Lamont, Stewart. 1986. *Religion Inc.: The Church of Scientology*. London: Harrap.

Larsen, Egon. 1971. *Strange Sects and Cults: A Study of Their Origins and Influence*. London: Arthur Barker.

LeBlanc, Doug. 1996. The Worldwide Church of God: Resurrected into Orthodoxy. *Christian Research Journal*, Winter.

Leonard, Harry. 2000. The Foundations of Adventism in the British Isles. In *A Century of Adventism in the British Isles*, 5–7. Watford, UK: British Union Conference of Seventh-day Adventists.

Lewis, James R. 1995. *The Gods Have Landed: New Religions from Other Worlds*. Albany, NY: State University of New York Press.

———. 2003. *Encyclopedic Sourcebook of UFO Religions*. Amherst, NY: Prometheus.

Lewis, James R., and Sarah M. Lewis, eds. 2009. *Sacred Schisms: How Religions Divide*. New York: Cambridge University Press.

The Lost Books of the Bible. 1963. New York: New American Library. First published 1926.

Lüdemann, Gerd. 1996. *Heretics: The Other Side of Early Christianity*. London: SCM.

Ludlow, Daniel H., ed. 1992. *Encyclopedia of Mormonism*. 4 vols. (continuous pagination). New York: Macmillan.

MacGregor, Geddes. 1959. *The Bible in the Making*. London: John Murray.

MacGregor, P. S. n.d. *How the Spell Was Broken*. Hounslow, UK: Bible and Gospel Trust.

Manley, G. T., ed. 1947. *The New Bible Handbook*. London: Inter-Varsity Fellowship.

Marcus, Amy Dockser. 2000. *Rewriting the Bible: How Archaeology Is Reshaping History*. London: Little, Brown.

Martin, Ernest L. 1994. *Restoring the Original Bible*. Portland, OR: Associates for Scriptural Knowledge.

Martin, Walter R. 1967. *The Kingdom of the Cults: Major Cult Systems in the Present Christian Era*. London: Marshall, Morgan & Scott.

Martin, William C. 1980. Father, Son and Mammon: How Evangelism Pays. *Atlantic*, March.

McCann, Kathleen. 2002. COGR Hung On, Then Moved On. *The Journal: News of the Churches of God*, June 30.

McGuire, Meredith B. 2002. *Religion: The Social Context*. 5th ed. Belmont, CA: Wadsworth.

McKenzie, Steven L. 2000. *King David: A Biography*. Oxford: Oxford University Press.

McNair, Marion J. 1977. *Armstrongism: Religion or Rip-off? An Exposé of the Armstrong Modus Operandi*. Orlando, FL: Pacific Charters.

McNair, Raymond F. 1996. *America and Britain in Prophecy*. San Diego, CA: Global Church of God.

———. n.d. Articles by Evangelist Raymond F. McNair, Church of God—21st Century. http://cog21.org/images/journalindex.html (no longer active).

Medici, David. 1999. Letter to the Global Church of God Board of Directors and Council of Elders. April. Available online at http://www.hoselton.net/religion/global/split/medici.htm (no longer active).

Melton, J. Gordon. 1977. *A Directory of Religious Bodies in the United States*. New York: Garland.

———. 1991. When Prophets Die: The Succession Crisis in New Religions. In *When Prophets Die: The Postcharismatic Fate of New Religious Movements*, ed. Timothy Miller, 1–12. Albany: State University of New York Press.

———. 1999. *Encyclopedia of American Religions*. 6th ed. Farmington Hills, MI: Gale.

Melton, J. Gordon, and Martin Baumann, eds. 2002. *Religions of the World: A Comprehensive Encyclopedia of Beliefs and Practices*. 4 vols. (continuous pagination). Santa Barbara, CA: ABC-CLIO.

Meredith, Roderick C. 1997. *Which Day Is the Christian Sabbath?* San Diego, CA: Global Church of God.

———. 1998. Living Church of God—Meredith Letter. CESNUR. December 21. Available online at http://www.cesnur.org/testi/Meredith.htm.

Meyer, Marvin, ed. 2005. *The Secret Gospels of Jesus: The Definitive Collection of Gnostic Gospels and Mystical Books about Jesus of Nazareth*. London: Darton, Longman & Todd.

Milks, Ralph, and Vivian Milks. 1996. Letter. *In Transition*, September 16.

Miller, Timothy. 1991. *When Prophets Die: The Postcharismatic Fate of New Religious Movements*. Albany, NY: State University of New York Press.

Mokarow, Art. 2004. *God's Puzzle Solved*. Montgomery TX: Evanow.

Morgan, Dale L. 1953. A Bibliography of the Churches of the Dispersion. *Western Humanities Review* 7 (Summer): 255–66.

Neal, Philip. 1996. Have We Flunked the Test on the Church? *In Transition*, October 28.

Nettlehorst, R. P. 1979. British Israelism: A Mirage. *Biblical Research Monthly*, June. Available online at http://www.theology.edu/journal/volume4/BritishIsraelism.htm.

Newton, Tim, ed. and comp. 2009. *The Forgotten Gospels: Life and Teachings of Jesus Supplementary to the New Testament; A New Translation*. London: Constable.

Nichols, Larry, and George Mather. 1998. *Discovering the Plain Truth: How the Worldwide Church of God Encountered the Gospel of Grace*. Downers Grove, IL: InterVarsity Press.

Nickels, Richard C. 1996a. Church of God—Adventist! *Servants News*, February. Available online at http://www.servantsnews.com/sn9602/cogadventist.htm.

———. 1996b. Did Christ Reorganize the Church? In *Early Writings of Herbert W. Armstrong*, 205–9. Neck City, MO: Giving & Sharing.

———. 1996c. *Early Writings of Herbert W. Armstrong*. Neck City, MO: Giving & Sharing.

———. 1996d. Herbert W. Armstrong: 1892–1986. In *Early Writings of Herbert W. Armstrong*, 213–33. Neck City, MO: Giving & Sharing.

———. 1999. *History of the Seventh Day Church of God*. Neck City, MO: Giving & Sharing. Available online at http://www.giveshare.org/churchhistory/historysdcog/index.html.

Niebuhr, H. Richard. 1957. *Social Sources of Denominationalism*. New York: Meridian.

Nugent, J. Timothy. 1976. Herbert W. Armstrong—A Legend in His Own Mind. *Ambassador Review*, June. Available online at http://www.hwarmstrong.com/ar/Legend.html.

Nyomarkay, Joseph. 1967. *Charisma and Factionalism in the Nazi Party*. Minneapolis: University of Minnesota Press.

O'Connor, Cornelius A. 1993. A Comprehensive Analysis of the History and Doctrines of the Worldwide Church of God (Armstrongism), Together with an Exegetical Commentary and a Discussion of some of the Radical Doctrinal Changes in the Post-Armstrong Era of the Church. PhD thesis. St. David's College, University of Wales, Lampeter.

———. 1997. Take One, It's FREE: The Story Behind the Worldwide Church of God and the Plain Truth Magazine. In *The Coming Deliverer: Millennial Themes in World Religions*, ed. Fiona Bowie, 163–201. Cardiff: University of Wales Press.

Ogwyn, John H. 1995. *God's Church through the Ages*. San Diego, CA: Global Church of God.

———. 1999. *What's Ahead for America and Britain?* San Diego, CA: Living Church of God.

———. 2003. *God's Church through the Ages*. Charlotte, NC: Living Church of God.

Orchard, Linda. 2008. U.S. Ministerial Conference 2008. *Church of God News*, September.

Orr, Ralph G. 1999. *How Anglo-Israelism Entered Seventh-Day Churches of God: A History of the Doctrine from John Wilson to Joseph W. Tkach*. http://armstrongdelusion.com/resources/.

Overton, Mac. 1999a. Members Moving Forward with New Church that replaces Global. *The Journal: News of the Churches of God*, November 30.

———. 1999b. WCGF, WCGR Leaders Explain Situation. *The Journal: News of the Churches of God*, July 30.

———. 2000a. CGCF President Resigns, Moves to Living Church. *The Journal: News of the Churches of God*, July 31.

———. 2000b. Leaders of Two Church Groups Begin Dialog. *The Journal: News of the Churches of God*, June 30.

Overton, Mac, John Robinson, and Linda Moll Smith. 1995. Did WCG Leaders Have Doctrinal Agenda? *In Transition*, August.

Pack, David C. 1999. *Except the Lord Build the House: Key Quotes from Herbert W. Armstrong.* 2nd ed. Akron, OH: Restored Church of God.

———. 2000. *Why the Restored Church of God?* 3rd ed. Wadsworth, OH: Restored Church of God.

———. 2001. Endless False Doctrines—How Most Are Still Being Fooled! *The Pillar of the Truth*, February.

———. 2003. *America and Britain in Bible Prophecy*. Wadsworth, OH: Restored Church of God.

———. 2008. *There Came a Falling Away*. Wadsworth, OH: Restored Church of God.

Partridge, Christopher, ed. 2003. *UFO Religions*. London: Routledge.

PCG (Philadelphia Church of God). 2009. Pastor General Visits Big Sandy, Acquires Sculpture. Philadelphia Church of God website, April 13. http://www.pcog.org/article.php?articleid=82.

Peake, Arthur S. 1948. *A Commentary on the Bible*. London: Thomas Nelson.

Peel, Robert. 1977. *Mary Baker Eddy: The Years of Authority*. New York: Holt, Rinehart & Winston.

Petersen, William J. 1975. *Those Curious New Cults*. New Canaan, CT: Keats.

Pierce, Robert L. 1977. Nurtured to Maturity in America. Chap. 7 of *The Rapture Cult: Religious Zeal and Political Conspiracy*. Signal Mountain, TN: Signal Point. Available online at http://www.reformed-theology.org/html/books/rapture/chapter7.htm.

Plain Truth. 1997. Advertisement. October.

Platt, Rutherford H., Jr., ed. 1980. *The Forgotten Books of Eden*. New York: Bell. First published 1926.

Quinn, D. Michael. 1976. The Mormon Succession Crisis of 1844. *BYU Studies* 16 (Winter): 187–233.

Rader, Stanley R. 1980. *Against the Gates of Hell: The Threat to Religious Freedom in America*. New York: Everest House.

RCG (Restored Church of God) website. Here Is The Restored Church of God. http://www.thercg.org/books/hitrcog.html.

Richardson, Alan. 1957. *A Theological Word Book of the Bible*. London: SCM.

Ritenbaugh, Richard T. 2000. Was Herbert Armstrong a False Prophet? *Forerunner*, January.

Roberts, Oral. 1970. *Miracle of Seed-Faith*. Tulsa, OK: Roberts.

Robertson, Suerae. 1997. Garner Ted Armstrong—"Getting Rubbed the Wrong Way." http://members.tripod.com/gavinru/tvtranscript2.htm.

Robinson, David. 1980. *Herbert Armstrong's Tangled Web*. Tulsa, OK: John Hadden.

Robinson, John. 1997. WCG Governmental History Traced up to Tkach Era. *In Transition*, January 31.

Rube, Kate. 1999. Worldwide Church of God. http://web.archive.org/web/20060829230806/religiousmovements.lib.virginia.edu/nrms/wcg.html.

Rumney, Gavin. 2008. Climb the Wall. *Ambassador Watch* (blog). August 24. http://ambassadorwatch.blogspot.com/2008/08/climb-wall.html.

———. 2009. Die Meistersinger—Zweiter Teil. *Ambassador Watch* (blog). June 20. http://ambassadorwatch.blogspot.com/2009/06/die-meistersinger-zweiter-teil.html.

———. 2011. The Community of Christ and Grace Communion International. *Cross-Pollination* (blog). Revision. http://otagosh.blogspot.com/2011/03/cross-pollination-community-of-christ.html.

———. n.d. The Letter W. http://homepages.ihug.co.nz/~gavinru/herb2.htm.

Russell, Ron. 1997. Honey, I Shrunk the Church. *New Times Los Angeles*, April 2. http://www.hwarmstrong.com/honey-i-shrunk-worldwide-church-01.htm.

Salyer, Larry. 2003. Standing for Truth—A Personal History. Sermon, Grand Junction, CO, December.

Sanders, J. Oswald. 1962. *Heresies and Cults*. Rev. ed. London: Marshall, Morgan & Scott.

Sanders, J. Oswald, and J. Stafford Wright. 1956. *Some Modern Religions*. London: Inter-Varsity Fellowship.

Scharf, Betty R. 1970. *The Sociological Study of Religion*. London: Hutchinson.

Schultz, Jim. 1995. Sex Suit Names TV Evangelist; Garner Ted Armstrong Denies Nurse's Accusations. *Houston Chronicle*, November 23.

Seekins, D., and J. N. Seekins. 2006. "Tell Me Please": British-Israel Identity Foundation Truths, pt. 2. *The Ensign Message*, June. http://www.ensignmessage.com/archives/Tellme2.html.

Simmons, John K. 1991. "Charisma and Covenant: The Christian Science Movement in its Initial Postcharismatic Phase." In *When Prophets Die: The Postcharismatic Fate of New Religious Movements*, ed. Timothy Miller, 107–24. Albany: State University of New York Press.

Simpson, Richard. 2002. The Political Influence of the British-Israel Movement in the Nineteenth Century. MA dissertation, Birkbeck, University of London. Available online at http://www.originofnations.org/books,%20papers/MA_dissertation_BI.pdf.

Sladek, John. 1978. *The New Apocrypha: A Guide to Strange Sciences and Occult Beliefs*. London: Panther.

Smart, Ninian. 1969. *The Religious Experience of Mankind*. New York: Charles Scribner's Sons.

———. 1987. *Religion and the Western Mind*. London: Palgrave Macmillan.

———. 1989. *The World's Religions: Old Traditions and Modern Transformations*. Cambridge, UK: Cambridge University Press.

———. 1996. *Dimensions of the Sacred: An Anatomy of the World's Beliefs*. London: HarperCollins.

Smith, William. 1967. *Smith's Bible Dictionary*. New York: Pyramid.

Stark, Rodney, and William Sims Bainbridge. 1985. *The Future of Religion*. Berkeley: University of California Press.

———. 1987. *A Theory of Religion*. New York: Lang.

Stark, Rodney, and Roger Finke. 2000. *Acts of Faith: Explaining the Human Side of Religion*. Berkeley: University of California Press.

Steinman, Murray. 1999. Transition Team to Fill Office of President at Church Universal and Triumphant. *Church Universal and Triumphant*, July 30.

Stevens, Anthony, and John Price. 2000. *Prophets, Cults and Madness*. London: Duckworth.

Stickland, Mike. n.d. *An Inside Look at Seventh-day Adventists*. Watford, UK: British Union Conference of Seventh-day Adventists.

Storm, Rachel. 1991. *In Search of Heaven on Earth*. London: Bloomsbury.

Storr, Anthony. 1996. *Feet of Clay: A Study of Gurus*. London: HarperCollins.

Stoyanov, Yuri. 2000. *The Other God: Dualist Religions from Antiquity to the Cathar Heresy*. New Haven, CT: Yale University Press.

Strangite Mormons. n.d. Famous Members. http://www.strangite.org/Famous.htm.

———. n.d. Seventh-day Sabbath Saturday. http://www.strangite.org/7th-day.htm.

Summerville, James. 2004. *The Divine Destiny of America*. Terrytown, LA: Church of God Ministries International. Available online at http://www.thecogmi.org/articles/divinedestinyofamerica.pdf.

Svarupa dasa, Ravindra. 1994. Cleaning House and Cleaning Hearts: Reform and Renewal in ISKCON—Part 2. *ISKCON Communications Journal* 4 (December): 25–33.

Tabor, James D. 2006. *The Jesus Dynasty*. London: HarperElement.

Taylor, Dan C. 1984. Where We Have Been! *Plain Truth*, February.

Thiel, Bob. 2003. Consider Candid Responses to 15 Accusations about HWA. *The Journal: News of the Churches of God*, February 28. Available online at http://www.cogwriter.com/hwaacc.htm.

———. 2006. News of Those Once Affiliated with the Global Church of God. http://www.cogwriter.com/5gnews.htm.

———. 2007. PCG Press Release: WCG Betrayed HWA. Available online at http://www.cogwriter.com/news/cog-news/pcg-press-release-wcg-betrayed-hwa/.

———. 2009. Church of God, an International Community. http://www.cogwriter.com/cogaic.htm.

———. n.d. Why Not the Restored Church of God? David Pack isn't HW Armstrong's Successor. http://www.cogwriter.com/rcg.htm.

Thompson, Damian. 1996. *The End of Time: Faith and Fear in the Shadow of the Millennium*. London: Sinclair-Stevenson.

Tkach, Joseph. 1997. *Transformed by Truth*. Sisters, OR: Multnomah Books.

Todd, Douglas. 2003. Leader Left Divine Light Behind Him. *Vancouver Sun*, September 29.

Trechak, John. 1985. The WCG—A Future after Herbert Armstrong? *Ambassador Report* 31 (March). Available online at http://www.hwarmstrong.com/ar/AR31.html.

———. 1989. Joseph W. Tkach—God's New Rep on Planet Earth. *Ambassador Report* 41 (March). http://www.hwarmstrong.com/ar/AR41.html.

Troeltsch, Ernst. 1931. *The Social Teachings of the Christian Churches*. Translated by Olive Wyon. London: Allen & Unwin.

Tucker, Ruth. 1996. From the Fringe to the Fold. *Christianity Today*, July 15.

Tuit, John. 1981. *The Truth Shall Make You Free: Herbert Armstrong's Empire Exposed*. Freehold, NJ: Truth Foundation.

Vincent, Rabon, Jr. 1999. *God vs. Evolution Y2K*. Avilla, IN: Eagle.

Waite, Roger. 2000. An Analysis of the WCG Doctrinal Changes and Crisis in the Church of God. Unpublished manuscript, available online at http://www.rogerswebsite.com/articles/Analysis-of-WCG-Changes.pdf.

Wallis, Roy. 1975. *Sectarianism: Analyses of Religious and Non-Religious Sects*. London: Peter Owen.

———. 1979. *Salvation and Protest: Studies of Social and Religious Movements*. New York: St Martin's.

———. 2003. Three Types of New Religious Movement. In *Cults and New Religious Movements: A Reader*, ed. Lorne L Dawson, 36–58. Oxford: Wiley-Blackwell.

Watch Tower Society. 1995. Can You Trust God's Promises? *Awake!*, June 22.

WCG (Worldwide Church of God). 1994. *We're Often Asked...* Pasadena, CA: Worldwide Church of God.

———. 1995a. *Statement of Beliefs of the Worldwide Church of God*. Pasadena, CA: Worldwide Church of God.

———. 1995b. Where We Have Been, Where We Are Going. *Welcome to Our Fellowship*.

———. 2009. Worldwide Church of God Announces Name Change. April 16. http://www.wcg.org/namechange.htm.

WCG (Worldwide Church of God): History. n.d. A Brief History of Grace Communion International. http://www.wcg.org/lit/aboutus/history.htm.

WCG (Worldwide Church of God): Israel. n.d. Church's Statement Regarding the Identity of Ancient Israel.

WCG (Worldwide Church of God): MOA. n.d. Mystery of Mysteries. http://www.wcg.org/lit/church/history/mysteries.htm.

WCG (Worldwide Church of God) website. Worldwide Church of God (UK): About Us. http://www.wcg.org.uk/about_us/index.htm.

Weber, Eugen. 1999. *Apocalypses: Prophecies, Cults and Millennial Beliefs through the Ages*. London: Hutchinson.

Weber, Max. 1948. *Essays in Sociology.* London: Routledge & Kegan Paul.

—. 1964. *The Theory of Social and Economic Organization.* New York: Free Press.

—. 1965. *The Sociology of Religion.* London: Methuen.

—. 1993. *Basic Concepts in Sociology.* Translated by H. P. Secher. New York: Citadel. First published 1925.

Weinland, Ronald. 2004. *The Prophesied End-Time.* Dallas, TX: The-end.com.

—. 2006. *2008: God's Final Witness.* Dallas, TX: The-end.com.

—. 2008. Second Witness. *Ronald Weinland* (blog). April 18. http://ronaldweinland.com/?p=75.

—. 2009. "In" the Final Three and One-Half Years." *Ronald Weinland* (blog). March 6. http://ronaldweinland.com/?p=80.

—. 2012a. The Day of Christ's Coming. *Ronald Weinland* (blog). May 30. http://ronald-weinland.com/?p=115.

—. 2012b. God's Time. *Ronald Weinland* (blog). June 15. http://ronaldweinland.com/?p=117.

—. 2012c. A New World. Sermon, May 26. Available online at http://www.cog-pkg.org/audio/docs/2012-05-26_A_New_World.pdf.

White, Craig. 2005. Herman L. Hoeh: A Salute to a Worldwide Church of God Pioneer. http://www.originofnations.org/HRP_Papers/Hoeh_Salute%20to%20a%20WCG%20Pioneer2.pdf.

—. 2009. *Herbert W Armstrong: Man of God!* Available online at http://www.originofnations.org/HRP_Papers/HWA_inspired_sifter!.pdf.

Wilson, Bryan R. 1961. *Sects and Society: A Sociological Study of Three Religious Groups in Britain.* London: William Heinemann.

—. 1967. *Patterns of Sectarianism: Organisation and Ideology in Social and Religious Movements.* London: Heinemann.

—. 1970. *Religious Sects.* London: Weidenfeld & Nicolson.

—. 1990. *The Social Dimensions of Sectarianism: Sects and New Religious Movements in Contemporary Society.* Oxford: Clarendon.

—. 2000. "The Brethren": A Current Sociological Appraisal. Available online at http://www.theexclusivebrethren.com/documents/academicstudy.pdf.

Wilson, John. 1971. The Sociology of Schism. In *A Sociological Yearbook of Religion in Britain* 4:1–20.

Worldwide News. 1986. God Restored These 18 Truths: How Thankful Are You for Them? *The Worldwide News,* August 25.

Wright, Jeff. 1998. Leap of Faith. *Eugene Register-Guard,* February 28. Available online at http://news.google.com/newspapers?nid=1310&dat=19980228&id=fnUVAAAAIBAJ&sjid=gusDAAAAIBAJ&pg=6777,7020286.

Wright, Stuart A. 1994. From "Children of God" to "The Family": Movement Adaptation and Survival. In *Sex, Slander and Salvation: Investigating The Family/Children of God,* ed. James R. Lewis and J. Gordon Melton, 57–70. Stanford, CA: Center for Academic Publication.

Yinger, J. Milton. 1970. *The Scientific Study of Religion.* New York: Macmillan.

Zald, Mayer N., and Roberta Ash. 1966. Social Movement Organizations: Growth, Decay and Change. *Social Forces* 44:327–40.

Zola, Margaret D. 1977a. Garner Ted Armstrong—Son of the Legend. *Ambassador Report.* http://www.hwarmstrong.com/ar/SonOf.html.

—. 1977b. The Missing Dimension In Ambassador College—Accreditation. *Ambassador Report.* http://www.hwarmstrong.com/ar/Missing.html.

INDEX

All churches and other organizations (except magazines, websites etc) which are direct or indirect offshoots of the Worldwide Church of God (WCG) are grouped together under **WCG offshoots**. Most doctrines are grouped together under **doctrines of the Churches of God**. With a few significant exceptions the titles of doctrinal books and booklets from WCG and offshoot churches are not listed.

Dispensationalism, 22

dissolution. *See* After the Founder Dies (model)

divergence. *See* After the Founder Dies (model)

divine revelation (revealed truths), 69–70, 72–73, 83, 103, 120, 125, 154, 165, 170, 171, 195

   see also offshoots

divorce and remarriage. *See* doctrinal changes (1970s)

doctoral theses on WCG, 244

doctrinal changes (1970s), 43, 61, 67, 83, 90, 151, 155, 171

   divorce and remarriage, 12, 70–73, 74, 90, 124, 192

   Pentecost, date of, 68–70, 72, 124, 192

doctrinal changes (1980s), 4, 9, 12, 27, 63, 85, 87–92, 95, 96, 125–6

   accommodation with, 127

   impact on reaffiliation, 120, 210–2

   justifying changes, 95–96

   ministers' reaction to, 92–97, 100, 102, 113, 121, 125, 126–7, 162, 245–6

doctrinal questioning by ministers (1970s), 67, 69, 70–71, 73–74, 81

   see also Systematic Theology Project

doctrine, importance of. *See* religious capital

doctrines of the Churches of God, 29–32

   Bible, literal truth of, 30

   biblical prophecy and the End Times, 30, 31, 34, 195; *see also* news, prophetic analysis of

   binitarianism and anti-trinitarianism, 24, 29, 89, 91–92, 211, 228, 237

   British-Israelism. *See* British-Israelism

   Christmas and Easter etc as pagan festivals, 30, 31, 99, 240

   church eras, 29–30, 31, 54, 55, 116, 139

   church government, 30, 38; *see also* governance

   crucifixion on Wednesday, 30, 48

   dietary restrictions and unclean foods, 24, 31, 33, 52, 93, 99–100, 240

   divorce and remarriage. *See* doctrinal changes (1970s)

   End Times. *See* millenarianism

   evolution, falsehood of, 30, 49, 91

   God family, 29, 39–40, 91, 121, 138

   healing, 89, 108, 211

Holy Spirit, 29, 91–92

Jesus, nature of, 29, 91, 138, 146

Jewish festivals, seven annual. *See* Holy Days

Kingdom of God, 30, 36, 83, 107

   makeup, 12, 47, 80–81, 108, 240

   members will be rulers in God's Kingdom, 30, 36–37, 152–3, 196

   obedience to God's law. *See* law, obedience to

   reward according to works, 30, *see also* salvation

   Sabbath-keeping, 93, 94, 99, 100, 101, 123, 211, 218, 228, 240; *see also* Sabbatarianism

   soul sleep, 30, 31

   stake, Jesus killed on, 111

   tithing, 30, 31, 33, 38, 51, 59, 60, 93, 94, 146

   tithing, second and third tithes, 30, 33, 72, 125

   unsaved are destroyed, 30, 31

   see also Systematic Theology Project

Does God Exist?, 111

Dugger, Andrew N., 52

Early Writings of Herbert W. Armstrong, 145, 246

Eddy, Mary Baker, 183, 192

Edwards, Norman S., 56, 146,

18 Restored Truths (article), 38, 87, 97, 152, 160

Elan Vital (Divine Light Mission), 189–90

Elim Foursquare Gospel Church (Pentecostal), 6, 7, 78–79, 122, 123, 209

Emissaries, the, 200–1

End Times, 20–23, 26, 35, 86–87, 112, 119, 142, 143–4, 165

Ephraim. *See* British Israelism

esoteric movements, succession in, 188

ethnography, 239

Eugene, Oregon, 50, 52, 68, 73, 206, 212, 218

European Community in prophecy, 35

Eusebius, 18, 19

Evangelical Christianity, 22, 33, 89, 90, 93, 94, 96, 99, 107, 112, 244

   organizations, 95, 97, 99, 102, 196

   see also born again doctrine; Worldwide Church of God

evolution. *See* doctrines of the Churches of God

living-room churches. *See* WCG offshoots

Living to Win (newsletter), 145

London, 27, 34, 112–3, 202

Luckmann, Thomas, 240

Luker, Dennis, 132

McBride, James, 136

McGuire, Meredith B., 218

McMichael, Sherwin, 173

McNair, Eve, 123, 185

McNair, Marion, 57, 199

McNair, Raymond F., 57, 74, 82, 123–4, 185, 217, 247n

Maharaji, Guru (Prem Rawat), 189–90

makeup. *See* doctrines of the Churches of God

Malachi's Message to God's Church Today, 117, 120

Manasseh. *See* British Israelism

man of sin, the, 116, 119

Mark of the Beast. *See* Sabbatarianism

Martin, Ernest L., 246, 247n

Martin, Ramona. *See* Armstrong, Herbert W.

Martin, Walter R., *See Kingdom of the Cults, The*

Mattson, Vern, 47, 76

Meakin, John, 131

meaningful order. *See nomos*, nomization; social construction of reality

Melton, J. Gordon, 23, 190, 193, 212, 218

membership,
    of offshoot Churches, 63n, 104–7, 118, 121, 126–7, 130, 132, 135, 137, 138, 139, 147, 159
    problems of definition, 98, 104–6, 147
    of WCG, 94, 97–99, 102, 105, 147

members' role, 107–8, 166

Meredith, C. Paul, 57

Meredith, Roderick C., 6, 58, 176, 192, 210
    in Global Church of God, 5, 110, 121–2, 162, 186
    in Living Church of God, 110, 112, 122–3, 124
    personality and attitudes to, 86, 123, 124, 159, 162–4, 169, 191
    succession from, 124, 201–2
    in WCG, 38, 57, 74, 82, 121, 123, 162, 170

methodology, 10, 239–41

Meyer, David J., 142

millenarianism, 11, 20–23, 34–37, 112, 237

Miller, William, 22–23

ministers, 11, 167–8, 208–10

ministries, 145–6

See also WCG offshoots

Miscavige, David, 181–2

Mohammed, 188

Mokarow, Art, 246

Moody, Dwight L., 22

Moon, Rev., 60

moral capital, 9, 12, 170, 205–6, 219–229, 232, 253
    see also leaders, negative experience of

Mormonism. *See* Church of Jesus Christ of Latter-day Saints

Mumford, Stephen, 19, 50

Mystery of the Ages, 37n, 113, 119, 161
    Armstrong's writing of, 113, 114
    copyright dispute, 110, 114–5
    court case, 114–5, 187
    importance, 113, 114
    withdrawal of, 37, 113, 212

Nathan, Peter, 128, 129, 209

New Beginnings (magazine), 127

New Covenant. *See* Old Covenant and New Covenant

New Horizons (magazine), 136

new religious movements, 11, 154, 235
    see also cults; sects

new revelation, 195
    see also offshoots

news, prophetic analysis of, 59, 64–7, 116, 121, 142, 195
    see also Signs of the Times

New Zealand, 128

niche-shifting, 103, 181

Nickels, Richard C., 53, 54, 66, 145, 154, 155, 246, 247n

Niebuhr, H.R., 6, 235, 237

1939 article. *See* governance of churches

1970s, 8–9, 41, 60, 61, 63–84, 91, 95, 123, 125, 133, 147, 153
    harm to the church, 168–9
    see also doctrinal changes (1970s); doctrinal questioning by ministers (1970s); schism(s); Worldwide Church of God

1975 in Prophecy, 64, 91

nineteen-year time cycles, 54, 56, 91

nomos, nomization, 17–18, 153, 159, 175, 211–2, 240 (definition)
    see also agonic model; social construction of reality

Number of the Beast, 142

obedience
 to Church leaders and ministers, 38, 69,
  128, 154, 155–6, 167, 208
 to God, 17, 20, 49, 152, 228
 see also law, obedience to
offshoots
 criticizing each other, 108, 109, 117, 118,
  125–6, 138, 160, 198
 differences between, 126, 147
 future of, 253–5
 membership. *See* membership
 mergers, possibility of, 123, 137, 253
 new revelation/doctrines, 117, 119,
  120, 169
 number of, 5, 73, 104, 137, 140, 141, 147,
  154, 253–5
 originating from Garner Ted Armstrong,
  104, 108, 109, 112, 129, 133–7
 personality of leaders, 200–1
 upholding Armstrong's teachings, 109,
  117, 125–6, 195–6, 218
 see also WCG offshoots
Old Covenant and New Covenant, 32,
 93, 94
only true church. *See* God's only true
 church
options available to members, 5–6
order. *See nomos*, nomization; social
 construction of reality
Oregon, 38, 52, 172
*Origin and History of the Church of God,
 International, The*, 133
orthodox or heterodox theology. *See*
 heterodox or orthodox theology

Pack, David C., 6, 110, 125–6, 129, 164,
 176, 192
Panacea Society, 184–5
Pasadena, WCG headquarters, 28, 38, 58, 65,
 89, 94–95, 100, 102, 118
Passover, date of, 68, 69
Pastoral Bible Institute, 186n
Patrick, Saint, 19
Paul, Saint, 187
Pentecost, date of. *See* doctrinal changes
 (1970s)
perceptions, different, 10, 42–44, 58–61,
 79, 88, 160, 205, 232, 239, 243,
 246, 248
personal communications, 241, 247–8
Peter, primacy of, 172

phenomenology, 205, 232, 239–40
 emic and etic accounts, 205, 239
  (definition), 248
Philadelphia Church (era), 30, 54, 55,
 116, 119
 see also doctrines of the Churches of God
Philadelphia Trumpet, The (magazine), 114,
 116, 118
Pike, Kenneth L., 239
place of safety, 66
Plain Truth, The (magazine), 3, 4, 29, 35, 42,
 52–53, 58, 59, 67, 81, 89, 111, 116,
 118, 121, 153, 162
Portune, Al, 71n
Prabhupada, A.C. Swami Bhaktivedanta, 184
progressives and conservatives, 109,
 132, 161
 see also hardline or liberal distinction
prophecy, failure of, 64–67, 91, 116,
 142, 144
 explanations for failure, 65, 142, 144
 see also Armstrong, Herbert W.
Prophecy Flash! (magazine), 142
Prophesied End-Time, The, 143
Prophet, Elizabeth Clare, 59n, 179n, 183
Prophets, Cults and Madness, 173–5
psychic coercion, 154–5
psychological studies of religious leaders,
 170–5
 See also Armstrong, Herbert W.

questioning leaders and doctrines, 136, 139,
 199–200, 215–6
questionnaire, 206–8, 215, 248
 demographics, 57, 207–8, 249–52, 254

racial issues, 28, 31, 37, 39, 108
 see also British Israelism; *Mystery of the Ages*
Rader, Stanley R., 60, 78, 81, 82, 86, 169,
 191, 192
 see also Against the Gates of Hell
Radio Church of God, 4, 41, 52, 57, 58,
 62, 76
 see also Worldwide Church of God
Radio Luxembourg, 56, 59
radio and TV, 43, 52–53, 56, 77, 94, 106,
 107, 111, 112, 121, 139, 145
 see also World Tomorrow, The (radio
  and TV)
Raelian Movement, 189, 200
Raising the Ruins, 115, 176, 244

Rajneesh movement (Osho), 197
rational choice theory, 9 (definition), 205,
     210, 228–9, 223, 232
reaffiliation, 8, 9, 132, 210, 217–29, 232, 240
     hypothetical situation, 223–9
reform/revolution. *See* After the Founder
     Dies (model)
religion and corporation, distinction, 114–5,
     122, 187
religious capital, 9, 12, 17, 102, 205, 210–2,
     217–9, 220–9, 232, 253
religious choice. *See* rational choice theory
religious niches, 103, 181
Remnant of Israel, The (magazine), 31n, 36
Reorganized Latter Day Saints, 40, 186
restoring the original truth, 39, 40, 50, 56,
     125, 153, 171
revealed truths. *See* divine revelation
Revelation, Book of, 21
rewriting of texts. *See* literature
Ritenbaugh, John, 138, 176
Ritenbaugh, Richard T., 66, 176
Rivera, Geraldo, 134
Robertson, Suerae, 134
Roberts, Oral, 59n
Robinson, David, 76, 123, 146, 173, 199
Robinson, John, 146
Roman Catholic Church, 89, 96, 178, 236
routinization of charisma. *See* authority;
     continuation of religion after
     founder's death
Rumney, Gavin, 39, 158–9, 206, 247
Rupert, Greenbury G., 31, 36
Russell, Charles Taze, 186
Ruth, Alan, 99, 104, 253–4,
Rutherford, Joseph Franklin "Judge", 186, 191

Sabbatarianism, 18–20, 23, 32–34, 38, 39,
     93, 139, 211, 228, 237, 249
     Armstrong discovers, 48
     in early Britain, 19
     Sunday-keeping the mark of the beast, 24, 89
Sacred Names, 141, 146, 249
Sadler, John, 26
Salem, West Virginia, 50, 52, 54
salvation, 107
     through faith or works, 30, 32–33, 92, 94
Salyer, Larry, 37, 92
Sardis (era), 30, 54, 55
     see also doctrines of the Churches of God

Scharf, Betty R., 155, 239n
schism(s), 5, 40, 68
     following death of founder, 178
     in the future, 186, 253–5
     keeping the true faith, 218
     in the 1970s, 8, 12n, 61, 63, 64, 67, 71, 72,
          78, 82, 83, 103–4, 129
     number of, 63, 104, 253–5
     practical consequences of, 110–1, 114–5,
          132–3
     theories of, 6–8, 93, 103, 155, 159, 178,
          208–9, 210, 233
     see also After the Founder Dies (model)
Scientology, Church of, 29, 61, 105–6,
     181–2, 194, 199
Scofield Reference Bible, 22
Scott, Gary, 114
Second Coming. *See* End Times
sects, 90, 155
     definitions, 11, 32, 235–7
     heterodox and orthodox, 4, 6, 8, 31, 32,
          39, 40, 102, 236–7 (definition)
     see also cults; new religious movements
Servants' News (magazine), 146
services, 45, 98, 106, 107–8, 110, 111–3,
     132–3, 158
Seven Laws of Success, The, 59n
Seventh-day Adventist Church, 11, 23–25,
     31–32, 49–50, 61, 65, 112, 119, 147,
     187–8, 237n
Seventh-day Baptists, 19, 23, 49
sexual morality, teaching on, 43, 75–76
sexual scandals, 74–77, 125, 172, 175
     justification of, 75, 76, 134
     see also Armstrong, Garner Ted;
          Armstrong, Herbert W.
Shakers, 194
Signs of the Times, 35, 59, 64, 90, 116, 121
     see also news, prophetic analysis of
small remnant, 54, 197
Smart, Ninian, 239
Smith, Harold, 138
Smith, Joseph, 39, 103, 186
social capital, 9, 12, 205, 212–4, 217–9,
     220–9, 232
social construction of reality, 3, 8, 13, 17–18,
     93, 102, 120, 153, 159, 181, 214,
     228, 231, 239, 240 (definition)
     see also nomos, nomization
Soka Gakkai International, 60

white supremacy. *See* racial issues
Who is "That Prophet"?, 117
Wilson, Bryan R., 4, 6, 7–8, 78–79, 103, 117,
    133, 147, 197, 208–9, 236
Wilson, John (British Israelite), 26, 27,
    34–35, 52
Wilson, John (sociologist), 6, 101, 114, 233
Wolverton, Basil, 64
Wonderful World Tomorrow: What It Will Be
    Like, The (and variants), 37, 110, 113
Work, the, 53, 62, 67, 77, 87, 107–8, 118,
    121, 123, 131, 200
World Ahead, The (magazine), 121
World Council of Churches, 236
world news analysis. *See* news, prophetic
    analysis of
world-rejecting groups, 181, 197, 214, 236
World Tomorrow, The (radio and TV), 52, 58,
    59, 66, 75
    see also radio and TV
Worldwide Church of God
    authoritarianism, 32, 60, 67, 87, 127, 136,
        156, 165, 168, 170, 235
    becomes Evangelical, 3, 4, 7, 9, 11, 84, 94,
        99, 103, 126, 129
    changes in doctrine. *See* doctrinal changes
        (1970s); doctrinal changes (1980s)
    criticized as a cult, 4
    doctrines. *See* doctrines of the Churches
        of God
    early history, 52–58
    finances, 51, 53n, 61, 63n, 75, 82, 94, 97
    God's only church. *See* God's only true church
    headquarters. *See* Pasadena, WCG
        headquarters
    literature. *See* literature
    marketing of the church, 46
    members content with changes, 6, 101–2
    members with old beliefs who stayed, 6,
        100–1
    1970s, 8–9, 41, 63–84
    organization, 193
    periods: historical, transitional, reformed,
        8, 10–12
    receivership (1979), 82, 243
    reformed Worldwide view of old
        Worldwide, 44
    schisms. *See* schism(s)
    see also Armstrong, Garner Ted;
        Armstrong, Herbert W.

WCG offshoots
    NOTE: Church of God, Churches of
        God, and Church of God's are
        listed together
    Associates for Scriptural Knowledge, 246
    Association for Christian Development, 71
    Barnabas Ministries, 253
    Christian Biblical Church of God, 68n, 82,
        246, 250
    Christian Churches of God, 138
    Christian Educational Ministries, 145,
        168, 175
    Church Bible Teaching Ministry, 146
    Church of the Eternal God, 124
    Church of God Big Sandy, 133, 140,
        168, 250
    Church of God, a Christian Fellowship,
        123, 124, 202, 208
    Church of God, the Eternal, 57, 69, 72, 83,
        103, 124, 145, 154, 169–70, 250
    Church of God's Faithful, 111, 112,
        118–9, 120, 140, 176, 250
    Church of God Faithful Flock, 140, 250
    Church of God Fellowship, 138
    Church of God – Front Royal, VA, 119, 120
    Church of God, International, 11, 34n, 78,
        105, 111, 133–7, 195, 250
    Church of God, an International
        Community, 105, 106, 109,
        112, 128, 129–31, 132, 161, 198,
        209, 250
    Church of God Ministries International,
        34n, 136
    Church of God New World Ministries,
        136, 140
    Churches of God Outreach Ministries,
        105, 106, 134, 136, 137, 250
    Church of God's Patience, 119
    Church of God in Peace and Truth, 139
    Church of God Preparing for the
        Kingdom of God, 143–4
    Church of God, Restored, 100–1
    Church of God, Talents Ministries, 68n
    Church of God in Truth, 68n, 139, 141
    Church of God – 21st Century, 123–4,
        185, 194
    Churches of God, UK, 112, 134, 136
    Church of God, a Worldwide Association,
        11, 104n, 105n, 109, 131–3, 136n,
        140, 161, 202, 253